Lecture Notes in Computer Science   8263

Commenced Publication in 1973
Founding and Former Series Editors:
Gerhard Goos, Juris Hartmanis, and Jan van Leeuwen

Bruce Christianson   James Malcolm
Frank Stajano   Jonathan Anderson
Joseph Bonneau (Eds.)

Security
Protocols XXI

21st International Workshop
Cambridge, UK, March 19-20, 2013
Revised Selected Papers

 Springer

Volume Editors

Bruce Christianson
James Malcolm
University of Hertfordshire
School of Computer Science
Hatfield, Hertfordshire AL10 9AB, UK
E-mail: {b.christianson, j.a.malcolm}@herts.ac.uk

Frank Stajano
Jonathan Anderson
University of Cambridge
Computer Laboratory
Cambridge CB3 0FD, UK
E-mail: {frank.stajano, jonathan.anderson}@cl.cam.ac.uk

Joseph Bonneau
Princeton University
Center for Information Technology Policy
Princeton, NJ 08540, USA
E-mail: jbonneau@gmail.com

ISSN 0302-9743   e-ISSN 1611-3349
ISBN 978-3-642-41716-0   e-ISBN 978-3-642-41717-7
DOI 10.1007/978-3-642-41717-7
Springer Heidelberg New York Dordrecht London

Library of Congress Control Number: 2013951245

CR Subject Classification (1998): K.6.5, E.3, C.2, D.4.6, H.4

LNCS Sublibrary: SL 4 – Security and Cryptology

Typesetting: Camera-ready by author, data conversion by Scientific Publishing Services, Chennai, India

Printed on acid-free paper

Springer is part of Springer Science+Business Media (www.springer.com)

Preface

This volume collects the revised proceedings of the 21st International Security Protocols Workshop, held in Sidney Sussex College, Cambridge during 19th and 20th March 2013.

The theme of the workshop was "What's happening on the other channel?" Many protocols use a secondary channel, either explicitly (as in multichannel protocols[1]) but more usually implicitly, for example to exchange master keys, or their hashes. The role of the Other Channel is fundamental, and often problematic, and yet protocol composers typically take them as a given. Sometimes the Other Channel really is completely covert, but sometimes it just has properties that are different. And it's not only security properties that are relevant here: bandwidth, latency and error rate are often important considerations too. Even a line-of-sight channel usually doesn't quite have the properties that we unthinkingly attributed to it. Moriarty has been subscribing to the Other Channel for years: perhaps it's time for Alice and Bob to tune in too.

As with previous workshops in this series, each paper was revised by the authors to incorporate ideas that emerged during the workshop. These revised papers are followed by an edited transcript of the presentation and ensuing discussion.

Our thanks to Lori Klimaszewska for the raw transcriptions of the audio, later revised by the speakers themselves, and to Vashek Matyas for serving with us on the Program Committee.

We hope that reading these proceedings will encourage you to join in the debates. If you have an idea that might spark an interesting discussion, why not write it up as a position paper and send it to us? There'll be another workshop next year.

September 2013

Bruce Christianson
James Malcolm
Frank Stajano
Jonathan Anderson
Joseph Bonneau

---

[1] LNCS 4631, 112–127.

Previous Proceedings in this Series

The proceedings of previous International Security Protocols Workshops are also published by Springer Verlag as *Lecture Notes in Computer Science,* and are occasionally referred to in the text:

20th Workshop (2012)	LNCS 7622	ISBN 978-3-642-35693-3
19th Workshop (2011)	LNCS 7114	ISBN 978-3-642-25866-4
18th Workshop (2010)	LNCS 7061	*in preparation*
17th Workshop (2009)	LNCS 7028	ISBN 978-3-642-36212-5
16th Workshop (2008)	LNCS 6615	ISBN 978-3-642-22136-1
15th Workshop (2007)	LNCS 5964	ISBN 978-3-642-17772-9
14th Workshop (2006)	LNCS 5087	ISBN 978-3-642-04903-3
13th Workshop (2005)	LNCS 4631	ISBN 3-540-77155-7
12th Workshop (2004)	LNCS 3957	ISBN 3-540-40925-4
11th Workshop (2003)	LNCS 3364	ISBN 3-540-28389-7
10th Workshop (2002)	LNCS 2845	ISBN 3-540-20830-5
9th Workshop (2001)	LNCS 2467	ISBN 3-540-44263-4
8th Workshop (2000)	LNCS 2133	ISBN 3-540-42566-7
7th Workshop (1999)	LNCS 1796	ISBN 3-540-67381-4
6th Workshop (1998)	LNCS 1550	ISBN 3-540-65663-4
5th Workshop (1997)	LNCS 1361	ISBN 3-540-64040-1
4th Workshop (1996)	LNCS 1189	ISBN 3-540-63494-5

No published proceedings exist for the first three workshops.

Table of Contents

Introduction:
What's Happening on the Other Channel?
(Transcript of Discussion)

Bruce Christianson

University of Hertfordshire

Welcome to the 21st Security Protocols Workshop, which means that we are indeed twenty years old this year, and it's nice looking round to see a few faces of people who were at the very first one twenty years ago. And it's also very nice to see a few new faces of people who haven't been here before. So for the benefit of those who haven't, and for the benefit of some of those who are regulars, I'll just go through the rules of engagement quickly.

This is a workshop and not a conference: the idea is to be spontaneous and to let ideas emerge, so when you're presenting you're expected to lead a discussion rather than power through your PowerPoint in the order in which you originally intended to give it. We do prepare transcripts but they're heavily edited, you'll get a chance to see it, and we won't let you say anything egregiously stupid on the record, so feel free to have a go, and if it doesn't work out we'll just delete it. Don't feel that you have to say what you planned to say when you stood up. On the other hand, if the answer that you'd give to a question is going to be less interesting than what you would have said anyway, please just use your skill and judgement to resolve that one.

We have a couple of small features designed to add to the spontaneity this year. One is that the pre-proceedings won't be available until tomorrow. And the second is that Vashek is currently snowed in on the runway at Brno airport, so if there's somebody who was planning to speak tomorrow and who's either already prepared their talk, or wasn't planning to prepare their talk at all, and is willing to give the same (or even a different) talk this afternoon, please make yourself known to me during the tea break and we'll do a swap round.

Every year we have a theme. This isn't intended to constrain what people say, it's just intended to give a conceptual framework to allow the ideas to develop, so you can think of it as a sort of drying rack to hang your ideas on while they're still a bit damp, and this year the theme is: "What's happening on the other channel?" There's been continued interest over the last few years in multi-channel protocols, probably the most famous being the Resurrecting Duckling, which was presented here quite a few years ago[1]. And I saw just the other day a new device for a cash-point in Japan, where you put your mobile phone on the cash-point and then place your finger on a scanner, you don't ever key any information into the cash-point, only ever on your mobile phone. There's

---

[1] LNCS 1796, 172–194.

B. Christianson et al. (Eds.): Security Protocols 2013, LNCS 8263, pp. 1–2, 2013.

no keyboard on the cash-point. You can have a think about that one over the tea break.

But just as we discover at some point that we've all been speaking prose for years, in the same way when we go back and look again at all the old protocols that we thought we understood, but with the perspective that looking at multi-channel protocols has given us, we usually realise that these protocols involved side channels as well. The difference is just that they're not on stage, they're either happening before the formal modelling that we do for the single channel protocols begins, or they're happening out of band, or they're happening afterwards when there's some sort of dispute resolution going on. But there's almost always something happening using some other means of communication than the one that's being modelled in the protocol, and the thought is that perhaps this is a helpful way of looking at things more generally.

Sometimes the other channel is a covert channel. We're used to thinking of covert channels as something that attackers use, but when we look at a number of authentication protocols we often find out that Alice and Bob are relying on being able to keep a covert channel open somewhere in order to prove that the authentication protocol has actually authenticated the parties that they think it has. Line-of-sight authentication is a classic example of this, once you start looking at how line-of-sight authentication actually works, there's an awful lot more going on there than you might think.

But one thing we can be sure of, which is that Moriarty being an evil genius has been looking very carefully for many years at what's happening on the other channel, and there is a danger that he's getting ahead. So part of our mission for the next two days is to redress that situation.

Towards New Security Primitives
Based on Hard AI Problems

Bin B. Zhu[1] and Jeff Yan[2]

[1] Microsoft Research Asia, Beijing, China
binzhu@microsoft.com
[2] School of Computing Science, Newcastle University, UK
Jeff.Yan@ncl.ac.uk

Abstract. Many security primitives are based on hard mathematical problems. Using hard AI problems for security has emerged as an exciting new paradigm (with Captcha being the most successful example). However, this paradigm has achieved just a limited success, and has been under-explored. In this paper, we motivate and sketch a new security primitive based on hard AI problems.

Keywords: Captcha as gRaphical Passwords (CaRP), passwords, cross-device authentication.

1 Thwart Password Guessing: A New Method

PassPoints [1] is a well-studied graphical password scheme, where a user clicks on an image and the ordered sequence of her click-points is used to derive a password.

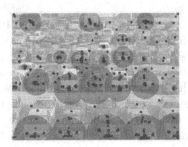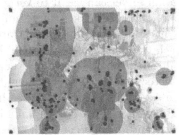

Fig. 1. Hotspots in PassPoints (taken from [2])

PassPoints has an inherent security weakness: it is easy for an attacker to automatically identify all salient points in an image using standard image processing methods. Then running through random combinations of salient points will lead to a brute force attack on passwords. To make things worse, when given

B. Christianson et al. (Eds.): Security Protocols 2013, LNCS 8263, pp. 3–10, 2013.

an image, people tend to prefer some image points (e.g. eye-catching ones) over others when creating passwords. These more popular points are 'hot spots' of the image, as shown in Figure 1, and an attacker can exploit them for an effective dictionary attack, significantly reducing the security of PassPoints [2,3].

To address the above problems, we have pondered a new approach to mitigating password guessing attacks.

Password guessing, on text or graphical passwords, online or offline, is typically a deterministic elimination process. Each guess reduces the remaining search space, and a next guess has a higher chance for success. While more and more password candidates get eliminated, the probability of a current guess being correct increases, and this probability finally approaches 1. Naturally, a classic defense is to increase the password space.

But, how about thwarting the deterministic elimination process? What if previous guesses do not contribute to reducing the password space, and thus a next guess is just like starting from scratch? Is this possible?

Salient points in PassPoints harm security but help memorability, as these points are often structural and they facilitate users to remember their clickpoints. It is impractical to force users to choose non-salient points, as these will be hard to remember. If we do not want to increase the image size to boost the password space, the only option remaining seems to make it hard for computers to exploit salient points. If the points a user clicks to login in a session cannot be correlated to the points she clicks in other sessions, then it is likely that a previous guess is not correlated with the next. One way of achieving this is the following: a different image is used for each session, and in each of the images, a user's password points appear in different forms, different locations, etc. This way, each automated guess will not reduce the password search space any more.

On the other hand, there must exist some invariant components in all the images used in different login attempts, otherwise users cannot use anything as passwords. We also need a password to remain the same for a user so that the authentication server can use it to verify her.

The above two requirements are similar to that of an ideal Captcha. In particular, as an established principle in Captcha design: to defeat machine learning attacks, each Captcha challenge should be computationally independent of the other [4]. If a new image is used in every login attempt and there is no computationally detectable correlation among these images, then the salient points or hotspots collected from previously used images will not help to locate the target points in the next image. As such, an adversary cannot build a dictionary with entries consistent for different login attempts to mount a dictionary attack.

The above thoughts have led to the concept of CaRP (Captcha as gRaphical Passwords), a new family of graphical passwords robust to online guessing attacks. Their relationship with Captcha also indicates how to construct CaRP schemes from various Captchas.

2   CaRP: Captcha as gRaphical Passwords

CaRP is a family of graphical password systems created with Captcha technology. Just like PassPoints, a user clicks on a CaRP image and the sequence of her clicks creates a password. However, each CaRP image is automatically generated by a Captcha generator, and thus is also a Captcha challenge. Just like a session key, a CaRP image is never reused across different sessions. Even for the same user, a new CaRP image is needed for every login attempt. To the contrary, in PassPoints a user always uses the same image to click her password, and many users use the same image for their password input, which leads to successful attacks exploiting hotspots.

Pinkas and Sander [5] introduced a protocol to protect passwords from online dictionary attack with Captchas[1]. Captcha and password are separate entities in this protocol, but are intrinsically combined in CaRP, which is *both a Captcha and a graphical password (scheme)*.

The notion of CaRP is simple but generic, and it can have multiple instantiations. Many Captcha schemes, regardless of whether they are text based or image recognition based, can be converted to a CaRP scheme. We provide a number of examples as follows.

2.1   ClickText

ClickText is a CaRP scheme built on top of text Captcha. Unlike normal text Captchas, a CaRP image should contain all the alphabet to allow a user to form any allowed password. Figure 2 shows a ClickText image with an alphabet of 33 characters. In ClickText images, characters can be arranged randomly on 2D space. This is another major difference from traditional text Captchas in which characters are typically ordered from left to right. Using ordinary text Captcha is not suitable in this context, as it is hard to arrange all the characters one dimensionally in a reasonably small space. Also, there is no order among characters in a CaRP image whereas the order is needed for characters in a normal Captcha image so that users can type them in. Therefore, we propose a new problem, 2D text segmentation, as the underlying hard AI problem for ClickText.

A ClickText password is a sequence of characters in the alphabet, e.g. $\rho =$ '$AB\#9CD87$', which is similar to a text password. To enter a password, the user clicks on the image the characters in her password in the order, 'A', 'B', '#', '9', 'C', 'D', '8', and then '7'.

When a CaRP image is generated, each character's location is tracked to produce a ground truth. The authentication server relies on the ground truth to

---

[1] In the PS protocol, a user is required to solve a Captcha challenge after entering her valid user name and password, unless a valid browser cookie from a previous successful login is available. If the user name and password pair is invalid, with a probability determined by a deterministic function, the user will receive a Captcha challenge to solve before being denied access to her account.

Fig. 2. A ClickText image with 33 characters

identify the characters corresponding to user-clicked points. The server does not store passwords in the clear, but their cryptographic hashes.

ClickText does not use visually-confusing characters. For example, letter 'O' and digit '0' may cause confusion in a CaRP image, and thus one of the characters should be excluded from the alphabet.

2.2   ClickAnimal

Captcha Zoo [6] is an image recognition scheme whose security relies on both object segmentation and binary object classification. It uses 3D models of two similar animals, e.g. dog and horse, to generate 2D animals with different textures, colors, lightings and poses, and then places them on a cluttered background. A user clicks all the horses in a challenge image to pass the test. Figure 3 shows a sample challenge where all the horses are circled red.

Fig. 3. A challenge in Captcha Zoo with horses circled red (taken from [6])

We can turn Captcha Zoo into a CaRP scheme, by introducing additional similar animals such as dog, horse and pig into the alphabet. In this new CaRP which we call ClickAnimal, a password is a sequence of animal names such as $\rho = 'Turkey, Cat, Horse, Dog, ...'$. For each animal, one or more 3D models are built. The Captcha generation process is applied to generate ClickAnimal images, wherein 3D models are used to generate 2D animals by applying different views, textures, colors, lightning effects, and, optionally, distortions. Different views applied in this step generate many different 2D shapes for the same animal, which, together with other anti-recognition mechanisms applied in this step, makes it hard for automatic recognition to identify the generated 2D animals. The resulting 2D animals are then arranged on a cluttered background such as grassland. Some animals may be occluded by other animals in the image, but their core part should not be occluded in order for humans to identify. Figure 4 shows a ClickAnimal image with an alphabet of 10 animals.

Fig. 4. A ClickAnimal image (left) and a 6 × 6 grid (right) determined by the red turkey's bounding rectangle

2.3 AnimalGrid

The number of similar animals is much less than the number of available text characters. ClickAnimal has a smaller alphabet, and thus it implies a smaller password space than ClickText does. CaRP should have a sufficiently-large effective password space to resist human guessing attacks. ClickAnimal's password space can be increased by combining a grid scheme as follows, leading to a new CaRP which we call AnimalGrid.

To enter a password, a ClickAnimal image is displayed first. After an animal is selected, an $n \times n$ grid appears, with the grid-cell size equaling the bounding rectangle of the selected animal. All grid cells are labeled to help a user identify them. Figure 4 shows a 6 × 6 grid when the red turkey in the left image was selected. A user can select zero to multiple grid-cells to form her password. Therefore a password is a sequence of animals interleaving with grid-cells, e.g. $\rho = $ '$Dog, Grid(2), Grid(1); Cat, Horse, Grid(3)$', where $Grid(1)$ means the grid-cell indexed as 1, and grid-cells following an animal means that the grid is determined by the bounding rectangle of the animal. A password must begin with an animal.

3 Application Scenarios

CaRP's typical applications include the following.

E-banking. Many e-banking systems have deployed Captchas to protect customers from automated online password attacks. For example, ICBC (http://www.icbc.com.cn/), the largest bank in the world, requires solving a Captcha for every login attempt. We envisage that it is faster and more convenient for people to use CaRP than the combined effort of entering a password and then solving a Captcha.

Cross-device authentication. Typing passwords is cumbersome on touch devices such as smartphones and tablets, where click/touch-based input is convenient. CaRP can offer the same password entry experience across different types of devices, including desktops, smartphones and tablets. Therefore, it is inherently a cross-device authentication mechanism, and a single implementation can simultaneously serve a wide range of different devices. On the contrary, text passwords are more friendly to desktop users, but less so to smartphone or tablet users.

Spam mitigation. CaRP can be deployed to increase a spammer's operating cost, and thus likely help reduce junk emails. For an email service that deploys CaRP, human involvement is compulsory to access an account; a spam bot cannot log into any account even if it knows the password. If CaRP is used together with a policy of throttling the number of outgoing emails allowed per login session, a spam bot will need regular human assistances, and each time it sends out only a limited number of emails. All these will reduce a spammer's productivity.

4 Security Analysis

The computational intractability of hard AI problems such as object recognition is fundamental to the security of CaRP. Existing analyses on Captcha security were mostly case by case or used an approximation approach. No theoretic security model has been established yet. Segmenting similar objects (e.g. characters) is considered as a computationally-expensive and combinatorially-hard problem [7], which modern text Captcha schemes rely on. According to [7], the complexity of object segmentation is exponentially dependent of the number of objects contained in a challenge, and polynomially dependent of the size of the Captcha alphabet. A Captcha challenge typically contains 6 to 10 characters, whereas a CaRP image typically contains 30 or more characters. Therefore, ClickText is much more secure than normal text Captcha. Furthermore, characters in a CaRP scheme are arranged two-dimensionally, which further increases segmentation difficulty due to an additional dimension to segment. ClickAnimal relies on both object segmentation and multiple-label classification. Its security remains an open question.

As a framework of graphical passwords, CaRP does not rely on the security of any specific Captcha scheme. If one Captcha scheme gets broken, a new and more robust Captcha scheme may appear and be used to construct a new CaRP scheme.

CaRP offers protection against online dictionary attacks on passwords, which have been for long time a major security threat for various online services.

Defending against online dictionary attacks is a subtler problem than it might appear. Intuitive countermeasures such as limiting the number of logon attempts do not work, for two reasons:

- They cause denial-of-service attacks (which were exploited to lock highest bidders out in final minutes of eBay auctions [8]) and incurs expensive helpdesk costs for account reactivation.
- They are vulnerable to global password attacks [5], where adversaries intend to break into any account rather than a specific one, and thus they try each password candidate on multiple accounts. This way, the number of guesses on each account is made below the threshold, thus avoiding triggering account lockout.

CaRP makes it much harder for bad guys to perform automated guess attacks. Even when a human is involved, the attack is still expensive and slowed down. CaRP also offers protection against relay attacks, which have been an increasing threat to online applications protected by Captchas. In a relay attack, Captcha challenges are relayed to humans to solve, with their answers returned.

CaRP is robust to shoulder-surfing attacks, if combined with Microsoft's dual-view technologies [9] that show two sets of completely different images simultaneously on the same LCD screen: one for private, and the other for public. When a CaRP image is displayed as private, attackers can capture a user's click-points but not the private image, but these points are useless for a next login session (where a new CaRP image will be used).

CaRP is robust to cross-site scripting attacks targeting at stealing users' graphical passwords, although other click-based graphical passwords such as PassPoints are vulnerable to such attacks.

However, a longitudinal evaluation is needed to establish the effective password space for each CaRP instantiation. CaRP is vulnerable if a client is compromised, and the image and user-clicked points can both be captured.

5   Usability

Initial user studies with several schemes proposed in Section 2 are encouraging. Still, CaRP requires a user to handle a Captcha-like challenge each time to login. This might have a usability impact, but it can be mitigated by serving CaRP images of different difficulty levels, according to an account's login history and whether a known machine is used for login.

The optimal configuration for achieving good security *and* usability remains an open question for CaRP, and further studies are needed to refine each implementation for actual deployments.

6   Summary

It is a fundamental method in computer security to create cryptographic primitives based on hard mathematical problems that are computationally intractable.

Using hard AI problems for security, initially proposed in [10], is an exciting new paradigm. Under this new paradigm, the most notable primitive invented is Captcha. However, the new paradigm has achieved just a limited success, if compared with the number of cryptographic primitives based on hard math problems and the wide applications of such primitives. We have showed that it is indeed possible to construct new security primitives based on hard AI problems.

Like Captcha, CaRP utilizes unsolved AI problems. However, a password is much more valuable for attackers than a free email account that Captcha typically protects. Therefore there are probably more incentives for the attackers to hack CaRP than Captcha. That is, CaRP can attract more efforts than ordinary Captcha does to the following win-win game: if the attackers succeed, they contribute to improving AI by providing solutions to open problems. Otherwise, our system stays secure, contributing to practical security.

Overall, CaRP appears to be a step forward in the paradigm of using hard AI problems for security. What else can be invented this way? We expect CaRP to inspire new inventions of AI based security primitives.

Acknowledgements. We thank Peter Ryan for very helpful discussions, and thank Tim Barclay for proofreading our camera-ready version, which improved the writing quality of this paper.

References

1. Wiedenbeck, S., Waters, J., Birget, J.C., Brodskiy, A., Memon, N.: PassPoints: design and longitudinal evaluation of a graphical password system. Int. J of HCI 63, 102–127 (2005)
2. Thorpe, J., van Oorschot, P.C.: Human-seeded attacks and exploiting hot spots in graphical passwords. USENIX Security (2007)
3. Dirik, A.E., Memon, N., Birget, J.-C.: Modeling user choice in the PassPoints graphical password scheme. ACM SOUPS (2007)
4. Zhu, B.B., Yan, J., Li, Q., Yang, C., Liu, J., Xu, N., Yi, M., Cai, K.: Attacks and design of image recognition CAPTCHAs. ACM CCS, 187–200 (2010)
5. Pinkas, B., Sander, T.: Securing passwords against dictionary attacks. ACM CCS, 161–170 (2002)
6. Lin, R., Huang, S.-Y., Bell, G.B., Lee, Y.-K.: A new Captcha interface design for mobile devices. In: Australasian User Interface Conference (2011)
7. Chellapilla, K., Larson, K., Simard, P.Y., Czerwinski, M.: Building Segmentation Based Human-Friendly Human Interaction Proofs (HIPs). In: Baird, H.S., Lopresti, D.P. (eds.) HIP 2005. LNCS, vol. 3517, pp. 1–26. Springer, Heidelberg (2005)
8. Wolverton, T.: Hackers attack eBay accounts. ZDNet (March 26, 2002),
   http://www.zdnet.co.uk/news/networking/2002/03/26/
   hackers-attack-ebay-accounts-2107350/
9. Kim, S., Cao, X., Zhang, H., Tan, D.: Enabling concurrent dual views on common LCD screens. In: Sig. CHI 2012, pp. 2175–2184 (2012)
10. von Ahn, L., Blum, M., Hopper, N.J., Langford, J.: Captcha: using hard AI problems for security. In: Biham, E. (ed.) EUROCRYPT 2003. LNCS, vol. 2656, pp. 294–311. Springer, Heidelberg (2003)

Towards New Security Primitives
Based on Hard AI Problems
(Transcript of Discussion)

Jeff Yan

University of Newcastle

OK, today I talk about 'Towards new security primitives based on hard AI problems'. We all know that actually most security primitives are based on hard math problems, such as integer factorisation and discrete logarithm, but in 2003, using hard AI problems for security purposes was proposed at CMU. Everyone knows that Captcha is the most successful example. The research question we have asked is very simple: what else can we invent along this line? Can we do anything else in security primitives based on hard AI problems?

My next slide, which some people in this audience have seen before, is taken from a talk I gave at a Cambridge Security Seminar in 2007. At the time I was busy designing a new graphical password scheme, which is now known as Background Draw A Secret. I had a look at a popular graphical password scheme, which is called PassPoints. In this scheme basically each user has an image, you click five points on this image, and derive your password. Apparently you can apply image processing techniques to automatically grab all those salient points, those eye-catching points. Therefore, if you do a random combination of those salient points you effectively do a brute-force attack on the passwords. And in this system, because multiple users will use the same image to create and enter their passwords, some salient points are more popular than others, therefore they lead to 'hotspots'. If the hotspots are detected then you effectively can launch a very successful dictionary attack to break PassPoints. The attack was demonstrated in two papers, one at USENIX Security'07 and the other at SOUPS'07.

I was considering how to address the problems, or the difficulties facing Pass-Points. We pondered over a new method for thwarting password guessing attacks. The idea is the following. If we look at the password guessing attack, we have the following angle. No matter whether the guessing is done online or offline, and no matter it is on text passwords or graphical passwords, guessing is a deterministic elimination process. Each guess reduces the remaining search space, and therefore a next guess will have a higher chance of success. While more and more password candidates get eliminated, the probability of a current guess being correct of course increases. And finally this probability approaches 1. This is the usual real world strategy of password guessing attacks, and therefore a natural defence is very simple: we just increase the password space, and make it harder and longer to finish this elimination process.

What we were thinking at the time is: how about failing the deterministic elimination process so that password guessing is less effective? For example, no matter how many previous guesses have been done, if the chance for a current

B. Christianson et al. (Eds.): Security Protocols 2013, LNCS 8263, pp. 11–18, 2013.

guess to be correct remains the same, then this would effectively make each guess fail to reduce the search space. So in a sense, this means that each password guess is independent of the other. [Pointing to an equation on the slide] This might not be mathematically a rigorous description, but anyway, the point is that if such a thing can be done then we can fail this elimination process.

We know, as I mentioned, salient points in PassPoints harm security, but they are essential, and they help memorability, because people have to use those salient points to remember passwords. It is unlikely to force people to choose non-salient points as their password click-points, as nobody could remember them. OK, so if we choose to not increase the image size to boost the password space then the only option remaining for us to defend against password guessing is to make it harder for computers to exploit salient points. So if a user still uses a sequence of salient points – and indeed a user needs a sequence of salient points to form a password – but if the salient points are displayed in different forms, different locations, etc, for each logon session, for example, we use a different image per session, what does this imply? Basically this means that a previous guess is not correlated with the next. This means each automated guess will not reduce the password search space any more.

Of course for the same user, her password points have to remain invariant across all the different images used for different logon sessions. But if we look at these two requirements: we need invariant points to form passwords, this is the first requirement; the second requirement is to make a previous guess independent of the next. These two requirements are exactly the same as for Captchas. For those who are familiar with Captcha design, we know there is an established principle in Captcha design: to defeat machine learning attacks, each Captcha challenge should be computationally independent of the other. Therefore we have a simple idea: we want to combine Captcha and graphical passwords. And what we have got is what we call a CaRP: Captcha as gRaphical Passwords.

The idea is simple: a CaRP is both a Captcha and a graphical password scheme. Just like PassPoints, a user clicks on an image to create her passwords. But unlike in PassPoints, in CaRP each image is actually a Captcha challenge, and it should be used only once, just like a session key. This CaRP notion is actually pretty generic. We can use either text or image-recognition Captchas to build such a graphical password scheme. Let me just show a few examples.

The first one is ClickText, a CaRP based on text Captchas. In my previous work, we looked at a lot of text Captchas, and all the text Captchas we have looked at were broken by us. Well just this morning, I apologised to some of the audience for making everybody's life hard, as our attacks made it harder for people to solve Captchas. What we have learned from our attacks is the traditional text Captcha doesn't work. Those are one line Captcha, where characters are displayed from left to right, just in one line. They will not work for this ClickText either, therefore we propose a new open problem, and we propose to form a new kind of Captcha. And we use this new Captcha to build a CaRP, which is called ClickText. So like text passwords, you still construct passwords using letters and digits, but with a limited alphabet. The server of course has to track each character's location as ground truth, so when the user logs on she clicks on an image and her click points will be mapped to the right characters by the server using the ground truth, and then the actual ground truth's hash is store in the server.

In our prototype implementation we used an alphabet of 33 characters, so if we ask users to form a password of eight characters, this gives us about 40 bits. The design choice of using 33 keys is just to make this scheme work for both laptops and touch devices. Of course you can use a larger alphabet, but ...

Frank Stajano: Could you tell us what the advantage would be compared to the password, because it looks that this is not going to be any more secure than passwords, there's more or less the same cognitive effort, perhaps more, because yours also have defined the characters, what's the benefit compared with passwords?

Saar Drimer: And you also have to click on the right place.

Reply: First, this one is better in terms of defending against online dictionary attacks. Secondly, this kind of design is suitable for a touch device like an iPad or iPhone. If we deploy this solution for e-banking on mobile devices, this will offer a lot of advantages.

Saar Drimer: If it's a touch device on the finger I just can't see it, like the bottom area, is it HK is it down there, where do you expect people to click it?

Reply: You're right, indeed sometimes a user will find it hard to figure out some distorted characters. So what they can do is to pass the confusing image and get another one.

Frank Stajano: I don't believe the claim is better for a dictionary attack because all that the programme has to do is segmentation, without even recognizing which characters, and then just try the stuff that goes in there.

Reply: Well the good thing is that this image will not be used again, so you have only one single chance to guess a password using this image, next time you get an entirely different image, so all the previous guesses will not contribute to your next guess. So all the guesses should now be started from scratch, that's why we claim this is good for defending against online dictionary attacks.

Frank Stajano: How is this different from just showing a keyboard that randomises each time?

Reply: Those keys can be easily recognized by image processing algorithms, so attackers can still know the locations of each character.

Frank Stajano: And then?

Reply: And then, they know where each character is, but if it's this design, the location of each character is in a different place for a different image.

Feng Hao: So if I understand correctly, if you are talking about a human attacker and he doesn't have an advantage over the traditional password authentication scheme, but if you're talking about the bot.

Reply: Yes, I'm talking about automated attacks.

Feng Hao: In that case, yes, it has some (inaudible).

Reply: Yes. For human attacks this slows down their guessing process.

William Claycomb: Isn't there still a finite number of combinations of pictures that you have as they will never be used again, is that really true, surely an infinite number of combinations that you can put on the screen?

Reply: Yes, that's definitely doable. The alphabet is fixed, but the location of a character can change each time, and the form and font of each character can change all the time. So this requirement is just like a requirement for ordinary Captchas, which of course is satisfied and practised by all the major companies.

Frank Stajano: I really don't see the differences here because if the point is that the password is just going to make mixed up characters like this, right, its password is not going to be word, right, otherwise you could just look for a word. Is it going to be something that has meaning, or is it going to be completely random characters?

Reply: I think actually you can use a word or a non-word, just up to your own choice, although I agree this choice of alphabet will put some constraints to users. But for the exact constraints I am not very sure at this moment.

Daniel Thomas: So this is like having a long hash function on a server, it will then take longer to attack, and instead of doing it on the client, the clients are forced to do a computational, so brute-forcing rather than the server having to do the work, so you're trying to slow down attacks by making people bruteforce lots of hashes, so you have can have a, your login process is slow because you're doing a lot of SHA-256 iterations, and making your server do it, but the client has to do its own recognition stuff, but each client has to do quite a lot of work in order to proceed.

Reply: I think the main point is that no matter what a client does, each guess doesn't reduce the password search space. So you cannot say, we definitely can crack this password with a definite number of guesses. So this process becomes probabilistic. You have to do a lot more guesses if we are talking about automated guessing attacks. But if it is about a human guess attack, that's a different story.

Daniel Thomas: So you must reduce the search space by one if you do character recognition and you know what your characters are you can ...

Reply: Basically the idea is that current recognition techniques cannot identify each character, and where each character is.

Daniel Thomas: So it would have to do random guesses?

Reply: Yes, that's the main idea. So you don't know which character is which, and you don't know where a character is.

Reply: Mike, you still have any questions?

Michael Roe: I think you've just answered my questions. What I was going to say was the reason this increases the entropy is because the program trying to do brute-force doesn't know which character is which, and so can't use its knowledge about what dictionary words are likely, and it just has to choose things, choose points randomly, I think you already covered in the answer.

Reply: Yes you are right, thanks.

Feng Hao: So from the usability perspective, if you have an eight character password, and the user will have to sit through eight random pictures, and then for each picture the user has to identify where to click. Is that quite tedious process for the user? Do you anticipate any usability issues?

Sandy Clark: Particularly because each image is going to have to contain every character, because you don't know which one they chose originally, so the images are going to be quite confusing.

Reply: We did run a usability study, and we got some interns at MSRA as the participants. The preliminary result is pretty encouraging. But of course a user study with general people would definitely be a plus.

Francesco Bergadano: It looks like those Captchas could actually be easier for this particular application with respect to Captchas where it used to use another application, because if the Captcha is defeated ...

Reply: You mean this is easier, right?

Francesco Bergadano: No, I mean, it could be an easier image, because if it's defeated then you don't get the property you want to get; next time the probability will be higher of finding the password.

Reply: But if the underlying Captcha is broken then this CaRP will not be secure because attackers can do an automated guess attack to guess your password.

Francesco Bergadano: if it's defeated one time then it's not a disaster for this particular application. And the consequence is that the image could be made a little bit larger, bigger and easier to use for the user especially on a touch screen.

Reply: Yes. OK, any other comments or questions?

Saar Drimer: This is implemented, and if it is broken, the image processing problem is not there any more.

Reply: This is indeed implemented and we trialed existing attacks and haven't succeeded yet.

Saar Drimer: I understand that it's implemented in the real world and used. What would be the solution to that if the image processing problem is no longer a hard problem, do you now need to train your users to a different system, how would you enhance your system so you increase the amount of work that the attacker has to put in? It doesn't seem to me like an easy incremental addition to how hard it is to circumvent What's your next step if it's easy to ...

Reply: If it's easy to break, you mean?

Saar Drimer: Yes.

Reply: Let me answer this question when I talk about the security analysis later on, OK? My slides will cover that. The next thing to show: we can use other types of Captchas to build CaRP as well. So this is a new CaRP instantiation which uses image recognition Captchas.

We took a Captcha in the literature, this is not designed by us, but an image recognition Captcha in the literature. The idea is that, they use two animals of similar 3D models, and then derive 2D animal images using their similar 3D models; different textures, colours, lightings and poses and etc are applied to those 2D animals, and then the animals are placed on a cluttered background. This Captcha design is currently not broken yet. In order to pass the test, a user has to click all the horse's images. In the original design there are two types of animals only, one is a horse, the other is a dog; their images look very similar.

We added a spin to this Captcha Zoo scheme in order to show that it's indeed possible to form a CaRP using image recognition Captchas. We create 10 animals of similar 3D models, then use these 3D models to derive 2D images. And this way, these animals are invariants in each logon session, and people use the animals to form a password. This of course is not as secure as ClickText because the search space is a lot smaller, but this is still stronger than PassFaces, a graphical password scheme whose password space is only about 10^4.

We can enhance the security of this scheme by adding some other tricks. For example, we introduced a grid scheme to create a new CaRP which we call AnimalGrid. Basically this is based on the ClickAnimal scheme I introduced a while ago. Once you click an animal then the system will show a grid. This grid has a grid cell size equal to the bounding square of the selected animal. So, for example, if people click 'turkey' then you will have this grid, then you can select any grid cell as your click point as well. So in this case a password is a sequence of animals interleaving with grid cells. Basically this is just to show, indeed we can make the password space larger. And in this design a password must begin with an animal. I give an example of a password here: the first click is a dog animal, then followed by Grid 2 and Grid 1. This means actually once this dog is clicked, a grid is displayed and the user just ticks two grid cells there. And for this cat, this next click, the user actually decided to choose no grid cells, then there's no grid cell there in the password, and so on. In this way we can make the password space larger.

OK, some application scenarios we have figured out for CaRP. I talked about this e-banking application already in answer to some of your questions. I think that another application, a pretty cool application, is to make a spammer's life harder. If you run an email service you know some accounts are more suspicious, they are more likely spam suspects, then OK for those accounts they have to use CaRP to login every time. This means that even if a spammer runs a bot, and this spammer knows the password, but they cannot login to their own account without human involvements. We're trying to sell this idea to Microsoft's product team. Probably one day if your account looks suspicious, you will be forced to use this CaRP all the time.

Just a little bit more about security analysis. As I mentioned, and some of you commented, computational intractability of hard AI problems is indeed fundamental to CaRP security. So far segmenting ClickText is still an open problem. And this problem is apparently much harder than cracking the usual text Captchas. And the security of Animal Zoo is also an open problem. And because we believe what we are proposing is not just individual constructions of CaRPs, what we are proposing is actually a framework of constructing graphical passwords using Captchas. Therefore we can claim that CaRP does not rely on any specific Captcha, so if a Captcha gets broken, a new and more robust scheme may appear, and then you can use that to construct a new CaRP. For example, if we have a scheme to make it more difficult to do segmenting attacks, this could be used for building a better ClickText, in response to Saar's question.

We also mentioned that this design makes it much harder to do an automated online guessing attack, even if a human is involved the attack is slowed down and still expensive. Some other new features are the following. Unlike a Captcha, CaRP is not vulnerable to a relay attack. We know for a Captcha protected system there is a relay attack, but a relay attack doesn't work on CaRP at all. We can also make a CaRP resistant to shoulder-surfing. A new technology, implemented into Microsoft Windows 8, is called dual-view support. This technology can show two views of the same screen. One view is shown as private, and the other is shown as public. This technology can help us to provide a shoulder-surfing defence. Why? Because if we display a CaRP image as private, and attackers of course can capture click-points each user is clicking, but these click-points are useless, because only when you get both the click-points and the CaRP image, the correlation of those click-points and the underlying image will tell you which character is which. But in this case, because the CaRP image is private and thus invisible to the attacker, and the next time a new image will be used, therefore this CaRP image is just like a session key. So all the click-points that attackers collect are useless, so they cannot do shoulder-surfing attacks anymore. I think CaRP would also be good at defending against cross-site scripting attacks, but it takes a lot more time to explain, that's why I've skipped that.

But the main reason why we have this feature, it goes to the main point: effectively the previous guess is independent of the next – this explains almost all the security advantages of CaRP.

But of course as a password scheme, it is essential to estimate its effective password space. We do not know yet what an effective password space is like for each CaRP instantiation we are proposing. To get an estimate for the effective password space, of course longitudinal user studies are needed.

I think actually this is my last slide. The take home message is that security primitives based on hard AI problems are pretty interesting stuff, and that this is an interesting new paradigm. And now we have Captcha and CaRP, so the question naturally we want to ask is, what's next, what else can we do, what else can we invent along this line? And I also encourage the audience to think, what other killer applications we can figure out for CaRP, whether there are some novel use of such primitives in security protocols. This's the last slide of my talk. If you have any questions... You can have a look at my adverts as well.

William Claycomb: So I understand the image itself on the back end for the system, the image itself is a grid thing, and at some point the user presses a point on the image, the machine recognises the point on the grid, and the machine knows what's supposed to be in that grid, whether an image or a combination this user has selected.

Reply: The server knows the click-points, because once the click-points are clicked they will be passed to the server, when generating each CaRP image, the server knows exactly where the character is. Such information is stored as the ground truth. So this design is not about defending against offline attack, it is mainly for dealing with online guessing attacks.

William Claycomb: So the attacker, you're trying to prevent somebody trying to guess the password, the password is CAT, and they have to determine where C A T are, and each different image changes every time. What about an attack where the attacker lets the system introduce the variability, I just click the same point, at the same time, every image I put the same point and let the variability happen at the backend so that the guessing ...

Reply: What vulnerability are you thinking about?

William Claycomb: Well eventually C A T will, the randomness will appear at the same point on three sets of images.

Reply: No, actually in theory that shouldn't appear in the same place with a limited amount of time, in theory that will be randomised.

William Claycomb: So in theory, when I'm like picking the letter for images for my password I will never by chance pick the same place on the screen twice in a row?

Bruce Christianson: There's always a possibility that you're going to get somebody's private key in RSA by being very lucky. (laughter)

Reply: Good point.

Michael Roe: But clearly, you cannot guess the password that way. It makes it much stronger to defeat, it takes many more guesses to guess it, that's why we're choosing them at random, than you would have done by using the dictionary, and knowing which words are active, choosing the right new words, because you've got an idea of which one is the most likely one.

William Claycomb: I'm just thinking about the key space; would a two-character password be secure in the scheme, or three or four, what's necessary.

Reply: Well I think you have a good point, if two, then this could be a problem, I think that's why we actually enforce in our study eight as the minimum length.

Bruce Christianson: It deprives the attacker of some opportunities to do systematic searching.

Reply: And we have to worry about human guessing as well. If the password is only two characters then this would be too weak. So for the real deployment it is not just about automated attacks, it is about human guessing attacks as well. So a minimum length is definitely needed.

Towards a Theory of Application Compartmentalisation

Robert N.M. Watson[1], Steven J. Murdoch[1], Khilan Gudka[1],
Jonathan Anderson[1], Peter G. Neumann[2], and Ben Laurie[3]

[1] University of Cambridge
[2] SRI International
[3] Google UK Ltd.

Abstract. Application compartmentalisation decomposes software applications into sandboxed components, each delegated only the rights it requires to operate. Compartmentalisation is seeing increased deployment in vulnerability mitigation, motivated informally by appeal to the principle of least privilege. Drawing a comparison with capability systems, we consider how a distributed system interpretation supports an argument that compartmentalisation improves application security.

1 Introduction

Application compartmentalisation decomposes applications into sandboxed components, each assigned only the rights it requires to operate. Motivated by the *principle of least privilege*, the focus of historic work on compartmentalisation has been primarily in access-control policy enforcement [25]. More recently, compartmentalisation has been employed in *vulnerability mitigation*: exploited vulnerabilities leak only the subset of overall application rights that are held by the compromised sandbox. For example, web browsers might be compartmentalised such that each web page visited is rendered in its own sandbox [22]. Successful exploitation of a JavaScript rendering bug might lead only to very limited leakage of system-centered rights (e.g., local files) and application-centered rights (e.g., username/password tuples for other web sites).

To date, application compartmentalisation has been intuitively grounded in the principle of least privilege, but without a theoretical foundation that permits the use of formal or automated reasoning. In this paper, we consider experience gained in developing and deploying compartmentalised applications, and its implications for new theoretical foundations. Our approach considers applications to be distributed systems, and is, therefore, a fundamentally protocol-centered approach. This viewpoint grants us access to a large existing literature on network and distributed system analysis: we reason about the gains attackers make in communicating with, and compromising, elements of the system as a network of components. One important outcome of this work will be a new approach to application security measurement.

B. Christianson et al. (Eds.): Security Protocols 2013, LNCS 8263, pp. 19–27, 2013.

2   Protection Model

Application compartmentalisation is premised on strong *isolation* between individual compartments: no communication is permitted except via controlled communication channels. This is a view long-espoused in security system design, ranging from microkernel- and security-kernel systems to programming-language virtual machines. Isolation deployed within applications typically follows a *sandboxing* model: code is encapsulated in a process or other execution container, and granted only specific rights delegated or forwarded from the containing system. We have previously observed an elegant alignment between the intersection of sandboxing features across operating system platforms and the *capability system model* [7,26].

Capability system models can be mapped into classic OS primitives (processes and IPC) if access to ambient authority is limited. This approachs falls naturally out of classic capability hardware and OS designs such as the CAP computer [27] and seL4 [12], but also hybrid capability systems such as Capsicum that allow selected processes to operate in a non-ambient "capability mode" [26]. Capability system models can also be layered over other substrates, such as distributed systems or programming languages such as Joe-E [17] or Caja [18].

All of these systems are able to represent non-hierarchical protection models: mutually distrusting program instances with disjoint sets of rights may safely interact. However, the efficiency of cross-domain calls involving mutual distrust varies significantly – programming languages such as Java provide this very efficiently through a blend of static and dynamic enforcement, whereas hardware-supported process models rely on slower message passing via a mutually trusted kernel. This variation introduces a necessary set of tradeoffs between performance and security – i.e., more granular compartmentalisations that better approximate the principle of least privilege may incur greater cost on some substrates.

In general, we believe that sandboxing schemes approximate capability systems, but with a not-uncommon problem that support for flexible delegation and fine-grained application-level access control may be limited by some substrates (e.g., SELinux with its static rule configuration [16]). It is unclear to us whether this rigidity improves performance; in our experience, however, it observably increases fragility in the presence of ongoing software development.

3   Applications as Distributed Systems

In Capsicum, the kernel and a small amount of userspace communications code act as the run-time Trusted Computing Base (TCB) [2]. Sets of sandboxes and their interconnections are able to represent different communication and trust relationships, including both purely hierarchical relationships (e.g., the HTTPS download component depends fully on the ambient component of `fetch`), non-hierarchical isolation (e.g., different renderer processes in a web browser), and non-hierarchical mutual distrust with communication (e.g., two components representing different stages in a firewall processing pipeline). This approach suggests a graph-oriented

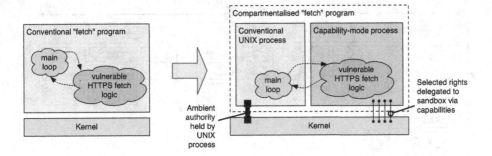

Fig. 1. Whereas conventional HTTPS `fetch` executes within a single process holding ambient user privilege, Capsicum's `fetch` executes TLS in a sandbox holding only delegated rights. This is a code-oriented compartmentalisation: selected risky code runs in a per-application instance sandbox.

analysis of program structure, in which nodes execute components with state (processes), and edges are IPC channels (perhaps sockets).

However, this graph captures only communications, and not trust (or perhaps more accurately, dependence), which may track communication edges (especially in a purely information-flow-centric analysis), but also span multiple edges via intermediate nodes. For example, microkernel systems often employ the notion of a service namespace manager, such as in Mach [1]; isolated components will necessarily trust the namespace manager in some form, but via the namespace manager they may indirectly trust the actions of other parties that are reachable via the shared namespace. As such, trust is more complex than simple annotations on communications edges in the graph.

This is fundamentally a distributed system view of application structure, allowing us to borrow an extensive literature on protocols, consensus, fault tolerance, and distrust, including Lamport's Byzantine Generals [13], and more recent work on understanding and managing compromise in distributed systems [23], software composition [19], and layering of compartmentalised software over microkernels and separation kernels [3].

4   Compartmentalisation Philosophies

Figure 1 illustrates the transformation of a conventional application, `fetch`, into a compartmentalised one via Capsicum. The kernel provides a capability system substrate; a portion of `fetch` operates with ambient authority, outside of the capability system, and a sandboxed HTTPS download component executes with only delegated rights. In this example, two types of rights have been delegated via *kernel capabilities*: a set of explicitly delegated files and sockets, and an IPC channel used to communicate with the parent.

Even a program as simple as `fetch` serves as a useful proving ground for exploring ideas about compartmentalisation – not least, by bringing to light the observation that a single program may have many different possible decompositions, with

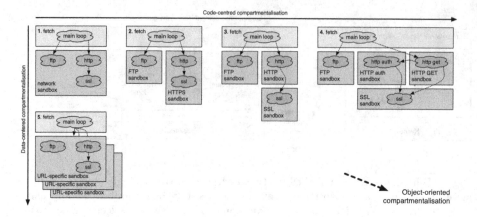

Fig. 2. `fetch` and `libfetch` can be compartmentalised along many different cut points, with different security, performance, and complexity tradeoffs

different security properties. The illustrated compartmentalisation is fundamentally *code-oriented*, in that two pieces of code, a main loop and a set of network functions, are separated from one another. Selection of a decomposition is often grounded in our understanding of *past vulnerabilities*: OpenSSL code has suffered a number of past vulnerabilities, both stemming from incorrect implementation and incorrect use. Frequently, these vulnerabilities have been remotely exploitable, leading to remote code execution, which can be mitigated by sandboxing.

However, further decomposition along *data-oriented* lines can also be justified: `fetch` can accept multiple URLs on the command line, and if an exploit originates from one web server communicated with, exploit code may have access to later files downloaded in the same code-oriented sandbox. We might, therefore, choose to further introduce sandboxes one per web site, pursuing the principle of least privilege. We might reasonably take the view that this is an *object-oriented partitioning*, instantiating an object to process each URL, based on a common class, even though the C programming language itself does not capture those higher-level programming properties. It is for this reason that we suggest that fine-grained compartmentalised applications adopt the *object-capability paradigm*; Figure 2 illustrates additional points on the code-based spectrum, including finer-grained compartmentalisations even within the processing of as single HTTPS connection.

We make several further observations about the nature of compartmentalisation. Finer-grained decompositions require tradeoffs between security goals, program complexity, and performance, as security-beneficial decomposition requires both programmer attention and incurs a run-time overhead. In designing decompositions, we are responding to informal notions of risk – properties of the code itself: past vulnerabilities, source code provenance (e.g., open-source supply-chain trojans), and risky code structures (e.g., video CODECs). However, we are also taking into account where data originated (a file or web site), its sensitivity (e.g., keying material), and how it will be processed. Notions of data provenance (informally, taint) and the nature of rights that could be leaked will all be inputs to this reasoning.

These are all aspects of compartmentalisation design that we would like to capture in a structured model.

5   A Graph-Oriented Analysis

Traditional graph representations of networks (whether of connected hosts, collections of applications on a host, or subsystems within an application) represent components as nodes and edges indicate permitted communication paths between components. This representation lends itself to compartmentalisation through blocking communication paths which are not necessary, using firewalls, mandatory access control, or capabilities as appropriate. Eliminating an edge in this model by blocking a communication path will improve security, but not all edges are created equal. Typically, there is some concept of the source of malicious activity (e.g. the Internet), and following connectivity from here to other nodes will show which nodes are at particular risk.

However, merely being connected to a potentially malicious node does not necessarily imply that that the network design is vulnerable. While some communication paths are highly dangerous (e.g. exposing an industrial control system designed without security in mind to the Internet), others may be far less problematic (e.g. connecting a hardened web server to the Internet). Including information about how vulnerable a particular node is can help, as it indicates the likelihood that a node may be compromised if it encounters malicious input. However, even this extension is not sufficient – for example while connecting the web server to the Internet may be fine, connecting its file system to a malicious file server is likely not.

The traditional model can capture connectivity, but not trust, and so has significant limitations when it comes to measuring the network. Instead each node can be modelled as a series of ports, and connectivity is from a port on one node to a port on another, forming a matrix of probabilities. Rather than a single vulnerability probability for a node, there is a probability assigned to each pair of nodes stating the probability that a malicious output will result from a malicious input. In the example of a web server, a malicious input on the socket input of the web server is unlikely to lead to malicious output and thus will be assigned a low probability, whereas a malicious input in the file system input of the same program will likely result in malicious output on all ports.

This approach captures both trust between nodes and vulnerability of applications, but a high probability does not necessarily mean that an individual node is somehow flawed. A router may forward malicious traffic (unless the router has a suitably configured firewall) even though it is operating as intended. To evaluate whether a network is secure it is necessary to establish the consequences of connectivity between malicious nodes and critical resources to be protected.

Defences can also be modelled in this approach. For example compartmentalising an application may not affect the probability that it will be compromised, and so will not be captured by assigning a single probability of compromise figure to the node. However, the matrix approach is more suitable – compartmentalisation results in the probability for malicious output will be lowered in cases where the input and output ports are in different compartments.

While powerful, the challenge of using the model is in its complexity. Extracting data to fill in the vulnerability matrix is challenging. Also the computational complexity of reasoning about the network is high, due to the number of network states growing exponentially with the number of states of each node. Therefore new techniques in data collection and simulation will need to be adopted for this model to be fruitful.

6   Related Work

Application compartmentalisation is a recasting of the microkernel hypothesis into the application space – in fact, contemporary monolithic applications are of a similar scale (millions of lines of code) to the monolithic kernels that motivated microkernel research. Past security-kernel research is concerned with providing a reliable TCB for decomposed components [15], and more recent microkernel research has likewise been interested in the verifiability of security properties when combining untrustworthy components over a formally verified separation kernel [3].

Karger originally proposed the use of capability systems to contain trojans [10], an approach later adopted by Provos in SSH privilege separation [21] and Kilpatrick in Privman [11]. While these application decompositions were concerned with UNIX root privilege, contemporary application compartmentalisation is more interested in limiting rights to ambient (unprivileged) user rights, as utilised by Reis et al in Chromium [22] and by the authors in Capsicum [26]. This is a response to the observation that, on a single-user machine, access to the single user's account is, in practice, almost as important as access to root privilege.

We are interested in capturing a variety of trust relationships in application compartmentalisation – not least, hierarchical trust models explored in Multics [24], non-hierarchical models, such as assured pipelines, from Type Enforcement [5], and the flexible programmer-driven models supported by capability systems that differentiate policy and enforcement, such as in CAP [27], PSOS [20], and Hydra [14].

Research into automation of application decomposition is also directly relevant, although not always well-supported by current theory. Brumley and Song developed Privtrans [6]; Bittau et al, Wedge [4], and most recently, Harris et al have used parity games to drive automata-based application of policies to compartmentalised software [9] – a policy- rather than least-privilege–oriented approach. Our own SOAAP toolchain attempts to take into account many factors in selecting (and trading off) application decompositions in a dialogue with the developer, which has motivated our search for formal grounding [8].

7   Conclusion

Our ongoing work with application compartmentalisation has driven us to begin development of theory helping us to justify and quantify program decompositions. Throughout, the principle of least privilege (together with desires for good software engineering practices such as abstraction, encapsulation, and facile composability) guides our approach, with a focus on providing vulnerability mitigation. In a broad sense, compartmentalisation represents the adoption of further distributed system programming paradigms in local systems: interconnected components are isolated in sandboxes used to construct larger user-facing applications, and subject to a variety of faults (malicious and otherwise). This has led us to a graph-oriented analysis that will provide the foundation for modelling application security through quantifiable comparisons of risk and rights exposure. This in turn will lead to the development of automated tools to help develop and reason about compartmentalisation strategies.

Acknowledgments. We would like to thank our colleagues on the Capsicum, CTSRD, and SOAAP projects for their thoughts and comments contribution to this paper, including Ross Anderson, David Chisnall, Brooks Davis, Pawel Dawidek, Steven Hand, Anil Madhavapeddy, Ilias Marinos, Will Morland, Michael Roe, and Hassen Saidi.

We gratefully acknowledge Google, Inc. for its sponsorship. Portions of this work were sponsored by the Defense Advanced Research Projects Agency (DARPA) and the Air Force Research Laboratory (AFRL), under contract FA8750-10-C-0237. The views, opinions, and/or findings contained in this report are those of the authors and should not be interpreted as representing the official views or policies, either expressed or implied, of the Defense Advanced Research Projects Agency or the Department of Defense.

References

1. Accetta, M., Baron, R., Golub, D., Rashid, R., Tevanian, A., Young, M.: Mach: A New Kernel Foundation for UNIX Development. Tech. rep., Computer Science Department, Carnegie Mellon University (August 1986)
2. Anderson, J.P.: Computer Security Technology Planning Study. Tech. rep., Electronic Systems Division, Air Force Systems Command, Hanscom Field, Bedford, MA 01730 (October 1972)
3. Andronick, J., Greenaway, D., Elphinstone, K.: Towards proving security in the presence of large untrusted components. In: Proceedings of the 5th Workshop on Systems Software Verification (October 2010)
4. Bittau, A., Marchenko, P., Handley, M., Karp, B.: Wedge: Splitting Applications into Reduced-Privilege Compartments. In: Proceedings of the 5th USENIX Symposium on Networked Systems Design and Implementation, pp. 309–322. USENIX Association (2008)
5. Boebert, W.E., Kain, R.Y.: A practical alternative to hierarchical integrity policies. In: Proceedings of the 8th National Computer Security Conference (1985)

6. Brumley, D., Song, D.: Privtrans: automatically partitioning programs for privilege separation. In: Proceedings of the 13th Conference on USENIX Security Symposium, SSYM 2004, vol. 13, p. 5. USENIX Association, Berkeley (2004)
7. Dennis, J.B., Van Horn, E.C.: Programming semantics for multiprogrammed computations. Commun. ACM 9(3), 143–155 (1966)
8. Gudka, K., Watson, R.N.M., Hand, S., Laurie, B., Madhavapeddy, A.: Exploring compartmentalisation hypotheses with SOAAP. In: Proceedings of the Workshop on Adaptive Host and Network Security (AHANS 2012). IEEE (September 2012)
9. Harris, W.R., Farley, B., Jha, S., Reps, T.: Secure Programming as a Parity Game. Tech. Rep. 1694, University of Wisconsin Madison (July 2011)
10. Karger, P.A.: Limiting the damage potential of discretionary trojan horses. In: IEEE Symposium on Security and Privacy, pp. 32–37 (1987)
11. Kilpatrick, D.P.: A Library for Partitioning Applications. In: Proceedings of USENIX Annual Technical Conference, pp. 273–284. USENIX Association (2003)
12. Klein, G., Andronick, J., Elphinstone, K., Heiser, G., Cock, D., Derrin, P., Elkaduwe, D., Engelhardt, K., Kolanski, R., Norrish, M., Sewell, T., Tuch, H., Winwood, S.: seL4: formal verification of an operating-system kernel. Commun. ACM 53, 107–115 (2009)
13. Lamport, L., Shostak, R., Pease, M.: The Byzantine generals problem. ACM Transactions on Programming Languages and Systems 4(3), 382–401 (1982)
14. Levin, R., Cohen, E., Corwin, W., Pollack, F., Wulf, W.: Policy/mechanism separation in Hydra. In: SOSP 1975: Proceedings of the Fifth ACM Symposium on Operating Systems Principles, pp. 132–140. ACM, New York (1975)
15. Lipner, S.B., Wulf, W.A., Schell, R.R., Popek, G.J., Neumann, P.G., Weissman, C., Linden, T.A.: Security kernels. In: AFIPS 1974: Proceedings of the National Computer Conference and Exposition, May 6-10, pp. 973–980. ACM, New York (1974)
16. Loscocco, P.A., Smalley, S.D.: Integrating Flexible Support for Security Policies into the Linux Operating System. In: Proceedings of the USENIX Annual Technical Conference, pp. 29–42. USENIX Association (June 2001)
17. Mettler, A., Wagner, D., Close, T.: Joe-E: A Security-Oriented Subset of Java. In: Proceedings of the Network and Distributed System Security Symposium, NDSS 2010 (February 2010)
18. Miller, M.S., Samuel, M., Laurie, B., Awad, I., Stay, M.: Caja: Safe active content in sanitized javascript (May 2008),
    http://google-caja.googlecode.com/files/caja-spec-2008-06-07.pdf
19. Neumann, P.G.: Principled assuredly trustworthy composable architectures. Tech. rep., Computer Science Laboratory, SRI International, Menlo Park (December 2004)
20. Neumann, P.G., Boyer, R.S., Feiertag, R.J., Levitt, K.N., Robinson, L.: A Provably Secure Operating System: The System, Its Applications, and Proofs, Second Edition. Tech. Rep. CSL-116, Computer Science Laboratory, SRI International (May 1980)
21. Provos, N., Friedl, M., Honeyman, P.: Preventing privilege escalation. In: Proceedings of the 12th Conference on USENIX Security Symposium SSYM 2003, vol. 12, p. 16. USENIX Association, Berkeley (2003)
22. Reis, C., Gribble, S.D.: Isolating web programs in modern browser architectures. In: EuroSys 2009: Proceedings of the 4th ACM European Conference on Computer Systems, pp. 219–232. ACM, New York (2009)
23. Robertson, P., Laddaga, R.: Adaptive security and trust. In: Proceedings of the Workshop on Adative Host and Network Security. IEEE (Septmeber 2012)

24. Saltzer, J.H.: Protection and control of information sharing in Multics. In: SOSP 1973: Proceedings of the fourth ACM Symposium on Operating System Principles. ACM, New York (1973)
25. Saltzer, J.H., Schroeder, M.D.: The protection of information in computer systems. Proceedings of the IEEE 63(9), 1278–1308 (1975)
26. Watson, R.N.M., Anderson, J., Laurie, B., Kennaway, K.: Capsicum: Practical capabilities for UNIX. In: Proceedings of the 19th USENIX Security Symposium. USENIX Association, Berkeley (2010)
27. Wilkes, M., Needham, R., The Cambridge, C.A.P.: Computer and Its Operating System. Elsevier North Holland, New York (1979)

Towards a Theory of Application Compartmentalisation (Transcript of Discussion)

Robert N.M. Watson

University of Cambridge

I would like to start by acknowledging a great many collaborators, some of whose names appear on the first slide.

Here is a plausible outline, we'll see how it goes. First I will tell you about application compartmentalisation. You have probably heard of this already, but you might know it by another name, perhaps privilege separation or another term. However, I want to reintroduce it using some specific vocabulary. I'm going to tell you very briefly about capability systems, as we are attempting to understand compartmentalised applications in terms of the vocabulary of capability systems. But the actual topic of this talk is how to write these compartmentalised programs. I'm going to suggest – and it might be true – that we could apply ideas from security protocols and distributed systems to understand the behaviour of these pieces of software. In particular we would like to get from a world where we have a very informal understanding of why we break programs into pieces and sandbox their components to a more formal one, and ideally more quantitative one. By appealing to the literature of distributed systems and security protocols, we can start to do that.

Very briefly, what is application compartmentalisation? The intuition is pretty simple. We start out with some application that historically will have had what we call "ambient rights" in the system – which is to say, pretty much everything. It contains vulnerable pieces of code – in this case we're going to talk about the fetch application on BSD, but you could think of wget or curl, or any other command-line tool that accepts a set of URLs and downloads the files. In the brave new world order we compartmentalise fetch: part of it continues to run with full rights – so it has the ability to open the files you ask it to open – but the remainder of it will run in a sandbox. The principle is fairly straightforward: when something goes horribly wrong, we'd like the horribly-wrong thing to be in the sandbox.

So how does this play out? We decompose the applications into parts; how to do that is the problem of interest. We will try to make each one run with only the rights it needs, the principle of least privilege, the granularity of which is an interesting question. And then we're going to claim that at the end of it we've mitigated vulnerabilities, that is, somehow the vulnerability has less impact because we're running things in a sandbox. This is all intuition-based today, and we'd like to go somewhere a little bit more structured if we can.

So what happens when things go wrong? Well when a vulnerability happens on this side of the slide, they get everything, and typically that's full access to

B. Christianson et al. (Eds.): Security Protocols 2013, LNCS 8263, pp. 28–38, 2013.
© Springer-Verlag Berlin Heidelberg 2013

your file system. On a single-user machine, which many machines are, that really is everything of value. On the other side of the slide, you leak certain very specific delegated rights. We're going to try and make life harder for the attacker because if they want to get larger sets of rights they have to break more things. Privilege separation is an idea popularised by Neil Provos in the late 1990s, but actually we can trace the idea back to Paul Karger, here at the Computer Laboratory, who proposed that we might use capability systems to mitigate Trojans. Today's interesting notion of a Trojan might be something that arrived in your software supply chain, but it might as well be a vulnerability that's been exploited, so the idea is fairly interchangeable.

This is what we term an "application TCB". Historically when we talked about trusted computing bases, we meant operating systems and the CPU; today applications are really important, because many of our applications are managing different security domains. They're dealing with data from many different origins, and perhaps we can use this compartmentalisation idea to try and make them run better in the same way we did for historic TCBs.

Let me give you a couple of examples. When you use your web browser, you visit many different sites – you would like to think that every one of those tabs is isolated from the other tabs. We can push it a bit further because each tab renders content from many different sites, and we might want to further compartmentalise there. Each site itself might present content from many different origins – images appearing in GMail are downloaded from Google, but you might not trust them equally, or at all. You would not want attachments in one e-mail to interfere with processing of attachments in another e-mail, despite both arriving in the browser side-by-side from GMail: you want them in separate boxes.

You can extrapolate from this to many other kinds of applications: office suites and your mail reader have these properties as well. You can imagine progressively finer- and finer-grained sandboxing improving security. It should be obvious that a failure of your application as a TCB allows all the data and rights to leak back and forth: access to your web banking from your webmail is not something that we want to encourage.

There was a class of systems called capability systems. Here's a notable capability system, the CAP Computer; you can go and see it at the Computer Laboratory. If you see it live it is in a pretty shade of blue, here it's black and white, a photo from the CL's relics archive. These systems were designed to implement the principles of least privilege: they're designed to have lots of compartments, and they have a model by which rights are passed around in the system. We call these things capabilities, and the textbook definition says that they are "unforgeable tokens of authority" that you can pass around, but are unable to simply make up; you have to have received them from somebody. You only have the rights (or capabilities) that are delegated to you; you're not allowed to access other things in the system without their capabilities. Delegation is a key part of the model; there isn't necessarily an access control policy inherent to the system, but we might layer one on top, so it is a protection mechanism, not a policy mechanism.

We can build interesting things on top. We can have policies about information flow, we can have policies about fine-grained delegation, and so on. This is an approach widely adopted in microkernels – the compartmentalisation story seems familiar as it is exactly the same story as microkernels: take a big piece of software, break it into pieces, and put them in compartments. We might wonder to ourselves why we care about compartmentalisation in applications today, and why did the microkernel story not go so well? One reason is need: we have real security problems we want to mitigate today, which is why people run their SSH daemons in a compartment. There's also performance: computers have gotten a lot faster and so we're willing to invest energy in places perhaps we weren't before.

A few years ago, in collaboration with several of the co-authors on this paper, we built a system called Capsicum. We attempted to take ideas from research capability systems and merge them with a conventional UNIX operating system. We did this so that we would have access to a large application corpus – real software is very complicated. Central to this is moving away from using access-control primitives for sandboxing, and moving towards an explicit protection primitive. An example of the former is using SELinux to create compartments using access-control rules; our approach is exactly the other way around, in which the fundamental primitive is the compartment. We bridge compartments, and we might use access-control to limit that, but the compartment is fundamental. In Capsicum, some pieces of your programme run with all the rights they've held previously; other pieces have only the rights they are delegated – hence being a hybrid capability system. We argue that makes Capsicum incrementally adoptable.

Once you have a system like that you begin to think: "how am I going to write these programmes that are so much better than they were before." You can think about it in lots of different ways. In fact, every application has a spectrum of possible compartmentalisations that might be interesting, which allow you to trade off performance, security, and complexity in different ways to get different results. Obviously one potential result is incorrectness, though we try to aim for correct programmes; I'll talk more about that in a moment. I have suggested that finer-grained decomposition gives you better mitigation of vulnerabilities. Intuitively this makes sense: the smaller the sandbox is, the fewer rights each has, the fewer rights you gain when you exploit a vulnerability. Not only that, you get network effects where you (as the attacker) can't reach every component, and because you can't reach it, perhaps it is less exposed as well.

I've suggested a number of axies, but let's look at the details. One axis might be data-centred compartmentalisation. For example, if we take the fetch web downloaded programme, we might decide that processing for each site belongs in its own sandbox. When we do the risky bit, which is the downloading of data and parsing of protocols, we want an exploit from one site to affect only other downloads from the same site. I've also suggested we might go further – perhaps rather than combining URLs downloaded from the same site in a single sandbox, we give every URL a separate sandbox. Another dimension is code-centred compartmentalisation. We observe, for example, that if we're processing HTTP within SSL, we could put HTTP and SSL processing in different sandboxes. If you have a vulnerability in HTTP processing you don't get access to the client cert, which might be on the SSL side. As you move across this dimension you get finer and finer-grained compartmentalisation. And, as your throw the code and data instances together, you inevitably observe that this sounds object-oriented; indeed, many people who build capability systems use an object-oriented programming style, with capabilities as references to objects (with rights) – a quite natural composition.

If we were to zoom in very slightly we might wonder, when you compromise one of these components, what do you get out of it? The answer depends on how we've distributed these system capabilities (files and so on), in Capsicum. But there is another notion, an application-centered object: sometimes your application itself has objects that are interesting – a database of objects, for example, and these are just as important, perhaps more important, than system objects. They're frequently expressed in terms of the system capabilities such that we have to be careful when we reason about this, and obviously the goal is to distribute things as carefully and minimally as we can. I suggested we might have this problem, via application-level keying material, with TLS and HTTP, which might be one reason we break things up. We might decompose things further: we could take HTTP processing itself, and break it into pieces so that the keying material used to authenticate to an HTTP proxy is not available for the processing of later MIME encodings of data. There are all sorts of possibilities here.

Naturally, having come up with this great solution we now have a new problem, which is that writing these programmes turns out to be very difficult. The first observation we made almost immediately was when you compartmentalise a program, it ceases to be a local programme in a classic sense – it becomes a distributed system. You have lots of parts running around, talking to each other, often using message passing, suffering various kinds of problems. We would prefer our programmes to do (almost) the same things when we're done compartmentalising as they did before: most of the time they should behave identically, and once in a while they behave differently, and that's when the sandboxing kicks in. But we found it was quite hard to do this, and particularly, as you start to replicate data between sandboxes, attempt to keep them consistent, and so on, you encounter classic data-synchronisation problems. We leave the programmer with this trade-off space: how should they determine what is the right trade off? Do they accomplish their security goals through various cuts through the system? And because compartmentalising requires work, do you become over-invested in a particular compartmentalisation? It is hard to change compartmentalisations after introducing them – so you want to explore the space without having to implement every one of them.

An important larger question is: if you've made all these changes to your programme, did you meet your security goals? We would like to be able to reason about this – and get away from the intuitive "ah, the principle of least privilege says we should do this" and towards a more structured analysis. We have a project named SOAAP, which I won't describe in detail: the aim of the project is to provide analysis tools for applications, which will provide advice to the programmer about compartmentalisation. The programmer describes hypotheses, annotating the programme with, "I was thinking about compartmentalising it this way, and I want to accomplish these security goals; could you help me figure out if that's true." Of course that requires a model of why it is that compartmentalisation helps, which is why we're thinking about some of these things. We are able to look at things like past vulnerabilities that are annotated in the programme – where have you found problems before? You could also have as an input to that an automated vulnerability analysis tool with false positives and false negatives: "there might well be a vulnerability here," or "this is the kind of code where you don't tend to find a vulnerability." We also perform information-flow analysis and call-graph analysis trying to figure out, if you have keying material, could it leak out using the APIs in the way that you have, so your SSL key escapes to the wrong place? Finally, we do some performance analysis, trying to predict whether, if you pick a particular compartmentalisation, will you meet your performance goals? So it's an analysis tool: it doesn't actually perform the compartmentalisation, it helps you reason about it, and play with it, and it's very cheap to use so you can trivially vary the annotations and get updated results.

What you get in return is advice: you can change your application, you can change your hypotheses, and iterate until you are satisfied. I also wanted to draw your attention to something on the left-hand side of the diagram: its inputs. There is the application author, but often the application author is not the person doing the compartmentalisation. We often have a security developer who turns up later and wants to take an application and add these. Despite being a very common structure, this causes lots of problems because the security developer doesn't understand the application; the application author doesn't understand the security goals; so we have to try and help them meet in the middle. And there's this last character – sometimes us – the person who provides the sandboxing platform, who must characterise its semantics because authors of portable applications want to know what the implications are when the application is moved from one platform to another with different sandboxing properties.

I've suggested this might be a distributed systems problem, or a protocol problem, so let's rearrange things a bit, draw dotted lines, and boxes, and now we have the same picture but differently represented. The dotted lines are communication channels, and we have the kernel, or TCB; some rights are delegated – this really thick one is intended to suggest ambient authority. This component really has all rights in the system, so it is necessarily part of the TCB. These other elements might arguably be part of the TCB, because something might depend on them for security: if SSL processing is wrong, then it's hard to imagine you're going to get HTTP processing particularly right. We could also add some labels to try and make it look more familiar to a security-protocol community: Alice and Bob, and Eve. You often have intermediate nodes in these structures – some component that sits in the middle and forwards messages, whether it's the kernel, or perhaps a name space service. Objects are advertised, and exchanged, and so on.

We could also, somewhat obviously, observe that the dotted lines that I've drawn mean that message passing is taking place. It might be performed by the kernel, it might just be initiated by the kernel, it could be capability oriented. One of the other interesting things is that we're allowed to pass around these capabilities: suppose this process has a capability; it sends a message and it can attach the capability. We have a vocabulary for this in security protocols literature – we call these capabilities "keys," and of course key is a term often used in capability systems. We likewise have distributed capability systems, so we could reapply that vocabulary. There's some transitivity: if I give you a capability then, in many capability systems, you're allowed to delegate it on, so you have a delegation-based model. In fact, we could make a comparison with systems like Kerberos, or cryptographically protected data services, and so on, try to reuse that vocabulary as well.

I mentioned reachability earlier, but I wanted to be explicit. Direct reachability is important: I can't talk to a node unless I have a communications channel. However, compartments may link multiple communication channels providing shared services such as file-system access. So reachability is important to understanding exposure, but it is not the only element, we can't simply assign probabilities to nodes, and then specify a probably of compromise, and extrapolate directly.

I'm going to touch on a few more specific topics – first, correctness. One element of system correctness has to do with minimising the set of capabilities assigned to each compartment while still retaining programme functionality. We're also interested in this data synchronisation problem: not classically a security problem per se, but we also do know that security problems arise out of synchronisation problems, so we have to be a bit careful, if we don't get that right it's not going to help things. And of course there's this pragmatic question: if I build a compartmentalisation, is it something that falls naturally out of the existing structure of my programme, or is it a ton of work? If I invest lots of energy trying to select this compartmentalisation, might I discover that I don't really like it? Performance in these systems is a first class property, so an interesting further question is, if I have a strategy, how will affect a workload I'm actually interested in? There are trade offs here, so one interest is in selecting performance bounds: will a given compartmentalisation lead to no more than a ten percent slowdown for my workload?

A more interesting question has to do with changes to the protection substrate. If I take code written for Capsicum and I reuse it on Linux, using SELinux for sandboxing, are the performance trade offs the same, and will that affect how I understand how the application is going to behave? We want to help the programmers reason about that. In classic distributed system performance parlance, a key part of that is avoiding or mitigating round trip times. There's therefore a tendency to adopt asynchronous programming styles to try and mitigate system calls and message passing. That unfortunately forces us to more complex application event models.

When we think about what the attacker is trying to accomplish, we can ask ourselves, "what will they gain when they compromise something?" The obvious benefit is data in the process, so we can perhaps gain access to the keying material associated with the TLS session, and so on. But we're also interested in system rights, such as local files – and also references to communication channels to other sandboxes. More generally we are interested in the leaking of computational resources; that tends to be less of a focus in our community, but we do like availability.

When we contemplate these relationships, it would be tempting to use the word "trust" – which we don't like very much as it's very broad – but certainly there is a notion of dependence. There is dependence entirely in a functional sense, "does one node depend on another node." There's also an attack surface associated with opportunity: if I compromise one node, I interface more directly with another that I want to attack – perhaps exploiting lower-level vulnerabilities in its RPC library, for example.

The most important part is security. Critically: does the compartmentalisation implementation I have limit the flow of rights through the system – has sandboxing actually bought me anything, or do I simply have a slower and more complicated programme? One way to think about this is to consider past vulnerabilities: if they exploit a vulnerability, can we reason about the effects? Well, in the distributed system view, when we look at capabilities held by the compromised component, and ones that depend on it, we can answer that question directly. For example, we can annotate in programme source code where the vulnerability took place (historically), perform a static or dynamic analysis, and report on what rights will be leaked. For the first time, we actually have quite useful information about the effects (and mitigation) of a vulnerability. We can also hypothesise about future vulnerabilities, reusing the literature on vulnerability analysis, and probabilistic understanding of where they might occur.

Another interesting case occurs if one of the pieces of my very large application pulled from a third party turns out to contain a Trojan. If you are the author of the Chromium web browser you might find that you have an application TCB footprint of around four million, perhaps six million lines of code. You have WebKit, you have image libraries, you have libpng, you have the works, and it is not impossible that someone has compromised one of the repositories from which you get code. We want to be able to reason about that – and we can in this world view: we can say, "where are all the compartments where this code could run?", "what rights are exposed to them?", and "what is the impact of discovering that we have a Trojan?" This is a very nice world view.

And finally there's this protection substrate question. What happens if I move from one platform to another? In particular, we have security refinements to file descriptors in Capsicum that don't exist in other UNIX systems, and so we are able to more finely compartmentalise programmes in terms of delegated rights. We need to know what the implications are of losing access to aspects of the model across different platforms: how does the set of potentially leaked rights change?

All this suggests that we're actually thinking about risk in a much more mature way, although we must use the word "risk" with some caution. We're trying to ask questions such as: what are the rights that will be leaked if there is a partial or total compromise of some specific component, and then we want to build from that out, spreading across a network of compartments, both in terms of direct and indirection communications and functional dependence. This in turn how affects attacker strategy, so we can lift ideas out of the space on attacker reasoning and modelling that say, well if the attacker's model of the system involves these features, how will they now apply those to our distributed system? Historically those models have been applied primarily to distributed systems because we were interested in attackers getting into middle nodes and firewalls, and then spreading out across the network – that applies entirely in the environment that I'm describing.

Sandy Clark: I find myself thinking that this would be extremely useful for not just in security but for privacy, because this compartmentalisation isolates things in such a way that, it might make things like wiretapping …

Reply: Yes I think you're right. We provide a protection substrate, and then we try overlay a network on top of it with properties of information flow, and so on, dependent on our protection substrate for isolation and bounded communication. It doesn't really specifically target information flow, but we do then layer an information flow analysis on top, so we do do information flow in programmes. And I'd like to do what you're describing.

Sandy Clark: Yes, it may not do this now, but this might be something that could be put…

Reply: Yes, it seems like the right thing, and you can make a comparison with some of the privacy work on Android, and in particular TaintDroid. Ideas like TaintDroid on top of the JVM work, in part because you have a protection layer under the hood, so you need protection somewhere.

I want to draw a couple of conclusions. First, there's a hypothesis: we're saying that compartmentalised applications are distributed systems. This means that we can take advantage of that model to give us robustness – for example, so that we can have nodes fail without the whole system failing. However, we also accept the distributed-system Byzantine failure mode, which is appealing to attackers: when I break into a node via a vulnerability, I'm not going to crash it and cause a fail stop necessarily – although that might be a side effect of a failed attempt. What I would rather do is subvert the node entirely and make use of its rights. However, we can reason about the impact of that as we know what rights have been delegated around the system.

We can also reuse notions of attacker modelling and protocol analysis. When I drew those pictures of messages going back and forth, and capabilities being delegated, it was hard not to think of cryptographic protocol descriptions – where things are encrypted and passed around. Having a protection substrate changes the narrative, because we now get our integrity properties from a different place. But in some ways, it's really the same story because, if you can access the key – that is, the capability – you could use all of its rights. You can be a middle node taking advantage of a middle spot in the network, and so on. And, in fact, if we look at sensor-network research in the past, we had this notion of node compromise there, and that applies entirely here.

Right now we're interested in automated analysis, what we'd like to move towards is automated transformation. Where we'd really like to end up is a quantifiable notion of applications security, because if you start assigning probabilities to nodes, and you start looking at the communication networks, then we really can start to quantify the behaviour of the system and the presence of a vulnerability being exploited. We can look at what is exposed, we can look attack surfaces. More generally, we can now answer the question: "is our application better from a security perspective?" which is not something we've able to do before, and it really requires this approach. It gives us a concrete set of strategies for tolerating and managing vulnerabilities.

Jeff Yan: Actually I'm just curious, the notion of "capability" actually has been there for a very long time. What were the reasons it didn't take off?

Reply: I think in some sense it did. You find lots of outcome from the capability literature in programming languages; such as ideas of unforgeable references in the JVM. You find these ideas all over the place – the microkernel literature, SeL4 and so on, are all entirely based on capability models.

Virgil Gligor: So it's very hard to say that they did or they did not.

Reply: Yes, it's the system of the future, and it always will be, yes.

Virgil Gligor: That's what Jim Morris used to say, capabilities are the way of the future and always will be.

Jeff Yan: In terms of security actually I think capability is a lesser requirement, right?

Virgil Gligor: Well yes, but there is a group of people who argue that strong typing is essentially embedded into capabilities, therefore it took off at the programming language level. But that view has a little bit of a problem because strong typing existed slightly before capabilities. So then you could say, well, capabilities propagated into different pieces of the system, for example, cryptographic capabilities; tickets in Kerberos might be considered to be capabilities, and of course those took off. And certificates might be considered to be capabilities, and of course those took off.

Jeff Yan: I think Kerberos is probably less successful.

Virgil Gligor: No, it's in your box!

Reply: You don't have Active Directory?

Virgil Gligor: Well maybe not in that one.

Reply: Oh it's probably there.

Jeff Yan: Is there anything changing that makes capabilities more relevant?

Reply: I think capabilities are a natural way to describe systems that require delegation and flexibility, and so when we say, "let's turn to capabilities," what we really mean is, we want to build systems that have natural delegation properties – not just overt policies, but the delegation of rights based on code and structure. And you're forced to end up in this place. There's no novelty in capabilities except that we can perhaps use them in some new ways, I think.

And they do seem to solve this problem nicely. When we did the original Capsicum work, for example, we looked at Chromium. One of the things that we like about Chromium is that they implemented a ridiculous number of different .sandboxing techniques. They used discretionary access control, and mandataory access control in other systems, and then capability systems, and so on, and because they want to run on top of all of these they have to actually choose a subset of the functionality. And intuitively what they're doing is, they're taking all these different policy-based systems, you know, SELinux and so on. They're building sandboxes, and they're creating constrained communication paths, and then they're delegating things across them, which is to say, somehow out of all these access-control systems they've derived a capability system. And so it was very natural to then take Chromium and say, "well let's make it a use capability system." And in fact when we counted lines of code: you know, using discretionary access control on windows is a very bad idea, so twenty thousand lines of code; and Capsicum took about a hundred lines of code, relative to an already effectively capability-based piece of software, it just seemed like a natural structure. And if you assume what you're doing is building distributed systems then it kind of makes sense, because in the distributed systems world we've seen lots of success of capabilities, certificate-like systems, and so on.

Bruce Christianson: Do you have a view about how fine grained it's appropriate for capabilities to be?

Reply: When we did Capsicum, we took the view that there were natural operating system objects, and that it was therefore natural that capabilities refer to instances of the objects. Then, there are two dimensions: "how fine-grained on instances do you go," and "how fine-grained on rights do you go?" In the operating system context, those choices were pretty much defined by the objects the OS provides. It's when you get into the application that it gets interesting, because the application might be very large – significantly larger than your operating system. We would argue the finer grained you get, the more potential protection benefit you get, although then you have to reason about where vulnerabilities could be. I think that's a very intuitive argument, and of course there are these trade-offs.

Hopefully this analysis and this approach allows us to start to reason about, when do you hit the point where you get diminishing returns. "I keep adding more complexity and I keep not getting any benefit", especially if you have some probabilistic notion of where vulnerabilities will be. I think we have some tools, there's been a lot of research on this basis to say, "this piece of code is pretty questionable," and "this piece of code is OK." The other nice thing you get out of this approach is the ability to take a view on where you should apply your effort, because you can now find the pieces of code which have the greatest impact and improve those. I think what you'll find is that it's the TCB: that's where you should be investing your effort. Anywhere that holds lots of rights, and potential vulnerabilities are enormous, those components are part of the TCB, and that means we actually now have a notion of a gradient of TCB, which we never had before. Ii's not just "the TCB" and "the not-TCB" – we have all these pieces with different levels of trust, which seems like the right thing, I think, as a security-oriented view.

Bruce Christianson: Sometimes another way you can go is to say that certain capabilities come with flavours, and if you give a capability a flavour that says it can only be used as part of a sequence in a compatible flavour.

Reply: I didn't really mention types much, but some capability systems have types, and others don't, and there's a very long literature of capability-derived systems that only had types, and then eventually just became types and no capabilities. SELinux I think is a quintessential example of that. Type Enforcement in SELinux was derived from Type Enforcement in in Sidewinder and so on, type enforcement in Fluke, DTMach, and so on, which were microkernel systems where they were types on capabilities. Somehow, this ends up in SELinux – the code is lifted from Flux and dropped in, despite there being no capabilities in Linux. And as you suggest, there's a temporal aspect, which we are also interested in. We have a recent joint publication with Harris, Jha, and Reps at the University of Wisconsin on reasoning about the delegation of capabilities. Their interest is primarily on system-oriented capabilities, they don't really take an application-centred approach, whereas we are more interested in the internals, but I think the analysis would apply.

Authentication for Resilience: The Case of SDN

Dongting Yu[1], Andrew W. Moore[1], Chris Hall[2], and Ross Anderson[1]

[1] Computer Laboratory, University of Cambridge
[2] Highwayman Associates Ltd.
{Dongting.Yu,Andrew.Moore,Ross.Anderson}@cl.cam.ac.uk,
Chris.Hall@highwayman.com

Abstract. Software Defined Networks (SDN) aim to deconstruct current routers into a small number of controllers, which are general purpose machines, and a large number of switches that contain programmable forwarding engines. The vision is that, instead of the ad-hoc mechanisms used in current routers, we can build programmable networks using proper computer science abstractions. This technology is now at the startup stage, and is being deployed in the data centres of large web service firms.

We are interested in protecting a future SDN. The current designs follow traditional security assumptions and do not consider many likely deployment scenarios. We discuss how SDN architecture can be structured to offer more security, the auxiliary services that such a network will require and the advantages that it can offer.

1 Introduction

SDN is gaining traction in traditional networking settings by offering a low-cost, programmable alternative to traditional proprietary routers. A large number of hardware switches are controlled by a smaller number of controllers, which are general-purpose computers running special software. This allows network operators to break free from vendor lockin and also holds out the prospect of making networks programmable, leading to the prospect that a number of services currently deployed in proprietary devices (such as firewalls, intrusion detection engines and botnet mitigation) might become applications. The initial deployments are mostly in datacentres where cost savings are paramount [4].

However SDNs will be deployed in less controlled environments too. The question that then arises is what new security problems and protection opportunities may arise in these environments, such as a large airport where 100,000 staff working for 1,000 companies may be sharing the facility owner's network. These airlines, baggage firms, travel agents, catering companies and so on are often competitors and sometimes the agents of states in conflict with each other. A future SDN will have to support good separation between rivals' virtual networks while also supporting dependable shared channels (e.g. of which aircraft is at which gate).

How will the controllers and switches in a complex environment such as an airport authenticate each other? The current standards simply state that SDN

B. Christianson et al. (Eds.): Security Protocols 2013, LNCS 8263, pp. 39–44, 2013.

systems may use TLS, but this is not always implemented and would be nowhere near enough. We need to work with, or in some cases replace, existing network security mechanisms such as MPLS, DNSSEC [1] and BGPSEC [5] while supporting resilience against local failures and service-denial attacks. In an environment like an airport, for example, many switches and some controllers will be on tenant premises and so may be open to occasional compromise. Existing mechanisms not only fail to support resilience; they are incompatible or ill-defined. For example, within an AS, iBGP authentication is not compatible with route reflectors, which cause source IP addresses to not work. (There's a proprietary extension by one router vendor to deal with this, but no standard.) Another example is bandwidth: there are proprietary mechanisms such as Cisco's IP SLA to probe network bandwidth to inform routing decisions, but no standard.

It is therefore time to update the threat model. Just as the traditional protocol research community started off in the days of Needham and Schroder from the assumption that all principals behave themselves, and then had to adapt to cope with misbehaving clients or servers, so also intradomain routing has been traditionally thought to need little authentication which will change as we move to more dynamic networks. The airport with a controller and six switches in a closet that a janitor can access is a very simple case; if and when SDN is deployed on the battlefield, engineers will have to design authentication to cope with devices being constantly added and lost, and occasionally falling into enemy hands.

Scaling also forces a rethink. As we move from current SDN deployments of perhaps 50 controllers and 500 switches in one data centre to global networks with tens of thousands of controllers and hundreds of thousands of switches, we can no longer assume that the threat only comes from outside. It is already an issue that when a network operator deploys a router in a remote location, this is usually done by an untrusted local contractor.

Our threat model must assume physical compromise of devices, along with associated attacks involving (for example) software that's old and vulnerable or that has been tampered with. We must assume that some devices in the field are unsafe; that a handful of switches, and sometimes controllers at the bottom of the hierarchy (which are deployed near switches), are compromised at any given time. Some communication channels are also insecure: the wires are subject to the same attacks.

In addition to the usual mechanisms for key generation, distribution, update and revocation, a resilient authentication infrastructure will also require a trustworthy mechanism to monitor and detect rogue devices in the rest of the SDN. This will alert operators when a device starts to act maliciously, so that appropriate action can be taken to revoke and exclude it. The scale and complexity are much larger than previously considered, but a broad range of data can be monitored: we can query a switch, its neighbours and their controllers for bandwidth information; and we can also launch data plane probes to cross-check. With a large corpus of live and historical network data, the operator can make better decisions when under attack.

2   Proposed Architecture

Architecture matters. We can get real benefit from the move from peer routers and switches, any of which can cause equal havoc if compromised, to a hierarchical system of switches and controllers. This means we can arrange things so that the compromise of a few switches will do no more than local damage.

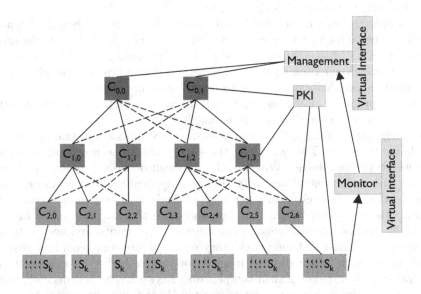

Fig. 1. An SDN setup with hierarchical controllers and switches. Solid lines denote connections, and dotted lines backup connections. Note that the PKI, management, and monitoring services are conceptually drawn, and may not be physically separate from the main hierarchy.

To illustrate this, an SDN currently deployed in a data centre, as illustrated in Figure 1, might have a bottom layer of 1,000 switches, with each ten switches driven by a level 2 controller, every ten level 2 controllers driven by a level 1 device, and the ten level 1 devices coordinated by a master controller. If we can arrange things so that only controllers can cause widespread outages if compromised, the number of critical components is reduced by a factor of ten. If we can further arrange things so that the compromise of a level 2 controller does little damage outside of its immediate neighbourhood, then we have reduced the number of points of serious failure by another order of magnitude.

Although Figure 1 illustrates an SDN hierarchy informed by datacenter practices, without much imagination it is plausible to map the components to those of an ISP (Network Operation Centre, Regional Offices, PoPs, etc.) and to the components of our airport example (where there are some central facilities, some in separate buildings and some on different floors of those buildings, connected in a hierarchy).

In terms of division of work, the two or more layers of 'middle management' controllers between its root controller and the switch fabric is where the 'work' will be done, of creating virtual networks and supporting virtual services. An operator will issue commands top down from level 0 and each level of controllers below will be responsible for translating the directives into rules suitable for their layer of abstraction. If there is virtualisation, it will also happen in the middle layers, at layers 1 and 2. Finally, the level 2 controllers issue the necessary primitive rules to the switches they control.

We assume the level 0 and level 1 controllers to be trusted, although with potential accidental configuration errors; and that there may be occasional compromises at level 2. However, there may be network application code (the software-defined applications) running on level 1 and level 2 controllers, which might misbehave, intentionally or not. As we noted, some proportion of the switches may be compromised at any one time; and, as the data packets being dealt with can come from anywhere, nothing is assumed of them.

We imagine that in time there will be many SDN applications that operators can choose to deploy. This will bring the same problems seen with application markets for mobile phones. Will we take the 'walled garden' approach of the iPhone, with some central authority that vets applications and developers, or the somewhat more freewheeling approach of Android, where all can play but applications are removed from the play store once they are considered harmful? Many applications will contain too much code to verify, and even if their developers are honest and competent, they may still face commercial incentives to collect as much information as possible, or to give higher priority to their own traffic at the expense of their competitors'. Network engineers deciding how much access to grant an app may be more sophisticated than the typical Android user trying to decide whether a social networking app that asks for the ability to send text messages is exploitative — but the difficulties encountered with the manifests for phone apps bear careful thought. How should we design the set of permissions that will define and constrain the behaviour of an SDN app? How should the access control policies look like? And what will be the practicality if a hundred different virtual networks are run on this fabric for different tenants – will it be at all practical to run different apps on behalf of different tenants on a number of controllers, or will we have to impose significant limitations (such as no shared state for apps on tenant networks, or across controllers)?

We believe this area that needs substantial and urgent research.

3   Auxiliary Services

Apart from the hierarchy of controllers and switches, we will need auxiliary services in the network. Switches are connected to a logical monitoring service which in turn feeds relevant data back into the management service, completing the loop by connecting to the root level controllers. If TLS is used, there may also be a PKI to support this; an alternative could be a Kerberos-type system.

Monitoring is a logical service in the network. The purpose of monitoring is to collect both control plane status and data plane statistics from the bottom level switches. Monitoring makes available its information to relevant users and operators so they can watch and intervene if needed. This service can perform both passive and active monitoring. Passively, it can measure statistics such as the number of packets matching a certain signature, or per-interface bandwidth usage. Actively, it can send a packet to a switch and observe the decision made by the switch on that packet. Because the monitoring service can observe all interfaces of a switch, it can see the result of a forwarding decision. Monitoring also exposes a new level of control to the network. The potential of using this for auditing and information flow analysis is immense. Among others, SDN makes available an interesting potential for tackling botnet outbreaks as well as adapting and reacting to other forms of network attacks [6,8].

The monitoring service also feeds data back into the management service. Since this knows all the commands issued from the top, it can check if they are followed, completing the loop. It can can also actively generate fake traffic to isolate devices that are dishonest. Most importantly, it links the human operator with the rest of the network. While the root controllers are the technical authorities in the control plane, the management service translates human operator intentions into control directives.

Both the management service and monitoring service expose a virtual interface for a users of the network, or to those to whom the operator delegates access, for example a network operator for an airline only needs partial access to the airport network. Each such user gets a separate virtual slice of the network along with relevant virtual devices, resources, and monitoring data. On the management side, the virtual interface deals with resource allocation and visibility; and the monitoring side only shows the part of the collected data that the user is authorised to view. There exist recent works [3,2,7] that caters to abstractions and virtualisations in network programming. It is not hard to adapt these works to be integrated into the architecture we have laid out.

4 Conclusions

Software defined networks are getting deployed because they are cheap, both for hardware capital expenditure and for operation. Yet the work on SDN security has only just started. As these technologies escape from the datacenter and get deployed in large heterogeneous networks, a lot of protection issues arise. An important first step is architecture. We propose a hierarchical model of SDN which reduces the number of points of serious failure by one or two orders of magnitude. The significance for protocol research is that while people have in the past talked about hierarchical deployment of both public-key and shared-key protocol mechanisms, this has so far been abstract (and was largely limited to the debate in the 1990s about which cryptographic technology scaled better). For the first time, SDN provides an environment with a real need for hierarchical security. This in turn raises the question of whether we can use delegation with public key mechanisms, or hierarchical Kerberos mechanisms, to support tiered security in networks.

Acknowledgments. We would like to thank Peter Neumann, Phillip Porras, Vinod Yegneswaran, Anil Madhavapeddy, and Charalampos Rotsos for helpful discussions in the early stage of this work. We would also like to thank the audience at the Security Protocols Workshop '13 for additional comments during the presentation.

This work was sponsored by the Defense Advanced Research Projects Agency (DARPA) and the Air Force Research Laboratory (AFRL), in part under contract FA8750-11-C-0249, and in part under contract FA8750-13-2-0023. The U.S. Government is authorized to reproduce and distribute reprints for Governmental purposes notwithstanding any copyright notation thereon. The views, opinions, and/or findings contained in this report are those of the authors and should not be interpreted as representing the official views or policies, either expressed or implied, of the Defense Advanced Research Projects Agency, the Air Force Research Laboratory or the Department of Defense.

References

1. Arends, R., Austein, R., Larson, M., Massey, D., Rose, S.: DNS Security Introduction and Requirements. RFC 4033 (Proposed Standard) (March 2005),
   http://www.ietf.org/rfc/rfc4033.txt
2. Foster, N., Guha, A., Reitblatt, M., Story, A., Freedman, M.J., Katta, N.P., Monsanto, C., Reich, J., Rexford, J., Schlesinger, C., Story, A., Walker, D.: Languages for software-defined networks. IEEE Communications Magazine 51(2), 128–134 (2013)
3. Gutz, S., Story, A., Schlesinger, C., Foster, N.: Splendid isolation: a slice abstraction for software-defined networks. In: Proceedings of the First Workshop on Hot Topics in Software Defined Networks, HotSDN 2012, pp. 79–84. ACM (2012)
4. Hoelzle, U.: OpenFlow @ Google, keynote address at the Open Network Summit (2012)
5. Lepinski, M. (ed.): BGPSEC Protocol Specification (February 2013),
   http://www.ietf.org/id/draft-ietf-sidr-bgpsec-protocol-07.txt
6. Porras, P., Shin, S., Yegneswaran, V., Fong, M., Tyson, M., Gu, G.: A security enforcement kernel for OpenFlow networks. In: Proceedings of the First Workshop on Hot Topics in Software Defined Networks, HotSDN 2012, pp. 121–126. ACM (2012)
7. Reitblatt, M., Foster, N., Rexford, J., Schlesinger, C., Walker, D.: Abstractions for network update. In: Proceedings of the ACM SIGCOMM 2012 Conference on Applications, Technologies, Architectures, and Protocols for Computer Communication, SIGCOMM 2012, pp. 323–334. ACM (2012)
8. Shin, S., Porras, P., Yegneswaran, V., Fong, M., Gu, G., Tyson, M.: Fresco: Modular composable security services for software-defined networks. Internet Society NDSS (to appear, February 2013)

Authentication for Resilience: The Case of SDN (Transcript of Discussion)

Dongting Yu

University of Cambridge

My name is Dongting and I'm here to talk about software defined networks and their resilience. It's joint work with Professor Ross Anderson. So what are SDNs? It's a fairly new concept of doing networking in the past three, four years. The basic concept is we take intelligent controllers, which are basic everyday computers, PCs, and we use them to drive the switching and routing logic inside switches, using programming languages. It's a separation of control and data plane, because the switchers and routers will just do their own stuff, and the controllers would be doing all the control plane logic. The goal of SDN is not to bring a new feature into networking, but rather to bring organisation and abstraction into networking, so you have much better manageable networks. And another goal is to cut cost because we can potentially replace large Cisco routers with a few of the cheaper switches and the general purpose PCs.

So where can SDNs be used? The traditional settings of datacentres and ISPs can almost directly benefit from SDNs, and in fact a lot of them are already deploying or almost deploying. There are some newer settings. Internet exchange points and control systems are what we can think of, and in fact Internet exchange points are actually moving towards SDN prototype as well. We can also think of next generation networking, for example, in battlefields or microclouds when we have Google Glass, and using a nearby microcloud for rendering, for example. We have a favourite example here, which is Heathrow Airport. The case of Heathrow Airport is that there are 180,000 staff, and 3,000 companies, including baggage handler companies, UKBA presence, there are also airlines that are representing countries at wor with each other, for example, Israel and Arabic nations. And there are many staff members at Heathrow, more than the population of Cambridge itself. So a terminal of Heathrow would be a very good use case for SDN, and we can keep that in mind when we talk about SDN.

Frank Stajano: When you describe this as a working example does it mean it would be a good way to envisage this, or it's already currently deployed there?

Reply: It's not deployed, but it's a good way to envisage this, because it's a very concrete example.

One question that people raise is, if we already have MPLS and OSPF, and all these existing networking technologies, why do we need SDN. What we realise is that SDN can reduce the number of points of serious failure in the network. So if you have MPLS network and you manage to take over one MPLS switch, then you can pretty much bring havoc to the whole network that the MPLS is part of. But with SDN you can reduce that because you can potentially make

B. Christianson et al. (Eds.): Security Protocols 2013, LNCS 8263, pp. 45–53, 2013.

the switches not the failure points. And it's a good idea, in the case of Heathrow again, when there are many people trying to take over your network.

So what's the threat model that we're considering? In the case of Heathrow, for example, we can think of a dozen, or a few dozen switches, being compromised at any time by malware or physical attack. If you are a janitor at Heathrow you probably can have access to some sort of networking device within the terminal. Or if you are an airline then you have access to the other computers and potentially you can do some damage as well. And we also consider once in a while a controller, especially the local controllers that we distribute everywhere, can get compromised. Once you compromise a hardware you can inject firmware, you can change software, you can add a new hardware, for example, you can install anything, so basically once you have access to something you can do a lot of damage.

So we want authentication in SDN. We assume many of the switches are physically vulnerable because they are out everywhere in the building. So protecting the controller is a more reasonable thing to do. At the same time, because SDNs will be deployed in many large networks, we also want authentication to scale. The classical order $log(n)$ way to do it, is to have a tree of things, so we have the most important controller on the top, and then recursively down into a hierarchy of controllers, and at the very end many, many switches. In the 1990s, there were discussions of shared keys versus PKIs and this can be applied into an SDN case.

So there are things we need to authenticate. Controllers need to be first considered. If we have a hierarchy of controllers in a shared network, or a dedicated network, the controller-controller communication is anything that the programmer writes, so it becomes pretty much a general distributed systems problem, where you can use any of the existing technology, or we can make new technologies to make them authenticate each other. BGPSEC is one of the possible candidates, but BGPSEC is not exactly written for this kind of situation, so it might have its own problems and cost overheads. We also need to think of revocation. What if you want to revoke devices as you maintain the network, or what if you want to revoke devices when you're being attacked, how do you do it within a reasonable time. And more importantly, how do you know what you want to revoke. If you see misbehaviour how do you know which ones are the ones exactly that you want to revoke.

We also have authentication of switches at the most bottom layer. In the OpenFlow specification, OpenFlow is one of the most popular implementations of SDN, and they say use TLS, and that's pretty much the only security word inside the whole specification. But TLS has its own problems, a lot of vendors are not implementing TLS, especially hardware switches. In software it's fairly OK because you have existing libraries, you can borrow them. Another thing is, how do we monitor switches, what kind of behaviour do we want to monitor in the switches. And if switches become so small then maybe a lot of existing assumptions do not hold anymore.

So that brings us to the problem of monitoring, and we argue that monitoring is needed in this situation. Controllers know exactly what logic they are sending to the switches, so they can query the switches and their neighbours to see if a particular switch is behaving correctly. We can have a large monitoring system where a lot of data continues to flow into a central repository of a database that operators can see, or they can write automated systems that detect malicious behaviour. And this monitoring system should be separate, because controllers can be compromised, and maybe not all the controllers can be trusted.

So how do we design a system that encapsulates all these desired properties. In turns out in datacentre design there's already a similar hierarchical view. So if we learn from the datacentre design we can build a hierarchical system where we have a couple of very important root controllers on the top, we have area controllers. And we have a hierarchy, going down we have local controllers, and each of the local controllers controls a whole bunch of switches, and these can be maybe fairly insecure, but the ones on the top should be pretty secure. And we have primary links, and we have backup links, similarly for all the all the other layers, for failover purposes. So we have a basic design of an SDN network, but in order to add authentication into it we might want a PKI which connects to all areas. It can be RPKI, for example, or it can be a general purpose PKI.

But the controllers are still a little low level for the operators, so we want a management interface. And in the management interface we can say things like, we want to create a new VPN consisting of so many switches and so many specific kinds of behaviour. And connecting to the switches we attach a monitoring service server, and this monitoring server collects data from all of the switches, statistically or by other means, and puts it into a central database. And what's good about this design is that the monitoring device can feed back into the management, so the management can say, I've issued these comments into the controllers and switches, does it match with the behaviour that I see. If it doesn't match then maybe somewhere something is misconfigured, or something is malicious. In the Heathrow case, because we have so many users and different companies, we want to have a virtualised interface for the monitoring and the management services. So in the management case a new airline carrier will say, well we are a new company, we want so many switches, a VPN that does so and so, submit. And the terminal operator can see the request and say, OK, we'll deploy into the controllers. In the monitoring case the same airline can say, well we want to see if our network is behaving correctly, give us some data, but at the same time you don't want to give the data that they shouldn't see to that company. So we're going to have a virtualised monitoring interface as well.

So what are the advantages of this design? Well we have minimal trust, because we don't need to trust all the devices, we only need to trust the higher ones. So if you only protect the root controllers, and maybe the area controllers in more protected rooms where the janitors cannot access. It might be OK to have the switches everywhere that people can launch physical attacks. We can also get faster convergence, for example, when there's a power failure and you're trying to boot up the whole network, in the traditional sense you need to have everyone participating in the convergence time, but right now we say that we can only do the root controllers, and then they all converge the area controllers, and each of them will converge the devices underneath. There is also a delegation of work. You can offload a lot of the computing power into the lower level controllers in this case, so the higher level ones only need to do the higher level coordination where the lower ones do the actual work.

So there are three highlights in the design that I just showed. One is the management system, they directly manage the root controllers, they do higher-level directions, so for example, give me a VPN, and then they will make sure that the controllers do the rest of the work. The management system also can be, for example, a general web interface that faces everyday users, airlines, so we need to have abilities to deal with different users. But the management itself is a trusted subject. Second thing we had in that diagram was virtualisation. In the case of Heathrow, for example, and similarly in other cases, such as shared datacentres and ISPs, you have many users that share the same resource. Each of them will want their own management interface, and also the monitoring interface. Virtualisation also works in the middle layer, so the roots do not virtualise, but they will control the virtualisations, and the virtualisation will stop just before the switches. The third thing we had was monitoring. So we need a monitoring system that stands on the side of the network and observes this whole network. We need to collect data from switches through multiple ways that are possible. The monitoring system sees everything, but it doesn't provide all of the information to every party that requests information. So we might want some kind of control, mandatory access control would be one of the ways to solve this.

So what we are seeing here is a change of scale. In the 80s and 90s we were concerned with thousands of users, and we were concerned about how to set up keys, the authentication channel. Later on we were concerned with millions of users, and we were concerned with the revocation channel, how do we tear down keys. And now with SDN and potentially many, many more nodes in the network, it's now shifting into the monitoring channel, which keys shall we replace.

So in conclusion, software defined networks are seen as a Cisco killer, so Cisco is now participating in this as well so they can control their share of this. In a large network especially a heterogeneous one such as Heathrow, by doing SDN we reduce the protection perimeter that we need in the network so that there is less chance of causing catastrophic failures. Mandatory access control is probably needed because you have so many users. But the real hard problem is monitoring multiple virtual networks efficiently and effectively. We have a mandatory thank you for the sponsor, and I will take the questions.

Bruce Christianson: You have a little box with the letters PKI written on it on one of your slides, tell us a little bit more about that, and in particular about the key replacement policy.

Reply: The key replacement policy. So the PKI serves as a querying service, so you can query for things, and if you see keys or certs you can ask the PKI if this is right. If it's not right then the logical thing to do is not to trust the information that comes with it. If you do see through the monitoring and management interface that something is misbehaving then you can revoke devices. In a system like BGP and BGPSEC it's hard to revoke because you have a very distributed system, and if you revoke your neighbour you don't necessarily know that your neighbour's neighbour will see your revocation, because that might be the only route downstream. But in this case because everything is controlled by the same domain, it might be easier. So we assume that these are more or less trusted, so if a switch is misbehaving then the controller can easily revoke this and programme the other switches, so takeover its function.

Bruce Christianson: Right, but how does that get propagated?

Reply: It doesn't need to be because the switches are the lowest level already. So the case of this versus the traditional network is that the switches don't need intelligence, they don't need to participate. So as long as the controller knows that this switch is misbehaving, it just needs to revoke this switch and tell the other switches to do something else. We also considered that the lowest level controller may be occasionally compromised so if that one is compromised then this controller will tell the needed parties that this one is being wicked, and we assume that other switches below are lost.

Bruce Christianson: Does the monitor need to know about any of this?

Reply: The monitoring reports activity so I would say the intelligence would be the management system, because it's only in the management system that you know the expected behaviour, and the observed behaviour.

Bruce Christianson: That PKI box needs to have about a billion dotted lines coming out of it.

Reply: It's to illustrate that it connects to all layers. I guess the lines are not very rigorous.

Robert Watson: I guess one of the problems with a software defined network is that, the way it talks to nodes is over the network, and so when you lose control of the nodes you risk not being able to talk to the nodes anymore, or any of the nodes that it's connected to. Do you take a view on structures we compose that help keep reachability working for the purposes of maintenance administration, or you take the view that that's kind of a policy?

Ross Anderson: We did have a slide on whether we needed heartbeat networks or not but we deleted it for reasons of time. There's a debate in a number of environments, such as the control systems world, for example, about whether you need an absolutely dependable core network with multiple layers of fallback and backup.

Robert Watson: Maybe in software defined networking you can implement that, right. It's all programmable, but you'd have to instruct switch vendors on how to construct these things, and it seems like a design pattern that might be useful.

Ross Anderson: We thought the interesting thing for this workshop though was that with an architecture like this, which strongly suggests it's sort of in this new technological world, the revocation problem that we've agonised over for so many protocols workshops becomes almost trivial.

Bruce Christianson: That's a really nice thing.

Ross Anderson: Not entirely trivial, because there are some residual intelligence things on the bottom, but that's almost trivial. But what then suddenly becomes of overwhelming importance is the audit trail, the block of fat old paper that we used to use to keep open the fire-door, all of a sudden this becomes where the intrinsic complexity of the system migrates, right, it becomes a big complex mandatory access control multi-level secure system, that is if you're going to do full network virtualisation and provide different decent separation between different VPNs. But it's become seriously hard.

Bruce Christianson: But at least you've got the sense that you're trying to solve the actual problem, whereas with revocation you always had the sense that you were trying to solve a problem that was an artefact of how you architected. Whereas here the audit information is all stuff that you need anyway.

Ross Anderson: Well with small systems the detection of faults was always down to the system administrator. The police would phone you up, or cert would phone you up, or a customer would phone you up and say, oh golly, or words to that effect, and you'd rush round and wonder what broke. But once you have billion node networks, you know, the oh golly approach to fault diagnosis doesn't work.

Bruce Christianson: It doesn't scale.

Robert Watson: Also taking a view on the work the applications are doing, the reason that you're seeing a pickup of SDN in high-end datacentres is that things like spanning tree don't scale, so in order to replace spanning tree, and say, provide applications, in a datacentre you might have one or two applications, or some larger number, but I suppose in some environment you might want applications to do load balancing or traffic engineering. Is that part of the model that you're interested in, or is that sort of a separate application.

Reply: So we're definitely interested in that. There are multiple things, right, so at the most connection area you need basic connection, and we say that you can have a physical connected network for, for example, for this layer, for the root controllers. And you have a more expanded network for the area controllers. And if something fails then you still have the core ones, and they can kind of boot the other ones up. So you have this layer, and once you establish connectivity you can do authentication on top of it, controller to controller and controller to switch. And once you have established a trusted perimeter of your authenticated devices then you can load applications on top of that.

Robert Watson: Yes, the basic question is, where does the application fit into this graph of communications and so on. Applications might run on the controllers, they might have applications by talk controllers of distance, but I guess there's an authentication piece there.

Reply: Applications are created in the management, and the management will convert the applications into directives into the controllers.

Ross Anderson: If you want to do this with the kind of tools you're working on, and you think perhaps in terms of a language where you can express a number of rules for the creation of the virtual networks, and you then compile these down through the various layers until you've got full rules you can apply to the switches. And of course extraction rules that can apply to the monitoring systems for putting out the relevant examples of facts.

Robert Watson: I've seen applications that would do much more sophisticated things like that, they look at flows, that come in and decide how to load balance across multiple service, or interactive things. So I wonder if, since this is a protocols workshop, the bit to blow up is the management bit, you need to figure out if there is another set of principles there, there is another set of authentication protocols. Obviously you have to have the substrate, which is what this is, to bootstrap in order to make it useful, but at the end of the day it's the applications that are going to need properties as well.

Reply: I would say the virtualisation is kind of an application in the general sense offered by the SDN

Audience: Virtualisation is one application is all I'm saying, there may be other applications.

Reply: So the other applications, such as load balancer, would work on top of the virtualisation layer, and only work with a device that the virtualisation provides. So in the case of Heathrow, the Heathrow administration would have a virtualisation app, and each airline can have their own load balancer or firewall apps within this virtualised SDN slice, and they don't even see it's a virtualised slice, they just think it's their own slice of SDN. So I guess there's a separate view, a separate portion in this diagram where a user through the management interface after receiving an allocated slice can then deploy their own applications on top of the available resources.

Ross Anderson: I expect load balancing would, and if you're doing that in part of that work in this fabric would probably run at the C2 layer.

Bruce Christianson: Is there an assumption that the controller hierarchy maps onto a switching hierarchy, or is the switching much more longer term in the story?

Reply: I don't think we need to have a hierarchy in the switches. So these can be tightly coupled, but we don't need the hierarchy in the switches.

Robert Watson: You can characterise this as an enterprise centred view of how SDN gets deployed, that is the enterprise owns all the switches therefore you don't need a switching hierarchy, or so on, or do you view it, what happens if you've got two enterprises with two networks, does somebody have to own all the switches to use this key, or can it be two different networks that switch it or talk to each other?

Reply: Even if you have two enterprises sharing physical resources, you always still need to have an owner.

Robert Watson: Someone has to own your switch. Some of the questions that came up in active networks, which is what the last round of software defined networking was called, were concerned with multiple enterprise networks, applications that span different networks, so they for example, were tracking down denial of service, and then suppressing at the origin rather than suppressing in the middleware. It isn't obvious how to do that. And so they would have to coordinate the applications so they would be allowed to talk to – well, they weren't controllers, but they might as well have been – at each one of the enterprises in order to suggest, this flow is no longer of interest, which led to a whole research area in, how do I identify, how do I authenticate, how do I decide what policies are appropriate to distribute. And so to my mind it would be appropriate to apply that vocabulary once you have a substrate like this one, which is why I asked the enterprise question. Within an enterprise, yes, you can say who owns a thing, who provides virtualisation, and so on, but when you've got multiple enterprises, there are actually quite interesting applications that could float one layer higher.

Ross Anderson: Well exactly, suppose you're US Airways, for example, you go and you rent yourself a VPN at Heathrow, you rent yourself a VPN at JFK, you stitch these together into your own corporate network, that's the sort of thing people want to do, and this is perfectly fine. Similarly if you're HM government, you want to rent a classified slice of network at Heathrow, and one at Gatwick, and one at Stansted and so on, and put them all together into your classified borders agency network, this is normal.

Robert Watson: You imply there's a layer above that and I think it would be interesting to draw the layer above, because the layer above obviously it wouldn't have these Ss in it, I think, right, and yet clearly it's a replication in some sense of that structure.

Reply: So yes, applications, especially if you write your own applications that stitch multiple networks, it would be interfacing with the management interface.

Robert Watson: And one way to interpret software defined networking is to look at software defined TLBs in conventional processes. So TLB uses a TCAM, you try to cache the collected information, and then once in a while you take an exception because there's a miss, and then you go out to a controller, which is to say the software page tables and so on, and it fills the TLB. So a classic failure of design there is how many rings do you want, do you want one ring, or two rings, do you want four rings, and the recent explosion of hypervisors in virtualisation was possible because, I think we should use that extra ring now. So one thing that would be nice to know is that this structure doesn't impose a bounded number of rings to the point you get a cliff in performance behaviour, or we have to fundamentally change your perimeter, but instead degrades, say, as a factor of load rather than a factor of a number of layers in virtualisation. So it would be interesting to look at that.

Ross Anderson: Well in practice how many layers of virtualisation would you expect to have, two or three max?

Robert Watson: Well that's not the direction things are going currently in software.

Ross Anderson: But networks maybe aren't quite the same. I don't know.

Robert Watson: Well, no, I think it's an open question, right, but it could be that by describing the APIs properly they've actually set it up so you can have unlimited layers of virtualisation, and efficiency is a property of load on the network, not on the number of layers. But it would be good to have security properties track that scalability if it exists in the underlying layer. Because I think you're right, I think layers of virtualisation is the natural place to put these applications, but how many layers of those can you have.

Jeff Yan: In addition to authentication, what other security properties do we need to reconsider in SDN and in particular OpenFlow?

Reply: Well in this talk we argue for authentication as a way to achieve resilience. In reality, in the very general sense, there are also integrity would be an immediate property that we would want to have. But that follows from authentication, so if you have an authenticated device then maybe integrity would be easier.

Jeff Yan: Are there some newer security issues for SDN?

Reply: Nothing comes to mind immediately, I mean, you can think of it as programmable network where you can match any bits in the switches. I don't think there's anything immediately different from a traditional networking example, of course other than what we're arguing here.

Rubin Xu: How do you gather reliable monitoring information from the switches?

Reply: We didn't really consider this part in detail, but you can think of, for example, a monitoring device that sends random messages into the switches once in a while in a round robin fashion.

Ross Anderson: Bear in mind that we're assuming that merely a dozen switches out of a thousand in an installation the size of Heathrow would be bad at any one time. So even if none of the switches is unconditionally trustworthy, most of them are working properly at any one time, and so there's a big literature on how you do sampling of network traffic, and you want to arrange things so that if you're looking at one packet in ten thousand then you see the same one packet in ten thousand going out from switch K to switch K+1 that you see coming in at switch K+1 from switch K again, because that way if a switch starts misconducting itself and lies about it, then you'll protect it faster. But the details of this are basically for future work.

Verifiable Postal Voting

Josh Benaloh[1], Peter Y.A. Ryan[2], and Vanessa Teague[3]

[1] Microsoft Research, Redmond, WA, USA
benaloh@microsoft.com
[2] University of Luxembourg
peter.ryan@uni.lu
[3] Department of Computing and Information Systems,
University of Melbourne, Australia
vjteague@unimelb.edu.au

Abstract. This proposal aims to combine the best properties of paper-based and end-to-end verifiable remote voting systems. Ballots are delivered electronically to voters, who return their votes on paper together with some cryptographic information that allows them to verify later that their votes were correctly included and counted.

We emphasise the ease of the voter's experience, which is not much harder than basic electronic delivery and postal returns. A typical voter needs only to perform a simple check that the human-readable printout reflects the intended vote. The only extra work is adding some cryptographic information into the same envelope as the human-readable vote.

The proposed scheme is not strictly end-to-end verifiable, because it depends on procedural assumptions at the point where the ballots are received. These procedures should be public and could be enforced by a group of observers, but are not publicly verifiable afterwards by observers who were absent at the time.

Keywords: electronic voting, verifiability, postal voting, vote by mail, end-to-end verifiable voting.

1 Introduction

There are no good options for voters unable to visit a polling place. Snail mail is slow, unreliable and easily intercepted, but it has one great advantage: ordinary people can see clearly what they have sent. This is the same advantage that has made a human-readable paper trail a focus of attempts to improve the integrity of polling-place DRE voting machines. Voters all over the world are clamouring for a substitute for postal voting, with its numerous inconveniences. Postal voting is also much less secure than attendance paper voting, being more susceptible to both privacy compromise and vote manipulation. It struggles to satisfy fast delivery requirements, in two directions, over what can be a very slow channel. Many people who haven't thought much about electronic security think that Internet voting is a great alternative. It's a pity about the human-readable paper record though.

B. Christianson et al. (Eds.): Security Protocols 2013, LNCS 8263, pp. 54–65, 2013.

One obvious improvement to postal voting is to deliver ballot information electronically and then ask voters to return paper votes by mail [JS12]. This cuts out the difficult half of the snail-mail delivery, and provides simple cast-as-intended verification, but it gives no more guarantees than ordinary postal voting of privacy, delivery, or accurate counting.

An alternative approach is to use cryptography to mitigate the vulnerabilities of (Internet-based) electronic voting. End-to-end verifiable systems such as Helios [Adi08] provide proofs that all the votes were counted as cast and correctly tallied. The most difficult part is allowing voters to verify that their votes were cast as they intended, even given the possible presence of malware on their computers. Helios voters are encouraged to perform a randomised protocol to test whether the vote is recorded in the way they intended. If the voters perform the protocol correctly, they get very good evidence that their vote was cast as they intended. It isn't necessary for all voters to perform this check—the important point is that a manipulating machine risks detection unless it can be confident the voter won't check. There is therefore a key assumption that regardless of the voter, a Helios client will never have prior certainty that the voter will not perform a check. Whether this assumption is valid depends, at least in part, on the population of voters. The IACR election is highly likely to have a large enough population of sophisticated voters that any cheating attempt has a high probability of detection. However, for some ordinary voters in government elections, it could be much easier for a malicious machine to predict that the voter will not check, or to trick them into not checking.

Our proposal is to try to get the best of both worlds, with a simple cast-as-intended check for most voters and a verifiable protocol demonstrating correct inclusion and counting. The scheme uses both an electronic and a snail-mail channel — blending the best properties of each.

We emphasise the ease of the voter's experience, which is not much harder than basic electronic delivery and postal returns. The extra cryptographic information needs only to be added into the same envelope as the human-readable vote. Mechanisms for assisting voters with disabilities could easily be incorporated into the process of filling in the ballot by computer (though not quite so easily into the process of putting the printouts in an envelope and posting it). The proposal provides a set of security properties not obtainable on other remote systems with such an easy voting experience.

The proposed scheme is not strictly end-to-end verifiable, because it depends on procedural assumptions at the point where the ballots are received. These procedures should be public and could be enforced by a group of observers, but are not publicly verifiable afterwards by observers who were absent at the time.

1.1   Related Work

A completely different approach is Code Voting [Cha01], in which voters receive a code sheet in the mail and then use codes to communicate their choices to the electoral authorities via an untrusted electronic device, or to check via a return code that the authorities received the correct choice. This style of remote voting has been used in government elections, for example in Norway [Gj10]. Chaum's original code voting scheme assumed an honest electoral authority. Although subsequent works have weakened this assumption substantially, all code voting schemes still require a secrecy assumption for the integrity of the election. In other words, a malicious device that learns the codes can manipulate the vote. PGD [RT13] allows the code information to be generated in a distributed way, and Remotegrity [ZCC+13] uses physical protections such as scratch strips to protect the data in transit, but there are still strong assumptions about the security of the (postal) delivery system. Furthermore, code schemes are difficult to use when the ballot is complex, such as in IRV/STV elections with many preferences [HRT10]. Our proposed system works for any voting or tallying scheme. One interesting difference is that code-based schemes send out a piece of paper and then receive the vote electronically, while our proposal sends ballot information electronically and then requires a paper return.

Two polling-place voting systems elegantly combine human-readable paper records with end-to-end verification. In the Wombat voting system [RTsRBN], voters produce both human-readable and encrypted versions of their votes. Because Wombat is an attendance voting system, the process of reconciling and then separating the two representations is performed by the voter, using a process similar to Benaloh's simple verifiable elections [Ben06]. In the StarVote system proposed for Austin, TX, [BBK+12], voters make both human-readable plaintext representations and encrypted representations, check that the former matches their intentions, and then either cast or audit their ballots. In addition, the plaintext representation is part of a risk-limiting audit in the style of SOBA [BJL+11]. Our question is how to achieve a similar set of security guarantees in a remote setting without asking the voters to do too much work.

Our proposal uses a different method of combining the benefits of cryptographic-style verification with randomised, publicly-observable checking of paper records. The rough idea is that each voter produces a human-readable paper record, and a (non-human-readable) encrypted record. Voters check that the former matches their intention, and submit the latter into a process of public auditing which verifies that with high probability the encrypted records match the paper ones. The following section describes the background assumptions. We then provide an overview of the protocol, followed by some important details, then a discussion of some possible variants.

2   Assumptions and Requirements

Some simple assumptions about voting:

1. *The electoral authorities maintain an accurate list of who is eligible to vote,*
2. *There is a public list linking a public key to each eligible voter.*

Some more complex assumptions about postal voting in particular:

3. *There is sufficient observation or proper process at the vote receiving location to ensure that votes are not lost upon arrival and some observable procedures are followed.*

We will require an unpredictable coin toss for each received vote. The trick is to design a process that provides good counted-as-cast evidence to observers. See below.

4. *There is an irrevocable process for separating pieces of paper that arrive in the same envelope, from each other and from the envelope.*

   This process varies somewhat from one country to another, but is used to separate the voter's identity, usually on an external envelope, from the contents of the vote, usually inside an(other) envelope. Traditionally the vote is mixed in a box with other votes. We will also use this to separate irrevocably pieces of paper that originated in the same envelope.

Like all end-to-end verifiable voting protocols, we assume we have a Bulletin Board, which is an electronic authenticated write-only broadcast channel with memory ("broadcast" means that everyone is guaranteed to see the same data). Some requirements for the system:

1. *Vote privacy.* It should be infeasible to link individual voters to their vote. However the system is not receipt-free (and hence not coercion resistant).
2. *Eligibility Verifiability.* The list of public keys of admitted voters is public.
3. *Cast-as-intended (individual) verifiability.* Voters should each have evidence that their votes were cast as they intended.
4. *Counted-as-cast verifiability.* Each observer should each have evidence that all votes were counted as they were cast. (Note that in end-to-end verifiable systems this is verifiable by voters; here it is verifiable by any observer who participates in the vote-opening protocol.) We have two different variants with different assumptions for counted-as-cast verifiability—see Section 3.3.
5. *Universally verifiable tallying.* Voters and observers alike can verify the correct tallying of all cast votes.

The scheme aims to defend against:

1. *An attacker who manipulates paper votes in transit.*
   This should be detected at audit time with probability at least $1/2$.
2. *A malicious voting device that misprints the plaintext paper record.*
   This should be detected by the voter.
3. *A malicious voting device that manipulates the encrypted record*
   This should be detected at audit time with probability at least $1/2$.
4. *A collusion of some of the electoral authorities opening envelopes and their observers.*
   One honest observer should be able to detect departure from the protocol.

It does not aim to defend against an attacker who drops postal votes—this can be detected, but cannot be distinguished from "honest" failures of the mail system. Nor does it defend against a complete collusion of all electoral authorities and all of the observers at envelope-opening time. In other words, at least one observer must be honest. Although the scheme defends against either a malicious voting device or an attacker who controls the postal voting channel, it is susceptible to collusion between those two attackers. There is also a strong assumption that the paper records, once received, are properly secured.

3 The Proposal

Voters receive voting information, such as candidate names, electronically. They fill out their vote on their computer, and print three representations of it on separate pieces of paper:

- VR, a human-readable plaintext vote,
- VE, an encrypted and signed representation of the vote, which identifies (in non-human-readable form) whose key it is signed with.
- VI, an encrypted but not signed representation of the vote, which is printed along with two large random values:
  - RI is the random value used to encrypt VR to produce VI,
  - RE is the random value used to re-encrypt VI to produce VE.

(These values may or may not be encrypted—see below.)

All three printouts go in the same postal envelope.

Each voter retains a copy of VE as a receipt (in printed or electronic form), but voters' computers are supposed to delete VI and the random values used to produce VI and VE.

The difficult part is to allow any observers present at the opening of the voting envelopes to get evidence that the votes are counted as cast, without compromising privacy. In other words, by checking that for each vote, VR and VE represent the same thing. We will do this by using the intermediate representation VI. Observers randomly choose whether to get evidence that VI matches VR or that VI matches VE. (This evidence consists of learning either RI or RE). The implementation details could vary with the voting scheme and the requirements of the paper delivery mechanism.

The result is similar to Randomised Partial Checking [JJR02]. On the bulletin board go the complete list of plaintext votes VR_1, VR_2, ... the complete list of intermediate representations VI_1, VI_2, ... the complete list of signed, encrypted votes VE_1, VE_2, ..., and, for each vote, either a value (RI_i) proving the link from VR_i to VI_i, or a value (RE_j) proving the link from VI_j to VE_j. Like RPC, privacy is reasonable but imperfect: each vote is anonymised among half of the set. See Figure 1.

The difficulty is to design an easy process for publishing (and proving) either the link from VI to VE or the link from VI to VR, while hiding or destroying the other link.

3.1 Details 1: How One Link Can Be Published and the Other Destroyed

One possibility (from now on called *the crypto option*) is to encrypt both RE and RI, print both encrypted values on the same piece of paper as VI, post both encrypted values on the Bulletin Board, and then decrypt only the one that is selected. The other value remains encrypted and hence does not reveal the link between VI and the other data item (VR or VE).

VR	**Physical shuffle or proven link**	VI	**Physical shuffle or proven link**	VE
VR_2	——————link (RI_2)——————	VI_2		VE_8
VR_5	——————link (RI_5)——————	VI_5	Physical Shuffle	VE_2
VR_7	——————link (RI_7)——————	VI_7		VE_7
VR_8	——————link (RI_8)——————	VI_8		VE_5
VR_3		VI_4	——————link (RE_4)——————	VE_4
VR_1	Physical Shuffle	VI_1	——————link (RE_1)——————	VE_1
VR_4		VI_3	——————link (RE_3)——————	VE_3
VR_6		VI_6	——————link (RE_6)——————	VE_6

Fig. 1. Information published on the Bulletin Board to demonstrate votes are counted as cast

A second possibility (from now on called *the paper option*) is to use physical paper mechanisms to separate and destroy the unused value. For example, RI and RE could each be printed on its own separate piece of paper. The selected value could then be attached to VI and published, while the unselected value was shredded. Alternatively, both values could be printed on the same piece of paper as VI, but the unused one could be detached and shredded.

These two options seem to achieve the same effect. The first option involves more cryptographic work; the second involves more fiddling with pieces of paper. The structure of the protocol is the same in each case.

3.2 The Rest of the Protocol

When the envelopes arrive at the electoral authority:

1. For each envelope, the signature on VE is verified without revealing to observers whose signature it is.
2. For each envelope, a coin is tossed which determines whether observers will later get a link from VR to VI, or a link from VI to VE. The piece of paper containing VI is accordingly stapled to either VE or VR, depending on the coin toss.

   If we are using the paper option, the appropriate random value (RE proving VI matches VE or RI proving VI matches VR) must also be stapled to VI, while the other value is shredded. With the crypto option both encrypted values and VI are printed on the same piece of paper and don't need special treatment here.
3. When all envelopes are opened there are four (nearly) equally large piles of paper:
   (a) VR with VI and (possibly encrypted) RI stapled to it,
   (b) VR without VI stapled to it,
   (c) VE with VI and (possibly encrypted) RE stapled to it,
   (d) VE without VI stapled to it.
   Each is shuffled in an ordinary ballot box, then retained as evidence.
4. The pile of VR with VI stapled to it has its RI values (proving the equivalence of VI and VR) published on the Bulletin Board. If we are using the crypto

option the encrypted value is published, then provably decrypted.[1] (The unused value doesn't need to be published, and should never be decrypted.)

5. The pile of *VE* with *VI* stapled to it has its *RE* values (proving the equivalence of *VI* and *VE*) published on the Bulletin Board. The crypto option is the same as for the *VR* with *VI* pile.

6. The other data contained in the other two paper piles (the lists of *VR* and *VE* unlinked to their corresponding *VI*) is also published on the Bulletin Board.

7. The list of encrypted, signed votes are cryptographically mixed (or homomorphically tallied) and verifiably decrypted.

Everyone can verify the proofs, but of course the cast-as-intended evidence depends on the coins being properly tossed so that the match of *VR* with the electronic data is verified.

Some care needs to be taken for the first of the above steps, *i.e.* verifying the signatures at envelope-opening time without revealing to the observers whose signature it was, or to the (electronic) signature reader which vote it was. Ensuring this separation is crucial for privacy, and has to be enforced procedurally. The signature would be in a format (such as a QR code) that's prohibitively difficult for humans to read or remember by sight. The electronic signature reader would scan only the signature on *VE*, and the observers would be forbidden from pointing technological devices at the ballots.

3.3   Details 2: How the Random Bit Selection for Each Ballot Should Be Performed

There are various sources of randomness. It's important that the source is unpredictable to whichever attacker tries to manipulate the vote. Here are two example sources:

The Voter, Using a Combination of the Electronic and Paper Channels. Individual cast-as-intended and counted-as-cast verifiability could be achieved by having voters themselves make the "random" selections as to which of *RI* or *RE* will be revealed after their ballots have been printed. This could be accomplished by explicitly indicating which of the two links should be revealed (perhaps by ticking a separate box). Diligent voters could remember which of *RI* and *RE* they had selected and see on the subsequent public postings that the correct one had been revealed.

One problem with this apporach is that humans are notoriously poor at making random selections, and this would need to be accounted for along with cases where no selection is made.

---

[1] It isn't entirely clear that a proof of correct decryption is necessary here given that we've assumed the paper trail is properly guarded after being received at the electoral commission. However, it seems important not to introduce an opportunity to pretend it matched a value different form what the voter saw.

A physical method of obtaining randomness from voters could work well here. The ordering or orientation in which the ballot paper(s) are placed in the envelope could be used as a source of random selections. (There are at least four distinct and easily distinguished orientations in which a — folded or unfolded — rectangular piece of paper can be placed in a slightly larger rectangular envelope. Two simple classes can be whether the leftmost printing of the front of the ballot is placed against the leftmost or rightmost printing of the front of the envelope.) Since every ballot must be oriented somehow within the envelope, there would always be a "random" selection — presumably not known in advance by the voter's computer. Knowledgeable voters could take note of this orientation and check that the correct value is subsequently revealed.

However, this approach has one important weakness: an attacker who controls the postal system (and can open envelopes and reseal them) can see which VR records will not be checked against VI. This allows the possibility of substituting VR undetectably. (A full mix and decryption of VE records will detect the anomaly—it just won't be clear what caused the problem, or which result is correct. See Section 5 for a longer discussion.)

It is preferable to ask the voter to send one bit in the paper envelope, and a separate bit electronically (via the same machine that they use for vote printing). The checking of VI against VR or VE could then be chosen by taking the XOR of that voter's two bits. The aim would be to prevent the machine from learning the "paper" bit (and hence manipulating the electronic bit and the encrypted records), and prevent anyone who intercepted the paper record from knowing the electronic bit (and manipulating the paper bit and paper record).

Voters could access their VE records and verify that the correct links had been opened. This reduces the trust assumptions on the observers to not knowing the electronic bit in advance, and not manipulating the paper records afterwards.

The Observers or Electoral Authorities Jointly, Using Jointly Generated Data and Data from the Vote. We could do a more traditional distributed randomness generation, either using cryptographic joint coin-tossing or the sort of machine used in lotto. In this case we're assuming that at least one observer at the receiving end honestly inputs some randomness, and there's a commonly available PRNG to expand the seed into a string of random bits.[2] This could be applied to ballots in some predetermined order, or combined with some randomness generated from the ballot itself. There are two options:

- **ballot order:** The ballot order would be fixed in advance, or drawn at random. The seed would be used to generate a pseudorandom string which was applied to each ballot choice in turn.
- **ballot contents:** The bit would be (part of) the output of a hash of both the seed and some data on the ballot. One possibility is to use only data

---

[2] One concrete possibility is to use Stark's tools for generating randomness for risk-limiting audits, available at
http://www.stat.berkeley.edu/~stark/Java/Html/ballotPollTools.htm

from *VE*, in which case anyone can use the data on the Bulletin Board to check that the correct link has been opened for each vote.

This reduces the trust assumptions on the observers to not arranging the envelopes with knowledge of their contents, and not manipulating the paper records afterwards.

Comparison of Approaches to Random Bit Selection. One way to compare the proposals is to think about an attacker with unsupervised access to a ballot at different times. Our attacker wants to substitute *VR*.

- If the attacker has the ballot before the envelope has arrived at the vote receiving location, and before the seed has been generated, then (with either method) the attack has at least a 1/2 chance of being detected.
- If the attacker has the ballot after the seed has been generated, and before it arrives at the vote receiving location (or before it's been properly accepted into a secure storage area), then with the "ballot contents" scheme the attacker knows which half of the ballots can be safely manipulated; with the "ballot order" scheme the attacker also has to arrange for the ballot order to be manipulated.
- If the attacker has the ballot before the seed has been generated, then with the "ballot contents" scheme the attack will still be detected with probability 1/2. With the "ballot order" scheme, the attacker will (still) need to collude with someone who manipulates the ballot order.
- An attack on the scheme where the voter chooses two bits has at least a 1/2 chance of being detected, assuming that the electronically-sent bit is secret and was randomly generated. (But this is possibly a too-strong assumption given that people are not good at choosing random values or keeping secrets.)

The crucial point with the keyed scheme is not to generate the seed until all the ballots are in, past the point where they're subject to manipulation. One option is to generate a new seed every day.

4   Privacy

Since voters mark their ballots electronically, there is no defence against eavesdroppers or malware such as keyloggers resident on the voter's computer system. The system otherwise provides reasonable (though not perfect) privacy but is not receipt-free. (We could encrypt the signature and the voter's ID so that only the electoral authority could identify whose it was. This would mitigate eavesdropping on the snail mail and not otherwise affect the protocol, except that it would require an additional decryption step when the vote arrives.)

When the envelopes are opened, all of the vote and identification data are present together. At the time the signature is verified electronically, the vote information is not supposed to be available to the electronic system. When the human-readable paper vote is exposed, the observers are not supposed to learn the identity of the signature that is being verified. Both of these need to be enforced by procedural mechanisms as the envelopes are being opened and the pieces of paper stapled together. Similarly, the proper shuffling of each of the four piles of paper is necessary for breaking the links between corresponding elements.

Voters are obviously supposed to erase VI and its associated randomisation/re-encryption factors. If they remember this data then they can prove how they voted. This is why the protocol is not receipt-free.

5   Verifiability

Cast-as-intended verifiability is achieved very straightforwardly by letting each voter print a human-readable vote VR and check it before placing it in the envelope. Universally verifiable tallying is achieved by publishing the paper votes in cleartext, so they can be tallied directly. Voters check that their electronic records have been properly received by looking up VE on the Bulletin Board.

Counted-as-cast verifiability consists of checking that VE matches VR. This is done by allowing observers to choose randomly whether to get a proof of VI matching VE or VR. Of course the quality of this assurance depends on the randomness. If the two options are chosen randomly and independently then the probability of successfully manipulating votes decreases exponentially with the number of manipulations. We have described two different proposals which give evidence of proper random generation to different sets of observers. One gives each individual voter control over their own random bit selection; the second gives a group of observers evidence about the proper bit selection of the collection of votes.

This system could be have been designed as two independent partially-verifiable systems: a simple paper system of electronic ballot delivery and (human-readable) paper returns, plus a (non-human-readable) computerised system in which the voter can use cryptography to verify proper inclusion and tallying, but not that their vote was cast as they intended. We could have simply compared the paper count to the cryptographically verifiable electronic tally and declared success if they matched. Numerous cryptographic schemes exist that are truly universally verifiable (*e.g.* [CGS97], [SK95]), and ensure that the probability of a single undetectable vote substitution by the authorities would be exponentially small. However, there is no cast-as-intended verification: if the electronic tally differed from the paper records, it would not be clear whether the paper record had been manipulated, or a malicious voting computer had sent the wrong vote.

The problem, of course, is that in any practical election they'd be unlikely to match perfectly, and it would be impossible to understand what had gone wrong. This would raise unanswerable questions about which tally to accept— the answer would depend on a guess about what had caused the inconsistency.

The auditing step suggested here, in which each ballot is checked for consistency between its encrypted and human-readable versions, ensures that the paper and electronic counts are very unlikely to differ by much. This should obviate the need to decide whether it's the paper count or the electronic count that's the "true" count.

There is still a firm assumption about proper care of the physical paper evidence, particularly the half that's not cryptographically linked to VI. This seems unavoidable with a simple VVPAT.

Although the scheme defends against an attacker who controls either the voting device or the postal channel, it does not defend against colluding attackers who control both. The malicious device could print a human-readable record that matches the voter's intention, but encrypted electronic records for a different choice, then the attacker could switch the human-readable record in the mail.

6   Other Variants and Discussion

It would be possible to ask voters to send VE electronically to the electoral authorities (as well as the printed version). This increases the complexity, but also has the benefit that the count could commence much sooner. It could be possible to mix and tally electronically "optimistically," meaning that the electronic record would be used, but the paper records would subject to audit in close races, or kept in case of a dispute.

One important practical complication is that some electronically delivered votes will not subsequently appear in paper form, due to failure of the mail. It's unclear what to do in this situation, but the simplest defensible thing is not to count them. (The alternative is to count them anyway, but then there is no cast-as-intended verifiability.) Hence the authorities must at least open each envelope and check which votes have arrived.

Another design direction worth investigating is to attempt to achieve everlasting privacy [MN10] by using perfectly hiding commitments rather than encryptions of VI and VE. This would mean that integrity depended on a computational assumption (that a computationally binding commitment could not be opened in more than one way), but this could be a reasonable tradeoff, especially since integrity depends on distributed randomness generation and associated procedures here anyway. It would require a way of either adapting or omitting the electronic tallying step.

7   Conclusion

This system makes strong, but observable procedural assumptions for both verifiability and privacy, but almost all parts of the process are individually or universally verifiable. This represents a reasonable tradeoff among the conflicting requirements of remote voting.

References

[Adi08]   Adida, B.: Helios: Web-based Open-Audit Voting (2008)

[BBK⁺12]   Benaloh, J., Byrne, M., Kortum, P., McBurnett, N., Pereira, O., Stark, P.B., Wallach, D.S.: Star-vote: A secure, transparent, auditable, and reliable voting system (2012)

[Ben06]   Benaloh, J.: Simple verifiable elections. In: Proc. 1st USENIX Accurate Electronic Voting Technology Workshop (2006)

[BJL⁺11]   Benaloh, J., Jones, D., Lazarus, E., Lindeman, M., Stark, P.B.: Soba: Secrecy-preserving observable ballot-level audit. In: Proc. USENIX Accurate Electronic Voting Technology Workshop (2011)

[CGS97]   Cramer, R., Gennaro, R., Schoenmakers, B.: A secure and optimally efficient multi-authority election scheme. In: Fumy, W. (ed.) EUROCRYPT 1997. LNCS, vol. 1233, pp. 103–118. Springer, Heidelberg (1997)

[Cha01]   Chaum, D.: SureVote: Technical Overview. In: Proceedings of the Workshop on Trustworthy Elections, WOTE 2001 (2001)

[Gj10]   Gjsteen, K.: Analysis of an internet voting protocol. Cryptology ePrint Archive, Report 2010/380 (2010), `http://eprint.iacr.org/`

[HRT10]   Heather, J., Ryan, P.Y.A., Teague, V.: Pretty good democracy for more expressive voting schemes. In: Gritzalis, D., Preneel, B., Theoharidou, M. (eds.) ESORICS 2010. LNCS, vol. 6345, pp. 405–423. Springer, Heidelberg (2010)

[JJR02]   Jakobsson, M., Juels, A., Rivest, R.: Making Mix Nets Robust for Electronic Voting by Randomized Partial Checking. In: USENIX Security Symposium, pp. 339–353 (2002)

[JS12]   Jones, D.W., Simons, B.: Broken Ballots: Will Your Vote Count? University of Chicago Press (2012)

[MN10]   Moran, T., Naor, M.: Split-ballot voting: Everlasting privacy with distributed trust. ACM Transactions on Information and System Security 13, 16:1–16:43 (2010)

[RT13]   Ryan, P.Y.A., Teague, V.: Pretty Good Deomcracy. In: Proceedings of the Seventeenth International Workshop on Security Protocols 2009 (2013)

[RTsRBN]   Rosen, A., Ta-shma, A., Riva, B., Ben-Nun, J.(Y.): Wombat voting system

[SK95]   Sako, K., Kilian, J.: Receipt-free mix-type voting scheme. In: Guillou, L.C., Quisquater, J.-J. (eds.) EUROCRYPT 1995. LNCS, vol. 921, pp. 393–403. Springer, Heidelberg (1995)

[ZCC⁺13]   Zagórski, F., Carback, R.T., Chaum, D., Clark, J., Essex, A., Vora, P.L.: Remotegrity: Design and use of an end-to-end verifiable remote voting system. In: Jacobson, M., Locasto, M., Mohassel, P., Safavi-Naini, R. (eds.) ACNS 2013. LNCS, vol. 7954, pp. 441–457. Springer, Heidelberg (2013)

End-to-End Verifiable Postal Voting
(Transcript of Discussion)

Vanessa Teague

University of Melbourne

[Uninterrupted explanation of the paper, omitted.]

Conclusion: So the argument is supposed to be that this process of randomly choosing one link or the other is supposed to give you confidence that the set of pieces of paper on the far left-hand side that the voter has actually looked at matches the set of encrypted things on the right-hand side that the voter has signed with their public key. But you didn't actually get to learn for any individual vote which signature matches which plaintext.

Michael Roe: So the human-readable one isn't identifiable as to which vote it is?

Reply: Correct. It's just a completely ordinary vote. In Australia, this is an ordinary piece of paper with a vote on it and without a unique ID. More questions? The obvious question is, what's the process for choosing this random bit in a way that makes anybody believe that this process is being done correctly? Because clearly if you can manipulate the bit-choosing process, then you can also manipulate the vote, one way or another, even without being able to forge signatures.

There are some simple ways to choose the random bit. You could throw some dice at the receiving point, you could use one those random beacons from astronomical noise or something, and assume that it's more expensive to manipulate, to pay off the people at the telescope, than it is to manipulate the election in other ways. Or a more complicated, but I think more credible, way of choosing the random bit, goes like this: Everybody agrees before voting on a keyed hash function, but you don't determine the key until after the votes have come in. Once voting has ended and you've got an ordered list of votes sitting in the room you're using to count the votes, let's assume that there's some set of observers who are present, maybe party scrutineers, or election observers, or whatever, who can join in some distributed process for generating a key together, which could be a fancy crypto process, or possibly could be something more simple involving envelopes and people writing numbers on it, or filling out lotto tickets or something, depending on whether your group of observers is sophisticated enough to accept the crypto protocol. And then for each ballot we're going to take the keyed hash, and take some kind of data from the ballot, and combine them together to get one bit which says which side of that table gets opened. And so then the argument is supposed to be that anybody who might have tried to manipulate the votes isn't going to be able to predict which side gets opened, and therefore is going to get caught with 50-50 probability.[1]

In summary, nobody really knows how to do usable, verifiable remote voting, and anyone who says differently is selling something. This proposal gives a reasonable combination of security properties. It's not strictly end-to-end verifiable, but the bit that isn't publicly verifiable is verifiable because the coin-tossing step is verifiable among a group of people who are standing around in a room. And the great virtue of it is that it has a very simple cast-as-intended step that really could be used in practice by ordinary voters, even using very complicated voting systems. Questions?

Michael Roe: So what protects the voter against the voting authority opening all of them and then working out where they voted?

Reply: So, yes, that's a good question. Whenever you've got a person attached to an encrypted representation of the vote, there's always going to be a possibility that all the people who can decrypt that vote will get together and figure out what it says. So I guess there are two different ways that a person's vote might be exposed in this system. One is what you said, one is that at the point where all their pieces of paper are in the same envelope, somebody could just open the envelope and carefully look through all the pieces of paper and identify whose signature it is. And the other is that whoever holds the key that their vote was encrypted with before it was signed could use that. You would usually distribute that key among a set of people, but that set of people could maliciously get together and decrypt a particular individual's vote if they wanted to.

So when I wrote the proposal here I made a lot of the "what's happening on the other channel" theme, and actually when I first wrote it the thing that struck me as being nice about the paper channel was the fact that it's evident to everybody exactly what they sent on it. So the big advantage of the paper channel is that you don't have to do anything clever to see what information you sent on a piece of paper. But it strikes me that the other thing that is really nice about the pieces of paper, that wouldn't be so nice about sending that equivalent data electronically, is that once you've opened the envelope and split the pieces of paper apart they're irrevocably split. If you had that all coming in as electronic data you'd really have to work hard to make sure that you completely deleted all of the possible places where that data might have been copied by anybody. But in the paper case you've only got one copy of it and so you can just put it in different piles.

Ross Anderson: It's not that simple because, if you have got two halves of a piece of paper you can join them, if you've got two pieces of paper from the same pack then there's going to be forensic stuff, so you have to have a procedure surrounding the eventual destruction of the paper. What about the procedures surrounding the mechanism whereby the user's public signature verification key gets shared between the user and the authority? Because of course the verification key need not be public in the sense that it's posted on the front page of The Times.

---

[1] The updated version of the paper includes more detail and some new techniques for performing this random selection.

Reply: Right, that's a good question, and that's out of scope for this work, but you're right, it's a really important question in practice.

Ross Anderson: That's perhaps the missing link in a system like this because if you are going to enrol people in a professional society, you presumably have their email addresses, but if you're enrolling them for a national election there will be some mechanism whereby people get a piece of paper in the letterbox, or whatever.

Reply: They have to register and do something.

Ross Anderson: And there's then a protocol whereby they run an app which generates a key, and they interact with the website, and you know, that website could be under the control of a different authority. The end-to-end design, in other words, would have to take a view of the likelihood of attackers compromising a system which consisted of the registration mechanism, and also the voting system, and also the mechanism for ultimately destroying the papers after the losing candidate has bought the election.

Reply: That was three different things, so let me try and go through them one at a time. So the registration phase, you're absolutely right, the registration phase for this kind of thing is by far the most vulnerable point of such a system. So in some ways it's a bit unfair to...

Ross Anderson: And in the UK the very biggest organised attempts to mess with elections have been in Northern Ireland where each of the factions wants to register many more voters of their type than actually exist.

Reply: Yes, it's true. So, I mean, the argument that I've been trying to run is that, at least in principle, if you get people to register once, and then continue, and then use their registration credentials over and over again, it's still completely insecure at the point that they actually register, but at least the capacity for, re-manipulating every time a new election is run is a little bit harder. I'm not saying that that solves the problem, but I'm saying that I don't know how to solve the problem really.

Ross Anderson: What are reasonable assumptions around the challenge of that sort of thing? In domestic elections in the UK you simply go and state your name to the Returning Officer, and if it turns out that somebody already voted in your name they register a protest, which will be investigated only if the margin between the winner and the losers is so low that it matters.

Reply: We have similar secure procedures.

Ross Anderson: All these other surrounding procedures tend to be ignored by designers of e-voting systems, but putting them in a design as well could make the whole problem an awful lot more interesting and tractable.

Reply: I don't understand how you can establish that kind of authentication mechanism within the design.

Ross Anderson: There's an assumption in the UK that the voter roll is verifiable because in principle at least it's published. There are some privacy ifs and buts around that, you could be on the roll that isn't really public, the roll that's only made available to the political parties, but maybe there is challengability in that if one party registers a whole lot of dead people to vote for it, the other party can pick that up and challenge it.

Reply: So that's true, but it's still hard to make sure that you've attached a particular public key to a particular individual who is eligible to vote. Compulsory voting in Australia actually makes it hard, because there's a strong expectation that everybody votes, but if anything there are people who would pay somebody else to save them the trouble. So it's very hard to say with any confidence that anybody would bother to protect their voting credentials, or prevent somebody else from registering on their behalf.

Ross Anderson: But this is then an assumption that perhaps no-one in this community has considered, that people might wish not to vote, and to find a cheat that will enable them to get out of the duty to vote.

Reply: I don't know how to solve that one either.

Sandy Clark: Or better yet sell their vote.

Reply: Yes, right, I guess the vote-selling thing assumes that...

Bruce Christianson: But I guess you're trying to make it so that it's no harder or easier than the manual voting-in-person protocol.

Reply: Yes, exactly.

Daniel Thomas: But this way, you could give someone an app, a sort of steal-my-vote app, you give him some money and then it takes the credentials away, and in your scheme that would be easier than getting someone to turn up in person.

Reply: Yes, very true.

Ross Anderson: Well how this is typically done in Britain is that the politician who's buying or harassing your vote, comes and sits in your front room and helps you fill out the postal ballot form.

Reply: Right, which is very labour intensive.

Ross Anderson: But certain parties have a large amount of labour, they have lots of supporters, people who want to be councillors, and so on.

Peter Ryan: But they also have lots of people who could go along perhaps impersonating you, in person.

Bruce Christianson: There's a protocol for the New Zealand postal votes where you print off two papers, one of which is the voting paper that's the same for everyone, one of which is the paper that identifies you as the person that casts that particular vote. And then you put your vote in an envelope and you put that with the other piece of paper in another envelope. And the obvious protocol is followed with the chain of officers at the receiving end. It's similar in some ways to what you're proposing.

Reply: So do you have any evidence that nobody changed your vote in transit?

Bruce Christianson: Only by the protocol for sealing envelopes, and sign and pass them back, chain of custody. So that you're relying on the Post Office to provide you with a chain of custody.

Reply: That's interesting, I'll have to look that up. And you need a special envelope, like you need to fit one envelope into the other envelope.

Bruce Christianson: You need to fold one envelope into the other.

Reply: I'll have to find out about that. I think in Victoria we've done something similar, but I think they decided that it was really clever to get the voter to print out the special envelope, and then carefully cut it out and fold it up. The result was it wasn't a very popular scheme.

Independent Computations for Safe Remote Electronic Voting

Alec Yasinsac

School of Computing
University of South Alabama
Mobile AL, 36688
yasinsac@southalabama.edu

1 Introduction

In a world where a high percentage of citizens carry a smart phone or iPod and most households have one or more computers, it is difficult to understand why we have not been able to leverage powerful personal computing devices to allow citizens to cast their ballots electronically. The argument turns on security weakness in all kinds of network computing and on theoretical limits on the ability to protect critical applications.

Though there are several voting system vendors that provide Remote Electronic Voting (REV) services, the SERVE Report [1] and its subsequently published version [2] continue to define REV security discussions. One of the most serious security concerns with REV is the danger of malware on the voter's client machine. Malware can easily be designed to prevent the voter from successfully voting, or to violate the voter's privacy by sending a copy of the ballot to a third party, or even to surreptitiously modify the voter's choices before the ballot is encrypted for transmission so that the wrong vote is transmitted and counted without anyone knowing. While we have no solution to the first two kinds of malware threats, in this paper we present an all-electronic protocol that greatly reduces the likelihood that malware can modify a ballot without detection. To date, we have not seen an Internet voting solution proposed for real elections whose design effectively addresses ballot integrity on a computer that is malware infected.

In this paper, we propose a verifiable, paperless Remote Electronic Voting protocol that leverages independent computations, one for voting and one for verification, to prevent acceptance of any ballot on which malware on the voting client has altered the voter's selections. Our solution reduces the likelihood that malicious software on the voting client or assistive device can alter REV voter selections. While our approach requires device properties that may not be widespread in the general population, we contend that these protocols are well suited for use by some constituencies, such as the U.S. military members and federal service employees serving overseas.

The rest of this paper is organized as follows. In the next section, we give an overview of Internet Voting architectures and follow with a description of our protocols, the prerequisites of the voting environment, and provide details of the

B. Christianson et al. (Eds.): Security Protocols 2013, LNCS 8263, pp. 71–83, 2013.
© Springer-Verlag Berlin Heidelberg 2013

system's properties, specifically including things that the protocol does not do. We close with summary and concluding remarks.

2   Internet Voting Architectures

Voting integrity is commonly considered in terms of the voter's ability to have justified confidence in three serial steps, i.e., that their selections are:

a. Cast as Intended
b. Recorded as Cast
c. Tallied as Recorded

These steps form the core of the five Voter Integrity Phases (VI Phases) shown in Table 1

Table 1. Voter Integrity Phases

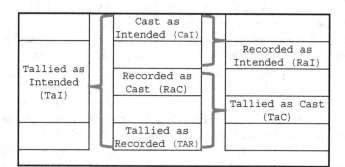

"Cast as Intended" (CaI) involves ensuring that the voter is able to find their preferred candidates/choices on the ballot and that they are able to unambiguously indicate their selections. This is usually managed through user interface activities such as ballot design, analysis and testing for paper ballots and electronic ballot engineering for electronic voting devices.

The latter two self-descriptive VI Phases are beyond the capabilities of current election practice. That is, with existing voting technology (e.g. Precinct Count Optical Scan and touch screen Direct Recording Electronic devices) the voter has a limited ability to prove that their ballot is either recorded as cast or that it is properly included in the final tally.

Cryptographic voting systems leverage mathematical formula in order to attempt to provide voters the full spectrum "Tallied as Intended" (TaI) proof. Computer scientists have been developing cryptographic voting protocols that can have provable security and accuracy properties for years, e.g. [3–5]. The key to many cryptographic voting systems is that they leverage a voter feedback channel. That is, at the time of voting, each voter receives, or generates, something that they can use after results are reported to ensure the accuracy of the voting process. Of course this information is most useful if it also allows them to make corrections if they detect an error or malicious entry.

The following three phrases are often used synonymously: Cryptographic voting systems, End-to-End voting systems, and Universally Verifiable voting systems. The latter two are subsets of the former; that is, end-to-end voting systems and universally verifiable voting systems are distinct subsets of cryptographic voting systems. Differences in the two include the number of voters, the type of feedback channel, and the VI Phase that is involved.

Universal Verification (UV) provides strong voter integrity, giving the voter procedures that can provide strong confidence that ALL published votes were legally cast and accurately counted. Voting systems that provide UV [4, 6] rely on a public broadcast medium, e.g. a public bulletin board, to broadcast all the voting information necessary to confirm the election results. Usually, that includes the voter rolls and some form of each voted ballot that is cryptographically manipulated to both ensure election integrity and to preserve voter anonymity.

End to End (E2E) voting systems provide voters information that is sufficient to allow them to have a high level of confidence that their own votes are Recorded as Intended (RaI)[1]. This is a weaker standard because voters in E2E systems are not necessarily able to verify all ballots because their proof of inclusion is at the recording, rather than tallying, level.

The E2E feedback channel may be in the form of a text message, e-mail, or some other type of serial communication between the elections office and the voter. Like UV systems, E2E voter feedback may also take the form of a public broadcast medium, such as posting on a bulletin board or webpage, but the broadcast is not necessary to meet the E2E feedback requirement.

Voting client malware is the one of the greatest threats to Internet elections, so being able to ensure that the voting client is not infected can dramatically increase the security of an Internet voting system that leverages remote attestation. One approach to improving confidence in networked applications systems is for nodes to rigorously assess one another to determine whether or not either node is malware infected, this is a technique known as remote *attestation*. There is substantial research in literature that details the approaches and technologies that can enable remote attestation with a high level of competence [7–10]. Once these solutions are fully mature, voting applications may leverage remote attestation to mitigate voting client malware risks.

3   Voting Protocols with Independent Computations

We propose to protect integrity for Remote Electronic Voting by requiring voters to create a signed, electronic version of their ballot that is independent of the voting client. The security of this approach turns on the voter's ability to safely enter the signed ballot into the voting client.

If the voter can generate the signed ballot without the help of a computer, then malware alterations can always be detected. Unfortunately generating a digital signature is a complicated operation that requires automated assistance.

---

[1] Many equate E2E systems with those that offer universal verification. In this paper E2E has a slightly different meaning, reflecting transmission from the voter to the elections official but without universal verification.

Two of our protocols rely on the voter using two cooperating devices [11, 12]. In our case, the devices are a voting client and an assistive device to compute digital signatures. If the voting client and assistive device are strongly independent, then a voting client malware attack must independently infect both the voting client and the assistive device in order to undetectably alter a voters ballot, making the attack much more difficult.

3.1   Preliminaries

Voters must first generate a public/private key pair and register the public key with a Certification Authority from which election officials can retrieve a certificate for the voter's public key. For the protocols that use two computing devices, the voter must have a smart assistive device with a camera/scanner, proper computational ability, and an appropriate voting application.

The assistive device holds the voter's private key which must not be accessible to the voting client. The primary computation on the assistive device during voting is to decode a barcode and to compute a hash and signature.

3.2   Device and Malware Independence

The phrase "device independence" can have many connotations. We are concerned about device relationships relative to malware infection, as given in the following definition.

Definition #1. Two electronic computing devices are *malware independent* if and only if, in the threat environment they are both embedded in, the probability that the two devices will be infected by a pair of cooperating malware modules at the time of voting is the product of the probabilities that either of them will be infected by one of the malware modules separately.

The significance of this independence property is that the protocols that we describe can only be defeated when *both devices* are infected by a pair of malware modules *that were designed to cooperate to subvert the voting process*. If, for example, there is a 10^{-2} probability that one device is infected with one of a pair of malware modules that can undermine our protocol and a 10^{-3} probability that the other device is infected with another malware module that can cooperate with the first one, then we want to be able to say that there is only a 10^{-5} probability that they are both infected with a cooperating malware pair, and if that is true, then the devices are malware independent.

Of course there are circumstances that can undermine malware independence. If the devices communicate directly with each other before the election and one of them is infected, the malware might be able to pass a cooperating malware infection to the other device, in which case the probability that both are infected can be almost as high as the probability that the first one is infected. If the two devices communicate indirectly with each other, or both communicate with the same third device or server, e.g. by visiting the same web page, they are also less malware independent.

Other factors affecting malware independence include the hardware and software architectures of the two devices. Sharing the same processor, motherboard, or disk drive model reduces independence, as does running the same operating system, device drivers, or other software because it makes it easier for the same malware module [with similar proliferation strategies] to infect both machines.

It is common for smart phone users to connect their phone directly to a laptop, e.g. to synchronize files or download mobile applications. Some smart phones tether to the laptop to provide remote connectivity. Devices that are directly connected dramatically reduce malware independence. Any connection, wired or wireless, can allow a sophisticated intruder to install cooperating malware on the connected devices. So, in order to maintain the strongest malware independence, one of the two devices would never be network connected. In our protocols, only one message is sent to the assistive device and this as its last protocol action. This minimizes the amount of connectivity, and optimizes the devices' malware independence.

3.3 Digitizing the Ballot

Our protocols leverage properties of a ballot's binary representation and there are many ways to digitize a ballot. For our purposes, it is beneficial to have a representation that minimizes the ballot size and that the voters can compute themselves.

In the sample ballot shown in Figure 1, the fourth row represents a voter's selections reflecting the traditional 'x' in the box. The fifth row is the translation of the votes into their binary representation. Of course binary representation is not intuitive, or convenient, for voters. By partitioning the digital ballot into six-bit groups, we can translate the selections into an alphanumeric form a base-64 representation using digits 1-0, letters a-z and A-Z, and special symbols '@' and '*' to reflect the base-64 values. In Figure 1, the character string "kAo" represents selection of Hunt, Arthur, Snow, Went, Beck, and Good and no others.

Federal Contests									State Contests								
President		US Senator			US Congress				State Senator		State Representative		General		State Attorney General		
Doran	Hunt	Katz	Arthur	Ford	Mack	Snow	Clay	Jeff	Went	Rick	Trip	Smith	Beck	Good	Farmer	Clark	Davis
	x		x			x			x				x	x			
0	1	0	1	0	0	1	0	0	1	0	0	0	1	1	0	0	0
k						A						o					

Fig. 1. Sample Digital Ballot

000000	0	001000	8	010000	g	011000	o	100000	w	101000	E	110000	M	111000	U
000001	1	001001	9	010001	h	011001	p	100001	x	101001	F	110001	N	111001	V
000010	2	001010	a	010010	i	011010	q	100010	y	101010	G	110010	O	111010	W
000011	3	001011	b	010011	j	011011	r	100011	z	101011	H	110011	P	111011	X
000100	4	001100	c	010100	k	011100	s	100100	A	101100	I	110100	Q	111100	Y
000101	5	001101	d	010101	l	011101	t	100101	B	101101	J	110101	R	111101	Z
000110	6	001110	e	010110	m	011110	u	100110	C	101110	K	110110	S	111110	*
000111	7	001111	f	010111	n	011111	v	100111	D	101111	L	110111	T	111111	@

Fig. 2. Binary to Base 64 Conversion Table

We do not suggest this as a regular, general election voting approach. However, we argue that it is not unreasonable for certain constituencies, such as the U.S. military and federal service employees serving overseas, to be able to enter their votes using a ballot constructed as shown in Figure 1 and a conversion table as shown in Figure 2 to cast their ballot in base-64 format.

3.4 Quick Response (QR) Code Technology

In simplified terms, a QR Code ™ is a high capacity barcode definition[2]. QR codes store data in images that can be captured via a camera or scanner and translated with image-interpreting software.

Reading a QR Code from the screen of one device through the camera of another device offers several positive security properties. The communication is short range, with no repeaters, amplifiers, switches, routers, or other devices, and no software required between sender and receiver. Unlike electronic communications media, the "sender" is passive; it is the "receiver" that performs the active role. No network is necessary, no MAC address, IP address, phone number, or Bluetooth addresses are needed. The receiving device need not be discoverable or detectable other than to the intended sender.

4   Voting-Client-Malware Safe Voting Protocols

4.1 A Two-Pass Protocol

The *de facto* standard remote electronic voting configuration is for the voting client to reside on a classic networked workstation, such as a desktop or laptop computer, which provides a full suite of user interface tools. Most importantly, the workstation model provides a full screen display to allow the voter to effectively understand their options and accurately capture their intended selections. We refer to this workstation as the "voting client".

---

[2] http://www.iso.org/iso/iso_catalogue/
catalogue_ics/catalogue_detail_ics.htm?csnumber=30789

For our protocols, the voter selects a second, independent device as described above, to generate a computation that cannot be spoofed by the voting client. An obvious selection would be for the voter to use their smartphone or personal digital assistant for that purpose. We call this the *assistive device*.

Once the voting client and assistive device software and the other prerequisites are met, the voter attains a blank electronic ballot. The blank ballot may be delivered via electronic network or out of band as long as the ballot is delivered safely and does not compromise the cooperative voting devices malware independence.

With the proper blank ballot loaded the voting protocol proceeds as follows:

1. The voter enters his or her selections on the voting client.
2. The voting client translates those selections into a digital ballot representation and presents it on its display screen as a QR code to the voter.
3. The voter scans the QR code, containing the voted ballot, with the assistive device.
4. The assistive device presents the voter's choices on its display for verification.
5. On voter approval, the assistive device generates a hash of the ballot representation, signed with the voter's private key.
6. The voter scans the signed hash into the voting client via QR code generated by the assistive device.
7. The voting client returns the signed hash along with the voter's ballot to the voting server.
8. The voting server calculates the hash of the ballot and compares it to the hash that it received.
9. If the hashes match, the voting server sends a success message to the voter on both devices, confirming his or her selections.
10. If the hashes do not match, the voting server refuses the ballot and sends a failure message notifying the voter of the problem.

The concept is straightforward, with the voter entering their selections into the voting client, transferring them to the assistive device via QR code signing the ballot on the assistive device, and then transferring the signature back to the voting client. The voting client then submits the digital envelope, containing ballot and signature, to the voting server where the signature is verified. When the votes are transferred between the assistive devices, they are presented to the voter for verification.

This protocol defends against the following three possible malware attacks:

a. Ballot manipulation on an infected voting client. Since the voting client does not have access to the voters private key, the voting server will detect any ballot manipulation through malware on the voting client, reject the ballot, and notify the voter.
b. Ballot manipulation on an infected assistive device. The voting client submits the original ballot that the voter entered into the voting client. The assistive device has no access to, thus cannot manipulate, the ballot. The most that a malware-infected assistive device can do is to generate a false signature, which would be detected by the voting server and reported to the voter.

c. <u>Denial of Service</u>. The voter can detect a denial of service attack by either the voting client or the assistive device by noticing that the success notice does not arrive on both devices (specifically, it will not arrive on the uninfected device).

4.2   A One-Pass Protocol

In electronic communications protocols, every message transmission introduces vulnerability. If voters are willing and capable of making their selections on their assistive device, they may reduce the number of communications between the cooperative voting devices using the following steps.

1. The voter enters his or her selections on their assistive device.
2. The assistive device translates the voter's selections into a binary ballot representation, generates a hash of the ballot signed with the voter's private key, and presents it on its display screen as a QR code to the voter.
3. The voter scans the QR code containing the digital envelope containing the voted ballot and signature into the voting client, which decodes the ballot and presents the ballot choices to the voter.
4. The voter verifies his or her selections on the voting client and authorizes the voting client to return the signed hash with the voter's ballot to the voting server.
5. The voting server generates the same hash, decrypts the voter-provided hash using the voter's public key, and compares the two.
6. If the hashes match, the voting server sends a success message to the voter on both devices, confirming his or her selections.
7. If the hashes do not match, the voting server refuses the ballot and sends a failure message to the voter, notifying them of the problem.

The security properties of this protocol are similar to the previous protocol, except that in this protocol, there is only one electronic message between the cooperative voting devices.

4.3   Independent Computation with No Device-to-Device Communication

Two vulnerable components of the protocol given in Section 4.2 are: (1) The image processing software in the voting client (as described above in Section 3.4) and (2) The scanning device itself, which contains sensitive components. In addition, the PC-connected scanners that are needed to collect barcode messages at the voting client are in declining demand.

In the following protocol, the voter casts their ballot on the assistive device, but there is no "transmission" to the voting client. Rather, the voter enters an alphanumeric string that represents their encrypted ballot directly into the voting client.

An additional prerequisite to this protocol is for the voting client to hold a valid public key certificate for the voter.

1. The voter enters his or her selections on their assistive device.
2. The assistive device:
   a. Translates the voter selections into a binary ballot representation.
   b. Generates a hash of the binary ballot signed with the voter's private key.
   c. Appends the signed hash to the binary ballot to form the digital vote envelope.
   d. Translates the digital vote envelope into a base-64 format.
   e. Presents the vote envelope on its screen to the voter as a base-64, alphanumeric string.
3. The voter enters the base-64 digital vote envelope into the voting client via the voting client keypad.
4. The voting client verifies the hash using the voter's Public Key and displays the voter's selections on its display screen.
5. The voter verifies their selections and authorizes the voting client to deliver the digital vote envelope to the voting server.
6. The voting server generates the same hash, decrypts the voter-provided hash using the voter's public key, and compares the two.
7. If the hashes match, the voting server sends a success message to the voter on both devices, confirming their selections.
8. If the hashes do not match, the voting server refuses the ballot and sends a failure message to the voter, notifying them of the problem.

The security properties of this protocol are similar to the previous protocols; however, in this protocol, there are no electronic messages between the cooperative voting devices. The user enters their choices on the assistive device and manually transfers the ballot and signature to the voting client, where the voter verifies their votes.

5   Experimental Results

A team implemented the two-pass protocol in a system that included necessary elements of the voting server, voting client, and assistive device [13]. The project demonstrated the efficacy of the protocol that captured voter selections, exercised hashing and public cryptography to protect ballot integrity, passive communication capabilities to transfer data between the devices, and return messaging to allow voter verification.

QR Code software is openly available and the system effectively encoded, transferred, and delivered the ballots using QR Codes to communicate between the voting client and the assistive device. The implemented system meets the design functionality and demonstrated that the protocol is practical in prototype.

6   Security Review

We simplified these protocols to focus on the power of independent computations to protect against voting client malware. We do not claim that these protocols provide comprehensive security.

In this section, we discuss our protocols security strengths and weaknesses. We also describe the security properties that these protocols alone do not improve over existing remote voting methods.

6.1   Voting Client Malware

The goal of these protocols is to protect the integrity of cast ballots against voting client malware attacks. Independent computations in each protocol accomplish strengthened malware protection by isolating the voter's private key to protect it from compromise. In the second and third protocols the assistive device application does not receive any data other than through the keypad.

Consider the probability that any arbitrary Voting Client 'a' (vca) is infected with a specific Voting Malware version 'b' (vmb). If that probability is non-absolute then:

$$0 \le P(vca, vmb) \le 1$$

This probability is difficult to assess, but is certainly dependent on the protective measures taken by the device and network administrators. If the probability is low, it complicates the attacker's job and reduces the possible impact that an attacker could have

6.2   Computation Independence Attacks

As we noted above, in order for protocols 4.1 and 4.2 to conclusively prevent malware attacks on the voting client, the two computers used to conduct computations must be independent. Network-based software applications offer opportunity for sophisticated intruders to corrupt different devices with cooperating malware that could defeat our protocols. However, our protocol complicates the attacker's job in several ways.

First, the attacker must have cooperating malware versions that match the voting client and the assistive device that the targeted voter uses. Second, if the voting client and assistive devices are never connected, the attacker must infect the two devices independently, in which case, using the notation above, the Probability of a Successful Attack is:

$$PSA = P(vca, vmb) * P(ada', vmb')$$

Where ada' is the assistive device that matches voting client 'a' and vmb' is voting malware that can collaborate with vmb and is able to attack assistive device b.

On the other hand, like any other data transfer protocol, barcodes offer an avenue for intruders to introduce malware. That is, if there are software flaws in the barcode interpreter, an intruder might be able to construct a barcode that can inject malware into the interpreting device. Protocols 4.1 and 4.2 may be susceptible to barcode malware attacks.

6.3 Voting Server Malware

The protocols that we present are designed to prevent malware attacks on the voting client, but they are not intended to prevent attacks that install malware on the voting server. Our protection can ensure that the voter's ballot is cast to the voting client as intended and that an honest voting server can identify and refuse to accept a manipulated ballot.

Our protocols provide only "Recorded as Intended", not "Tallied as Intended", confidence. An infected voting server controls the interactions with the voter so could interact inappropriately with the voter (i.e. provide the results as the voter expects), but could tabulate maliciously without the voter being able to detect the changes.

REV systems that utilize our protocols must implement other protections against voting server malware attacks.

6.4 Cryptographic Key Protection Vulnerabilities

Like most schemes that depend on cryptography, key management is critical to our protocol's success. If the voter's secret key is divulged to a malicious intruder, that malicious intruder could masquerade as the voter.

6.5 Receipt-Freeness

Our protocols are receipt free-neutral. That is, none of the three protocols that we present address the issue of receipt-freeness or coercion resistance [14]. Because the voter is unsupervised, similarly to vote-by-mail, voters could demonstrate to a third party how they vote.

On the other hand, our protocols are simply designed for delivering verifiable results from the voter to the voting server and are in no way inconsistent with methods for preventing vote buying and voter coercion. So, coercion resistance could be handled via other mechanisms, many of which are in the literature, see e.g. [15–18].

6.6 Voter Privacy

Similar to vote-by-mail, our protocols do not protect voter privacy. The voting application would need to incorporate standard network encryption to prevent transmission eavesdropping and elections officials would need to incorporate rigorous application operation procedures to ensure that voter privacy is not compromised.

Additionally, if the voting client is infected with malware, that malware can send a copy of the voted ballot, with voter identification, to a third party. Again, receipt-freeness and coercion resistance techniques could mitigate this effect.

6.7   Denial of Service

As we noted above, the protocols can detect denial of service through a feedback loop. If notification is sent to both devices, neither can be used to independently accomplish undetectable denial of service.

7   Conclusions and Future Work

Malware on the voting client is one of the most challenging problems to overcome in remote electronic voting. Cryptographic voting protocols have attempted to provide systems that can overcome malware attacks by allowing voters to verify that their votes were Tallied as Intended independent of the voting platform.

Our approach provides *Recorded as Intended* confidence even in the face of malware infection. We offer three voting protocols that leverage *independent computations* to prevent acceptance of any ballot on which malware on the voting client has altered the voter's selections. These protocols are simple in design and rely on voters using two independent devices to cast their ballot.

By leveraging *malware independence* we ensure that the difficulty of malware infestation is factored across the two platforms. We also leverage the positive security properties of barcode transmission to reduce the likelihood of malware transfer between the voting devices and offer one protocol in which no electronic communication between the devices is necessary.

Because of the properties of our protocols, specifically the properties of the voting devices, this protocol may be best suited to military voters, where both of the voting devices may be government issued and professionally maintained.

In order to move these protocols to the general voting public, it may be necessary to incorporate a third voting device that is never network connected, but that only communicates via keyboard and QR codes. This research is ongoing.

In this paper, we introduced the concepts of *independent computations* and *malware independence* and leverage the positive security properties of QR Codes ™ for safe device-to-device communication. We propose three protocols that reduce the prospective impact that a malware attack on either the voting client or the assistive device can have.

Acknowledgments. Many thanks to David Jefferson for many important suggestions and to Matt Bishop and Paul Syverson for their helpful comments on an early version of this paper. We also acknowledge the contributions of the University of South Alabama students that implemented this system (Erin Pettis, Naquita Hunter, Son Le, and Mengchu Lin) and their mentor, Terri Gilbert.

References

1. Jefferson, D., Rubin, A.D., Simons, B., Wagner, D.: A security analysis of the secure electronic registration and voting experiment (SERVE). Technical report (January 2004), http://www.servesecurityreport.org/

2. Jefferson, D., Rubin, A.D., Simons, B., Wagner, D.: Analyzing internet voting security. Communications of the ACM 47, 59–64 (2004)
3. Chaum, D.L.: Untraceable electronic mail, return addresses, and digital pseudonyms. Commun. ACM 24(2), 84–90 (1981)
4. Cohen, J.D., Fischer, M.J.: A robust and verifiable cryptographically secure election scheme. In: Proceedings of the 26th Annual Symposium on Foundations of Computer Science, SFCS 1985, pp. 372–382. IEEE Computer Society, Washington, DC (1985)
5. Sako, K., Kilian, J.: Secure voting using partially compatible homomorphisms. In: Desmedt, Y.G. (ed.) CRYPTO 1994. LNCS, vol. 839, pp. 411–424. Springer, Heidelberg (1994)
6. Adida, B.: Helios: web-based open-audit voting. In: Proceedings of the 17th Conference on Security Symposium, SS 2008, pp. 335–348. USENIX Association, Berkeley (2008)
7. Coker, G., Guttman, J., Loscocco, P., Herzog, A., Millen, J., O'Hanlon, B., Ramsdell, J., Segall, A., Sheehy, J., Sniffen, B.: Principles of remote attestation. Int. J. Inf. Secur. 10(2), 63–81 (2011)
8. Yasinsac, A.: Identification: Remote Attestation. In: Wireless Sensor Network Security, Cryptology & Information Security Series (CIS), ch. 11. IOS Press (November 2007) ISBN: 978-1-58603-813-7
9. Seshadri, A., Luk, M., Perrig, A., van Doorn, L., Khosla, P.: Scuba: Secure code update by attestation in sensor networks. In: Proceedings of the 5th ACM Workshop on Wireless Security, WiSe 2006, pp. 85–94. ACM, New York (2006)
10. Shi, E., Perrig, A., van Doorn, L.: Bind: a fine-grained attestation service for secure distributed systems. In: 2005 IEEE Symposium on Security and Privacy, pp. 154–168 (2005)
11. Yasinsac, A., Bishop, M.: The dynamics of counting and recounting votes. IEEE Security & Privacy 6(3), 22–29 (2008)
12. Bruck, S., Jefferson, D., Rivest, R.L.: A modular voting architecture (frog voting). In: Chaum, D., Jakobsson, M., Rivest, R.L., Ryan, P.Y.A., Benaloh, J., Kutylowski, M., Adida, B. (eds.) Towards Trustworthy Elections. LNCS, vol. 6000, pp. 97–106. Springer, Heidelberg (2010)
13. Pettis, E., Hunter, N., Lin, M.: S. Le. Military Remote Electronic Voting Protocol. Senior Project, School of Computing, University of South Alabama (December 6, 2012)
14. Delaune, S., Kremer, S., Ryan, M.: Coercion-resistance and receipt-freeness in electronic voting. In: Proceedings of the 19th IEEE Workshop on Computer Security Foundations, CSFW 2006, pp. 28–42. IEEE Computer Society, Washington, DC (2006)
15. Hirt, M., Sako, K.: Efficient receipt-free voting based on homomorphic encryption. In: Preneel, B. (ed.) EUROCRYPT 2000. LNCS, vol. 1807, pp. 539–556. Springer, Heidelberg (2000)
16. Juels, A., Catalano, D., Jakobsson, M.: Coercion-resistant electronic elections. In: Proceedings of the 2005 ACM Workshop on Privacy in the Electronic Society, WPES 2005, pp. 61–70. ACM, New York (2005)
17. Clarkson, M.R., Chong, S., Myers, A.C.: Civitas: Toward a secure voting system. In: IEEE Symposium on Security and Privacy, SP 2008, pp. 354–368 (2008)
18. Kuesters, R., Truderung, T.: An epistemic approach to coercion-resistance for electronic voting protocols. In: Proceedings of the 2009 30th IEEE Symposium on Security and Privacy, SP 2009, pp. 251–266. IEEE Computer Society, Washington, DC (2009)

Independent Computations for Safe Remote Electronic Voting
(Transcript of Discussion)

Alec Yasinsac

University of South Alabama

So this is a good follow-on to the previous papers. I've been working on electronic voting for several years, and as a retired U.S. Marine, I voted absentee for 20 years, and having not known much about voting and the electoral process when I was voting, when I began studying the electoral process I realized how many times I sent my ballot in and it wasn't counted, because, for example, in the military when you make a mistake you cross it out with a pencil and you initial it. Well when I did that on my ballot, that ballot went in the trashcan. Of course I had no idea. So since I've been involved with information security for a while, when I retired from the Marine Corps, I made this a focus of my research.

And I come at it from a perspective that's slightly different from many of my colleagues, and as a matter of full disclosure, my objective is to find a way for military members to deliver a voted ballot electronically. My objective is not to say, "is there possibly a way"; my objective is to find a way.

The notion here is pretty foundational. From a theoretical perspective, digital verification is hard. The Halting Problem says that using one computer program to verify another computer program is folly; you can't do that for arbitrary programs. That's the theoretical result. More practically speaking we know that it is hard because malware is pervasive, and in fact one of the hardest problems with remote electronic voting is being able to verify that you are doing these things with code that is unflawed.

There's a notion out there now of software attestation that would be a great thing to have for remote voting, and I've spent some time working on that too, but that's a little bit further down the road. Once you can be sure that the software that's running on that computer is the software that's supposed to be running there, that gives you a lot more flexibility to come up with protocols that can make voting safe. Still, I well-understand the reasons why many of my colleagues don't believe it's possible to vote remotely over electronic media today. What I'm here to offer you is, what I think is a fundamental difference in the ability to verify these ballots at the end and to make the argument that there are practical voting systems out there today that have some of the properties that could allow this to happen in a real election. So that's the goal of this paper today. I want to acknowledge several students, because they worked very hard, and they worked mostly independent of me: Erin Pettis, Son Le, Naquita Hunter, and Mengchu Lin. I gave them a copy of the paper, and their mentor, Terri Gilbert, and they implemented it as their senior, capstone project.

B. Christianson et al. (Eds.): Security Protocols 2013, LNCS 8263, pp. 84–93, 2013.
© Springer-Verlag Berlin Heidelberg 2013

They put it together and they wrote a voting system that actually implemented all of these concepts. It's not been used in any kind of election, but this is my fifth paper at the Security Protocols Workshop, so I know very well that you all know that the devil is in the details. It's awfully nice to have these high level protocols that have all these properties that you can prove, but then when you actually put them in the computer and in a machine, you know, it just didn't work out the way you thought it was going to work out. So that's a major contribution, from my perspective, that we have a system that actually runs, and it runs with handheld devices in the Android environment with a laptop computer, and that we made these things work in the laboratory. So I appreciate the work that they did, it gives me a little bit more confidence.

Now I want to back up just a minute and talk about this notion of universal verifiability, end-to-end voting systems. This terminology is not really well understood, even by some that have been doing this for a long time. The notion here regards the three steps in the middle that are the canonical steps in the voting integrity process. Have you cast that ballot as is intended? Now I argue that from a real perspective it's almost impossible to measure, because the intent of that voter is in that voter's mind. It may be that a voter doesn't have an intent that you can even describe. Maybe they voted for candidate A because they didn't like candidate B, or because they liked candidate A's name, or because candidate A was the first position on the ballot. We don't know what the voter's intentions are, so the metric that I have used is, "is it voter verifiable", i.e. can the voter look at what they cast and in some way say, yes, that's what I want to vote. So when they take a second look, they get a chance to be able to fix a mistake.

Now that's a very weak form of Cast as Intended, but it's probably, at least in my opinion, about as good as you can do. Now the real point of this slide is the difference between these two, "Recorded as Cast" and "Tallied as Recorded". The notion of Recorded as Cast is: I have some way to be able to determine that the local elections official that I sent my ballot to actually received the ballot in the form that I intended it to be delivered. Are all the selections on the ballot that the local elections official has the same as those that I intended for them to have? Now that is far better than the system that we have in place today. The gold standard of the voting elections community, is a Precinct Count Optical Scan system where you take your ballot, and you mark your ballot, put it in an envelope (or not), and you feed it in to this machine that scans it right there. Or maybe it scans it; maybe it's actually a shredder. It may well be that all those machines in some precincts really aren't counting those ballots, they may be shredding the ones that are received and dumping one that is in a bin underneath that shredder into the counted pot, that could really well be what's happening in all of those precincts throughout the United States.

So we do not have "Recorded as Cast" confidence today. While we think we have the gold standard in the United States, PCOS voting integrity system is Cast as Intended. Now I argue here that getting down to Tallied as Intended, or Tallied as Recorded and Tallied as Intended, is actually not an important distinction for us to make. It's hard to really capture what it means for the voter to be able to say, "I know my vote counted, because I can look at this piece of paper and see my ballot up there on the bulletin board, so I know it was counted". No, if I see it on the bulletin board all I know is it was Recorded as Intended. If I have some way to know that my ballot is on that bulletin board, I know that the local elections official got my ballot.

In order to be able to say that it's Tallied as Intended, I have to have some mathematics behind it. There must be some kind of abstraction that connects what I intended to be counted to the actual count at the end. So I can count all those ballots that are up there, and then I know my vote is in that count. Well in order for it to be Tallied as Intended I then have to know that all of those other ballots are legal, right, and that no other ballots were counted in the final count that was used to make this election. Well that's a really difficult process to do, it requires a whole lot of knowledge and understanding that most voters aren't able to get. And again, my argument is it doesn't give that much value to the electoral process and it provides a set of new attack vectors.

So the goal of the system that I'm presenting is to produce a Recorded As Cast electronic voting system.

The paper introduces the concept of malware independence; it's in the paper, so I won't go through this in detail. Malware independence is a property that two devices have, for two devices to have cooperating malware, they had to have been implemented independently. If the probability of putting malware A on machine X is Y, then the probability of putting malware B on machine C is a different probability, you have to multiply those together to get the probability of getting both of them. Remember the goal of this definition is to describe the complexity of being able to infect two independent devices. So if the voter uses two independent devices to cast a ballot, for malware to be able to change that vote without the voter being able to detect it, both of those devices would have to be infected by cooperating malware.

If a voter casts their ballot using two cooperating devices, they want to be sure they're not both infected with cooperating malware. Let's say a voter has a cellphone and a laptop, which are the two devices that really probably fit this bill. These devices are not malware independent if the voter plugs them together because as soon as they connect, one device could infect the other. There are other things that have an impact on whether two devices are independent or not, and I think that's the important point of this slide.

Another way that we try to reduce the likelihood that we're going to share malware between devices is through passive communication. Vanessa talked about using QR codes, but she didn't mention that was the form of the ballots that she took, the intermediate form, and then the encrypted form of her ballots, were essentially in QR codes. But the beauty of QR codes in this process is that it's passive communication; there is no IP address, there are no repeaters, you can't sit back and listen to this stuff at the back of the room, you can't have devices that are able to intercept the communications between a QR code and the scanner that reads the QR code. That reduces the attack surface because it doesn't have to be on a network. If it's on a network you can attack it from anywhere in the world. QR codes are local communication; they're passive communication. No electrons are exchanged and it reduces the likelihood that it will be able to inject malware into the system again.

QR codes are not perfect. One limitation is length. This slide quickly shows that QR code is 15 characters captured, you've got 185 characters here. Obviously if you've got a large ballot you're not going to be able to make those ballot representations, and there's some information in the paper about how you create digital representations of ballots that are optimized too, but it's not the paper's focus.

You could use multiple QR codes per ballot if you needed to, but in our prototype we wanted to get it down to one and they were able to do that with just a reasonably complex looking QR code to be able to make this work.

So the protocol overview for these independent computations, and essentially these are independent channels, which fits the theme; I know James will be proud, as there are independent channels, multiple channels working in this protocol. The notion is this: the voter gets their electronic ballot on the voting client. They make their selections, and transmit that to their assistive device through QR code. The assistive device then generates a ballot signature, a signed hash, whatever that may be, whichever works best, and the assistive device will then be the confirmation agent. So the voter can mark their ballot on their laptop, then when they receive it on their assistive device they can look at it right there on the assistive device; that's the voter verification. You have a second voter verification opportunity on the laptop, but again, if there's malware on the laptop, the laptop can show you the same ballot at the same time.

This is what the protocol looks like. Again all of this is right out of the paper so I won't go through that, but it's a blank ballot to the voting client. The voted ballot to the assistive device, the signed voted ballot, or the signature to the voted ballot back to the voting client. The ballot then comes to the State voting system and the confirmation goes back up to the assistive device, and life is good. Silence in the room.

Sandy Clark: Do you know that Norway actually implemented something like this about three years ago?

Reply: I do. Yes.

Vanessa Teague: You probably know what I am going to say, which is that it's hard to know a good criterion for real malware independence. So in particular, I agree that the examples you've given which demonstrate that the two devices are not malware independent, but it strikes me that there are other examples as well that could make the devices malware dependent. For example, some malware is propagated by infecting a website the person is likely to visit and encouraging the person to click on a link. If you as an individual own both these devices and you like that website you could very well visit independently once on each device, and then probability of your two devices getting infected by the same malware is much greater.

Reply: Absolutely true, there are many, many mechanisms that can allow these devices to be infected by cooperating malware, there's no doubt, because you have those same kind of interests, that's a great point. In fact I think in the long term a third way to do this is to have a third device that does nothing but those computations, OK, a widget, what I would call a widget. But in this case the answer may be, and going back to what my motivation was, that I shared in full disclosure when I began, in a military environment, many military members are given a handheld device, and they generally don't surf the web with that handheld device, you see. So the laptop that they vote on would be a machine that would be protected from malware from websites because maybe they don't use that machine for websites, their handheld they don't use for going to websites, and so that reduces the possibility of a coordinated malware attack.

Frank Stajano: In point number 6 you have the voter's countersigned hash to the voting client by the QR code generated by the assisted device. Usually the assistive device is the one that has a camera, but the laptop doesn't really have a camera, so how do you scan the QR code.

Reply: That's an excellent point and that's part of the challenge here is that the laptop would have to have a scanner associated with it for this particular protocol to work. In order for the laptop to be able to scan that in they would have to have a scanner. Of course scanners are cheap. It's just not an expensive proposition to have a scanner, but it creates more of a usability problem. Again, if you go back to the environment...

Frank Stajano: Is there a necessity of doing this via QR code as opposed to some other means? Are you exploiting any properties of the QR code channel in that particular step 6 is what I'm asking you.

Reply: That's an excellent point. There's no theoretical reason, no physical reason, why you couldn't use Bluetooth. The reason that I don't use Bluetooth is because I'm promoting this notion of passive communication that can't be intercepted, that can't be injected, it is a one-way communication that doesn't require any transmission.

Frank Stajano: But then you are exploiting features of that particular channel, because that's what makes it better than Bluetooth.

Reply: OK, thank you, yes I am exploiting features of that channel, thank you. But not in terms of speed or size, in fact the size is a limitation, but it is the security nature of that channel that makes it most useful. Yes.

Ariel Stulman: How do you know that the voting client doesn't inject in the QR some exploitable something that your assistive device would conflict?

Reply: That is absolutely in the paper. We mention that it is not impossible to be able to attack a device through the transmission that is in that QR code.

Ariel Stulman: That's the missing link because you guys clearly need independence.

Reply: No, it's not a missing link. We addressed this in the paper, that again there's no computer, and I mentioned it in my very first slide. Practically it's folly to try and verify one machine with another machine, but we can mitigate many of the risks by using this passive communication. The QR code technology is very well known, very well understood, and the amount of communication that can occur across it is very, very limited. So as you know, when we try and verify very large programs we have really hard problems; when we try and verify very small programs we have a much better chance of being able to do that. So being able to keep malware out of QR codes is much easier, even than being able to try and keep malware out of a user entry space where they're trying to enter their name. The QR code is small enough that you have a much better capability essentially of being able to do brute-force verification for every opportunity for transmission across that channel because it's so small. But it's a good point, and again, it's identified in the paper that I know many of you folks haven't seen yet, because you don't have the pre-proceedings just yet. Yes?

Peter Ryan: Perhaps you're going to say this in a minute, but what form does this confirmation message take?

Reply: That's a great question. The assistive device would create the signed hash, and that's what it was. But that's not necessarily the best form that it should take. Again, if you go back to the fundamentals of the Needham and Schroeder protocols, sending back that same signed hash is probably not a really good mechanism.

Let me confess here too that one of the things I didn't try to do in this paper was to do too much. One of the challenges of being able to offer an approach that we can reach some agreement on, is to try and not do too many things at one time. I don't know exactly the process this would take in an implemented system. The way we did it in our prototype was to send back the same signed hash. That's probably not what we would do in practice.

One thing that you might do to try and reduce some of the communications between those QR codes in the different machines is to receive that blank ballot on the assistive device. You get the blank ballot on the assistive device, you make all your votes there, then you would pass that signed voted ballot to the voting client, where you could verify your votes, so that if the assistive device has malware on it, you can still detect the change in votes that came from that assistive device, send that back here, and back with the confirmation to the assistive device again. So it's just a second protocol, only one pass required. You can see the second computation here where it's checked and the ballot is verified, and then to the local elections official.

Feng Hao: Isn't it required to have a private key to sign everything.

Reply: Yes, you have to have a key with the local elections official to be able to make this work.

Feng Hao: So problems of key distribution pertain here too?

Reply: Again, if you look right there in the paper, I mention all the standard disclosures, disclaimers, about the key handling and key management apply, if you're going to use cryptography, you've got to use keys. If you want to say that you can't use keys because you can't maintain them, then we'll throw those away too. But the bottom line here is, yes, you do have to use keys; you have to have a key infrastructure to make it work. Again, in the military that key structure is in place, it's on the cards. And again, I go back, the ability to verify in the

United States military is done on a card, all the ID cards have chips in them. That type of capability is not available in the general population, but it is in the military.

Feng Hao: But again, that becomes the source of your lack of independence, because if two machines need to get the key from some key distribution center then they are both accessing the same place.

Reply: Which two machines need the key?

Feng Hao: The assistive device and the voter client.

Reply: No, the voting client doesn't have the private key.

Feng Hao: How is it decrypted, how can it verify what's in the assistive device?

Reply: In the single pass protocol, the voting client need not decrypt anything. Rather, integrity is protected by the signed hash. The ballot that's displayed the voter could verify and then send that ballot and the signed hash to the local elections official. If that signed hash didn't match the ballot then it would be rejected by the voting server, which needs only hold the voter's public key. This ballot could be sent in the clear with a signature, with a signed hash of the ballot. Then when that gets here if they don't match the local elections official will reject, and notify. In order to protect privacy, the voting client, not the assistive device, would need to have the voting server's public key, but we did not incorporate that aspect because our focus is overcoming the malware threat.

Jeff Yan: So why do you need the voting client here, why not just one device?

Reply: You could do that, but then malware could convince the voter that the voter had created a ballot. The assistive device, without this device there's no voter verification. The malware on the assistive device could create a bad ballot, change the votes, create a hash and send that to the local elections official, but display the ballot that the user had intended to have vote. Does that make sense?

Bruce Christianson: But the assistive device can do that anyway can't it, by sending a voted ballot to the voting client that doesn't correspond to that, and then it's signed. The voting client has no way to know whether the signature that it's got matches the hash of the ballot that's been sent.

Audience: But in a local election the official would correct it.

Ross Anderson: Well they can, presumably the client can verify the signature if you assume the verification key is public.

Reply: That's correct.

Ross Anderson: And it can verify the signature against the display of the text.

Bruce Christianson: So it has to be done like that.

Reply: That's correct. Thank you Ross.

Ross Anderson: But that means in this particular design you lose the benefits of having a signature verification key that is in some sense not public.

Reply: Right. Well again the question here is, if the voting client doesn't have any key of any type, if the ballot is in the clear, but the signed hash accompanies the ballot, then when the voter looks at it, if it's the wrong ballot then they reject, and they go back and they start the process again. But if the ballot is what they intended they could send that with the signed hash to the voting server, and the only impact would be if they don't match it will be rejected.

Ross Anderson: No there's still an attack because if I'm the black bagman for the Republicans and what I arrange is a temporal sense of the time if somebody votes for the Democrats, I put in a signature that's mathematically wrong. Now if the voting client cannot verify that then I've managed to spoil ten percent of the Democrats ballot without a voter realizing it.

Reply: But the notification goes back and the voter starts over.

Bruce Christianson: The verification goes back to the assistive device, which is corrupt, and displays it as a positive acknowledgment.

Ross Anderson: Correct.

Reply: A ha.

Bruce Christianson: There's only one loop through the voting client and you can't do it with only one loop.

Ross Anderson: So what this means is that voting client must have the verification key corresponding to the signing key.

Bruce Christianson: Or must receive a confirmation.

Audience: Which means they can be attacked.

Ross Anderson: Which means it's difficult, not impossible, but it just makes it more difficult for the verification key to be non-public.

Bruce Christianson: You just need one more loop.

Reply: That's right.

Vanessa Teague: What happens if the assisted device could talk back to the local elections official, and is there anything that stops it spoofing the voting client? So, for example, if I were a corrupt assistive device, could I send one signed version of the ballot for the way that I wanted to cast, back to the local elections official, and then a few seconds later send, so the voter's got a properly signed vote that the voter wanted to cast back to the voting client, and then I guess I'd try and interfere with that message, the message number 3, and try and stop the voting client from sending back to the elections official.

Reply: So if, you're saying if the assistive device is malware infected and it has taken over the device and it decides to act as an adversary, an active adversary, by sending multiple messages, for example, to the local elections official. I mean, so what we would have then is the local elections officials would receive multiple ballots from the same voter.

Vanessa Teague: Yes, it would.

Feng Hao: It does not have to be a multiple, because the voting client doesn't have any secret keys so the assistive device can simply bypass that voting client and the elections official.

Reply: But the end user is using the voting client to verify the ballot, so they will know. They can't bypass the voting client in this case because the voter is looking for the ballot here.

Daniel Thomas: But if the voting client is tethered to the assistive device via wifi, then the assistive device could drop message 3, and just send message

2 directly to the election official. Because there's no change that happens in the voting client, if the assistive device actively accepts then the voter client won't know.

Reply: How could the assistive device prevent message 3 from being sent?

Daniel Thomas: If the voting client is connecting to the local elections official via the assistive device, for example, if they're using wi-fi tethering through 3G through the assistive device, then that would be possible.

Reply: Right, but we said we weren't going to do that, right, I mean, that was an assumption. If you violate the assumptions then the protocol doesn't work. So back to your question Vanessa, What you were saying is if this device sends a ballot to the local elections official then what you would have is either it would not send a vote here, and the voter would know, or there would be a second ballot that goes here and the local elections official would know.

Vanessa Teague: That's true. So in order to do it without the local elections official knowing you would have to find a way to interfere with the voting client's communications.

Reply: So this is the argument that we make, usual key management disclaimer that you ask for, receipt-free-neutral; maybe not. Maybe it actually diminishes receipt free properties because folks get back confirmations of how they voted that could be verified. But there is not intention to inject capabilities for coercion resistance, or vote buying or selling, that's not part of this paper.

The notion here, really the focus of this paper, is the technology to mitigate the impact of malware on independent voting clients, which has been an important problem. If you folks remember the SERVE Report, everybody that does voting knows the SERVE Report in 2004, the gang of four wrote a letter to the New York Times and ended up stopping a voting project by the U.S. Department of Defense, and one of the most important arguments they made was the issue of end-user device malware. So that's what this paper is intended to provide, at least a step forward in that area. No impact on voter privacy, the same as all remote electronic voting, and also denial-of-service, it at least in most cases will allow you to detect denial-of-service, but those are the ones that are in there.

That's really the paper I think. Again, it's recorded as intended, not counted as intended. And they are voter verifiable; passive communications are important, malware independence is important.

Jeff Yan: I am curious about the military chip. You showed us the card, so what was the underlying key mechanism, the PKI-based stuff? Basically how does the system enable an individual key for a person? So basically how does the card you showed to us work?

Reply: Oh I'm sorry, OK, so I confused things here, I apologize, this doesn't have anything to do with the talk, when I pulled out my card he asked how the card works in the US military. It's just simply a smart card, that's all it is, it allows you to have a personal ability to create cryptography. They use them in Estonia's voting system. Norway has the same kind of thing.

So in the United States, using electronic voting for remote voting is going to be very difficult without some type of strong authentication in the general population. In the US military you can use that card if you need to. I didn't leverage the strength of that card in this paper, but I did want you to know that that is a capability that the military has to be able to do that kind of thing with their card, in their handheld device, and in the laptops that they would have access to be able to cast their ballots. So it's a good question, just confused me, I'm sorry.

Michael Roe: And in that case is the US military has a reasonably good idea of who its employees are and how to identify them, whereas in general doing elections, let's say the UK government, had a rather poor idea of who the people are, of how to authenticate people who are going to vote, so you have a better starting position.

Reply: Well that's exactly right. There are probably hundreds of reasons why the military establishment is an excellent establishment to target remote electronic voting; lots and lots of really good reasons. There are also a lot of reasons why it's a political hot button issue because at least in the US the military is seen as being more affiliated with one party than the other. So every time somebody talks about increasing the availability of voting to the military you get into political discussions as opposed to the technology discussions, which is really what I'm here to talk about. So, I'm sorry, I'm taking up your time rambling, I appreciate it very much. Thank you.

ReDABLS: Revisiting Device Attestation with Bounded Leakage of Secrets

Jun Zhao, Virgil Gligor, Adrian Perrig*, and James Newsome

CyLab and ECE Department
Carnegie Mellon University
Pittsburgh, PA 15213
{junzhao,gligor,perrig,jnewsome}@cmu.edu

Abstract. Many commodity operating systems and applications become infested with malicious software over time, primarily due to exploits that take advantage of software flaws and operator errors. In this paper, we present the salient features of a system design which allows remote-device authentication by a verifier, reaching malware-free memory states, and trusted application booting in the presence of malicious software that is controlled by a network adversary. Our system design revisits the notion of *device attestation with bounded leakage of secrets* (DABLS), and illustrates both the significant challenges of making it work in practice and how to overcome them.

1 Introduction

During the past decade, Professor Moriarty, the fictitious genius and evil adversary, has acquired new attack capabilities and now poses an unprecedented challenge for the wizards of the Security Protocols Workshop (SPW). Not only can he fully control communication networks (e.g., in man-in-the-middle style) connecting remote devices with device-attestation hosts, but also he can now inject malware into those devices, making them behave in a Byzantine manner and/or leak their secrets. In the past, the wizards were able to counter either one of these attack capabilities or the other, but not both together.

For example, if Moriarty controls all network communications but not end hosts and devices, the wizards of SPW could deploy secret encryption keys in the commodity cryptographic modules; e.g., the Trusted Platform Modules (TPMs) [11] of remote hosts and devices, and take advantage of Moriarty's bounded computational power to counter his attestation attacks with provable-secure protocols. Or, if he could only insert malware in some of the remote devices but not control any network communications, remote connections to devices could be authenticated without device secrets; e.g., by using network front-ends, which remain beyond the reach of device malware, for remote devices. In this setting, the wizards could deploy sufficiently many additional devices beyond Moriarty's

---

* Current address: Computer Science Department, ETH, Zurich, Switzerland.

B. Christianson et al. (Eds.): Security Protocols 2013, LNCS 8263, pp. 94–114, 2013.
© Springer-Verlag Berlin Heidelberg 2013

reach to detect Byzantine misbehavior by the malware-infected ones, and enable host reliance only on clean devices. The strategy of relying on secret keys could be safely foregone and the significant challenge of secure, remote key management on malware controlled commodity hardware[1] avoided, in this setting. However, if use of secret keys would still be desired, each device could store a key fragment and rely on threshold cryptography - with the appropriate assumptions – to assemble a shared secret key that Moriarty could not obtain from the set of devices he controls.

Three of the questions faced in designing attestation protocols for remote devices are as follows.

(1) How could a host authenticate a remote device, when adversary Moriarty controls *both* the communication network (i.e., via network adversary M_{out}) and the remote device software (i.e., via device malware M_{in}), but not its commodity hardware (e.g., physical device configuration, components, channel bandwidth)? Clearly, device authentication requires that a device's secret be protected, and if secrets protected by commodity hardware could be discovered by Moriarty's malware M_{in} and exported to his network adversary M_{out}, he could then use his own bogus device to masquerade as the authentic remote device. Could we exploit hardware architecture features to perform software-based device authentication without depending on long-lived, hardware-protected secrets; e.g., without physically unclonable functions (PUFs) [2, 5], TPMs?

(2) How could a remote device prove that it has reached a malware-free memory state to an attestation host *after* Moriarty has inserted malware M_{in} into that device? Remotely re-booting device software and initializing a memory state could not be performed with significant assurance since malware M_{in} itself could compromise the reboot operation. Even if device authentication could be performed in the presence of malware M_{in} (e.g., by using special hardware, such as PUFs), proving the establishment of a malware-free memory state on a commodity device to an attestation host remains a challenge. Is there a way to clean up the device remotely and eliminate malware M_{in} despite the network adversary M_{out}?

(3) How could a remote device prove that it has performed a *trusted boot* of application software to an attestation host? Notice that between the time that a malware-free memory state is demonstrated to an attestation host and the time that trusted boot of application software is completed, the device could be compromised by Moriarty's malware M_{in} again. Could a proof of correct device authentication be composed with one of malware-free memory state establishment and further with one of trusted boot of application software?

---

[1] For example, a secure key update in response to side-channel attacks – as prescribed by leakage-resilient cryptography – could not be performed with significant assurance, even if a host could reach a remote device using secure network communication channels, now assumed to be beyond an adversary's control. Device malware could always respond correctly to key update commands using the already captured device key.

In this paper, we provide preliminary answers to the above questions in the context of commodity devices, *without assuming* that malware is prevented from accessing secrets stored on commodity devices and communicating with an external network adversary which controls it. Instead, we present a system that limits the bandwidth of the device's output channel to D_{ban} bits per second, updates secrets periodically and prevents the leakage of an entire pool of secrets. In effect, our system *confines* malware M_{in} sufficiently to enable a remote verifier established the three desirable properties outlined above, namely (1) remote-device authentication, reaching malware-free memory states, and trusted (re)boot of application software. Specifically, we revisit the notion of *device attestation with bounded leakage of secrets* (DABLS) and system description provided by Tran [10], and provide new operating conditions and modes, called ReDABLS, which appear to be practical for large classes of *different* system types and configurations. In particular, we argue that in contrast to the overhead rate of DABLS, which makes it impractical for large classes of intuitive operating conditions, ReDABLS can yield much lower overhead rates, particularly when acceptable probabilistic upper bounds are found for an adversary's success in attacking it.

ReDABLS also differs from the better-known software-only root of trust (SWORT) mechanisms [1, 3, 4, 6–9] in three ways. First, SWORT mechanisms do not provide device authentication directly since they have been introduced to achieve only *authentication of program execution* on any device of the *same* type and configuration. Second, without additional mechanisms, SWORT does not usually guarantee uninterruptable composition of malware-free memory state establishment and trusted boot of application software; i.e., malware could reinstall itself into the device after the establishment of a malware-free state and trusted software boot. Third, the ReDABLS verifier would be less susceptible to timing variations in the speed of the computing device (e.g., processor speed), since it would have to tolerate larger (e.g., network) delays, by design. For these reasons, practical answers to the three questions posed for ReDABLS above would provide stronger, more robust guarantees than SWORT.

We envision the use of ReDABLS for several applications that require periodic attestation of malware-free state and secure initialization for (1) hypervisors of remote devices, (2) control software of autonomous devices, and (3) software of unattended smart-grid devices (e.g., smart meters).

2 A Brief Overview of DABLS

In DABLS, a remote device is initialized with a device-unique, large pool of secrets S comprising N blocks of b bits each, prior to deployment;[2] viz., Fig. 1. The pool is updated by using a device local function $f(n_i, S)$ in response to a nonce n_{i-1} sent by a remote Verifier, in every T_s seconds, where T_s represents the device computation time dedicated to application execution. The time used for updating the N blocks of the pool and responding to the Verifier is denoted

---

[2] The initialization of pool S is done using a pseudo-random number generator, PRNG, which yields statistically unique pool values for reasonable sizes of N and b.

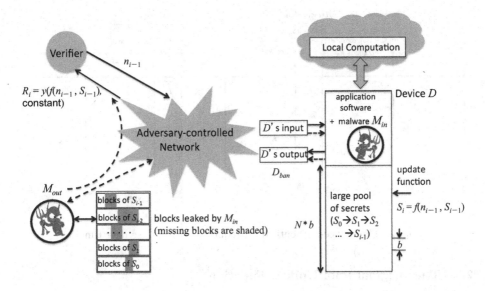

Fig. 1. A snapshot of the DABLS operation

by T_{up}. At the end of each update time, T_{up}, the device sends response $R_i = y(f(n_{i-1}, S_{i-1}), constant)$ to the Verifier, where y is a message authentication code function based on the updated secret pool state $S_i = f(n_{i-1}, S_{i-1})$. Failure to respond by the end of T_{up} or to produce an incorrect response R_i causes the Verifier to signal an exception. As a result of pool initialization to state S_0, and subsequent updates, the secret pool goes through a number of device unique states $S_0, S_1, \cdots, S_{i-1}$, unless a Verifier exception interrupts this sequence and causes re-initialization. A snapshot of the DABLS operation is illustrated in Fig. 1, and the device-authentication request and response over time are illustrated in Fig. 2.

We note that pool update function can use a variety of cryptographic primitives, such as pseudo-random functions (PRFs) and one-way functions (OWFs), to ensure that entire past pools can be computed and future pools cannot be anticipated unless all pool blocks of a given state are available, except with negligible probability. Let the speed of the cryptographic primitive used by the pool update function $f(n, S)$ be C_{P_n} seconds per pool block. The *overhead rate* of the update operation is T_{up}/T_s, and the system *feasibility condition* is $T_{up}/T_s < 1$.

In this paper we argue that the overhead rate has a lower bound $N \times C_{P_n} \times D_{ban}/b$, for a large class of pool update functions. We illustrate one of the challenges posed by the design of DABLS by showing that intuitively efficient pool update functions – not just those initially considered for DABLS [10] – fail to satisfy the system feasibility condition. This motivates our introduction of *probabilistic* pool update functions and additional operating modes for ReDABLS; viz., Section 4 below.

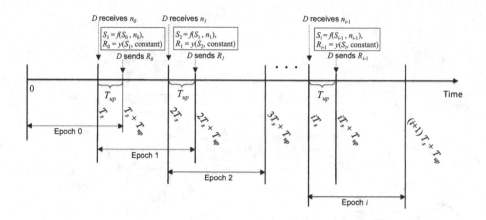

Fig. 2. The device-authentication request and response over time

2.1   The Original Pool Update Function

DABLS presents a pool update function f_1 by using a *non-invertible* pseudo-random function (PRF) as the basic tool. Let P be a family of non-invertible PRFs. A particular non-invertible PRF P_n is selected from that family by using the nonce n; i.e., $P : \{0,1\}^{|n|} \to P_n$. An instance P_n takes as input k blocks of size b bits, and produces one block of output; namely, $P_n : \{0,1\}^{k \cdot b} \to \{0,1\}^b$.

A secret pool S is broken into N blocks of size b bits: $S[0], S[1], \ldots, S[N-1]$. $S[i]$ is referred to as block i of the pool S, where $0 \le i \le N-1$. As specified by Equation (1), the recursive function g takes an index i as input and produces a single block g_i as output. g_i equals $S[i]$ for $0 \le i \le N-1$, and is computed by inputting the N previous blocks $g_{i-j}|_{j=N,N-1,\ldots,1}$ to the PRF P_n for $i \ge N$. Finally, f_1 is realized according to Equation (2) below, where $\lambda \ge N$.

$$g_i = \begin{cases} S[i], & \text{for } 0 \le i \le N-1, \\ P_n(g_{i-N}\|g_{i-(N-1)}\|\ldots\|g_{i-1}), & \text{for } i \ge N. \end{cases} \tag{1}$$

$$f_1(n, S) = g_\lambda\|g_{\lambda+1}\|\ldots\|g_{\lambda+N-1}. \tag{2}$$

2.2   DABLS Fails the Feasibility Condition

With f_1 used as the pool update function in DABLS, a necessary condition for preventing the external adversary M_{out} from obtaining a complete secret pool is $(T_s + T_{up})D_{ban} < N \times b$, which leads to $T_s < N \times b/D_{ban}$. Let C_{P_n} be the time cost to compute P_n on each input block. Then $T_{up} = N \times \lambda \times C_{P_n}$. Therefore, the overhead rate $T_{up}/T_s > \lambda C_{P_n} D_{ban}/b \ge N C_{P_n} D_{ban}/b$. However, as illustrated in Table 1, this lower bound $N C_{P_n} D_{ban}/b$ of T_{up}/T_s is greater than 1 for typical devices, rendering DABLS infeasible in practice.

Table 1. Examples of system parameters. P_n uses AES as the block cipher and the CBC-MAC-like as the mode of encryption, as illustrated by DABLS [10]

$|S|$ (MB)	b (bits)	N	D_{ban} (MB/sec)	b/C_{P_n} (MB/sec)	T_{up}/T_s
0.16	128	10^4	0.001	1.2 (on ARM 1176-482MHz)	> 8.3
1.6	128	10^5	0.01	107 (on Intel Core 2-1.83 GHz)	> 9.3

Several possible approaches to reduce the lower bound $N C_{P_n} D_{ban}/b$ of T_{up}/T_s are available. For example, to decrease C_{P_n}, P_n could use a $5 - 8$ times faster primitive; e.g., XoR-universal hash functions. Furthermore, given a fixed $|S|$, the block size b could be set larger to decrease N. Finally, commodity hardware front ends or network interfaces that remain beyond the reach of device malware could be used to effectively decrease the outbound network bandwidth limit of the device depending on other system parameters; e.g., an increased T_s, a decreased pool size $|S|$.

3   The New Pool Update Functions for ReDABLS

DABLS fails to provide a feasible pool update function for achieving the three desirable security properties discussed in the Introduction; i.e., remote-device authentication, reaching malware-free memory states, and trusted boot of application software. In ReDABLS, we rely on similar protocols as those in DABLS but introduce new pool update functions in an attempt to make the system overhead rate practical.

The challenge one faces in designing new pool update functions is that intuitive optimizations do not necessarily work. For example, one could attempt to use smaller input sizes than that of $f_1(n, S)$ without compromising update security; i.e., the number of input blocks could be smaller than N. However, this would not necessarily decrease the overhead rate; viz., function f_2 below. Another way would be to also use more efficient cryptographic primitives for the function implementation. Although, this could decrease the overhead rate, it would not necessarily satisfy our feasibility condition; viz., function f_3 below. For these reasons, we introduce probabilistic update functions (viz., f_4 and f_5 below), which can reduce the overhead rates of update functions such as f_2 and f_3 to feasible levels.

3.1   The Pool Update Function f_2

We assume that N is a product of two positive integers q and m; i.e., $N = qm$, where $m \geq 2$. Now we explain how $f_2(n, S)$ is computed given a nonce n and a secret pool S. S consists of N blocks: $S[0], S[1], \ldots, S[N-1]$. g_i is updated as follows. g_i equals $S[i]$ for $0 \leq i \leq N - 1$, and is computed by inputting $(q + 1)$ blocks $g_{i-jm}|_{j=q,q-1,...,1}$ and g_{i-1} to the PRF P_n for $i \geq N$; namely,

$$g_i = \begin{cases} S[i], & \text{for } 0 \leq i \leq N - 1, \\ P_n\left(g_{i-qm}||g_{i-(q-1)m}||\cdots||g_{i-m}||g_{i-1}\right), & \text{for } i \geq N. \end{cases} \quad (3)$$

Finally, similar to the design of f_1, the function f_2 is still defined as the last N blocks after computing λ blocks of g; i.e., $f_2(n, S)$ is set by

$$f_2(n, S) = g_\lambda||g_{\lambda+1}||\cdots||g_{\lambda+N-1}. \quad (4)$$

With function f_2 used as the pool update function, we have derived a set of conditions which are both necessary and sufficient for preventing the external adversary from obtaining a complete secret pool. (A detailed analysis of these conditions is provided in Appendix A.) The set of conditions indicates that the overhead rate T_{up}/T_s is at least $NC_{P_n}D_{ban}/b$, the same lower bound as in the case where f_1 is used as the pool update function. Therefore, a system implemented with f_2 would also fail the feasibility condition $T_{up}/T_s < 1$. Note that function f_1 can be regarded as a special case of function f_2 with $q = N$.

3.2 The Pool Update Function f_3

Consider a pool update from a secret pool S to the next secret pool $f_3(n, S)$. S consists of N blocks: $S[0], S[1], \ldots, S[N - 1]$; $f_3(n, S)$ consists of N blocks: $y_0, y_1, \ldots, y_{N-1}$. For $i = 0, 1, \ldots, N - 1$, block y_i is computed by inputing to PRF P_n w blocks with a sliding window of length w; specifically,

$$y_i = P_n(z_{j+i}||z_{j+i+1}||\cdots||z_{j+i+(w-1)}),$$

where $j \in \{0, 1, \ldots, N - 1\}$ is determined by the nonce n and block z_t is defined by

$$z_t = \begin{cases} S[t], & \text{for } 0 \leq t \leq N - 1, \\ y_{t-N}, & \text{for } t \geq N. \end{cases}$$

Here we set P_n as the MD5 hash function, whose computation cost on an input block is lower than that of CBC-MAC-AES.

With f_3 used as the pool update function, we have also proved that a necessary condition for preventing the external adversary from obtaining a complete secret pool is $T_{up}/T_s \geq NC_{P_n}D_{ban}/b$. (The proof is omitted due to space limitations.) If P_n is implemented with the MD5 function, f_3 also fails the feasibility condition $T_{up}/T_s < 1$, as illustrated in Table 2.

Table 2. Examples of system parameters. P_n is the MD5 hash function.

$|S|$ (MB)	b (bits)	N	D_{ban} (MB/sec)	b/C_{P_n} (MB/sec)	T_{up}/T_s
0.16	128	10^4	0.001	2 (on ARM 1176-482MHz)	> 5
1.6	128	10^5	0.01	268 (on Intel Core 2-1.83 GHz)	> 3.7

3.3 The Probabilistic Pool Update Functions f_4 and f_5

We consider probabilistic pool update functions and show that they can reduce the overhead rates of the three non-probabilistic functions discussed above to feasible levels.

Random Permutation. The idea of using a random permutation is that, given a random nonce, we can derive a permutation from the nonce that will change the ordering of the N blocks of the old secret pool randomly before the pool update. The intuition behind the overhead rate T_{up}/T_s reduction is that the external adversary M_{out} still cannot obtain a complete secret pool even though the internal adversary M_{in} leaks more blocks per epoch than in the three cases above where a random permutation is not used. This is the case because M_{in} can no longer be sure which pool blocks will be useful as the input for the update function in future epochs. Instead, the external adversary M_{in} has to predict the usefulness of blocks in future epochs.

We introduce a pool update function f_4, which is the random permutation version of function f_2, as shown below. Given a secret pool S, we now explain the computation of $f_4(n, S)$. S consists of N blocks: $S[0], S[1], \ldots, S[N-1]$. Then, based on the external nonce n, blocks $S[0], S[1], \ldots, S[N-1]$ are randomly permuted to blocks $S'[0], S'[1], \ldots, S'[N-1]$, which are inputs to the recursive block computation. Similar to (3), we define g_i as follows:

$$g_i = \begin{cases} S'[i], & \text{for } 0 \le i \le N-1, \\ P_n\big(g_{i-qm}||g_{i-(q-1)m}||\cdots||g_{i-m}||g_{i-1}\big), & \text{for } i \ge N. \end{cases}$$

Then the same as (4), $f_4(n, S)$ is set by

$$f_4(n, S) = g_\lambda||g_{\lambda+1}||\cdots||g_{\lambda+N-1}.$$

With f_4 used as the pool update function in ReDABLS, one can prove that the overhead rate is reduced by a constant factor that depends on system architecture (e.g., the ratio of the local memory size over the pool size $|S|$), compared with the case where f_2 is the pool update function.

Partial Pool Update. Consider a pool update from secret pool S_i to S_{i+1}. A fixed number of blocks in S_i are propagated to S_{i+1} without any change, while the remaining blocks in S_i are updated. The purpose of partial pool update is to reduce the number of blocks in each pool update to be updated by P_n, and thus to reduce T_{up}, which helps decrease the overhead rate T_{up}/T_s. Also, we need to enforce that the external adversary M_{out} still can obtain a complete secret pool with only a negligible probability.

We introduce a pool update function f_5, which is the partial pool update version of function f_3, as detailed below. In computing $f_5(n, S)$, let the number of propagated blocks in S be G. The G blocks are randomly selected based on the nonce n and are uniformly distributed among the N blocks of S. Without knowing the nonce n, the attacker cannot predict the G blocks.

Table 3. Examples of system parameters. The units of $|S|$, b, D_{ban} and b/C_{P_n} are MB, MB/sec, bits and MB/sec, respectively. P_n is the MD5 hash function; and Pr* is Pr[M_{out} succeeds in obtaining a complete secret pool].

$|S|$	b	N	D_{ban}	b/C_{P_n}	G	w	h	T_{up}/T_s	Pr*
0.16	128	10^4	0.001	2 (on ARM 1176-482MHz)	$9N/10$	$10N/11$	$N/11$	> 0.56	2.3×10^{-39}
1.6	128	10^5	0.01	268 (on Intel Core 2-1.83 GHz)	$29N/30$	$30N/31$	$N/31$	> 0.13	1.0×10^{-45}

The maximal number of blocks leaked or saved blocks in any epoch should be less than the sliding window w; otherwise, M_{out} could splice these leaked or saved blocks and update them, obtaining at least w blocks of secret pool S_0 at the end of epoch 0, at least $(w + 1)$ blocks of secret pool S_1 at the end of epoch 1, ..., and a complete secret pool S_i at the end of epoch $(N - w)$. We denote that number by $(w - h)$ since it is less than w, where $h \geq 1$. Clearly, $(w - h)$ is at least $T_s D_{ban}/b$, the maximal number of blocks leaked within T_s. Then $T_s \leq (w - h)b/D_{ban}$. Noting that $T_{up} = (N - G) \cdot w \cdot C_{P_n}$, we finally obtain

$$T_{up}/T_s \geq \frac{1 - G/N}{1 - h/w} \times N C_{P_n} D_{ban}/b.$$

The goal is to let the probabilistic-update factor $\frac{1-G/N}{1-h/w}$ be small and have a negligible probability for M_{out} succeeding in obtaining a complete secret pool. First, to ensure $\frac{1-G/N}{1-h/w} \leq 1$, it follows that $G \geq h$.

Given the leaked or saved $(w - h)$ blocks in an epoch and the G propagated blocks, if there are at least w consecutive blocks among them, then M_{out} succeeds in splicing the w blocks. Consider that the $(w-h)$ blocks have i (resp., j) number of the G propagated blocks to their immediate left (resp., right), where $i, j \geq 0$. M_{out} succeeds in splicing if $i + j \geq h$.

We have

$$\Pr[(i \geq h) \cap (j \geq 0)] = \binom{N - h}{G - h} \bigg/ \binom{N}{G},$$

and for $t = h - 1, h - 2, \ldots, 0$,

$$\Pr[(i \geq t) \cap (j \geq h - t)] = \binom{N - h - 1}{G - h} \bigg/ \binom{N}{G}.$$

Then

$$\Pr[M_{out} \text{ succeeds in obtaining a complete secret pool}]$$
$$\leq \Pr[i + j \geq h].$$
$$= \binom{N - h}{G - h} \bigg/ \binom{N}{G} + h \cdot \binom{N - h - 1}{G - h} \bigg/ \binom{N}{G}$$
$$\leq (h + 1) \times (G/N)^h.$$

Table 3 presents examples of system parameters.

4   Additional Operational Modes for ReDABLS

In this section, we briefly outline two additional operational modes intended to enhance the usability of ReDABLS.

First, a commodity network-interface device that is beyond the reach of malware M_{in} can be connected to the remote application device to limit the malware's output bandwidth independent of any length of T_s. All other hardware communication channels of the application device are disabled so that the network-interface device provides the only Internet connection service for the remote application device. We denote by D'_{ban} the effective outbound network bandwidth limit of the device enforced by the interface device. D'_{ban} can be set to be much smaller than D_{ban}, the device D's maximum outbound network bandwidth in the absence of the interface device. This means that T_s can be increased and/or $|S|$ decreased more than before to ensure a small overhead rate.

Second, ReDABLS can have an infrequent-activation mode based on a separate private but slow/expensive channel between the verifier and a remote human operator who would be located in the vicinity of the device and could visually identify it. The verifier-operator channel is secure, since it connects the verifier to an operator's phone via an encrypted cellular network connection, which remains beyond the reach of the network adversary M_{out}. That is, we assume that the network adversary M_{out} does not control the cellular communications, and the device owner's phone or any potential malware on it. For example, this operational mode could consist of the following specific steps.

1) The verifier sends a short secret seed over the secure channel to the device owner's phone. Note that this channel would be expensive to use for the direct transfer of the entire secret pool S from the verifier to the remote device. Instead, the secret seed is used to generate the pool on the device owner's phone.

2) The device owner's phone generates a secret pool S by seeding a PRNG with the short secret, and sends S to the device via a fast private channel (e.g., through a USB cable connecting the phone to the device).

3) The verifier can now authenticate the remote device, enable a multi-epoch establishment of malware-free state, and perform a trusted boot.

Note that this operational mode would be used only infrequently. Thus even if its overhead rate would be high, the overall overhead would be acceptable because it would be chargeable only to a small portion of the device operation. This operational mode also offers an opportunity to optimize $|S|$, the size of pool S. On the one hand, $|S|$ cannot be very large since S is generated on a phone with limited battery power, and on the other, $|S|$ cannot be very small because, otherwise, secret pool S could be leaked to the network adversary M_{out} by malware M_{in} before it gets updated.

5   Conclusions

In earlier work, Tran [10] presented DABLS – a system that attempts to achieve remote-device authentication, reaching malware-free memory states, and trusted boot of application software, in the continuous presence of device malware that can access device secrets and leak them to a network adversary. However, DABLS was infeasible in practice, leaving us with the substantial challenge of designing new operating conditions and modes for bounding the leakage of device secrets in a practical manner. To this end, we introduced a set of *probabilistic* update functions that decrease the update overhead rates in ReDABLS, and outlined new modes of operation to further decrease the relative system overhead. We now believe that the feasibility of device attestation with bounded leakage of secrets can be established conclusively.

Acknowledgments. The first author was supported in part by Lockheed Martin's CyLab Corporate Partners membership funds.

References

1. Armknecht, F., Sadeghi, A.-R., Schulz, S., Wachsmann, C.: A Security Framework for Analysis and Design of Software Attestation. In: Cryptology ePrint Archive: Report 2013/083 (February 18, 2013)
2. Gassend, B., Clarke, D., van Dijk, M., Devadas, S.: Silicon physical random functions. In: Proceedings of ACM Conference on Computer and Communication Security (CCS), pp. 148–160 (2002)
3. Kovah, X., Kallenberg, C., Weathers, C., Herzog, A., Albin, M., Butterworth, J.: New results for timing-based attestation. In: Proceedings of the IEEE Symposium on Security and Privacy (May 2012)
4. Li, Y., McCune, J.M., Perrig, A.: SBAP: Software-based attestation for peripherals. In: Acquisti, A., Smith, S.W., Sadeghi, A.-R. (eds.) TRUST 2010. LNCS, vol. 6101, pp. 16–29. Springer, Heidelberg (2010)
5. Pappu, R.: Physical One-Way Functions. PhD thesis, MIT School of Architecture and Planning, Program in Media Arts and Sciences (March 2001)
6. Seshadri, A., Luk, M., Perrig, A., van Doorn, L., Khosla, P.: SCUBA: Secure code update by attestation in sensor networks. In: Proceedings of ACM Workshop on Wireless Security, WiSe (September 2006)
7. Seshadri, A., Luk, M., Shi, E., Perrig, A., van Doorn, L., Khosla, P.: Pioneer: Verifying integrity and guaranteeing execution of code on legacy platforms. In: Proceedings of ACM Symposium on Operating Systems Principles (SOSP), pp. 1–16 (October 2005)
8. Seshadri, A., Perrig, A., van Doorn, L., Khosla, P.: SWATT: Software-based attestation for embedded devices. In: Proceedings of the IEEE Symposium on Security and Privacy (May 2004)
9. Shaneck, M., Mahadevan, K., Kher, V., Kim, Y.: Remote software-based attestation for wireless sensors. In: Molva, R., Tsudik, G., Westhoff, D. (eds.) ESAS 2005. LNCS, vol. 3813, pp. 27–41. Springer, Heidelberg (2005)
10. Tran, A.: DABLS: Device attestation with bounded leakage of secrets. Master's thesis, Carnegie Mellon University (July 2011),
    http://www.cylab.cmu.edu/files/pdfs/tech_reports/CMUCyLab13009.pdf
11. Trusted Computing Group. Trusted platform module main specification, Part 1: Design principles, Part 2: TPM structures, Part 3: Commands. Version 1.2, Revision 103 (July 2007)

A   Analysis of ReDABLS with Pool Update Function f_2

In this appendix, we provide a detailed analysis of ReDABLS only for the pool update function f_2.[3]

A.1   Minimum Amount of Leakage Necessary

In this update function, we enforce the condition

$$\lambda \geq N + m - 1 \tag{5}$$

to ensure that any block of the updated pool $f(n, S)$ ultimately needs all N blocks of previous secret pool S as inputs. If this condition is satisfied, then the internal adversary (i.e., malware) M_{in} needs to leak *at least* $N = m \cdot q$ blocks to succeed in leaking an entire secret pool.

Let S be the concatenation of N blocks $x_{D+i}|_{i=0,1,...,N-1}$, where $D \geq 0$. For $j = 0, 1, \ldots, m - 1$, we define $Y_j := \{x_{D+j+\ell m}\}|_{\ell=0,1,...,m-1}$. Clearly, the computation of block x_{D+N+j} needs $x_{D+N+j-1}$ and all blocks in Y_j. Therefore, by a recursive analysis, the condition $j \geq m - 1$ is necessary and sufficient to ensure that block x_{D+N+j} ultimately needs all blocks in $\bigcup_{j=0}^{m-1} Y_j$.

We denote the initial secret pool by S_0 and denote the N blocks of S_0 by $x_0, x_1, \ldots, x_{N-1}$. Let the secret pool obtained in the ith pool update be S_i. In the ith pool update for $i \geq 1$, pool S_{i-1} is updated to S_i. We let A_i be the set of blocks computed by the update. Then for $i \geq 1$, set A_i consists of all λ blocks with indices at least $(i - 1)\lambda + N$ and at most $i\lambda + N - 1$; i.e., $A_i = \{x_{(i-1)\lambda+N}|_{j=0,1,...,\lambda-1}.\}$. We also define A_0 as the set of N blocks $x_0, x_1, \ldots, x_{N-1}$; i.e., $A_0 = \{x_j|_{j=0,1,...,N-1}.\}$. Note that blocks in A_i can only be leaked after time iT_s for $i \geq 0$.

A.2   Preventing the Leakage of N Contiguous Blocks

Another necessary condition for attack success is for the external adversary M_{out} to obtain an arbitrary group of N *contiguous* blocks among the blocks leaked by malware M_{in}. (Note that we do not consider brute-force attacks whereby the adversary attempts to discover a few pool bits that are not available in the leaked blocks). We call a leaked block x "useful" in satisfying the contiguity condition, if x is used in at least one intermediate computation to obtain one of the final N desired blocks or if x itself is one of the final N desired blocks. Without loss of generality, we only consider attacks in which all the leaked blocks are useful. The *index stretch* of an attack is defined as the result of the highest index of useful leaked blocks minus the lowest index of useful leaked blocks.

For the external adversary M_{out} to obtain the final N consecutive blocks, the internal adversary M_{in} has to leak at least N blocks. For any successful attack with a certain number of useful leaked blocks, we derive the maximal index

---

[3] For simplicity, we sometimes drop the subscript of f_2 and just use f to denote f_2.

stretch of the attack to see how M_{in} might be able to spread the leaked blocks in multiple epochs so that only a small number of blocks needs to be leaked in each epoch. To this end, we establish Theorem 1. Preventing the maximal index stretch will deny M_{in} the opportunity to leak useful blocks.

Theorem 1. *The maximal index stretch of a successful attack with a fixed number M of useful leaked blocks is $(M - N)m + qm^2 - 2m + 1$, where $M \geq N$.*

We use the following Lemmas 1-4 in the proof of Theorem 1. The proofs of Theorem 1, and Lemmas 1-4 are given in Section A.5 of the appendix.

Lemma 1. *The maximal index stretch of a successful attack with N useful leaked blocks is $qm^2 - 2m + 1$.*

Lemma 2. *For the external adversary M_{out} to obtain J blocks out of N consecutive blocks $x_{G+i}|_{i=0,1,\ldots,N-1}$, where $G \geq 0$ and $1 \leq J \leq N$, the internal adversary M_{in} has to leak at least J blocks with indices at most $G + N - 1$.*

Lemma 3. *Consider the following attack with M leaked blocks, where $M \geq N$. With $y := (M - N) \bmod q$ and $a := M - N - qm$, the internal adversary M_{in} leaks the following M blocks:*

$$x_{A-ym-iqm+jm}\big|_{\substack{i=0,1,\ldots,a; \\ j=0,1,\ldots,q-1}}, \; x_{A+im}\big|_{i=q-y+1,\ldots,q-1},$$

$$x_{A-ym-iqm+qm-1}\big|_{i=0,1,\ldots,a}, \; x_{A+iqm-i+jm}\big|_{\substack{i=1,\ldots,m-1; \\ j=0,1,\ldots,q-1}}.$$

Then the external adversary M_{out} can obtain any block with index at least $qm^2 - qm - 2m + 2$; and the index stretch of this attack is $(M - N)m + qm^2 - 2m + 1$.

Lemma 4. *If adversary M_{out} obtains blocks $x_{A+iqm-i-(\sum_{\ell=1}^{i} \beta_\ell)m+jm}\big|_{j=0,1,\ldots,q-1}$ and $x_{A+(i+1)qm-(i+1)-(\sum_{\ell=1}^{i} \beta_\ell)m}$ for $i = 0, 1, \ldots, r$, where $r \geq 1$, then adversary M_{out} can acquire blocks in*

$$\mathcal{B}_i :$$
$$= \{x_{A+iqm-i-(\sum_{\ell=1}^{i} \beta_\ell)m+zm}\big|_{z=0,1,\ldots,(r+1)q-iq-\sum_{\ell=i+1}^{r} \beta_\ell}\}, \tag{6}$$

for $i = 0, 1, \ldots, r$.

A.3   Non-circumventable Time-Space Tradeoff

The internal adversary (i.e., malware) M_{in} faces a space-time tradeoff in its attempt to leak N contiguous pool blocks to M_{out}, whenever the output bandwidth D_{ban} prohibits the transfer of all N block in a single epoch. This is the case because M_{in} would either have to save the blocks not leaked in an epoch in freely usable system memory, denoted by L_{mem} below, for leakage in future epochs or perform the pool update computation using fewer than N blocks, or both. Hence, either (1) the memory size of L_{mem} is large enough to hold most, if not all, the blocks not leaked in an epoch or (2) M_{in} would have to use extra update computation time, if not enough memory space is available in L_{mem}. In the latter case, some of the N pool blocks would have to remain unused during the update, and thus extra computation time would be needed. However, if both L_{mem} and the pool update time T_{up} are upper-bounded by appropriately small values, M_{in} will either not have enough memory space to leak all blocks or will exceed the update time and be detected by the verifier. We call this the *space-time tradeoff* faced by M_{in}. If M_{in} cannot circumvent this tradeoff, it could not leak all the contiguous N blocks of any complete secret pool S.

Upper Bound on Memory Freely Usable by Malware. We derive the upper bound on L_{mem}, the amount of memory freely usable by malware M_{in}, so that it cannot circumvent the time-space tradeoff.

From Theorem 1, for any successful attack with $(N + y)$ leaked blocks, where $y \geq 0$, its index stretch is no greater than $(qm^2 - 2m + 1 + ym)$. Recall that $A_i = \{x_{(i-1)\lambda+N+j}|_{j=0,1,\ldots,\lambda-1}\}$ and $|A_i| = \lambda$ for $i \geq 1$, $A_0 = \{x_j|_{j=0,1,\ldots,N-1}\}$ and $|A_0| = N$. Therefore, the $(N + y)$ blocks leaked by M_{in} fall in at most $\left(\left\lfloor \frac{qm^2-2m+ym}{\lambda} \right\rfloor\right) + 2$ (denoted by L hereafter) number of successive sets among $A_i|_{i=0,1,\ldots}$. Assume the $(N+y)$ leaked blocks fall in h successive sets $A_H, A_{H+1}, \ldots, A_{H+h-1}$, where $1 \leq h \leq L$. Let F_i be the set of bits which are leaked by M_{in} and are among the bits in blocks of A_i, for $i = H, H + 1, \ldots, H + h - 1$. Recall that blocks in A_i can only be leaked after time iT_s for $i \geq 0$. We actually give adversary M_{in} more power by assuming that M_{in} can leak blocks in A_i at any time instance immediately after time iT_s, since the computations of blocks in A_i start from time iT_s and finish before $iT_s + T_{up}$.

After time HT_s, adversary M_{in} can leak bits in F_H. At time $(H + 1)T_s$, the number of bits in F_H that M_{in} has not leaked is at least $\max\{|F_H|-T_sD_{ban},0\} \geq |F_H| - T_sD_{ban}$. After time $(H + 1)T_s$, adversary M_{in} can leak bits in F_{H+1} or leak those bits in F_H that has not been leaked. At time $(H + 2)T_s$, the bits in $F_H \cup F_{H+1}$ that M_{in} has not leaked is at least $\max\{\max\{|F_H| - T_sD_{ban},0\} + |F_{H+1}| - T_sD_{ban},0\} \geq |F_H| + |F_{H+1}| - 2T_sD_{ban}$.

This process continues iteratively. Then, at time $(H + h)T_s$, the bits in $\bigcup F_{H+j}|_{j=0,1,\ldots,h-1}$ that M_{in} has not leaked is at least $\sum_{j=0,1,\ldots,h-1} |F_{H+j}| - hT_sD_{ban}$. From time $(H+h)T_s$ to $(H+h)T_s+T_{up}$, the pool S_{H+h-1} is updated to S_{H+h}; and the set of computed blocks is A_{H+h}. At time $(H+h)T_s+T_{up}$, the bits in $\bigcup F_{H+j}|_{j=0,1,\ldots,h-1}$ that M_{in} has not leaked is at least $\sum_{j=0,1,\ldots,h-1} |F_{H+j}| - (hT_s + T_{up})D_{ban}$. If all blocks of S_{H+h} are in the memory, L_{mem} is the available space to store the bits in $\bigcup F_{H+j}|_{j=0,1,\ldots,h-1}$ that has not been leaked. Therefore, to ensure that malware M_{in} cannot circumvent the space-time tradeoff and leak all bits in $\bigcup F_{H+j}|_{j=0,1,\ldots,h-1}$, we impose the condition

$$\sum_{j=0}^{h-1} |F_{H+j}| - (hT_s + T_{up})D_{ban} > L_{mem}. \tag{7}$$

Given $\sum_{j=0}^{h-1} |F_{H+j}| = (N+y)b$ and $1 \leq h \leq L$, where $L = \left(\left\lfloor \frac{qm^2 - 2m + ym}{\lambda} \right\rfloor \right) + 2$, then we obtain

L.H.S. of (7)

$$\geq (N+y)b - \left[\left(\frac{qm^2 - 2m + ym}{\lambda} + 2 \right) T_s + T_{up} \right] D_{ban}. \tag{8}$$

R.H.S. of (8) increases as y increases if

$$b\lambda \geq mT_s D_{ban}. \tag{9}$$

Therefore, we enforce (9) and

$$N \cdot b - \left[\left(\frac{qm^2 - 2m}{\lambda} + 2 \right) T_s + T_{up} \right] D_{ban} > L_{mem}, \tag{10}$$

so that (7) follows for any $y \geq 0$ and $h = 1, 2, \ldots, L$.

Computation Cost of Pool Update. Using the terminology of DABLS [10], we call the case when all $|S|$ bits of memory are used for the computation of $f(n, S)$, the *benign case*, and the case when fewer than $|S|$ bits of memory are used for computation, the *malicious case*. The following theorem gives the computation cost of $f(n, S)$ in both the benign and malicious cases.

Theorem 2. *For a pool update $f(n, S)$ in the benign case, the computation cost is $\lambda(q+1)C_{P_n}$. For a pool update $f(n, S)$ in the malicious case, if $\lambda \geq N + m - 1$ and c blocks of memoization cache [10] are used, where $c < N$, then the computation cost is at least $[2^{\lceil \frac{\lambda - 1 - c}{m} \rceil - 2} m(m+1)(q+1) + c(q+1)]C_{P_n}$.*

The proof of Theorem 2 is given in Section A.5 of this appendix.

Remark 1. *If q is a constant and does not scale with N, then the computation cost in the benign case is linear with λ.*

When $|S| - 1$ bits are used, this leaves $c = N - 1$ blocks to cache intermediate blocks. Given $c = N - 1$ and Theorem 2, we enforce the relation:

$$\lambda(q+1)C_{P_n} < T_{up} < [2^{\lceil \frac{\lambda - N}{m} \rceil - 2} m(m+1)(q+1) + (N-1)(q+1)]C_{P_n}. \tag{11}$$

A.4   Summary of ReDABLS Parameter Conditions for $f_2(n, S)$

From the above analysis, the required parameter conditions are (5), (9), (10), and (11), whenever $N = m \cdot q$ and $m \geq 2$.

A.5   Proof of Theorems 1, 2 and Lemmas 1-4

Proof of Theorem 1. Among the successful attacks with a fixed number M of useful leaked blocks, where $M \geq N$, let $\mathcal{A}_M$ be an attack which maximizes the index stretch and I_M be the index stretch of $\mathcal{A}_M$. As explained in Section A.2, all leaked blocks in $\mathcal{A}_M$ are "useful." We regard $M \geq N + 1$ below.

Let $x_{B+j}|_{j=0,1,\ldots,N-1}$ be the N consecutive blocks that the external adversary M_{out} finally obtains. Note that M_{out} can further use $x_{B+j}|_{j=0,1,\ldots,N-1}$ to get any block with an index of at least B. Denote the useful block with the lowest index in attack $\mathcal{A}_M$ by x_A. To make x_A useful, the external adversary M_{out} should obtain $x_{A+jm}|_{j=0,1,\ldots,q-1}, x_{A+qm-1}$ to compute x_{A+qm}. Since x_A is the useful block with the lowest index, all of $x_{A+jm}|_{j=0,1,\ldots,q-1}, x_{A+qm-1}$ can only be leaked instead of being computed, given the fact that if at least one of $x_{A+jm}|_{j=1,2,\ldots,q-1}, x_{A+qm-1}$ is computed, then at least one block with an index lower than A should be leaked. Clearly, x_A is not used in computation(s) other than that of x_{A+qm}.

We note that the highest index among the leaked blocks is $B+N-1$ since any block with index greater than $B+N-1$ is useless in inducing $x_{B+j}|_{j=0,1,\ldots,N-1}$. Then the index stretch I_M is at most $B + N - 1 - A$. Lemma 3 presents a successful attack with a fixed number M of useful leaked blocks and with an index stretch of $qm^2 - 2m + 1 + (M - N)m$. Hence, it follows that

$$B + N - 1 - A \geq I_M \geq qm^2 - 2m + 1 + (M - N)m. \tag{12}$$

Given $M \geq N + 1$, $N = qm$ and (12), it holds that for $i = 1, 2, \ldots, m - 1$,

$$B > A + iqm - i. \tag{13}$$

Consequently, block $x_{A+iqm-i}$ is not one of the final desired blocks $x_{B+j}|_{j=0,1,\ldots,N-1}$ for each $i = 1, 2, \ldots, m - 1$.

We have the following observation. If x_{A+qm-1} is used in computations in addition to that of x_{A+qm}, then there exists $\beta_1 \in \{0, 1, \ldots, q - 1\}$ such that adversary M_{out} obtains $x_{A+qm-1-\beta_1 m+jm}|_{j=0,1,\ldots,q-1}$ and $x_{A+2qm-2-\beta_1 m}$, which are together used to compute $x_{A+2qm-1-\beta_1 m}$. If $x_{A+2qm-2-\beta_1 m}$ is used in computations in addition to that of $x_{A+2qm-1-\beta_1 m}$, then there exists $\beta_2 \in \{0, 1, \ldots, q-1\}$ such that adversary M_{out} obtains $x_{A+2qm-2-(\beta_1+\beta_2)m+jm}|_{j=0,1,\ldots,q-1}$ and $x_{A+3qm-3-(\beta_1+\beta_2)m}$, which are together used to compute $x_{A+3qm-2-(\beta_1+\beta_2)m}$.

This process continues iteratively. Then we have the following two cases. 1) There exist $\beta_\ell \in \{0, 1, \ldots, q - 1\}$ for $\ell = 1, 2, \ldots, m - 1$ such that $x_{A+iqm-i-(\sum_{\ell=1}^{i-1} \beta_\ell)m}$ is used in computations in addition to that of $x_{A+iqm-(i-1)}$ for $i = 1, 2, \ldots, m-1$. 2) There exist $\gamma \in \{1, 2, \ldots, m-1\}$ and $\beta_\ell \in \{0, 1, \ldots, q-1\}$ for $\ell = 1, 2, \ldots, \gamma - 1$ such that $x_{A+iqm-i-(\sum_{\ell=1}^{i-1} \beta_\ell)m}$ is used in computations in addition to that of $x_{A+iqm-(i-1)-(\sum_{\ell=1}^{i-1} \beta_\ell)m}$ for $i = 1, 2, \ldots, \gamma - 1$; and $x_{A+\gamma qm-\gamma-(\sum_{\ell=1}^{\gamma-1} \beta_\ell)m}$ is not used in any computation other than that of $x_{A+\gamma qm-(\gamma-1)-(\sum_{\ell=1}^{\gamma-1} \beta_\ell)m}$.

We first consider case 1). Defining $\sum_{\ell=1}^{i} \beta_\ell = 0$ for $i = 0$, then by an iterative analysis, we know that for $i = 0, 1, \ldots, m-1$, adversary M_{out} has $x_{A+iqm-i-(\sum_{\ell=1}^{i} \beta_\ell)m+jm}|_{j=0,1,\ldots,q-1}$ and $x_{A+(i+1)qm-(i+1)-(\sum_{\ell=1}^{i} \beta_\ell)m}$, and use them to compute $x_{A+(i+1)qm-i-(\sum_{\ell=1}^{i} \beta_\ell)m}$. From Lemma 4, adversary M_{out} further acquires all blocks in $\cup_{i=0}^{m-1} \mathcal{B}_i$, where $\mathcal{B}_i$ is defined by (6). Define

$$T := A + (m-1)qm - (m-1) - \left(\sum_{\ell=1}^{m-1} \beta_\ell\right) m \qquad (14)$$

Then given $\beta_\ell \in \{0, 1, \ldots, q-1\}$ for $\ell = 1, 2, \ldots, m-1$, the lowest index among the blocks in $\mathcal{B}_i$ is $A+iqm-i-\left(\sum_{\ell=1}^{i} \beta_\ell\right)m$, which is at least $T+(m-i-1)$; and the highest index among the blocks in $\mathcal{B}_i$ is $A+mqm-i-\left(\sum_{\ell=1}^{m-1} \beta_\ell\right)m$, which equals $T + qm + (m-i-1)$. Therefore, for $i = 0, 1, \ldots, m-1$, adversary M_{out} obtains at least all the blocks whose indices modulo m give $(T-i-1) \bmod m$ and whose indices are at least $T+(m-i-1)$ and at most $T+qm+(m-i-1)$. In other words, adversary M_{out} obtains at least all the blocks whose indices are at least T and at most $T + qm + m - 1$. Clearly, M_{out} acquires blocks $x_{T+j}|_{j=0,1,\ldots,qm-1}$ without leaking x_i for any $i > T + qm - 1$. Given obtained $x_{T+j}|_{j=0,1,\ldots,qm-1}$, M_{out} can further compute x_i for any $i > T + qm - 1$. Then M_{out} obtains any block with index at least T. From (13), $B > T$ follows. Hence, M_{out} gets the final desired N blocks $x_{B+j}|_{j=0,1,\ldots,N-1}$ without leaking x_i for any $i > T + qm - 1$. Then it further follows that I_M (i.e., the index stretch of attack $\mathcal{A}_M$) is at most $T + qm - 1 - A$, which is at most $qm^2 - m$ given the definition of T in (14) and $\beta_\ell \geq 0$ for $\ell = 1, 2, \ldots, m-1$. This contradicts with (12) which shows that I_M is at least $qm^2 - 2m + 1 + (M-N)m$ and thus at least $qm^2 - m + 1$, given $M \geq N+1$. Hence, case 1) does not hold.

Then we consider case 2). Noting $\sum_{\ell=1}^{i} \beta_\ell = 0$ for $i = 0$, we know that for $i = 0, 1, \ldots, \gamma-1$, adversary M_{out} has $x_{A+iqm-i-(\sum_{\ell=1}^{i} \beta_\ell)m+jm}|_{j=0,1,\ldots,q-1}$ and $x_{A+(i+1)qm-(i+1)-(\sum_{\ell=1}^{i} \beta_\ell)m}$, and use them to compute $x_{A+(i+1)qm-i-(\sum_{\ell=1}^{i} \beta_\ell)m}$. Note that given $\beta_i \in \{0, 1, \ldots, q-1\}$, block $x_{A+(i+1)qm-(i+1)-(\sum_{\ell=1}^{i} \beta_\ell)m}$ belongs to $x_{A+(i+1)qm-(i+1)-(\sum_{\ell=1}^{i+1} \beta_\ell)m+jm}|_{j=0,1,\ldots,q-1}$. We define T as the N consecutive blocks with indices starting from $A + (\gamma-1)qm + 1 - (\sum_{\ell=1}^{\gamma-1} \beta_\ell)m$ and ending with $A + \gamma qm - (\sum_{\ell=1}^{\gamma-1} \beta_\ell)m$. Let T_1 be the set of blocks which belong to T and whose indices modulo m give $(A - i) \bmod m$ for $i = 0, 1, \ldots, \gamma-1$. Then $|T_1| = \gamma q$. From Lemma 4, adversary M_{out} obtains at least all blocks in T_1. Other than $x_{A+\gamma qm-\gamma-(\sum_{\ell=1}^{\gamma-1} \beta_\ell)m}$ and the blocks in T_1, among the blocks in T, let T_2 be the set of remaining blocks that adversary M_{out} obtains. Then among the blocks in T, adversary M_{out} obtains $T_* := T_1 \cup T_2 \cup \{x_{A+\gamma qm-\gamma-(\sum_{\ell=1}^{\gamma-1} \beta_\ell)m}\}$. From Lemma 2, to acquire T_*, adversary M_{in} has to leak at least T_* blocks with indices at most $A + \gamma qm - (\sum_{\ell=1}^{\gamma-1} \beta_\ell)m$.

We refer attack A_M as A_M^* when M_{in} leaks exactly the following $T_* = (\gamma q + |T_2| + 1)$ blocks among the blocks with indices at most $A + \gamma qm - (\sum_{\ell=1}^{\gamma-1} \beta_\ell)m$:

$$x_{A+iqm-i-(\sum_{\ell=1}^{i}\beta_\ell)m+jm}\Big|_{\substack{i=0,1,\ldots,\gamma-1;\\j=0,1,\ldots,q-1.}} \tag{15}$$

$$x_{A+\gamma qm-\gamma-(\sum_{\ell=1}^{\gamma-1}\beta_\ell)m}, \text{ and all blocks in } T_2. \tag{16}$$

Then the number of leaked blocks with indices at most $A+\gamma qm-(\sum_{\ell=1}^{\gamma-1}\beta_\ell)m$ in any instance of A_M is at least that in any instance of A_M^*. Therefore, considering that (a) the number of leaked blocks with indices greater than $A + \gamma qm - (\sum_{\ell=1}^{\gamma-1}\beta_\ell)m$ in any instance of A_M is at most that in any instance of A_M^* as the total number of leaked blocks is M for both A_M and A_M^*; and (b) for both the instance of A_M and the the instance of A_M^*, T_* is the set of all obtained blocks in the N consecutive blocks T, we know an instance of A_M^* which maximizes the index stretch is also an instance of A_M which maximizes the index stretch. Hence, we can just let A_M be A_M^* in the analysis. Accordingly, we can assume the $(|T_1| + |T_2| + 1)$ blocks given by (15) (16) are leaked in attack A_M.

Given attack A_M, we construct attack A_{M-1} as follows. The $(\gamma+1)$ blocks $x_{A+iqm-i-(\sum_{\ell=1}^{i}\beta_\ell)m}\big|_{i=0,1,\ldots,\gamma}$ leaked in A_M are not leaked in A_{M-1}. The γ blocks $x_{A+iqm-(i-1)-(\sum_{\ell=1}^{i-1}\beta_\ell)m}\big|_{i=1,2,\ldots,\gamma}$ not leaked in A_M are leaked in A_{M-1}. Other than the $(2\gamma+1)$ blocks mentioned above, the remaining blocks leaked in A_M are still leaked in A_{M-1}. Then the blocks which are leaked in A_{M-1} and have indices at most $A + \gamma qm - (\sum_{\ell=1}^{\gamma-1}\beta_\ell)m$ constitute the set

$$\left\{x_{A+iqm-i-(\sum_{\ell=1}^{i}\beta_\ell)m+jm}\Big|_{\substack{i=0,1,\ldots,\gamma-1;\\j=1,\ldots,q-1.}}\right\}$$

$$\cup \left\{x_{A+iqm-(i-1)-(\sum_{\ell=1}^{i-1}\beta_\ell)m}\Big|_{i=1,2,\ldots,\gamma.}\right\} \cup T_2$$

$$= \left\{x_{A+iqm-i-(\sum_{\ell=1}^{i}\beta_\ell)m+jm+m}\Big|_{\substack{i=0,1,\ldots,\gamma-1;\\j=0,1,\ldots,q-1.}}\right\} \cup T_2. \tag{17}$$

Therefore, each block given by (15) and leaked in A_M is now replaced with a block with index adding m in A_{M-1}. Similar to the proof of Lemma 4, we can show by mathematical reduction that in A_{M-1}, with leaked blocks

$$x_{A+iqm-i-(\sum_{\ell=1}^{i}\beta_\ell)m+jm+m}\Big|_{\substack{i=0,1,\ldots,\gamma-1;\\j=0,1,\ldots,q-1.}}, \tag{18}$$

adversary M_{out} can obtain all the blocks whose indices modulo m give $(A - i) \bmod m$ and whose indices are at least $A + iqm - i - (\sum_{\ell=1}^{i}\beta_\ell)m + m$ and at most $A + \gamma qm - i - (\sum_{\ell=1}^{\gamma-1}\beta_\ell)m$. Then (a) in attack A_{M-1}, among the blocks in T, adversary M_{out} obtains $T_1 \cup T_2$. It's straightforward to see that any block given by (18) is useful in inducing $T_1 \cup T_2$. Then since all the M blocks in attack A_M are useful, all the $(M - 1)$ blocks in attack A_M are also useful. (b) Recall that in attack A_M, among the blocks in T, adversary M_{out} obtains $T_1 \cup T_2 \cup \{x_{A+\gamma qm-\gamma-(\sum_{\ell=1}^{\gamma-1}\beta_\ell)m}\}$, but $x_{A+\gamma qm-\gamma-(\sum_{\ell=1}^{\gamma-1}\beta_\ell)m}$ is not used in any computation other than that of $x_{A+\gamma qm-(\gamma-1)-(\sum_{\ell=1}^{\gamma-1}\beta_\ell)m}$, which is also a block in T and is leaked in A_{M-1}. Note that (c) in attacks A_M and A_{M-1}, the leaked blocks with indices greater than $A + \gamma qm - (\sum_{\ell=1}^{\gamma-1} \beta_\ell)m$ (i.e., the highest block index of T) are the same. Therefore, from (a) and (b) and (c), among the blocks with indices greater than $A + \gamma qm - \gamma - (\sum_{\ell=1}^{\gamma-1} \beta_\ell)m$, the blocks that M_{out} can obtain in attacks $\mathcal{A}_M$ and $\mathcal{A}_{M-1}$ are the same. From (13), the lowest block index (i.e., B) among the final desired blocks $x_{B+j}|_{j=0,1,...,N-1}$ is greater than $A + \gamma qm - \gamma - (\sum_{\ell=1}^{\gamma-1} \beta_\ell)m$. Then since adversary M_{out} obtains $x_{B+j}|_{j=0,1,...,N-1}$ in attack $\mathcal{A}_M$, M_{out} also obtains $x_{B+j}|_{j=0,1,...,N-1}$ in attack $\mathcal{A}_{M-1}$. Because x_A is the leaked block with the lowest index in $\mathcal{A}_M$; block x_{A+m} is leaked in $\mathcal{A}_{M-1}$; and the highest block index in $\mathcal{A}_{M-1}$ is no less than that in $\mathcal{A}_M$, then the index stretch of attack $\mathcal{A}_M$ minus m. Recall that $(M-1)$ blocks are leaked in attack $\mathcal{A}_{M-1}$; and I_{M-1} is the maximal index stretch of a successful attack with $(M-1)$ useful leaked blocks. Therefore, for $M \geq N+1$, it follows that $I_{M-1} \geq I_M - m$, which together with Lemma 1 and (12), leads to $I_M = qm^2 - 2m + 1 + (M-N)m$. □

Proof of Lemma 1. Here we also let $x_{B+j}|_{j=0,1,...,N-1}$ be the final N consecutive blocks that the external adversary M_{out} wants to obtain. Given $N = mq$, we divide $\{x_{B+j}|_{j=0,1,...,N-1}\}$ into m sets $R_i|_{i=0,1,...,m-1}$, where $R_i := \{x_{B+jm+i}|_{j=0,1,...,q-1}\}$ for $i = 0,1,...,m-1$. We will prove that for adversary M_{out} to acquire $x_{B+j}|_{j=0,1,...,N-1}$, the internal adversary M_{in} has to leak at least N blocks in the union of m sets $G_i|_{i=0,1,...,m-1}$, with $G_i := \{x_{\alpha_i m+jm+i}|_{j=0,1,...,q-1}\}$, where α_i is a positive integer, for $i = 0,1,...,m-1$. Given $i = 0,1,2,...,m-1$, if all blocks of R_i are leaked, we just set G_i as R_i. Then we consider that at least one block (denoted by x_I hereafter) of R_i is not leaked given $i = 0,1,2,...,m-1$, where $I \mod m = i$. Computing block x_I needs blocks $x_{I-jm}|_{j=q,q-1,...,1}, x_{j-1}$. If the q blocks $x_{I-jm}|_{j=q,q-1,...,1}$ are all leaked, $x_{I-jm}|_{j=q,q-1,...,1}$, then we set G_i as $x_{I-jm}|_{j=q,q-1,...,1}$. If there exists a j_* such that x_{I-j_*m} is not leaked, the analysis continues iteratively as computing block x_{I-j_*m} needs blocks $x_{I-j_*m-jm}|_{j=q,q-1,...,1}, x_{j-1}$. Therefore, at the end M_{in} should always leak G_i to let M_{out} get G_i.

To maximize the index stretch, we consider the m sets $G_i|_{i=0,1,...,m-1}$ do not "cross" with each other. In other words, there exist distinct $i_0, i_1, ..., i_{m-1}$ which are from $\{0,1,...,m-1\}$ such that the highest block index of $G_{i_{j-1}}$ is less than the lowest block index of G_{i_j}, where $j = 1,2,...,m-1$. Then it's straightforward to see

$$(\alpha_{i_j}m + i_j) - [\alpha_{i_{j-1}}m + (q-1)m + i_{j-1}]$$
$$= m-1, \forall j = 1,2,...,m-1, \tag{19}$$

so that adversary M_{out} can use $\{x_{\alpha_{i_{j-1}}m+\ell m+i}|_{\ell=0,1,...,q-1}\}$ and $x_{\alpha_{i_j}m+i_j}$ to compute $x_{\alpha_{i_j}m+i_j+1}$. Given (19), with $A := \alpha_{i_0}m + i_0$, adversary M_{out} leaks the following N blocks: $x_{A+iqm-i+jm}|_{\substack{i=0,1,...,m-1; \\ j=1,2,...,q-1}}$. With $x_{A+iqm-i+jm}|_{\substack{i=0,1,...,m-1;; \\ j=0,1,...,q-1}}$, adversary M_{out} can further acquire any block with index at least $qm^2 - qm - 2m + 2$. In addition, any leaked block is useful in obtaining N consecutive blocks with indices at least $qm^2 - qm - 2m + 2$. The index stretch of this attack is

$$(m-1)qm - (m-1) + (q-1)m = qm^2 - 2m + 1.$$

$\square$

Proof of Lemma 2. The J blocks that adversary M_{out} wants to obtain can be divided into m sets $L_i|_{i=0,1,\dots,m-1}$, where L_i consists of blocks which are part of the J blocks and whose indices modulo m all give i, for $i = 0, 1, \dots, m-1$. Note that $|L_i| \leq q$. We show that for M_{out} to obtain L_i, M_{in} has to leak at least $|L_i|$ blocks whose indices modulo m all give i. This is true when all blocks of L_i are leaked, and is also true in the case where at least one block (say block x) of L_i is computed instead of being leaked because in that case, at least q blocks whose indices modulo m all give i should be leaked to compute block x. Hence, to obtain J blocks out of $x_{G+i}|_{i=0,1,\dots,N-1}$, adversary M_{in} has to leak at least J blocks with indices at most $G + N - 1$. $\square$

Proof of Lemma 3. First, given $x_{A-ym-iqm+jm}|_{\substack{i=0,2,\dots,a; \\ j=0,1,\dots,q-1}}$, $x_{A-ym-iqm+qm-1}$ $|_{i=0,2,\dots,a}$ and $x_{A+im}|_{i=q-y+1,\dots,q-1}$, adversary M_{out} can obtain $x_{A+jm}|_{j=0,1,\dots q-1}$. Then as explained in the proof of Lemma 1, with $x_{A+iqm-i+jm}|_{\substack{i=0,1,\dots,m-1; \\ j=0,1,\dots,q-1}}$, adversary M_{out} can further acquire any block with index at least $qm^2 - qm - 2m + 2$. In addition, any leaked block is useful in obtaining N consecutive blocks with indices at least $qm^2 - qm - 2m + 2$. It's straightforward to derive that the index stretch of this attack is $(M - N)m + qm^2 - 2m + 1$. $\square$

Proof of Lemma 4. We prove that adversary M_{out} can get $\mathcal{B}_i$ for $i = 1, 2, \dots, r$ by mathematical reduction with the following two steps ① and ②. ② Given $i = 1, \dots, r$, if M_{out} obtains the blocks in $\mathcal{B}_i$, then M_{out} can further get the blocks in $\mathcal{B}_{i-1}$.

① We show how adversary M_{out} acquires the blocks in $\mathcal{B}_r$. Given $x_{A+rqm-r-(\sum_{\ell=1}^{r}\beta_\ell)m+jm}|_{j=0,1,\dots,q-1}$ and $x_{A+(r+1)qm-(r+1)-(\sum_{\ell=1}^{r}\beta_\ell)m}$, adversary M_{out} can calculate $x_{A+(r+1)qm-r-(\sum_{\ell=1}^{r}\beta_\ell)m}$. Therefore, adversary M_{out} have all the blocks in $\mathcal{B}_r$.

Second, to prove ②, we demonstrate that given $i = 1, \dots, r$, if M_{out} gets all the blocks in $\mathcal{B}_i$, then M_{out} can also acquire all the blocks in $\mathcal{B}_{i-1}$. We first prove that adversary M_{out} gets $x_{A+iqm-(i-1)-(\sum_{\ell=1}^{i-1}\beta_\ell)m+zm}|_{z=0,1,\dots,(r+1)q-iq-\sum_{\ell=i}^{r}\beta_\ell}$. also by mathematical reduction with the following two steps ❶ and ❷. ❶ For $z = 0$, adversary M_{out} uses $x_{A+iqm-i-(\sum_{\ell=1}^{i-1}\beta_\ell)m}$ in $\mathcal{B}_i$ and $x_{A+(i-1)qm-(i-1)-(\sum_{\ell=1}^{i-1}\beta_\ell)m+jm}|_{j=0,1,\dots,q-1}$ to calculate $x_{A+iqm-(i-1)-(\sum_{\ell=1}^{i-1}\beta_\ell)m}$. ❷ Let adversary M_{out} obtain $x_{A+iqm-(i-1)-(\sum_{\ell=1}^{i-1}\beta_\ell)m+zm}|_{z=0,1,\dots,z_*}$, where $z_* \in \{0, 1, \dots, (r+1)q - iq - \sum_{\ell=i}^{r}\beta_\ell - 1\}$. From the condition, M_{out} also gets

$$x_{A+(i-1)qm-(i-1)-(\sum_{\ell=1}^{i-1}\beta_\ell)m+jm}|_{j=0,1,\dots,q-1}$$
$$= x_{A+iqm-(i-1)-(\sum_{\ell=1}^{i-1}\beta_\ell)m+zm}|_{z=-q,-(q-1),\dots,-1}.$$

Hence, M_{out} has $x_{A+iqm-(i-1)-(\sum_{\ell=1}^{i-1}\beta_\ell)m+zm}|_{z=-q,...,z_*}$. It's straightforward to see block $x_{A+iqm-i-(\sum_{\ell=1}^{i-1}\beta_\ell)m+(z_*+1)m}$ belongs to $\mathcal{B}_i$. Then M_{out} utilizes $x_{A+iqm-i-(\sum_{\ell=1}^{i-1}\beta_\ell)m+(z_*+1)m}$ and

$$x_{A+iqm-(i-1)-(\sum_{\ell=1}^{i-1}\beta_\ell)m+zm}|_{z=-q+z_*+1,-q+z_*+2,...,z_*}$$
$$= x_{A+(i-1)qm-(i-1)-(\sum_{\ell=1}^{i-1}\beta_\ell)m+(z_*+1)m+jm}|_{j=0,1,...,q-1}$$

to compute $x_{A+iqm-(i-1)-(\sum_{\ell=1}^{i-1}\beta_\ell)m+(z_*+1)m}$. Owing to ❶ and ❷ above, M_{out} acquires

$$x_{A+iqm-(i-1)-(\sum_{\ell=1}^{i-1}\beta_\ell)m+zm}|_{z=0,1,...,(r+1)q-iq-\sum_{\ell=i}^{r}\beta_\ell},$$

which with $x_{A+(i-1)qm-(i-1)-(\sum_{\ell=1}^{i-1}\beta_\ell)m+jm}|_{j=0,1,...,q-1}$ also obtained by M_{out} compromise set $\mathcal{B}_{i-1}$.

The result follows given ① and ②.   □

Proof of Theorem 2. Let $\mathcal{C}_{ben}$ and $\mathcal{C}_{mal}$ be the computation time for a pool update in the benign case and in the malicious case, respectively.

It is straightforward to derive $\mathcal{C}_{ben} = \lambda(q+1)C_{P_n}$.

Then we compute $\mathcal{C}_{mal}$ in the malicious case.

For $i \geq 0$, we also use C_i to denote the time cost in the malicious case to compute the unmemoized block $g_{nS}(N+c+i)$. For $-N \leq i < 0$, we define C_i as 0 only for ease of notation. Note that for $-N \leq i < 0$, C_i is not the time cost in the malicious case to compute the unmemoized block $g_{nS}(N+c+i)$. We have for $i \geq 0$,

$$C_i = C_{i-1} + \sum_{j=1}^{j=q} C_{i-jm} + (q+1)C_{P_n}. \tag{20}$$

From (20), we obtain $C_i \geq 2C_{i-m}$ for $i \geq m$ and $C_i = (i+1)(q+1)C_{P_n}$ for $0 \leq i \leq m-1$. Then for $i \geq 0$, it follows that $C_i \geq 2^{\lfloor \frac{i}{m} \rfloor}[(i \bmod m)+1](q+1)$.

The total cost $\mathcal{C}_{mal}$ equals the cost to compute $g_{nS}(N+i)|_{0 \leq i \leq c-1}$, plus the cost to compute unmemoized blocks $g_{nS}(N+c+i)|_{\max\{\lambda-N-c,0\} \leq i \leq \lambda-1-c}$. Then

$$\mathcal{C}_{mal} = c(q+1)C_{P_n} + \sum_{i=\max\{\lambda-N-c,0\}}^{\lambda-1-c} C_i$$
$$\geq [2^{\lceil \frac{\lambda-1-c}{m} \rceil-2}m(m+1)(q+1) + c(q+1)]C_{P_n}.$$

□

ReDABLS: Revisiting Device Attestation
with Bounded Leakage of Secrets
(Transcript of Discussion)

Virgil Gligor

Carnegie Mellon University

Our work on device attestation with bounded leakage of secrets (DABLS) started in early 2010, when Adrian Perrig described an idea he had in an area that interests me quite a bit, namely how to obtain desirable security properties *without* relying on secrets. Briefly, he suggested that a Verifier might be able to authenticate a remote device, D, even if the device is contaminated with malicious software (malware) that could access *any* of D's secrets. If both device D and Verifier could be initialized with the same large pool of high entropy secrets, S, *and* if the device's output bandwidth, D_{ban}, could be appropriately limited, then after deployment the device malware could not leak the entire secret pool S to a network collaborator before the Verifier would cause the device software to update and overwrite pool S to a new verifiable state $S' = f(n, S)$. Here, n is a Verifier-sent public nonce that has to be used in the pool update and f is the update function. The Verifier would send a fresh nonce to D every T_s units of time, the device would use T_{up} units of time to compute the pool update $f(n, S)$ and respond to the Verifier's challenge. The response would be computed with a message authentication code (MAC) function using the new secret S', namely $MAC(S', constant)$. Adrian thought that we could find an update function f, which would preserve pool entropy, prevent the external malware collaborator from ever discovering an entire secret pool S, and successfully masquerading device D in response to a Verifier's nonce-based challenge. Clearly, neither the device malware nor its external collaborator could predict a nonce n and construct a *future* state of pool S, given that the external collaborator's power is bounded.

Soon after, we realized that an additional requirement would become necessary, namely that the external collaborator must also be prevented from recovering an entire *past* state of S by updating and splicing blocks of different past pools over time, and thus the problem became more challenging than anticipated. We both thought that one of my graduate students, Andy Tran, would be able to design a suitable update function f for an appropriate device memory size, pool size $|S|$, output bandwidth, and time units T_{up} and T_s, so that device authentication would be possible even if the entire content of the secret pool S were accessible by device malware (but not by the external malware collaborator). Furthermore, our colleague Jon McCune suggested that, once we solve the *device authentication* problem, we could extend the solution to obtain remote *device attestation*. After authentication, the Verifier could then send some additional high entropy E, where $|E| \ll |S|$, to device D, which would be used by

B. Christianson et al. (Eds.): Security Protocols 2013, LNCS 8263, pp. 115–122, 2013.
© Springer-Verlag Berlin Heidelberg 2013

D's ROM-implemented boot program to initialize all D's processor-accessible memory outside the pool S region (e.g., primary memory, graphics card memory) with a bit pattern that could not be predicted by the malware collaborator in the network. The ROM program would be inaccessible to the device malware. Then device D would return a response $MAC(E||S')$ to the Verifier, and receive the new code to be booted C, and $MAC(E||S', C)$, which would authenticate code C to the boot program.

DABLS has the following advantages over the better known *software root of trust* (SWORT) establishment[1] on device D because SWORT does *not* (1) provide device authentication, *nor* (2) does it typically guarantee uninterruptable composition of malware-free memory state establishment and trusted boot of application software, without additional mechanisms (i.e., malware could re-install itself into the device after the establishment of a malware-free memory state and trusted software boot), *nor* (3) does it allow *remote* verification of program execution on a device, since it is usually very susceptible to much smaller timing variations than those experienced over the Internet.

Designing DABLS proved to be harder than anticipated, despite a clever construction for update function f supplied by our colleague Jim Newsome; i.e., function f_1 defined in the accompanying paper. While the update function and system parameters chosen allowed Andy Tran to prove the security of DABLS, the system design was infeasible since $T_{up}/T_s \gg 1$. This would imply that device D would spend a lot more time updating pool S than performing useful work. Andy Tran's Master Thesis[2] presents the DABLS analysis in some detail, and suggests that this problem is similar in spirit with that of bounded leakage of secrets in cryptography – a problem area started about 2006[3].

In 2012, Jun Zhao, another of my graduate students, revisited the DABLS problem, and this presentation summarizes the progress we made to date. We call the new system ReDABLS. In particular, we analyze two new additional pool update functions, namely functions f_2 and f_3 of the accompanying paper,

[1] F. Armknecht, A.-R. Sadeghi, S. Schulz, and C. Wachsmann, "A Security Framework for Analysis and Design of Software Attestation." Cryptology ePrint Archive: Report 2013/083, February 18, 2013.

X. Kovah, C.Kallenberg, C. Weathers, A. Herzog, M. Albin, and J. Butterworth. "New results for timing-based attestation." In Proceedings of the IEEE Symposium on Security and Privacy, May 2012.

Y. Li, J. M. McCune, and A. Perrig. "SBAP: Software-based attestation for peripherals." In International Conference on Trust and Trustworthy Computing (TRUST), June 2010.

A. Seshadri, M. Luk, A. Perrig, L. van Doorn, and P. Khosla. "SCUBA: Secure code update by attestation in sensor networks." In Proceedings of ACM Workshop on Wireless Security (WiSe), Sept. 2006.

[2] Andrew Tran. "DABLS: Device attestation with bounded leakage of secrets." Masters Thesis, Carnegie Mellon University, July 2011.

[3] G. Di Crescenzo, R. Lipton, and S. Walfish "Perfectly Secure Password Protocols in the Bounded Retrieval Model," in Proc. of the Theory of Cryptography Conference, LNCS 3876, Springer 2006, pp. 225-244.

which help us prove secure remote authentication in the presence of device malware and an external malware collaborator. Unfortunately, these functions also lead to an infeasible system despite somewhat improved performance; i.e., their overhead rate $T_{up}/T_s > 1$. Their analyses help illustrate the challenges faced by the ReDABLS design. Finally, we illustrate two new *probabilistic* update functions (i.e., denoted by f_4 and f_5 defined in the accompanying paper) and argue that these types of functions can lead to feasible system designs (i.e., their overhead rate $T_{up}/T_s \ll 1$), although they allow a very small probability of network adversary success in forging remote device authentication by collaborating with the device malware.

Note, again, that the embodiment of our adversary comprises two collaborating entities, both of which could easily be operated by the fictitious Professor James Moriarty – the evil genius and Cambridge graduate of Arthur Connan Doyle fame. The first entity is M_{in}, the malware operating inside the computing device, and the second M_{out}, the external network collaborator to whom M_{in} tries to leak a complete pool S during some epoch T_s of device operation. If this were possible, M_{out} could obtain the current value of some secret pool, past or present, and using the collected nonce, could generate a correct response to a Verifier's current challenge. However, given the design of ReDABLS with functions f_4 and f_5 defined in the the paper, and the bounding of the amount of leakage by M_{in}, this would be unlikely, except with a very small probability.

Observe that M_{in}'s network collaborator, M_{out}, controls the network in the same way that the Dolev-Yao adversary would. Hence, Professor Moriarty is much more powerful than a Dolev-Yao adversary, since he also operates and controls M_{in}. In fact, Moriarty is one of the most powerful adversaries that we faced at the Security Protocols Workshop (SPW) during the past decade. Clearly, if Moriarty could not insert, operate, and control M_{in} in device D, his power would degrade to that of a classic Dolev-Yao adversary, and SPW participants could easily counter his attacks using known techniques. Similarly, if Moriarty were deprived of M_{out}'s services and had to rely only on M_{in}, we would also be able to design a scheme for device authentication; e.g., perhaps using simple and secure network front-ends. Other techniques used in cryptography, such as proactive security based on threshold cryptographic functions, could also be used, at least in theory.

In short, this is the setting of the ReDABLS problem.

Frank Stajano: I have a question on the scheme as shown in the previous slide. I understand that the basic idea of software attestation is that, if you can say that the device was found in a certain state, then there's nothing else running on the device, so long as you already know what the device is like from a hardware viewpoint?

Reply: Yes, in software attestation one verifies a carefully-crafted program's timed execution on a known device, which essentially means that there is no running malware code during that program's execution. For timed execution to work, one has to know all the device details, not only of the processor timing. One has to know the timing of the buses, for example. In short, one has to know the very precise timing of the device to enable the Verifier to attest to the program execution on a certain device type.

Frank Stajano: For example, if someone has twice as much RAM in the device, then that could make a timing difference.

Reply: Yes, in attesting to a program's execution on a device, the device has to have a fixed configuration a priori known to the Verifier. More importantly, one cannot let the device communicate with an *outside proxy* device, which could be faster and simulate a correct response to a Verifier's challenge.

Frank Stajano: So, in this new scheme the adversary also controls the network.

Reply: Yes.

Frank Stajano: So, it seems that the Verifier would have no way of knowing whether it is talking to a device of the given hardware configuration, or not. In that case, how can you guarantee that the relevant part of the device RAM was overwritten in full when you don't even know how much RAM there is?

Reply: Oh no, the device configuration is fixed and known to the Verifier. In fact, part of the design of this scheme is determining how to choose the device parameters, for a given update function, for example. The hardware is fixed, and the Verifier has to know its parameters. In all attestation cases, the Verifier knows (at least some of) the hardware configuration, whether software or hardware attestation.

Frank Stajano: So please tell me if the following is part of your attacker model. Assume I am Moriarty, I get one of your devices, I open it up by consulting with Sergei [Skorobogatov], and then I take a much bigger computer in which install all the stuff (e.g., secret pool) that I got out from your device. Then, using this bigger computer, I start responding to your Verifier's challenges.

Reply: This adversary attack cannot be handled by our scheme. In our model, after device D and the Verifier are initialized locally with the same pool of secrets and the Verifier has the device configuration, the device can be deployed. After deployment, Moriarty has no physical control over the device. The only thing he can do is to install malware M_{in}. Or, perhaps, he has already managed to install M_{in} in the shrink-wrapped operating system code, which was loaded into the device prior to deployment. So Moriarty is able to either control the distribution of the device software or penetrate the system after deployment during normal device operation by exploiting software vulnerabilities, or both.

Frank Stajano: So Moriarty can only do a software attack on these devices. There's no hardware attack in your model.

Reply: Correct.

Frank Stajano: Or maybe some tamper resistance prevents hardware attacks.

Reply: No, we are simply not assuming any hardware tampering. The key idea is that this scheme would feasible for commodity hardware devices whose deployment and operation is beyond Moriarty's physical reach. Sorry for not having mentioned this earlier.

Mohammed Almeshekah: Sorry, just going back to the previous slide, did you say that you reset the RAM every time you reload software? So, if I understood you correctly, you minimize the bandwidth for output, and then every time you reset, you erase the pool of secrets that you have, right?

Reply: The RAM reset is done online, unless there is an authentication failure. We don't take the device off line to clean its memory of malware. However, if the Verifier detects that the device response was incorrect, or didn't arrive on time, then the Verifier would know that there is an authentication failure. In that case, the device operation would have to be restarted. One would have to reset the device offline, install a fresh pool (which erases the old one), and start the authentication protocol over again. However, so long as all the responses are correct and arrive on time, one would clean up the device memory only occasionally. The Verifier would send a command that says: "please clean up, here is some fresh high-entropy information E, erase whatever you have in memory outside pool S, use the additional entropy to fill out all this memory area with pseudorandom bits, and send the response back to me." That's basically the second part of the process, which follows device authentication protocol. And the third part would be to load the device with Verifier-provided software, after the device-accessible free RAM is overwritten with the pseudorandom sequence.

Returning to our authentication protocol, it is quite important that updating the large pool of secrets S be done efficiently, and not only efficiently, but be done in a feasible way. This means that the time to update the pool of secrets and send a response, namely time T_{up}, has to represent a small fraction of the device operation time; i.e., T_s the time until a new challenge arrives. Why is this the case? During epoch T_s the device performs the actual application computation, namely real application work. Hence, we want the overhead rate T_{up}/T_s to be much less than 1, or as close to 0 as possible. So what would be a reasonable overhead rate? In security typically unreasonable high rates would exceed 8 - 10%. Desirable overhead for security checks usually are between about 4 - 5%. If this rate comes close to 1, or if it's over 1, our scheme couldn't possibly work, so that's why the feasibility condition $T_{up}/T_s \ll 1$ is very important. And as it turns out, satisfying this feasibility condition is not easy at all.

The system operation, including the periodic pool update in response to receiving a nonce from the Verifier, is illustrated in Figures 1 and 2 of the accompanying paper. Please note the definitions of the first two update functions f_1 and f_2; viz., the accompanying paper. These functions satisfy the following three requirements that are necessary for the proof of secure pool updates, and yet they fail the feasibility condition. First, any block of the updated pool $S' = f(n, S)$ needs all N blocks of previous secret pool S as inputs. If this condition is satisfied, then the device malware M_{in} needs to leak at least all the N blocks of a secret pool to succeed in leaking the entire pool. Second, the collaborating network adversary M_{out} needs to obtain an arbitrary group of N *contiguous* blocks of a pool among the blocks leaked by device malware M_{in}. Third, the design of the functions must force M_{in} in a space-time tradeoff when attempting to leak N *contiguous* pool blocks to M_{out}. If the the device output bandwidth D_{ban}

prohibits the transfer of all N blocks in a single T_s epoch, then M_{in} would either have to save the blocks not leaked in an epoch in freely usable system memory, L_{mem} for leakage in future T_s epochs or perform the pool update computation using fewer than N pool blocks, or both. Hence, either (1) free memory L_{mem} is large enough to hold most, if not all, of the blocks not leaked in a T_s epoch or (2) M_{in} would have to use extra update computation time beyond T_{up}, if L_{mem} is too small. Hence if both L_{mem} and pool update time T_{up} are upper-bounded appropriately, M_{in} will either not have enough memory space to leak all blocks or will exceed T_{up}, which be detected by the Verifier. If M_{in} cannot circumvent this tradeoff, it could not leak all the contiguous N blocks of any complete secret pool S.

So the question is, what can we do now that neither function is feasible? Well, we try another function, f_3. Here, one runs a sliding window w, where $|w| < |S|$ over pool S, which is the input to a hash function, to generate a single block of the update pool. Then, the update function shifts the input window to the right over S by one block and produces a second block of the updated pool. This proceeds in a circular way over pool S, and once all the blocks of S have been processed, the updated pool S' is obtained. Note that f_3 uses a smaller input, $|w| < |S|$, for each block of the updated pool than f_1 and f_2, and a hash function instead of a PRF to generate a block of the updated pool, so we expected a significant performance improvement. Unfortunately, the feasibility condition could still not be satisfied.

Frank Stajano: So in all of these schemes you keep on generating new secrets, but still from the initial pool of the first epoch.

Reply: Yes, from the initial pool also committed in the Verifier.

Frank Stajano: So maybe I fail to understand some part of the scheme, but I thought that you said you needed to make sure that the malware inside the device could not leak the secret pool content, and you would do that by keeping on making the secret pool bigger, and bigger, and bigger.

Reply: No, the pool always has a fixed size $|S|$. It's not growing bigger and bigger when it is being updated.

Frank Stajano: So what is the part that prevents the malware from leaking, maybe slowly, the initial N secret blocks after which the network can simulate the whole device no matter how far the pool updates have gone.

Reply: We'll see that in a minute, but let me give you the short answer now. If I can leak only, say, three blocks out of a two hundred block pool during an epoch, T_s, in the next epoch the previous two hundred pool blocks are gone, since they're overwritten with the updated set of blocks.

Frank Stajano: After enough epochs have passed that I have leaked everything, I can leak an entire pool.

Reply: Yes, you are anticipating an important problem. Let me explain it now. Clearly, even if the scheme restricts malware M_{in} to leaking only a small part of the secret pool S before it is overwritten by the next set of values S', the outside network collaborator M_{out} can gain increasingly more pool values. As you anticipate, M_{out} could collect all the nonces sent by the Verifier, and apply the update function to the partial pool blocks (e.g., the three blocks mentioned above) it receives from M_{in} in epoch 1 to generate blocks of epoch 2. Then it could combine the updated blocks with the blocks leaked by M_{in} in epoch 2, and thus M_{out} would already exceed the three-block limit of epoch 2 leakage imposed on M_{in}. And M_{out} repeats this process for leaked blocks of epoch 3: with the collected nonces, it updates the blocks it has for epoch 2 and combines them with the leaked blocks of epoch 3, and thus it constructs a larger part of a secret pool outside the device. Eventually, adversary M_{out} can construct an entire pool for some epoch and wins. So the question is this: what prevents the adversary from carrying out this pool splicing process? That is your question.

Briefly, update functions f_1, f_2, and f_3 are designed to satisfy the three necessary conditions summarized above, namely (1) M_{out} needs at least N blocks, (2) it has to have contiguous blocks of some pool, and (3) M_{in} has to circumvent the space-time tradeoff in order to enable M_{out} to obtain the entire pool S of some epoch. (The appendix of the accompanying paper illustrates the use of these conditions in the security proof for function f_2.) However, none of these functions led to a performance-feasible system, as all have an undesirable lower bound on the overhead rate T_{up}/T_s. The challenge we faced caused us to doubt the feasibility of the entire idea of ReDABLS for a while. However, we could not prove that a suitable update function could not exist, and hence we had to try some other type of update function. The idea was to construct a *probabilistic* pool update function that could have about $1/100$ of the overhead rate of the previous functions, which would obviously be practical, even if the probability of adversary's success would not be zero. The goal was to design an update function that would have a small overhead rate and would only allow a very small probability of adversary success. Thus we defined functions f_4 and f_5 (viz., the the accompanying paper) and obtained feasible overhead rates $T_{up}/T_s \ll 1$.

This part of the presentation covered the first part of device attestation with bounded leakage of secrets, namely the authentication of a remote device. The second part is that of obtaining a malware-free memory state, and I will not go over it in detail because it's pretty straightforward. Once the Verifier authenticates the remote device D at epoch i, it can send it a bunch of entropy, E, where $|E| \ll |S_i|$, to D over a clear line. A ROM-stored program of D could overwrite everything in D's accessible memory outside the secret pool S_i with pseudorandom bits derived from E. The secret pool would be updated to S_{i+1} and then D would respond to the Verifier essentially confirming that this new memory state has no malware in it.

Ariel Stulman: I think I missed something in the previous slide. You send entropy E to the device over a network that's controlled by an adversary.

Reply: Yes.

Ariel Stulman: So, first of all, you assume M_{out} will send entropy on.

Reply: The point is that entropy E arrives at the device over clear lines. E augments the secret pool, which the network adversary M_{out} can only have in an incomplete way. So even if the adversary M_{out} gets E completely, it would not have the union of E and S_{i+1}; e.g., $E||S_{i+1}$. However, the device has $E||S_{i+1}$

and could respond correctly to the Verifier's challenge E. Remember that the device has to prove that it has $E||S_{i+1}$.

Ariel Stulman: It proved a union?

Reply: Yes, we've already shown that a secret pool cannot be leaked completely. Now if the adversary M_{out} has an incomplete pool and the complete entropy, he will still be unable to respond correctly to the Verifier, say with the result of a MAC function over the union $E||S_{i+1}$.

Ariel Stulman: The device is not sending back S_{i+1}, only?

Reply: No. We already have the complete pool S_{i+1} by now.

Ariel Stulman: On the device and Verifier?

Reply: Yes.

Ariel Stulman: Independently?

Reply: Yes, the device and Verifier independently generate S_{i+1}. That's exactly what they're supposed to do. And now the device says to the Verifier: "I'm done with the entropy E, and here is my response." And it takes a MAC over $E||S_{i+1}$ and sends it back to the Verifier. The Verifier checks that the response received is correct, and if it is, clearly all is well because the adversary M_{out} would not have been able to send this response since M_{out} only has entropy E, but not the complete pool S_{i+1}.

Enhancements to Prepare-and-Measure Based QKD Protocols

Peter Y.A. Ryan[1] and Bruce Christianson[2]

[1] University of Luxembourg
peter.ryan@uni.lu
[2] University of Hertfordshire
b.christianson@herts.ac.uk

Abstract. We propose some simple changes to a class of Quantum Key Distribution protocols. The first enhancement ensures early detection of any attempted Man-in-the-Middle attack and results in less leakage of key material to any eavesdropping attacker. We argue that this version is at least as secure as the original BB'84 scheme, but ensures a closer binding of the key establishment and authentication components of the protocol. Further proposed enhancements lead to a doubling of the key rate, but the security arguments become more delicate.

We also touch on the need to enhance the models used to analyze both the classical and quantum aspects of QKD protocols. This is prompted by the observation that existing analyses treat the quantum (key-establishment) and classical (authentication etc) phases separately and then combine them in a simple-minded fashion.

1 Introduction

The purpose of this paper is twofold: to present enhancements to existing prepare-and-measure Quantum Key Distribution (QKD) protocols, and to argue that we need to enrich our models for the analysis of QKD protocols, in particular to deal with this enhancement, but also for QKD protocols in general.

QKD exploits features of quantum mechanics, in particular Heisenberg's Uncertainly Principle and the No-Cloning Theorem, to ensure that any attempt by an eavesdropper to monitor the quantum channel will, with high probability be detected. Typically, QKD strives to provide unconditional secrecy, i.e. secrecy against an adversary with unbounded computational power. This contrasts with most classical crypto, where the security properties are typically based on hard computational problems and therefore assume an adversary with bounded computational power.

In this paper we focus on enhancing the BB'84 protocol due to Bennett and Brassard, [BB84]. The first enhancement proposed here is very simple but appears to be rather effective. After a quantum phase, protocols such as BB'84 involve a first classical step of agreeing for which photons the receiver used the "correct" measurement basis, followed by a step in which Anne and Bob agree a subset on which they

B. Christianson et al. (Eds.): Security Protocols 2013, LNCS 8263, pp. 123–133, 2013.

will compare their bits to detect any eavesdropping/noise on the quantum channel. In existing schemes, the agreement on the correct set and the eavesdropping detection subset is done by open negotiation, and so is known also to an attacker, indeed could potentially be manipulated by the attacker. Some form of end-to-end authentication and integrity property is required for the channel over which this negotiation takes place, and in practice this is provided by cryptographic means that require Anne and Bob to pre-share a secret authentication key. In our enhancement, Anne and Bob compute the subset for comparison separately and secretly, as a function of entropy derived from the previously established, secret authentication string. This results in less leakage of information to any eavesdropper and provides early, implicit authentication of the protocol.

The second enhancement is rather more audacious: we propose that the preparation/measurement bases, rather than being chosen purely randomly, are determined as pseudo-random functions of the prior, shared secret. Thus Anne and Bob are able to independently compute the basis sequence. Thus Bob can use the correct basis to measure all the photons emitted by Anne, rather than just guessing as for the conventional BB'84. This results in a doubling of the resulting bit rate, but now the security arguments become more delicate. A crucial observation that emerges from the analysis is that any measurements performed on a single photon by an eavesdropper, Yves, leak no information about the preparation basis. Consequently Yves cannot determine the seed of the pseudorandom function even with unlimited computational resources, as he cannot gain any information about the output from it. This, rather surprising observation is key to showing that this enhancement does not sacrifice security.

The third, even more radical, enhancement involves checking all the bits, not just a subset, without revealing anything about them. In certain circumstances, this makes the protocol more efficient.

We discuss the need for suitable models for the analysis of such protocols. Existing analyses typically use a physics (quantum mechanics based) model to argue that any eavesdropping on the quantum channel will be detectable during the classical phase, and any information leakage can be strictly bounded. The proofs are essentially reduction proofs: violation of these properties would imply the existence of a way to violate principles of quantum mechanics: Heisenberg Uncertainty and the no-cloning theorem for example. It is usually then argued that Man-In-The-Middle attacks can be thwarted by using unconditional authentication mechanisms on appropriate steps of the classical exchanges. Authentication is typically achieved using MACs based on universal hash functions such as the Carter-Wegman class. Most descriptions of QKD protocols in the literature are rather vague or inconsistent as to which of the classical exchanges should be authenticated.

Such a proof strategy is worrying: it treats the key-establishment and authentication phases separately and then composes them in a rather simple-minded fashion. We know from decades of experience analyzing classical protocols and primitives that great care needs to be taken in composing modules and arguments. We also know that it is essential that the key-establishment and authentication be inextricably bound together.

2   Background

BB'84, or variants of it, constitute the form of QKD that are most advanced in terms of implementation and commercialization. Similar constructs to those presented here apply to other QKD protocols, e.g. entanglement based protocols such as Ekert'91, [Eke91], but we'll stick to BB'84 based protocols for the purposes of this paper.

First we briefly outline the steps of conventional (prepare and measure) QKD protocols. We describe the idealized flow of the protocol, assuming a sufficiently low level of noise on the quantum channel and ignoring complications such as maintaining synchronization of the photon indices, multiple photon pulses etc. We then describe the changes to the eavesdropping detection and key sifting steps that constitute the enhancements proposed here.

As is standard, we assume that Anne and Bob share a secret bit string s prior to starting the protocol, and that this will be used to authenticate the key establishment. Note that, in order to achieve unconditional guarantees, none of the initial string should ever be re-used. If we use a stretch of the s string, say to authenticate a message using a MAC style mechanism, then this stretch of s must be discarded after use.

We assume that Anne possesses a device capable of emitting individual photons circularly polarized in one of four states: ($\uparrow$) 0° ($\nearrow$) 45° ($\rightarrow$) 90° ($\searrow$) 135°. Bob possesses a polarization measurement device that can be set to measure either in the horizontal ($\oplus$) or diagonal ($\otimes$) basis. We take the convention that in the $\oplus$ basis, a 0° photon encodes a 1 and a 90° photon encodes a 0, and in the $\otimes$ basis, 45° encodes a 1 and 135° a 0.

We will not go into the details of the "operational semantics" arising from the quantum mechanics, except to remark that when the circular polarization of a photon is measured with the "correct" basis the state will collapse to the correct eigenstate with 100% probability. If the "wrong" basis is used, the wave function will collapse into either of the eigenstates with 50% probability. Thus, for example, if a $\uparrow$ photon is measured in the $\oplus$ basis it will collapse to the $\uparrow$ state. If a $\nearrow$ photon is measured in the $\oplus$ basis it will collapse to a $\uparrow$ state with 50% probability and a $\rightarrow$ state with 50% probability, and similarly for the other combinations. More generally, if the angle between the photon state and an eigenstate is θ, then the probability that it will collapse to this eigenstate is given by $cos^2(\theta)$.

2.1   Phase 1 : The Quantum Channel

Anne emits a stream of photons over a suitable channel, e.g. optical fiber or free space. Each photon will be polarized in one of the four possible polarizations chosen randomly and independently. The source of this randomness is pure as opposed to pseudo-random. Anne keeps a record of the chosen polarization of each emitted photon. We will assume that mechanisms are in place to allow Anne and Bob to label each photon with a unique and consistent index, e.g. numbered consecutively. We'll refer to this indexing set as ϕ. Typically Anne emits a large number of photons, perhaps tens of thousands. Bob, at the other end of the quantum channel, measures each incoming photon in one of the two bases, chosen independently at random (again, really random). Bob keeps a record of the bases he used for each measurement and the outcome of the measurement (as a bit).

We now move to the classical phases of the protocol in which Anne and Bob exchange classical information over conventional, classical channels. These channels are not assumed to be secret, but are where necessary provided with integrity and endpoint authentication using information-theoretically secure MACs based on the prior shared secret string s.

2.2   Phase 2 : Key Sifting

Once the transmission and measurement of the photons is finished, Anne and Bob need to agree for which photons Bob used the "correct" measurement basis (the $\oplus$ basis in the case of 0° and 90° polarization, and the $\otimes$ in the case of 45° and 135° polarization). For these photons, in the absence of noise or eavesdropping on the quantum channel, the bit corresponding to the outcome of Bob's measurement should match Anne's bit. Where Bob used the "wrong" basis, the outcome of the measurement will be a random choice of 0 or 1. This agreement is established over open channels and so any attacker eavesdropping the classical channel will also learn this information.

To this end, for example, Bob reveals his choice of measurement basis for each photon (index). Anne responds by stating for which indices his choice was correct, but without revealing the polarization (i.e. the corresponding bit). At the end of this phase they have agreed the subset of the indices on which, aside from noise, they should have agreement between their bits. We'll refer to this set as ϕ_1. The complement set of ϕ_1 in ϕ is discarded.

2.3   Phase 3 : Detection of Eavesdropping

Now Anne and Bob need to agree a subset of ϕ_1 on which they will compare their bits to establish whether any eavesdropping occurred on the quantum channel. We will refer to this subset of ϕ_1 as ϕ_2. It is essential that ϕ_2 is chosen at random after the quantum phase is complete, but it is not, in the existing protocols, assumed that it is kept secret, rather it is established by open discussion and hence assumed known to the attacker.

Once they have agreed on ϕ_2, Anne and Bob compare bits for each index in ϕ_2. In the absence of eavesdropping and noise, they should agree on all these bits. In practice, due to noise on the quantum channel, there will be some level of disagreement, but as long as this is low enough to be compatible with the noisiness of the channel they conclude that there was either no eavesdropping or any possible eavesdropping is bounded to a sufficiently low level. If the level of disagreement exceeds an appropriate threshold, typically around 11%, they will conclude that a significant level of eavesdropping is likely and abort the protocol run. Note that they cannot distinguish between noise and eavesdropping. In line with the literature, we refer to this level of discrepancy as the Quantum Error Rate (QER).

2.4 Phase 4: Information Reconciliation

Assuming that they have not aborted after phase 3, Anne and Bob proceed to phase 4: where they start to construct the new session key. They now work with the complement of ϕ_2 in ϕ_1, which we will call ϕ_3. Thus ϕ_3 is the set of indices of photons for which Bob used the correct basis but for which they have revealed no information about the corresponding bits. For the bits indexed by ϕ_3, Anne and Bob should each have a string of bits which, aside from noise and eavesdropping, will match. The attacker should know at most a bounded amount about these bits. The problem is that there will inevitably be some disagreement between their bits strings due to the QER. They need to eliminate these mismatches while revealing as little as possible to an attacker eavesdropping on the classical channel about the actual bit strings. This is usually done using a "cascade" protocol [BS93]. This is quite standard and will be used unchanged in our first two enhancements, so we will not go into the details here. However our third enhancement will propose an alternative approach.

2.5 Phase 5: Secrecy Amplification

We assume that after completing phase 4 above, Anne and Bob share identical bit strings. An attacker should have at most a bounded amount of information about these strings, gleaned possibly from some "below the radar" level of eavesdropping on the quantum channel and by monitoring the classical channel, in particular from monitoring phase 4. Anne and Bob can use the QER they observed in phase 3 to bound the information that Yves might extract. This information now needs to be reduced to a negligible level by a process of "secrecy amplification". In essence the string is "distilled" down to a shorter string with purer entropy from the attacker's perspective. Again, the procedure here is perfectly standard and will be unchanged in our enhanced protocol so we omit details, [BBCM95].

2.6 Phase 6: Key Confirmation

Finally, to confirm that Anne and Bob indeed share the same distilled key and to authenticate the key, they can perform a final key confirmation step. They can for example each compute a keyed universal hash over the key, keyed using a fresh stretch of the initial shared string s, and exchange parts of the output. These values reveal no information about the session key to an eavesdropper, but if these values agree then Anne and Bob can be confident that they possess the same session key, and that the key has been shared with the correct counterparty.

They now have a confirmed secret key that can be used for secure communication in a One-Time-Pad (Vernam) encryption mode to provide unconditional secrecy, or in conjunction with a universal hash function to provide unconditional integrity. Alternatively, the key could be used for encryption under a suitable block cipher such as AES, but in this case the security properties are no longer unconditional.

Anne and Bob should set aside a suitable stretch of this freshly established key to use for authentication in the next run of the protocol.

Note that in existing descriptions of the protocol, these classical exchanges are over public channels and so the attacker knows the index sets ϕ_1, ϕ_2 and ϕ_3 and indeed the bits of the string indexed by ϕ_2. Descriptions vary as to which of these exchanges are authenticated and how, but these details are not relevant for our purpose here. The point for us is simply that at least some of the exchanges must be authenticated, and that in practice this requires a pre-established shared authentication secret.

3   The First Enhancement

The first proposed enhancement to the above style of protocol is very simple and modifies only phase 3: rather than have Anne and Bob agree the subset ϕ_2 in a public fashion, we provide a way for each of them to compute it in a secret fashion. Besides leaking less information, this approach also provides early, implicit authentication. For this they will use an agreed stretch of the shared initial shared secret string s, say the first 128 bits, call this s', to compute ϕ_2.

The details of this construction can be varied as necessary, but it should have the following properties:

- It must be a deterministic function of the secret string s'. Thus, given s', Anne and Bob should compute the same set of indices.
- It should be able to deal with an input of any given length (corresponding to the size of index set for which they establish that Bob used the correct measurement basis, i.e. the size of the ϕ_1 set).
- It should be able to accept a value p $(0 < p < 1)$ as a parameter and extract a proportion p of the ϕ_1 indices.
- An attacker, who knows p but does not know s', should not have a strategy for guessing ϕ_2 that is significantly better than guessing at random with probability p, even if the attacker has been "lucky" in guessing a higher than average proportion of the bits of s'.

An example of a simple way to realize such a construction is for Anne and Bob to use the s' value as a key for AES in Counter mode to generate a pseudo-random string w. The reason for this is that block ciphers are designed to have the property that that streams produced by even slightly different keys will be uncorrelated. Note that we are not using difficulty of inversion: Yves has unlimited computational power but cannot, even indirectly, observe the cipher stream.

Suppose, for illustration, that Anne initially transmits 1024 photons to Bob. For approximately 512 of these they will establish that Bob used the correct measurement basis, i.e. the ϕ_1 set. Suppose that they want to select 25% of these to compare, i.e. approx 128 indices to form the ϕ_2 set on which they will compare bits to check their level of agreement. They each use s to produce a string w. They segment w into pairs of bits, and for each 00 pair they select the index in ϕ_1. The 01, 10, and 11 pairs are not selected. This will yield approximately 128 bits. Anne can now transmit the first 64 bits to Bob and Bob transmits the last 64 bits to Anne. They do not reveal publicly the positions to which these bit values correspond.

More generally, suppose Anne and Bob want to select approximately $1/m$ of the ϕ_1 bits on the set to form the ϕ_2 set, where m is an integer. The stream w can be segmented into pieces w_i of length at least $\log_2 m$, and interpreted as select for $w_i = 0$, not select for $0 < w_i < m$ and ignore for $w_i \geq m$.

The point of this construction is fourfold:

- An attacker, whom we assume does not know s (or hence s'), will not be able to compute ϕ_2, hence he does not know which photons Anne and Bob will use for their comparison.
- We have implicit authentication: an attacker cannot masquerade convincingly as either Anne or Bob. Even if he tries a MITM attack and say, measures all the photons emitted by Anne, he will not be able to provide Anne (or Bob) with a string of bits matching her (or his) bits without knowledge of ϕ_2.
- The process of key establishment and authentication are inextricably intertwined in the protocol.
- In contrast to the standard protocols, we leak only partial information about the bits in the ϕ_2 set. Consequently we have the possibility of using these in the final session key, as long as we use suitable privacy amplification. Thus the resulting bit rate will be higher than with previous QKD protocols. It is worth noting also that an attacker knows less about the bits of the ϕ_3 string: even if he has managed to surreptitiously measure some of the photons in this set, he will not know exactly where these sit in the final key string.

3.1   Discussion

As mentioned previously: the new approach leaks much less information to the attacker (about the ϕ_2 and hence the ϕ_3 set) and provides early implicit authentication. In fact, with our modification, we do not even have to explicitly authenticate the classical exchanges between Anne and Bob, hence we do not need to consume so much of the s string (for example via universal hash functions) in order to ensure integrity.

From the attacker's perspective, the protocol is unchanged aside from the fact that he does not now learn the ϕ_2 set. The security of this variant of BB'84 is thus reducible to that of the original BB'84.

The new approach also provides a counter to the Photon Number Splitting (PNS) attack [GBS00]: this can occur when photon pulses have more than one correlated photon and, in principle, the attacker could measure one (or more) of the photons in the pulse while leaving one untouched. This provides a way to eavesdrop on the quantum channel without triggering the detection mechanisms (the photon that Bob measures has not been interfered with by the attacker). Such attacks are worrying, as in practice it is very difficult to eliminate completely the occurrence of multiple photon pulses, and they break the abstractions on which previous correctness proof models were based. This has prompted proposed counter-measures, such as the SARG protocol [SARG04]. The SARG protocol is however significantly more complex that the one proposed here, in particular it involves Anne and Bob having to throw away 75% of the photons at the first step as opposed to 50% in the original BB'84. With the enhancement proposed here, even an adversary who succeeds in measuring some photons undetectably in this fashion cannot masquerade successfully during the eavesdropping/authentication step. Furthermore, even if he manages to extract some bits of the key stream in this fashion, Yves will not know exactly where they lie in the final key stream.

Another important point is that, from experience in the analysis of classical AKEs, we know that it is essential that the key establishment and authentication be explicitly bound together. The approach proposed here achieves this: the bits that they compare, and hence the bits retained to form the key ultimately, are derived from the pre-shared secret authentication string s, because the indices that are identified for the comparison step, the ϕ_2 set, are computed as a function of s.

In the event that bits from the ϕ_2 set are used in the final key, an issue to consider is the possibility of belated leakage of information about the s string. This is analogous to a "forward secrecy" property for a purely classical scheme. To avoid this threat Anne and Bob should ensure that the utilized parts of s are deleted as soon as they have served their purpose.

4   The Second Enhancement

Now we introduce the second innovation: rather than generating the basis sequence purely randomly, we propose that Anne and Bob also compute the basis sequence b_i as a pseudo-random function of the shared s string. Anne now generates a true random bit sequence z_i and prepares the ith photon according to the coding convention mentioned earlier. Bob, for his part, measures the i-th photon using the b_i basis. Thus, in the absence of noise or eavesdropping, Bob should recover the z_i sequence exactly as generated by Anne. They now perform a comparison of a randomly selected set of elements of the z sequence as before. They could of course combine this second enhancement with the first enhancement, and secretly compute the comparison subset pseudorandomly.

4.1 Discussion

An important, and rather surprising, observation that emerges from the analysis is that, in the absence of an PNS attack, any measurement that the attacker may perform on the photons during the quantum phase leaks no information about the basis sequence. A simple calculation using the "operation semantics" of the measurement operator shows that Yves will get a 0 with probability $\frac{1}{2}$ and a 1 with probability $\frac{1}{2}$, regardless of which generation basis was used by Anne, and which measurement basis Yves uses, including oblique ones. This calculation is based on the assumption that the z sequence and the basis choice have the same statistics as pure random.

The significance of this observation is that it thwarts the obvious strategy that Yves might attempt: measure lots of photons early in the quantum phase and try to improve his guesses at the bases further downstream. We also need to ensure that Yves cannot benefit from a better-than-average guess at the string s. As argued before, the use of a good block cipher such as AES in counter mode to provide the PRNG should ensure an adequate lack of correlation.

Suppose that we use a 128 bit string as the seed to generate the basis sequence. The property we require of the PRNG is that if the attacker gets even one bit wrong in his guess at the seed, then the xor of the resulting guessed sequence and the real basis sequence will be essentially random. Using a good block cypher such as AES in counter mode has exactly this property, by construction. Hence, unless the attacker gets really lucky and guesses the 128 bits exactly right, he faces the same challenge as the conventional protocol with a strictly random basis sequence. This, along with the observation that (in the absence of PNS style attacks) no observation he can make on the quantum channel can extract any information about the basis sequence, implies that the security of the enhanced scheme is essentially the same as that of BB'84.

The above argument is based on the assumption that the attacker has at most negligible information about the authentication string. This assumption is standard for BB'84 and QKD protocols in general. We need to take additional care though with such an assumption for our second enhancement: having non-zero information about the authentication key for one run may help the attacker launch a more effective attack in a subsequent run. In conventional BB'84, as the basis sequences are pure random, this is not an issue. In our case, there is the possibility that a lucky guess in one run might be amplified in subsequent runs. However, as long as the PRNG has the properties stated above, a better than average guess at the authentication string will not yield any advantage over a simple bitwise guessing at the basis sequence, and hence confers no advantage for a subsequent run of the protocol.

However the second enhancement is vulnerable to PNS attacks: for example, if Yves measures two photons (out of three) in the same basis and they are different, then he knows that the basis choice is wrong. With his infinite computational power, he can then eliminate approximately half of the potential values for s' for each such measurement.

On the other hand, vulnerability to PNS is an unsatisfactory feature of most QKD protocols - for example SARG itself is insecure if Yves can block all pulses with fewer than three photons (and half of the three-photon pulses) [SARG04].

One possible response is to stipulate that if Yves is to be equipped with a reliable photon counter then it is only fair for Anne to have one too. In this case Anne can eliminate PNS attacks simply by deleting pulses with more than one photon, and under this assumption protocols incorporating the second enhancement are invulnerable.

Of course, informal arguments such as the ones given above need to be made formal in the context of an appropriate model that encompasses both the quantum and classical aspects.

5   The Third Enhancement

The most radical of our proposals involves Anne and Bob effectively testing all of the bits in ϕ_1, and not merely a subset. To do this we use a trick from the Vintage Bit protocol of Christianson and Shafarenko [CS09]. The protocol sequence proceeds as usual (Section 2) until the end of Phase 2. At this point Anne has a bitstream z corresponding to the elements of ϕ_1 and Bob has a bitstream z' which is the same as z apart from the QER (including any eavesdropping.) Instead of Phases 3 and 4, Anne and Bob proceed as follows:

Anne and Bob have set aside a segment p of a previously agreed key stream. This is now used as One-Time Pad to conceal a Forward Error Correcting Code F and a collision-resistant hash h of the key stream z currently being agreed. Specifically:

$$A \to B : [F(z) \mid h(z)] \; \texttt{xor} \; p$$

Bob now recovers $F(z)$, applies this to z', and checks that the result hashes to $h(z)$. If not, then Bob aborts the protocol, otherwise Anne and Bob proceed with Phase 5 as usual.

5.1   Discussion

Note that the property of the hash h being relied upon here is not non-invertibility (since Yves can never learn any bits of the hash value) but a particular form of collision resistance: Yves cannot manipulate the values for z or $h(z)$ plausibly without knowing p. Note also that no authentication or integrity is required for the open channel communication between Anne and Bob used to transmit the encoded $F(z)$ in this enhancement. Privacy amplification can be done deterministically by Anne and Bob, with no further communication. Of course, the hash could be replaced by the conventional use of an information-theoretically secure MAC at the end of the protocol; but equally, Step 6 could be replaced by an authenticated confirmation to Alice by Bob that the corrected value of z' has the correct hash[1].

---

[1] For example, $B \to A : p'$ where p' is another segment of a previously agreed key stream.

The requirement to use key bits from a previous run for p appears to be an additional burden, but this step replaces Phases 3 and 4 of the conventional protocol. Although the number of bits required for $F(z)$, and hence for p, is of the order of twice the maximum allowable QER for z, under the third enhancement no bits are lost from z by the need to reveal bits to detect eavesdropping, or to apply a cascade protocol.

The approach with the third enhancement has the advantage that any suitably aggressive FEC protocol can be used off the shelf, without concern for security issues, and Bob can count exactly how many of the bits in z needed to be corrected.

The third enhancement can be combined with the second enhancement, with similar caveats about PNS.

6   Conclusions

We have proposed some simple but effective enhancements to the BB'84 based QKD protocols. These enhancements explicitly ensure a closer binding between key-establishment and authentication than for previous protocols. They ensure very early detection of any MITM or masquerade attacks as well as the possibility of higher bit rates and an effective counter to PNS style attacks.

We have also argued that we need more powerful models, that encompass both the quantum and classical aspects of QKD protocols, in order to deal with richer threat models.

References

[BB84]   Bennett, C.H., Brassard, G.: Quantum cryptography: Public key distribution and coin tossing. In: Proceedings of IEEE International Conference on Computers, Systems, and Signal Processing, India, p. 175 (1984)

[BBCM95] Bennett, C.H., Brassard, G., Crepeau, C., Maurer, U.M.: Generalized privacy amplification. IEEE Trans. Inf. Theor. 41(6), 1915–1923 (1995)

[BS93]   Brassard, G., Salvail, L.: Secret key reconciliation by public discussion. In: Helleseth, T. (ed.) EUROCRYPT 1993. LNCS, vol. 765, pp. 410–423. Springer, Heidelberg (1994)

[CS09]   Christianson, B., Shafarenko, A.: Vintage bit cryptography. In: Christianson, B., Crispo, B., Malcolm, J.A., Roe, M. (eds.) Security Protocols. LNCS, vol. 5087, pp. 261–265. Springer, Heidelberg (2009)

[Eke91]   Ekert, A.K.: Quantum cryptography based on bell's theorem. Phys. Rev. Lett. 67, 661–663 (1991)

[GBS00]   Mor, T., Brassard, G., Lütkenhaus, N., Sanders, B.C.: Limitations on practical quantum cryptography. Physical Review Letters (2000)

[SARG04] Scarani, V., Acín, A., Ribordy, G., Gisin, N.: Quantum cryptography protocols robust against photon number splitting attacks for weak laser pulse implementations. Phys. Rev. Lett. 92, 057901 (2004)

Enhancements to Prepare-and-Measure-Based QKD Protocols
(Transcript of Discussion)

Peter Y.A. Ryan

University of Luxemburg

OK, so I'm going to talk about a little idea for what I believe will enhance quantum key distribution, in particular the BB84 style of prepare-and-measure protocol, so I guess it fits in the theme in the sense that we're dealing with quantum channels and classical channels, and in particular the relationship between the two, which I think is particularly intriguing. Can I just take a quick poll? Most people in this room have probably come across things like quantum key distribution and BB84, hands up. A fair number, OK. I was planning to just go very quickly through it to refresh and then to introduce the new idea.

As probably most of you realise, quantum key distribution relies on a completely different kind of premise from the usual classical security crypto protocols, namely principles of quantum mechanics like the Heisenberg Uncertainty Principle and the non-cloning theorem. Classically, we assume the eavesdropper can take copies of anything that travel across the channels, and can try and do computations on them, but he is limited in what he can do computationally, subject to assumptions about computationally hard problems. Here what we are assuming is that he can't actually make copies, if he tries to eavesdrop and take copies of the data that's travelling on quantum channels, he will inevitably, according to Heisenberg, perturb that and we set the protocol up in such a way that we ensure that we can detect that with high probability. We'll see this shortly.

So the basic idea, the quantum part, is a really beautiful concept, and in a sense it's a kind of Diffie-Hellman in the realm of the quantum. Of course the difficulty is that, just as in the classical world, you have to worry about authentication. There's no point having key establishment if you don't have authenticated key establishment. And one of the things we've learnt very clearly in the classical realm is that you really have to be very careful to intertwine these two processes. If the adversary can somehow disentangle the two, even if you've got perfect key establishment and perfect authentication, you can still get man-in-the-middle attacks and so on. One of the concerns that I've had for quite a while is whether the arguments that are presented in the QKD literature are intertwined properly.

I've looked at a bit of the literature, and I've spoken to some of the experts here and there are beautiful proofs, some of you may have seen them, in the quantum world at least, subject to certain idealised assumptions, and I can see Ross looking over, I'm in very dangerous water here I know. But anyway, if you buy quantum mechanics there are very nice proofs that show that the key

B. Christianson et al. (Eds.): Security Protocols 2013, LNCS 8263, pp. 134–142, 2013.
© Springer-Verlag Berlin Heidelberg 2013

establishment works quantum mechanically speaking. But then when you quiz people to say, well OK, but how do you intertwine the authentication, the answer I've had from several people is, well that's fine, we do it unconditionally using MACs, Carter-Wegman hashes and so on and so forth, that's fine. And I for one feel uneasy about this, I don't know about other people in this room. I haven't managed to attack any of these protocols. The other comment I should make is that when you look at the literature, it seems to be very vague and inconsistent about what parts of the classical exchanges should be authenticated, and how and when, and so on. There may be people in the room who know the literature better than I in fact, in which case I'm open to comments.

OK so I'm clearly not going to go into the depths of quantum mechanics, I'll just outline a few very elementary facts which are relevant for this talk, and most of them probably you know them already. So the basic premise of quantum mechanics is that the state of a system is represented by a vector in a Hilbert space, and when you make a measurement you collapse that state into one of the eigenstates of that measurement operator. And typically this will be a probabilistic collapse, you can't predict which way it's going to go. So now I just want to switch quickly to a couple of coding conventions, which I prepared earlier. So for BB84, again, probably most of you are familiar with this, we assume that we're working the circular polarisation states of photons. So we assume in the protocol that Anne and Bob will use four polarisation states, and the recipient will choose between two measurement bases. You can write a kind of operational semantics if you like, for this, so if Bob uses this basis to measure an incoming photon in a state it will come out right in the sense, it will collapse to that. On the other hand, if he uses an incorrect basis, for example, the diagonally polarised here, the photon here, it will collapse into either of the eigenstates of this operator with a 50-50 probability, and so on and so forth.

OK, so the crucial point is, if you use the incorrect measurement basis, and of course if you're do things randomly a 50-50 chance that it will be incorrect, you will scramble the bit. I should also add there's a coding convention here translating these into classical bits, OK, in this basis, this is a 0 and this is a 1, and in the diagonal basis this is a 0 and that's a 1. OK, got the gist of it, I think that's about all you really need to know. So don't worry too much about the Copenhagen interpretation of what's going on underneath that. For authentication we typically assume that there's an initial shared secret between Anne and Bob.

OK, so for the quantum phase, Anne sends a stream of photons, we assume that she has a device that can send a pulse containing one photon; in practice that's not easy, but let's leave that aside. And for each of these she chooses a polarisation randomly chosen from these four possibilities. OK, so it's sent across the quantum channel, and Bob, for each of these, makes a random choice of these two bases, to measure them in. And both of them record the appropriate information. And so at the end of the quantum phase then we move into some classical phases. Yes.

Ariel Stulman: There's one thing I don't understand, if there's an initial shared secret, so Eve could target that, what do you have to know?

Reply: Yes, we assume that there's a fairly short string, that they're going to use for authentication. When they run this they can send an unbounded number of photons essentially. So the point is to be able to amplify, bootstrap from a short string up to an unbounded string. Does that answer your question, is that your point?

Ariel Stulman: We can always do that, you can always go up out of the quantum, if I have a shared secret with Mark, I can fill up a secure channel.

Reply: Classically or quantumly?

Ariel Stulman: Classically, so why bother with quantum?

Reply: Yes, there are classical protocols which do this kind of thing. Perhaps I should have stressed more: the point about this is that it's meant to give you unconditional security guarantees, right, not subject to any computational assumptions about the adversary's computational power. If you do it classically then, you use, Diffie-Hellman or something, if that what you're thinking of, that's not unconditional.

Feng Hao: Well that depends on the condition that you distributed the MAC key securely, otherwise how do you get an authenticated channel.

Bruce Christianson: Let him go on for a bit (laughter).

Reply: Well, you have to assume that at time zero they share a secret string at some point, yes, I mean, I'm glossing over some details.

Bruce Christianson: At some point they've met in a desolate place.

Reply: Yes, precisely. And, the other point is, you have to iterate this. They run the protocols so they generate a large string, but they have to set aside a bit of that string to authenticate the next run.

Feng Hao: OK, I thought this s was set before the photons were sent?

Bruce Christianson: Yes, but you can use s to agree a long string, you then use some of that long string as the s for the next run. And you only have to agree s_1.

Feng Hao: But if you agree on s and then probably some computation of Diffie-Hellman, or bootstrapping to get that shared secret.

Reply: Not if they meet in a desolate place, no.

Bruce Christianson: Yes, it's an insoluble problem, they have to have some other way of agreeing on a secret string to start off with.

Reply: Is that OK. I thought you were all saying you were all familiar with this stuff already! (laughter)

Bruce Christianson: To be fair all these books that explain this are very vague about how the authentication is done.

Reply: Precisely, that's part of the point of the talk, yes, exactly.

So I think we've done the quantum phase.

So now there are a series of classical phases which I'll try and go through quickly. Anne and Bob are choosing these things at random, and that should be pure random ideally. So the net effect is that for roughly half of these photons Bob will have chosen the right measurement basis. So the first thing they have to do is determine for which photons Bob used the correct basis, and by the way I'm assuming glibly that they're able to index these photons in a consistent way, which is not trivial either, but let's leave that aside. Typically this is just done in the open by conversation, they just tell each other. Bob, for example, announces which basis he used for each photon, and Anne tells him which were correct, but without announcing of course the bit. So they do that. And so let's call that index set that they establish for the correct photons I_1.

OK, now we move into phase 2, which is where they're going to try and detect if there's been any eavesdropping by Yves in the middle. So now they choose a random subset of this I_1 set, which I'm going to call I_2, and again, typically the way this is described it is just done by open discussion: they exchange the messages in the clear, and they decide some random subset which is unpredictable to the adversary, and on this set they're going to compare their bits. In the absence of noise or eavesdropping, as you can see from the little semantics I put up there, they should agree on all the bits. Assuming that the noise-level disagreement is sufficiently low, they'll conclude either there's been no eavesdropping or at least if there was it's sufficiently low that it can be eliminated basically later in phase 3 when they do privacy amplification. OK, does that make sense? So they're happy that there's been at most a bounded level of eavesdropping by Yves.

Bruce Christianson: Although they seem to have to make some assumptions about Moriarty's computational bound to get the authentication to work, even at that stage.

Reply: Well so far I haven't actually said anything about authentication.

Bruce Christianson: It was on the previous slide.

Reply: Oh yes, OK. Well actually what people here typically say is that you use a universal Carter Wegman type hash MAC, you use a piece of that string, and you don't re-use it, to do the authentication. And the claim is it gives you unconditional authentication. I don't want to get too deeply into that because the point of my talk is to sidestep that. The claim is that that is achievable unconditionally. It's probabilistic I guess, Yves does have a negligible probability of faking it, but it's not computationally conditional.

So now what they do is they switch to the compliment of I_1 in I_2, which I will call I_3. So this is the subset of bits for which they should have agreement, but about which they've revealed nothing. In the I_2 set they were revealing their bits to do the comparison. In I_3 they haven't revealed anything about those bits. So in principle this should be a bit string, which they are pretty much in agreement modulo some degree of noise, but which is secret to the eavesdropper. But the difficulty is they will inevitably detect some noise, there will be some level of mismatch, so they have to eliminate that because ultimately they want a precisely matching secret string. So there's something called, well typically it seems to be the "cascade protocol", for which again, I'll skip over the details, but by basically comparing parities of randomly chosen blocks they can detect blocks that have mismatches and eliminate them. Of course in this process they will be leaking some information, and we'll come to that in a second.

I'll go through this very quickly, are people comfortable with this? Shout at me if I'm going too fast. OK. So in principle after phase 3 they should now have this secret, exactly matching bit string, which can be in some sense unboundedly long depending on how many photons they sent off in the quantum phase. But we know that there's potential for Yves to have some level of information about this string. So he may have managed to get away with a little bit of eavesdropping in the quantum channel, kind of under the radar, but we can bound that in the detection phase. And of course, if he's been monitoring this classical phase 3, he will also have got some information via parities of blocks etc. So we now go through a secrecy amplification phase, which basically distils the string down into, in a sense, a purer entropy string, about which Yves will have negligible information. So we can in principle, the claim is, reduce the information leakage to the adversary to a negligible level by appropriately distilling.

So now they have a secret shared key, they can do a key confirmation, for example, and at the very least, if you do that at the end presumably you get some authentication, confirmation of the key and implicit authentication, that it really is Anne and Bob, i.e. the two people who have shared that initial secret s.

Michael Roe: And it's an information-theoretically–secure hash rather than just a computationally-secure one like SHA-1?

Reply: It's Carter Wegman type stuff again, yes. And then of course you can run it either as a one-time pad, or sometimes it's suggested you use a block cipher or something, but then of course you drop the unconditional secrecy of the communication.

So that's got me through the preamble. So as I think we've sort of agreed there seems to be a real problem in the literature that it's very vague about how really the authentication is done, which parts of the communications are authenticated, and so on and so forth. I for one feel concerned about this, but when I talk to people in the field they say, oh it's not a problem, it's all unconditional authentication on the classical channels, there's no problem. But I felt uneasy about this. And it's in the process of mulling over this that we come to the twist, which is really what the talk is about.

So it's I think a very simple idea, almost embarrassingly simple, and it's possible it's somewhere out in the literature, but I haven't been able to find it. If someone knows of it, or knows of something similar, please let me know. So the simple thought was, well in all the conventional descriptions, as far as I can see, they talk about this I_2 being agreed in public, so it's known to the adversary. But why can't we compute it, secretly independently at Anne and Bob using part of the secret string, perhaps using unconditional hash functions or something. And we may want to include some fresh entropy, maybe they exchange some further entropy in the clear, which is also folded in, or maybe they derive some entropy from the communications that have happened during phase 1, the agreement on the correct set. So in principle they should be able to compute I_2 independently in secret, not communicate it to the adversary. And having done that they can then start exchanging bits between each other drawing from this index set, but the adversary doesn't know what these indices are. So Anne could say, send a bunch of these bits that she's computed at her end, and Bob can check they agree with his, and vice versa. So they do the eavesdropping detection phase, but they're also folding in mutual authentication into the process. So that's basically the idea.

So what are the features of this idea? Well one thing is, as I'm trying to stress, I think it does entwine the key establishment and the authentication steps much more tightly than, as far as I can see, it's done in any of the conventional protocols. It also gives you authentication at a very early step, almost as early as you can get it, sort of for free, as a spin-off of the eavesdropping detection process. You can also argue that you can perhaps get a better bit rate out of this whole process. It's kind of interesting: you could in principle use some of the bits from I_1. And you've got a rather interesting information theory problem here. You know that there's some long bit string, and you've leaked some of these bits to the adversary, but the adversary doesn't know where these bits fall in the string. So you obviously leak some information to him, but arguably not that much. And I haven't had time to do the information theory computations here, but you could presumably work out a bound on the information leakage in that process, and in principle you could actually use some of the entropy from the I_1 set that you would normally have to bin in the conventional approach.

Of course you'd have to be rather careful about this, so you probably might have to do a more ferocious distillation, so on balance I'm not quite sure how much of a gain you get. And I guess another thing which occurred to me a few weeks back is that there may be an issue of forward secrecy: a danger that at some later time information about the secret s leaks, then that could cause some additional leakage that you hadn't originally anticipated, so that might be a problem. How serious a threat that is I'm not quite sure. In principle, in these protocols we always of course assume that s is kept secret, but I guess conventionally you only have to assume it's secret until the end of the protocol. Here you'll potentially have to assume it remains secret indefinitely, which is maybe a little bit tricky. But maybe if you implement things carefully, and the secret is destroyed locally immediately after the run of the protocol, maybe you can make that assumption that it remains secret fairly strong, but that's something certainly to think about.

There's also a little technicality that this scheme also seems to help with something called the multiple photon counter attack, which again, some of you may of heard of. As I hinted earlier, a lot of these models are very idealistic of how the concept, the protocol, is implemented. In practice producing single photon pulses is far from trivial, and so in practice you often get two or three, you get a Poisson distribution, probably a fairly tight Poisson distribution, but a Poisson distribution nonetheless. And so in principle, an attacker, if he could detect that a particular pulse had more than one photon, and he could just pick one out and measure it nicely and let the others go through, then he's got a nice attack. Now as far as I know, this is still way beyond the current technology, but who knows, there are smart guys out there. And people worry about this, at least in theory, and so, for example, there is a protocol called the SARG protocol, which is designed to counter this, and I won't go into the details of it now, but it actually involves throwing away effectively 75% of the original bits that you sent, rather than the 50% that we had originally. So its bit rate is even worse than normal. But I think I would argue that my protocol seems to help counter this attack. I'll let you think about it, or we can discuss it later.

So, conclusions: it's a little tweak, a fairly simple tweak, it's a ludicrously simple tweak, and I'm kind of surprised that I've not been able to find it in the literature already, but it doesn't seem to have been used. It does seem to entangle, or entwine perhaps I should say, perhaps entangle is not the right word here, the key establishment and authentication in a much tighter sense. It does seem to result in somewhat higher bit rates, that's maybe not such a big deal because it's probably rather marginal, but it throws up some interesting little information theory problems. And I think it also points up just a more general issue in this whole field that, I for one have not really seen any convincing analyses which combine both the classical and the quantum parts of QKD. There are beautiful analyses of the quantum part, and beautiful analyses of the classical part, but then the arguments combining them seem rather loose, they're just sort of saying, oh it's fine, the authentication of the classical part makes everything fine. And I for one feel uneasy about this, and I think we need better approaches to either analysing these two channels together, or better ways of combining the arguments, the analyses of each individually. And that's about it. Thank you.

Bruce Christianson: Is there any reason why you couldn't use s to agree the sequence in I_1?

Reply: I_1 is the correct basis set, right, the....

Bruce Christianson: Yes, suppose that Alice and Bob have a convention that, instead of randomly choosing the alignments, they do it pseudo-randomly, based on s.

Reply: Well in fact I think there is one paper I came across which does something a bit like that, it does, there is a sort of pre-agreement.

Bruce Christianson: Because then you don't have to throw any bits away at all.

Reply: Yes, and I think that was precisely the point of this paper. You could. I for one feel rather uneasy about this. Yes, I think he even did a sort of periodic repeating of the pattern I think as he went through the photons.

Bruce Christianson: Now that's the point where I start to get uneasy.

Reply: You're saying just do it with a pseudo-random sequence generator either side?

Ross Anderson: But that reduces the security of the whole system to somebody guessing the pseudo-random generator.

Bruce Christianson: If somebody can guess the pseudo-random generator then they can masquerade as Bob, and the game is over anyway. Even in the standard quantum approach you have no more security than s to begin with.

Ross Anderson: Exactly so. You can secure the path, but you need over $30,000 of equipment to do that.

Bruce Christianson: Precisely so, yes. So pseudorandom generation of I_1 doesn't change the security parameters[1].

Reply: Right, and that's supporting your question, why couldn't you do that. I suppose in principle you could.

Bruce Christianson: You could then do a similar trick to the one that Alex Shafarenko and I do in the Vintage Bit Cryptography paper[2] where you essentially use very aggressive forward error correction. So instead of comparing things through a sample, you just do very aggressive forward error correction on the whole sequence. Xor the error correction code with a surplus piece of the transmitted sequence, and openly exchange that value along with a hash of the sequence that you're trying to agree (xored with another surplus piece of the transmitted sequence), and if that agrees then you're done.

Reply: Yes, it may work, I kind of thought about that sort of thing, I felt a bit uneasy. I mean, one of the beauties of the original scheme is that you are using these pure random strings, and you know, if you're gunning for unconditional secrecy that feels ...

Bruce Christianson: Well you are, you're using a purely random string that you've shared with someone. But the authentication of this, in the classical quantum protocols, comes entirely from this relatively tiny bit sequence that you've shared in a pub somewhere beforehand. And OK you're using it in a protocol that's information-theoretically secure, but that doesn't get you any more entropy. I really like your idea, it's a neat trick.

Reply: Well, maybe this is something we can talk about at greater length.

And you are injecting more entropy into the whole process just because you're generating these photons in a pure random fashion. So you are getting more entropy, fresh, genuine entropy in that sense.

But yes, I agree, what you are suggesting is certainly interesting and worth thinking about. I thought about it but I kind of felt a bit nervous about it somehow. The proofs will certainly get trickier, put it that way, it may end up being arguably perhaps as secure, but the proofs will certainly be difficult, it will be harder. But yes, that's certainly something that would be interesting to think about some more, yes. Any other questions, comments.

Michael Roe: Did you say you hadn't done the proof of correctness for this yet? The thing that is interesting about this is how then you prove something like this is correct.

Reply: Yes. I haven't done it, no. And that's one of the open questions, and well as I say, I'm not even convinced it's done properly for the original schemes.

Bruce Christianson: Yes, you've only got to do better than them.

Reply: Yes, right. And yes, that's the next thing to do, and do the information theory and analysis, and so on, which I suspect is probably sort of standard somewhere in the literature, but I'm not so familiar with that literature, I don't

---

[1] All that distinguishes Alice and Bob from Moriarty in BB84 is knowledge of s.

[2] LNCS 261–275.

know where to, which book to pull off the shelf. But of course, the whole basis of this might be completely flawed.

Ross Anderson: I'm very sceptical of the robustness of many of the definitions that are used in this field.

Reply: Which particular definitions?

Ross Anderson: The whole field of quantum crypto and quantum computing doesn't seem to suggest it's had anything like as much adversarial critique as things normally are in our field. But that is a story for, you know, a different workshop.

Reply: Yes. OK, you're not going to rise to the bait[3], OK.

---

[3] Ross Anderson and Robert Brady, 2013, "Why Quantum Computing is Hard – and Quantum Cryptography is not Provably Secure", arxiv.org/abs/1301.7351

Simple Defences against Vibration-Based Keystroke Fingerprinting Attacks

Rushil Khurana[1] and Shishir Nagaraja[2]

[1] IIIT Delhi, India
rushil09040@iiitd.ac.in
[2] University of Birmingham, UK
s.nagaraja@cs.bham.ac.uk

Abstract. Smartphones are increasingly equipped with sensitive accelerometers that can analyse acoustic vibrations on a physical surface. This allows them to gain a covert understanding of the surrounding environment by combining accelerometer sampling with sophisticated signal processing techniques. In this work, we analyse keyboard-sniffing attacks based on acoustic (vibration) covert channels, launched from a malicious application installed on a smartphone. An important requirement of such attacks is access to reliable acoustic signals that can be distinguished from the noise floor by applying appropriate signal processing techniques. Our analysis indicates that state-of-the-art attack techniques are fragile; injecting randomised noise (jamming) via the vibration medium into the accelerometer, reduces the efficiency of the attack from 80% to random guessing. We conclude that our work presents an important step towards disabling the covert channel and ensuring full security.

1 Introduction

The accelerometer sensors of modern mobile devices are getting increasingly powerful (around 100Mhz). After circumventing weak access control systems, if any, a malicious application on a mobile device such as a smartphone, can analyse incoming accelerometer signals to covertly gain an understanding of activities in its physical surroundings in an unauthorised manner.

Past work [2,3,5,7,6], on exploiting accelerometers to sniff keystrokes required direct physical contact with the keyboard. However a smartphone based accelerometer can be used to recover keystrokes to some extent **without** direct contact with the keyboard: Marquardt et al. [1] devised an attack that uses accelerometer readings from a smartphone to recover text being typed on a victim's keyboard. The keyboard and the smartphone are separated by a few inches on the same table. Accelerometer readings are collected by a mobile application running on the smartphone. Machine learning techniques are then applied to decipher English dictionary words. Marquardt et al. report an accuracy of recovering around 80% of the typed words.

Since the Marquardt attack is based on analysing acoustic vibrations, it is vital to examine their attack model in the context of **all** acoustic vibrations that

B. Christianson et al. (Eds.): Security Protocols 2013, LNCS 8263, pp. 143–151, 2013.
© Springer-Verlag Berlin Heidelberg 2013

are present in a reasonable setting including the keystrokes' acoustics and then test the effectiveness of the attack. Our contributions are as follows:

- We propose simple and usable defences based on injecting acoustic (vibration) noise into the covert channel to reduce the effectiveness of sophisticated signal processing techniques.
- We analyse and report on the practicality of the Marquardt attack within the original threat model [1]. We found that it attack effectiveness is much lower than a laboratory setting.

The Marquardt attack exploits weak OS access control mechanisms which allow smartphone applications to access the accelerometer sensor without explicit user permission. However, a major challenge they needed to overcome in comparison to past work is that the sampling rate of the accelerometer sensor present in a mobile device is a full two orders of magnitude less than that of the devices used in the previous works [2]. As a result, naive approaches involving direct mapping between signal features to keyboard input do not work. To overcome this challenge, they chose to apply the well known technique of bi-gram analysis where the statistical characteristics of the vibration signal can be uniquely mapped to two consecutive keypresses instead of a single keypress.

Vibration based side-channels pose an important threat to user security as they can leak confidential information. Such attacks leverage the fact that most users tend to place their mobile devices next to the keyboard. The attacker installs a keylogger via a social malware attack [8] on to the victim's mobile phone, which can record and relay stolen information (keystrokes) to the attacker.

The use of machine learning techniques to analyse vibrations caused by keystrokes or other sensitive information has given rise to fresh concerns about user security. However, we find that it is fairly straightforward to induce error into such attack techniques. In this paper, we analyse the robustness of the Neural Network technique, a supervised machine learning technique. We find that the attack is surprisingly ineffective when dealing with low levels of noise. Careful application of periodic acoustic noise alone can bring the classifier accuracy close to that of random guessing. It is clear that the attack is rendered completely ineffective by the application of pseudorandom noise.

We start by describing the Marquardt attack and explore the effectiveness of the attack under various common-day scenarios where random noise accompanies the acoustic vibrations produced by full-size desktop keyboards.

2   Keystroke Fingerprinting Attack Using Neural Networks

In the following section, we describe the Marquardt attack for fingerprinting vibrations caused by keyboard usage. Consider a desktop computer user operating the computer through a keyboard placed on a desk. Now consider a smartphone placed on the same desk a few inches away from the keyboard. The Marquardt keysniffing attack leverages a acoustic covert channel between the keyboard and a malicious application running on the smartphone. Vibrations induced by key-presses on to the desk shared by the smartphone and the computer keyboard are captured by the smartphone accelerometer. The collected information is then analysed by the malicious smartphone app (attacker) which applies a machine learning technique on the sampled vibration signals to infer the words typed in by the computer user (defender).

2.1 Marquardt's Keypress Fingerprinting Model

The sampling rate of accelerometers in mobile devices is too low to map the maximum amplitude of a vibration signal to a unique keypress (on a nearby keyboard). Therefore, the Marquardt adopts a bigram approach towards model-ing keypresses; instead of a single keypress, a pair of keypress events is modelled together. Let E_i and E_j be sequential keypress events. The following features have been used to characterise the event (E_i, E_j):

1. **Keyboard Position:** For each event E_i, $pos(E_i)$ is a feature that describes the relative position of E_i to a central line dividing the keyboard into two parts- *left(L)* and *right(R)*.
2. **Distance Between Successive Keypress Events:** For each pair of suc-cessive keypress events, $dist(E_i, E_j)$ is a feature that describes the distance between the two keypress events for a given pair. For a pre-determined value α, $dist(E_i, E_j)$ is either *near(N)* or *far(R)* where $N < \alpha$ and $R \geq \alpha$.

Each pair of successive keypress event (E_i, E_j) is represented by $pos(E_i)\|$ $pos(E_j)\|dist(E_i, E_j)$ where $\|$ represents feature concatenation. Any word can thus be represented by a sequence of concatenated features for each event-pair appearing in the word. For example, let $\alpha = 3$ and consider a partition of a QWERTY keyboard. All keys on the left of 't', 'f' and 'v' (inclusive) are assigned to the first partition named **Left**. The remaining keys are assigned to partition named **Right**. The word **rope** can then be represented as:

$$RO . OP . PE$$
$$LRF.RRN.RLF$$

It is clear from the above example that a word of n letters can be broken down into $n - 1$ constituent character representation in the attack model. This is a compact representation of words. The corresponding text can be extracted by processing it as shown in the following section.

2.2 Attack

The attack consists of two phases, supervised learning and analysis which we outline in multiple steps as follows.

Data Collection: When a key is pressed, the mobile application records the surface vibrations produced in the process and stores a three dimensional vector

(x, y and z axes) per sample in a log. The log thus generated, is a dump of raw accelerometer readings obtained using the victims phone.

Feature Extraction: Next, simple statistical metrics are computed over the collected data to yield a compact representation consisting of the following feature vector corresponding to each keypress.

$$Keypress(E_i) =$$
$$(mean, kurtosis, variance, min, max, energy, rms, mfccs, ffts)$$

Feature Labelling: To train the system, the above two steps are performed using a chosen dictionary of words. Next, each word in the training dictionary is broken down into a LR/NR (Left-Right Near-Far) representation. The model prepares a training data set by labelling feature vectors extracted in the previous step as either left(L) or right(R) for individual keys. For key-pair samples the feature vectors of each of the constituent letters is concatenated together and then this composite vector is labelled as either near(N) or far(F). After this step, we will have a training set containing labelled feature vectors.

Neural Network Setup: Two neural networks are created from the training set obtained — one for classifying left-right feature vectors (hereon, referred to as L/R classifier) and the near-far feature vectors (hereon, referred to as N/F classifier). After training using the labelled data from the dictionary; these two neural networks can be used to classify and label accelerometer readings from the log obtained from the victim as L/R or N/F.

Word Matcher: The word matcher assigns a score against each word in the dictionary to each of the word representation it obtains from the previous steps. The scored dictionary words are then sorted on the basis of their scores and the top k results are presented as predictions for the given representation.

2.3   Attack Efficiency before Application of Defences

As our first experimental step, we reproduced the Marquardt keyboard sniffing attack [1]. It involved two experiments to measure the accuracy of the two classifiers involved, and two experiments to measure the recovery of text. We obtained comparable accuracy results as the original authors. Marquardt et al. recovered 80% of the text from a self-built context-aware dictionary in the top 5 guesses. In comparison, we were able to recover 76% of the text.

3   Effectiveness of Marquardt's Attack under Random Noise

Given the relatively high accuracy of the attack, we devised a series of further experiments to analyse the Marquardt attack in a practical setting of a motivated defender. Specifically, we measured the susceptibility of the attack torandomised

Table 1. Table showing results of accuracy of L/R and N/F classifier measured with a single Harvard Sentence. Each column entry is the accuracy of each of the classifiers trained at a sampling rate of the corresponding row header and tested at the corresponding column header.

Sampling Rate	100	80	64	50
Trained at 100	88% (L/R), 76% (N/F)	85%, 70%	76% , 67%	76% , 64%
Trained at 80	85% (L/R), 73% (N/F)	85%, 76%	79% , 67%	73% , 64%
Trained at 64	79% (L/R), 70% (N/F)	79% , 70%	79% , 73%	67% , 64%
Trained at 50	70% (L/R), 64% (N/F)	70% , 67%	67% , 64%	61% , 58%

noise. For each of the following experiments, we measured the accuracies of the two classifiers involved in the attack. Their accuracy is a direct indicator of the rate of text recovery.

3.1   Variation across Keyboards

Marquardt et al claim that their attack does not require violating the physical security of the victim (unlike previous attacks). This implies that the attacker is unaware of the target's keyboard make and model. Therefore, we examine change in attack efficiency when the training keyboard is different from the keyboard on which the attack is applied.

Table 2. Table showing results of accuracy of L/R and N/F classifiers measured with a single Harvard Sentence. Each column entry is the accuracy of each of the classifiers trained with the data collected from the keyboard of the corresponding row header and tested with data collected from the keyboard of the corresponding column header.

Keyboards	K1	K2	K3	K4	K5
Trained K1	88%(L/R),76%(N/F)	76%,64%	70%,58%	52%,47%	52%,50%
Trained K2	76%(L/R),67%(N/F)	91%,70%	73%,61%	58%,50%	52%,52%
Trained K3	70%(L/R),61%(N/F)	73%,61%	85%,73%	64%,52%	58%,52%
Trained K4	58%(L/R),50%(N/F)	61%,55%	61%,58%	85%,70%	73%,73%
Trained K5	58%(L/R),52%(N/F)	55%,52%	64%,55%	76%,70%	79%,70%

We used the following keyboards in our set:

- K1: a HP KB-0316 keyboard.
- K2: a SK-1688 keyboard.
- K3: an Intex keyboard-M/M Rolex.
- K4: an iBall KB279 keyboard.
- K5: a Wipro SK-2030 keyboard.

We trained the attack classifiers on acoustic vibrations from one of the keyboards from the set followed by an attack targeting every other keyboard in the set. We evaluate attack efficiency by measuring classifier accuracy. The results are shown in Table 2.

Keyboards K1 and K5 have identical layouts but differ in terms of spacing between adjacent keys. Thus training on K1 and attacking K5, results in decreased attack efficiency. Similarly, keyboards K1 and K2 nearly identical spacing between keys resulting in similar attack efficiency.

3.2   Impact of Sampling Rate on Attack Efficiency

Apart from the accelerometer sensor itself, the sensitivity and resolution of the accelerometer is also dependent on the firmware settings and the mobile operating system's data handling and delivery mechanisms. We assume a broad spectrum of available accelerometer sampling rates and measure the accuracy of the attack. We do this by training the attack framework with a particular sampling rate and test it against data collected at a higher or lower sampling rate. We noted the accuracy of the L/R and N/F classifiers at various sampling rates, this is presented in Table 1. Each column in the given table indicates the accuracy achieved by the L/R and N/F classifier when Experiment 1 — Using a single Harvard sentence was conducted. The phone was trained with the sampling rate in the corresponding row header and tested with a sampling rate of the corresponding column header.

Table 1 shows that the sampling rate impacts accuracy of the attack. A attack classifier trained at a certain sampling rate has somewhat reduced efficiency at lower sampling rates. Roughly, a 20% reduction in sampling rate reduces attack accuracy by 10% to 15%.

3.3   Defensive Vibrations

So far we have considered the challenges faced during reproduction of the attack in a practical setting. We now consider automated defences against the entire class of covert-channel attacks that leverage vibrations induced on shared physical surfaces. Our approach to defence is to "sanitise" the physical surface supporting a user device using additional user-controlled devices that transmit **defensive vibrations** into the shared physical medium. Defensive vibrations can be introduced according to a variety of strategies. An optimal strategy would be to transmit well designed signals waveforms into the shared medium such that the user-dependent vibration signals are exactly cancelled out. A simpler and more obvious strategy is to introduce random vibrations which we explore in this section.

Therefore, in our next experiment we used a buzzer within a *defender* phone (of the type found on conventional mobilephones/pagers) to produce acoustic vibrations in various configurations (distances and angle) with respect to the locations of the attack smartphone. A defensive buzz (induced vibration from the buzzer) consists of switching the vibrator (defender's phone) on and off periodically for the duration of the attack. It depends on three parameters: relative location from attacker phone and keyboard, the signal amplitude (buzz volume), signal-on duration, and signal-off duration.

In our experiments, the attack phone and the keyboard were placed four inches apart while the defender phone was placed at various positions relative to them, as follows.

- Keyboard, attacker phone, and defender phone are placed in a straight line. Defender phone is placed between the keyboard and the attacker phone at a distance of one inch from the keyboard.
- Keyboard, attacker phone, and defender phone are placed in a straight line. Defender phone is placed one inch from the attacker phone.
- Keyboard, attacker phone, and defender phone are not placed in a straight line. Defender phone is placed one inch directly below the attacker phone.

At each of these positions, defensive buzzing was continuously applied for the duration of the attack at three different intensities from a Nokia-2100 phone — gentle (signal-on for 0.5 seconds signal-off for 2 seconds), medium (signal-on 0.5, signal-off 1 second), and aggressive (signal-on 0.5 seconds, signal-off 0.5 seconds). We trained the attack classifiers using a single Harvard sentence and calculated the accuracy of the L/R and N/F classifier at each of those points at each of the specified pace. We averaged out the results at each point for each of the specified intensity of defensive buzzing. The results are as shown in Table 3.

Table 3. Table showing results of accuracy of L/R and N/F classifier measured with a single Harvard Sentence while injecting noise with defensive buzzing at various paces. Each result in the column entry is averaged out from three pre-decided points.

Buzzing intensity	L/R	N/F
Gentle	85%	76%
Medium	79%	73%
Aggressive	70%	61%

We observe that aggressive buzzing is able to lower the classification rate to just 61%, which is ten percent better than a random guess. We believe that by better calibration, defensive buzzing can achieve much improved results.

3.4 Data Collector as a Source of Acoustic Noise

We now consider active defences where the victim's phone (so far referred to as the attacker phone) also participates in the defence mechanism. A possible defence allowed by the Marquardt threat model is the direct injection of noise into the attacker's data on the smartphone itself. Therefore, we analysed the effects of playing music on attacker/victim smartphone on attack efficiency. Again, a completely plausible scenario.

In this experiment, we played ten songs each from the following categories: Rock, Pop, Jazz, Classical, Blues, Hip Hop, R&B and Bollywood. We tried to pick as diversified songs as possible from the sub genres of each category. We measured the efficiency of the classifier in each case. The results are as shown in Table 4.

Table 4. Table showing results of accuracy of L/R and N/F classifier measured with a single Harvard Sentence while playing a song. Each result in the column entry is averaged out for 10 songs from each category.

Music Genre	L/R	N/F
Rock	44%	38%
Pop	47%	47%
Jazz	41%	38%
Classical	29%	41%
Blue	38%	44%
Hip Hop	29%	44%
R&B	38%	47%
Bollywood	29%	26%

For all categories, the accuracy was less than 50% which means that the classifier's detection rate at deciding the relative position of the keypress was worse than a coin toss.

Additional sources of noise: Calling/Receiving a phone and connecting via text messaging are among the most basic functionality of a mobile phone. In a real-world setting, the victim's phone could receive a text message, or receive a call, or buzz in response to event notifications. In workplaces, most of the phones are usually set to vibrate mode and even if not, phones often ring as well as vibrate. To understand the change in attack efficiency as a result of noise resulting from day-to-day operations, we ran the following experiments.

1. We generated a notification by text messaging the phone while the malicious application was running. This could be seen as any notification as usually the notification alert is similar (if not same) in android.
2. We called the victim phone while the attack was in progress. We however, did not receive the call as it would disturb the orientation of phone and the experiment is merely to understand the affect of vibrations produced by the phone. The attack obviously would fail if the victim picks up her phone from the table itself.

For each of the two scenarios, we conducted the experiment ten times and averaged out the results. In scenario one, the accuracy of the L/R classifier was noted to be 67% and the N/F classifier was only accurate 55% of the time. In scenario two, the accuracy of both the L/R classifier and the N/F classifier was noted to be 41% and 35% respectively. Therefore, suggesting that attack efficiency is very low if the victim receives a call during the attack.

4   Conclusions and Future Work

We have demonstrated that several simple defence options against the Marquardt attack are available to the motivated defender. Something as trivial as a periodic buzz can reduce the attack efficiency to 61%. Better defences are obtained by inducing low-frequency acoustic noise resulting in lowering attack efficiency to less than 50% (in a binary choice problem).

We have demonstrated that the attack can fail under various day-to-day scenarios. However, this is due to the limitations of the signal processing techniques which are not noise-tolerant. Overall, the application of machine learning techniques for statistical analysis of sensitive user data is fraught with difficulties. In particular, the ML technique used by Marquardt et al. is easily thwarted by random perturbations.

In future work, we will establish a comprehensive defence mechanism which can "cancel" the acoustic vibrations induced by a keyboard, hence moving towards a provably secure mechanism which can prevent the flow of data across the acoustic channels involved in the attack. The idea is to sanitise the nearby environment in a manner such that the sensor picking up data cannot differentiate between the instance of keyboard being typed on and the instance when it is not. That would ensure that irrespective of the attack mechanism or the algorithm used behind such an attack, it would be defended against.

References

1. Marquardt, P., Verma, A., Carter, H., Traynor, P. (sp)iPhone: Decoding Vibrations From Nearby Keyboards Using Mobile Phone Accelerometers. In: Proceedings of ACM Conference on Computer and Communications Security, CCS (2011)
2. Berger, Y., Wool, A., Yeredor, A.: Dictionary Attacks Using Keyboard Acoustic Emanations. In: Proceedings of the ACM Conference on Computer and Communications Security, CCS (2006)
3. Cai, L., Machiraju, S., Chen, H.: Defending Against Sensor-Sniffing Attacks on Mobile Phones. In: Proceedings of ACM SIGCOMM Workshop on Networking, Systems, Applications on Mobile Handhelds, MobiHeld (2009)
4. Mobile that allows bosses to snoop on staff developed BBC NEWS- Technology. Web (July 27, 2010), http://news.bbc.co.uk/2/hi/technology/8559683.stm/
5. Owusu, E., Han, J., Das, S., Perrig, A., Zhang, J.: ACCessory: Password Inference using Accelerometers on Smartphones. In: HotMobile 2012 - The 13th International Workshop on Mobile Computing Systems and Applications (2012)
6. Asonov, D., Agrawal, R.: Keyboard Acoustic Emanations. In: Proceedings of the IEEE Symposium on Security and Privacy (2004)
7. I.S. on Subjective Measurements. IEEE recommended practices for speech quality measurements. IEEE Transactions on Audio and Electroacoustics 17, 227–246 (1969)
8. Nagaraja, S., Anderson, R.: The snooping dragon: social-malware surveillance of the Tibetan movement. In: technical report UCAM-CL-TR-746, University of Cambridge (2009)
9. Schlegel, R., Zhang, K., Zhou, X., Mehool, I., Kapadia, A., Wang, X.: Soundcomber: A stealthy and context-aware sound trojan for smartphones. In: Proceedings of the 18th Annual Network and Distributed System Security Symposium, NDSS 2011 (2011)

Simple Defences against Vibration-Based Keystroke Fingerprinting Attacks (Transcript of Discussion)

Shishir Nagaraja

University of Birmingham

Good morning everybody, my name is Shishir Nagaraja, and I'm from the University of Birmingham. Welcome to the talk. This is a fairly practical talk where we are looking at vibration-based covert channels. The basic idea is very simple. You've got a phone, it sits next to a keyboard (laptop or conventional), when you press the keys, the phone tells you what keys were pressed by analysing the corresponding vibrations. OK, so that's a fairly simple setup.

In this work, we have analysed the machine learning techniques proposed for converting vibrations into keypresses. A second contribution is a threat model for covert channels. Covert channels have been used in the literature quite a lot, but often in the absence of a clear threat model. This makes it hard to get a handle on what the system can achieve, and what the limitations are.

The ability to meaningfully sense vibrations in human environments gives attackers access to a large amount of information. The potential risks are obvious: privacy invasion, and information theft. You type in keystrokes, your keystrokes are stolen, human drumming patterns on a chair or table can be similarly analysed to determine the person sitting there.

But there are also opportunities here, such as trustworthy information exchange. Together with vibration sensors and sources, you've got a relatively isolated network which doesn't require cables or special purpose infrastructure to set it up. So why would that be useful? It's well understood that a full-sized keyboard is an efficient way of typing, however carrying one everywhere is cumbersome and doesn't fit into the phone anyway. Using a vibration-based channel, this can be conveniently achieved with just a smartphone. I place the phone down on a table and I start typing on the same table, assuming a keyboard were present, and the phone picks it up. That's a constructive capability and you can build collaboration mechanisms over it. However, you can use vibration-based communication channels for stealing people's keystrokes. While a vibration based network is relatively isolated, you still need to tolerate attackers, both active and passive. How do you go about securing communication over vibration communication networks? We have a fairly conventional setup where one or more enemy phones share the communication medium with two or more friendly phones, all on the same table, and you want the authorised (friendly) phones to sense but not the unauthorised (enemy) phones. So that's the problem we're trying to solve. Note that the attacker doesn't actually have to physically place a phone on the table, they can do so by installing malware on a friendly phone using a targeted infection strategy.

B. Christianson et al. (Eds.): Security Protocols 2013, LNCS 8263, pp. 152–160, 2013.
© Springer-Verlag Berlin Heidelberg 2013

Right, so how do vibration-based communication channels actually work? Most smartphones possess a vibration sensor called the accelerometer. Any physical activity that induces vibrations into its surroundings can be sensed by the accelerometer. The accelerometer senses vibrations when you press keys. So you've got some 'traffic' which you are capturing using the accelerometer of the smartphone. You can build a PIN sniffer using this by putting a smartphone on the side of an ATM to read PINs, or you can build a virtual keyboard for smartphone users as we just discussed. So that's the setting.

Now let's briefly discuss the threat model. Often we see research which proposes a covert channel, the paper discusses various technical aspects such as bit-rate without any discussion of attacker capabilities or how easy or difficult it is to induce error in the covert channel. This is typically the way most papers are written in the covert channel literature unlike mainstream computer security literature. I argue that we've got to have a proper threat model in the first place to effectively evaluate covert channels. Of course this means we necessarily have to bring in an application context.

In the case of vibration-based covert channels, we envisage the following attacker capabilities: an obvious attacker is the active attacker who has full control of the smartphone on the table. An active attacker might purposely inject noise into the channel, for instance by engaging the phone's vibrator at well-chosen times. As usual, active attacks are observable which is usually against the interest of the attacker. A second setting is that of a passive attacker who just uses the accelerometer to sense and analyse vibrations. For instance, as a piece of malware running that does not interfere with other applications on the phone.

Aside from active and passive attackers, let me add a few more attacker types. The third type is a chosen-signal attacker. This attacker is modelled in the chosen-plaintext attacker from the security protocols literature. The chosen-plaintext attacker injects vibrations corresponding to keystrokes (plaintext) and tries to analyse the variation in the friendly phone's output caused by the vibration injection to gain an understanding about keyed mechanism used by the friendly phone to convert vibrations to ASCII. The fourth type of attacker model worth considering is the signal-replaying attacker, a weaker form of the chosen-signal attacker who can simply record and replay previous transmissions between friendly devices (keyboard and authorised phone). Finally, a fifth type is the signal-gathering attacker, who gathers multiple signal transmissions and tries to make useful inferences.

Let me briefly talk about the security requirements. This might clarify the motivation behind the threat model. One obvious requirement is secrecy—I don't want the adversary's smartphone to actually understand the keystrokes that I'm writing, but I want the friendly (authorised) phones to understand, so that's the secrecy property. Another requirement is covertness, which is, I don't want the adversary's phone to actually understand that there are any keystrokes being injected into the table in the first place. So the signal-replay attacker is a threat model that makes covertness really, really hard, because you can record a set of signals that's injected, you can repeatedly inject it into the medium, and you can look for differences in output.

To summarise the requirements, firstly unauthorised devices should not be able to read messages from the channel. Second is traffic analysis resistance, which is that unauthorised devices should not be able to distinguish whether the channel is under use or not.

Let me give an overview of the defence approaches we are considering for achieving these requirements. The first approach is to jam the channel. Jamming the channel means you're injecting arbitrary (pseudorandom) vibrations into the table. This can be done by injecting vibrations, say with a phone's vibrator or using a subwoofer facing down, among other techniques. Jamming in this manner disables the channel rendering it useless for both friendly and adversary devices. However that's not very good if you want to actually use it for creative purposes. Instead we propose pseudo-jamming which involves additional pseudorandom noise, which is the output of a key, into the communication medium. Devices which have the keys will be able to make sense of the transmissions but those that don't will not. To be effective, the noise has to be both additive and cancelling. Further, to achieve covertness it is necessary to ensure that the noise that you are adding is credible, because if the noise is not from the same space as normal traffic then clearly you cannot get any covertness, so that's a key requirement.

Earlier I mentioned the use of malware keylogger techniques. A recent paper was written on the topic by Marquardt et al. in CCS 2011 and they basically built a keylogger. Their essential design is as follows: the accelerometer signal coming from a phone is a time series where each element is a vector (X, Y, Z). The low sampling rate on the phones prevents you from mapping an accelerometer signal to a keypress directly. Instead, they map pairs of vibration signals to word pairs using a machine learning technique that requires two features. For example, let's take the word 'Rushil'. When 'r' and 'u' are pressed, or when 'u' and 's' are pressed, you try to distinguish between whether successive keystrokes were near or far. That's the first feature, the distance. The second feature is the position, as to whether each key pressed was to the left side of the keyboard or the right side of the keyboard. So the position of the attacker phone is assumed to be fixed and in addition, it has to be to be fairly close to the keyboard. However that's because of the low sensitivity of current smartphone accelerometers.

Once you've placed the attacker smartphone, you then run a training session to train the classifier. This is done by typing a set of sentences (ground truth) into the keyboard. The corresponding text is also supplied to the classifier on the phone to complete the training. Going back to the example of the word 'Rushil'. If you consider letters 'r' and 'u' then then the features recorded are: position – near (as the keys are close to eachother on a QWERTY keyboard), and distance – Left-Right. Thus position and distance features are recorded for each pair of keypresses. The authors use a neural network based classifier, however that's a rather poor choice amongst the available design options.

So the learning phase goes this way. You've got the raw accelerometer data, you get the feature extraction, which is the L R N or R L F kind of sequences that we just showed, and then you've got the training words with the corresponding representation. And then you just have this labelling part and that's essentially the inference algorithm. Once the attack model has been trained, you can carry out the attack phase, which means you get the raw accelerometer data and convert it into sequences which can be mapped into keystrokes.

It's instructive to try to understand the error tolerance of this mechanism, and then we can look at the attack tolerance. First we examine the effects of sampling. If you train at 100Mhz and then you carry out the attack at 100Mhz, the efficiency of the classifiers is between 88% and 76%. If you train 100 but use it at 50 then detection rate is seriously reduced. Generally, if you train at 100 you get a slightly higher detection rate than if you train at 50, it doesn't really affect it too much, but there's some impact. The other parameter is a change of the keyboard and then you see a bigger impact. Basically if you train it on a particular keyboard and use it on a different keyboard, then the attack doesn't work at all—it's close to the guessing rate because if you have a binary classifier that's working at 52% the detection rate is as good as tossing a coin. Our error tolerance analysis shows that in its current form the Marquardt attack isn't practical. However their limitations are down to the design of their inference algorithm's inability to deal with stochastic noise.

Daniel Thomas: So I am trying to understand what error rate means, I thought there should be two types of error rates, but you are only showing one here, which is success rate of recognising correct text, whereas there should be another one (false-positive rate).

Reply: Yes, so you are completely right, the reason I haven't discussed the false-positive rate is because I am first trying to determine the conditions under which detection will work. Without having a high enough true-positive rate it may not be worth discussing the false-positive rate.

Feng Hao: And your typist is always the same?

Reply: If you attenuate the signal then the error rate would go up, so if you put pads on the bottom and had the same typist, or changed the typist, then yes it does matter. The effects of changing typists is similar to the effect of increasing distance between the keylogger and the keyboard. If you increase that then the attack efficiency falls dramatically. This is due to the low sensitivity of current smartphone accelerometers.

Frank Stajano: And how sensitive is the attack to having the training session done in a completely different environment, because you can't really expect that you would be able to train on the desk where you are going to do the attack with the same guy, and the same computer, and so on. So presumably the attacker would have to train in his home, and then attack one of his acquaintances or friends?

Reply: Fairly sensitive, as you see, on some types of keyboards, so you just change the keyboard or the laptop, for example, on some it tends to work fairly OK, but on other places it's only as good as guessing.

Frank Stajano: I suppose it's not just the keyboard, it's also which table it's on.

Reply: Yes. Different tables can also lead to signal attenuation so these are sort of abstracted into the distance between the phone and the keyboard.

Frank Stajano: But there's plenty more here. What is the mechanical vibrations of the tables, it's completely different from the distance right?

Reply: Well in the sense that the signal gets attenuated by the distance, or it can get attenuated by the conductivity.

Frank Stajano: Is that the only variable, I mean, I have no idea. I'm surprised if that's the only effect, just attenuation. Surely there must be other things than inconvenient stuff that happened differently with different table resonance or other effects which are more interesting.

Reply: Right, OK, I see what you mean. No, I haven't looked at that.

Frank Stajano: How about the transfer function of different tables?

Reply: Resonance aspects and secondary vibrations are also interesting, you're right.

Michael Roe: It would be harder to implement but you could just imagine doing this with an unsupervised machine where there's no training set but you know the system is English so you've got the guy sitting there typing an email or something that gives you enough of a sample and you get vibration from it, and you don't know what their email was, but you have a reasonable guess it's in English, you know the statistics of English.

Robert Watson: And you could find out their character set, because you can send them an email that prompted them to send you an email.

Michael Roe: That would be a stretch?

Robert Watson: It would be a plaintext attack.

Michael Roe: So it's also if you get a known plaintext where you force him to type something, but even if you did, yes, I think you could in principle reconstruct given the unknown text, but knowing it's English, an unknown typist and unknown keyboard, you probably still could reconstruct it, so I think that has to be a threat model of possibility.

Reply: Yes I agree with you. The structure of the language is certainly helping here. I mean, the neural network-based machine learning technique is probably one of the worst candidates of the entire toolkit that machine learning offers. So you could certainly come up with much better machine learning techniques to exploit structural aspects.

Right, so let's now examine the attack tolerance. What happens if you add additional vibrations into the medium, for instance from resonance (Frank's comment)? What we do is inject defensive vibrations comprising sine waves at different frequencies. This is done using a simple desktop-style subwoofer with a 2.5 inch diaphragm, and 130 watts RMS. You place the subwoofer facedown on the table, and then play sine waves. That does quite a bit of damage to attack efficiency. At 1 kilohertz the attack success rate in reproducing sentences is reduced to about 50% of the text that you were getting earlier. At slightly higher frequences, at 50 kilohertz, the attack efficiency dramatically reduces. So if you inject random noise the attack efficiency dramatically comes down. So that I think answers your question to some extent, right Frank?

Frank Stajano: Well it's not quite the same because I'm just talking about, without external noise the transfer characteristics between the keyboard and the phone are literally dependant on the table.

Reply: Okay. The transfer characteristics primarily depend on the 'conductivity' of the table. Wood is an okay conductor, metal is much better. The resonance characteristics come into picture at certain frequencies only which is a function of table material as well as dimensions.

Daniel Thomas: If this just turned sideways, and there's no noise in it is there? This is a predictable sign wave?

Reply: It is a predictable sine wave, yes.

Daniel Thomas: So it's not noise, you could subtract it.

Reply: Yes.

Frank Stajano: If he has been trained without it then you have to guess that he has?

Reply: Yes.

Michael Roe: But a reasonable threat model is the attacker knows you're doing this and so does the obvious bit of processing to remove the sine wave.

Reply: Absolutely, yes, I think so. Better still as we've suggested in the paper, if you add random values to the accelerometer input that's coming into the smartphone, it becomes very hard for the attacker to make any sense out of it, right?

Frank Stajano: How annoying is this for the person who's at the table and have these things going bzzzz.

Reply: It can be pretty annoying because you can stand here and you can feel the vibrations, I mean, from the table.

Frank Stajano: But I'm just imagining you are in a situation like this and the guy behind you keeps shaking his leg against the chair, I mean, it's really annoying.

Reply: It's a little it, I mean, it's a bit faster than that because the frequency is a bit faster than that, because they don't do it 50 times a second.

Frank Stajano: Especially if you have the sine wave.

Audience: What about a room full of people each with their own? If it's a cube farm, a big office building, everyone has their desk, and they all are doing it, then could the building actually fall down?

Reply: Perhaps, if you hit the resonant notes with enough amplitude, but I am not sure.

Audience: To go back to the question from Frank, if you're in a cube farm you're sitting on something that's probably got some padding on it that might absorb those vibrations, and so I think it's really important that you consider the material that the phones are sitting on. I mean, have you done any testing, if you had a tablecloth on it as opposed to a solid surface?

Reply: No.

Audience: I see.

Reply: OK, so if you don't have a subwoofer, the other even more irritating alternative is to actually use a couple of defence phones on vibratory mode, and

you can do a sort of gentle 50 milliseconds followed by a two second silence, I
don't know which one is more irritating, or a more aggressive one, which is 50
milliseconds followed by 100 milliseconds of silence, and on the classifier you can
start to see that with the aggressive one you can start pushing down the attack
efficiency to some extent.

Audience: How about a real vibrator?

Reply: A real vibrator?

Audience: What people really mean when they say vibrator.

Reply: OK, so jamming is basically denial-of-service, but we can do something slightly better, a pseudorandom alternative which is what I'm currently
working on. Basically you generate random noise from a seeded uniform distribution. The seed acts as a key, and all devices which share the key with
synchronised boundaries can infer the correct vibrations while the unauthorised
devices sense noise alone.

Frank Stajano: Well just plug in some music, why does it have to be annoying, you can just listen to your favourite ?

Reply: Yes you can do that, and it works pretty well, as could several other
alternatives mentioned in the paper.

But I think basically it has the same problem as using a sine wave because
it's going to have structure, and then you can use the structure to isolate and
discard the blinding effects of the acoustic wave. Therefore, you have to have a
uniform distribution over frequencies. In addition, you need to have the combined
effects of wave energy addition and cancellation. Note that if you had only one
of them then the shape energy envelope of the keystrokes would still be in the
distribution, and then you could extract the keystroke from that.

So the main point is this gives you some secrecy but there's no covertness in
it. So I have a uniform pseudorandom generator, it's obviously not covert, even
my neighbours know that I have the jamming switched on, right, because they
might feel it through the floor.

Sandy Clark: Are you sure it's not because you're just having a party?

Reply: I am not too sure, yes, maybe it goes to what Frank was saying
about the vibrator. So spying on other people's keystrokes using smartphone,
you know, accelerometers isn't trivial, they are fairly easy to break, so that's
one thing. It's easy to defend basically by jamming the tabletop network, you
saw that picture already. So better defences are achieved by pseudo-jamming
based on shared keys, but achieving covertness is going to be hard because what
you'd have to do is, you'd have to simulate vibrations from the distribution of
whatever keystrokes based vibration is injected into the table. So you'd have to
draw from that distribution, and you'd have to probably come up with some
pretty neat ways of directional injection of waveforms to cancel the keystrokes
perhaps, that's going to be future work.

Frank Stajano: Covert, and so you're pretending you're not typing?

Reply: Well the phone doesn't know whether you're typing or not, yes, but
the jamming should not be obvious either.

Frank Stajano: Is the assumption that, of course the guy who wants to be covert doesn't know that the phone is tracking him? Why does it have to be? I'm not too sure I understand.

Reply: If you're using the table as a communication channel it shouldn't be obvious whether you're communicating or not.

Frank Stajano: Right, but if you're worried about it why don't you check whether there are any phones on the table?

Reply: That may not be obvious.

Audience: If I want to record your keystrokes that way I probably would stick my cellphone to the bottom of the table.

Reply: There are lots of ways.

Frank Stajano: Right, then I am still worried about whether when I type people detected I typed or not.

Audience: You can put another mat under the keyboard, and a tablecloth for either table, does that mean that that there is no longer a channel?

Reply: No, it just reduces the amplitudes of the signal, but it's not equivalent to signal absence; a more sensitive accelerometer will pick up the signal. What you actually want is the signal cancelling out. Otherwise, you're on weak ground as you are fighting an arms race with the sensitivity of the accelerometers and hoping to win.

Audience: Yes, but there's an amount of noise being derived anyway, and if you're pushing the noise to the noise limit

Reply: Well remember that you also want your smartphone to work in the same situation, so if you jam it, or you reduce it to a noise floor, that's not going to happen.

Audience: But do you get initially good signal to your phone that you can type on your keyboard and it would work effectively?

Reply: It is an app on the market.

Audience: OK.

Frank Stajano: Is the phone that is listening to you your own phone?

Reply: So you've got one phone, which is your own phone, and you pretend it's a keyboard and type and it understands, and then the attacker phone, which is trying to get the same stuff but that shouldn't work.

Audience: In that case it's not a covert channel, it's an intentional channel.

Reply: So that's an intentional channel, yes.

Frank Stajano: But you can't plausibly want to use this iPhone app and be covert in your typing, right.

Reply: You might want to be. The friendly phone running the app obviously understands, but you are covert in your typing as far as the enemy phone is concerned (the one that doesn't have the secret key).

Alec Yasinsac: If you're using the iPhone app you want the iPhone to know you're typing.

Reply: Yes.

Frank Stajano: But you want nobody else to know that you're typing.

Reply: Yes.

Robert Watson: Have you looked at the power use implications of this?

Reply: Not too bad, I think, but I haven't measured. Essentially you're just having the accelerometer on to collect the data, and the processing is done offline.

Robert Watson: I was wondering about the power use of vibrating the further relay and things like that.

Reply: No, I didn't look at that, no.

Daniel Thomas: When you have the accelerometer on it's basically free if you've only got a CPU on?

Michael Roe: I seem to remember something in the book Spycatcher, where they're not just, where they're doing the roll thing of Tempest, when they're looking at electromagnetic emanations from cipher machines, but they also look at the audio emanations from the electromechanical cipher missions of the era, so this idea that you might be able to monitor what the Russians are sending by listening to the teleprinter chatter from their cipher machines. And I think it's something that goes back a way in the literature. So it's a similar sort of thing.

Communication Setup in Anonymous Messaging

Francesco Bergadano

Dipartimento di Informatica
Università degli Studi di Torino
francesco.bergadano@di.unito.it

Abstract. In anonymous group messaging any group member may wish to send a message anonymously to the other members, and all members follow a defined protocol. Not all members can be trusted, meaning that some may disclose relevant information to an adversary, and our adversary could have complete access to network communications.

We will discuss here the protocol setup and start-up phase in anonymous messaging: this phase is highly critical and can actually compromise the anonymity of subsequent communication the very goal we wanted to achieve. The start-up phase actually represents a secondary communication channel, where relevant information is released, that can be caught by an adversary.

Two cases will be discussed: onion routing (section 1) and token passing (section 2).

The first case dates back to Mix-nets [1], and has being addressed in substantial later research [13–15]. Here we will specifically refer to the newest real-world Internet implementation of Tor, as described in [2]. In Tor, we have a free topology, where the actual path of messages within the onion router (OR) network is chosen at the source. This path-setup phase can be seen as part of communications on a secondary channel, that can provide useful information to an adversary.

The second case is based on new protocol, based on token passing over a fixed ring topology. The method can be related to some characteristics of DC-nets [6, 16, 17], and in particular to the Dissent [3] system. In the token passing system a start-up phase requires choosing the node that will first transmit relevant information, as well as guaranteeing that any node will be able to communicate (anti-starvation policy). The start-up phase, again, may contain secondary channels that will need special attention. The discussion is limited to 3 nodes, and the general n-node case is left for future work.

1 Onion Routing

Onion routing, as implemented in Tor [2], is based on the operation of so-called Onion Proxies (OPs) and Onion Routers (ORs). ORs have the same role of mixes in [1], while OPs interface to the user systems. Because Tor is a practical, real-world Internet system, it has to deal with the fact that, for efficiency reasons, encryption will have to be symmetric, and not only based on public key cryptography as was the case for Mix-nets.

B. Christianson et al. (Eds.): Security Protocols 2013, LNCS 8263, pp. 161–169, 2013.
© Springer-Verlag Berlin Heidelberg 2013

Because of this need for symmetric encryption with short-term keys, such keys will have to be distributed and shared between the OP and the first OR in a desired path, and between adjacent ORs on the path. A path and the corresponding keys will determine a so-called "circuit", allowing to send anonymous messages.

Let us first discuss the general Mix-net case, we will then come back to Tor and to the problems connected to the setup phase, where a circuit is created.

1.1   Mix-nets and Traffic Analysis

In mix-nets, some message M_A, sent by user A, is encrypted n times for a number of intermediate mixes $R_1, ,R_n$. Every encryption also carries the address of the next mix, and a random value N_i, needed to prevent someone from guessing the encryption input from the previous step.

Although this work is very well known, we will briefly review it, and then restate it in a modified context, so as to understand more clearly some consequences for anonymity when network-wide eavesdropping is possible. In the original proposal of mix nets, message M_A is sent from A to B through a sequence of mixes $R_1, ,R_n$. Initially, A sends to R_n the following message:

$$E_n(N_n, R_{n-1}, E_{n-1}(N_{n-1}, R_{n-2}, E_{n-2}(\ldots(E_1(N_1, B, E_B(N_B, null, M_A)))\ldots)))$$

where E_i is the encryption for R_i, e.g. encryption with the public key of R_i. R_n will then strip the outer encryption layer, throw away the random value N_n, and forward the following message to R_{n-1}:

$$E_{n-1}(N_{n-1}, R_{n-2}, E_{n-2}(\ldots(E_1(N_1, B, E_B(N_B, null, M_A)))\ldots))$$

Finally, B will strip the last encryption layer, and obtain the message M_A. Each mix only knows its predecessor and its successor, but does not know the rest of the chain.

It is well-known that, if there is a global eavesdropper, the above discussion will be insufficient when anonymity is desired [2]. Suppose, in an extreme case, that only one message is sent through the network, and it goes from A to B through the n mixes as explained above. For the global eavesdropper, seeing all the messages (though unable to decrypt them), it will be evident that the message is from A to B. If the message is then published by B, it will be clear that A is the origin. When many messages run through the onion routers, traffic and timing analysis will be more difficult, but in general not impossible if further assumptions are not made. The situation is informally depicted in Fig. 1.

In running onion routing infrastructures, one is faced with two contrasting needs:

– It is desirable to have many mixes, so that the user will not have to trust just a few mixes, that might collude and break the user's anonymity. E.g.,

Sender2 → R1 → R2 → R3 → Receiver
Sender1 → R6 → R2 → R4 → Receiver

Fig. 1. Mix-nets and traffic analysis

when using the Anonymizer [4], the user will need absolute trust in that one system, because the Anonymizer proxy could itself trace all of the user's traffic. In Tor, more than 30 mixes are used in different countries, and all would need to collude to link messages to users in the general case.

- It is desirable to have lots of messages going through mixes [2], otherwise traffic analysis may link initial input to final output, hence allowing an eavesdropper to identify message origin. To have many messages traverse the mixes, however, one should have a smaller number of mixes, to be used by the highest possible number of users.

1.2   Circuit Setup in Tor

In Tor the same Mix-net framework is used, but encryption is done with symmetric keys. The user communicates with an Onion Proxy (OP), and subsequent nodes are Onion Routers (ORs). A circuit has then to be constructed, so that, upon receipt of a cell, an OR knows which OR to forward the cell to, and what symmetric encryption key to use.

In order to setup a circuit:

1. The OP will send a first 'create' message to a first OR (call it OR1), specifying a new circuit link name (call it C1), and her own half of a DH handshake.
2. OR1 will reply with the other half of the DH handshake, so that OP and OR1 share a key.
3. To extend the circuit, the OP will send an 'extend' message to OR1, specifying the same circuit link name C1, and the next OR in the circuit to be constructed, say OR2, as well a DH information needed for generating the key to be shared by OP and OR2, encrypted with OR2's public key.
4. OR1 will now send a 'create' message to OR2, forwarding OP's DH handshake, and a new circuit link name, say C2. OR1 maintains a table that links OP's C1, with C2 and OR2, but this correspondence need not be known to OR2.
5. OR2 will then reply to OR1 with its own DH info.
6. OR1 will forward OR2's DH info to OP, so that OP and OR2 will now share a secret key.
7. The same circuit extension process (steps 3 to 6) is repeated by substituting OR2 to OR1 and OR3 to OR2. The communication actually goes through OR1, too, as if it contained application data to be relayed.

The above process is depicted in Fig. 2 - arrows may correspond to multiple messages over ORs.

$$- \to^1$$
$$\text{OP \ OR1 \ OR2 \ OR3}$$
$$\leftarrow -^2$$

$$- - -- \to^3$$
$$\text{OP \ OR1 \ OR2 \ OR3}$$
$$\leftarrow - - --^4$$

$$- - - - - - \to^5$$
$$\text{OP \ OR1 \ OR2 \ OR3}$$
$$\leftarrow - - - - - -^6$$

Fig. 2. Circuit Setup Pattern

Once the circuit is set up, data can be relayed over the circuit as in Mix-nets, but symmetric keys are used. So, in the example of Fig. 3, the OP will encrypt data for OR3, then again for OR2, and finally for OR1, and send it to OR1 specifying C1 as a circuit. OR1 will decrypt once, find the content to be still encrypted, then relay data to OR2, with circuit name C2. OR2 will do the same. OR3 will finally receive a data relay cell, decrypt it, and find it to be plain content, non-encrypted. OR3 will then route the traffic as simple TCP/IP connections.

$$- \to^1 - \to^2 - \to^3$$
$$\text{OP \ OR1 \ OR2 \ OR3} \leftrightarrow^4 \text{TCP responder}$$
$$\leftarrow -^7 \leftarrow -^6 \leftarrow -^5$$

Fig. 3. Data Relay Pattern

Every OR, as a Mix in Mix-nets, will know the preceding and following OR, but not the rest of the circuit, nor the originating OP. However, TOR relay data cells are subject to traffic analysis by a global eavesdropper, just as discussed for Mix-nets in the previous subsection. Moreover, the circuit setup phase can be detected by an eavesdropper.

The circuit setup and data relay patterns are different and can be detected by eavesdropping. Even though the content of messages is not known, the particular sequence of messages may give evidence of a circuit being constructed, with the identity of the participating ORs.

In Fig. 2 (circuit setup), in fact, the sequence of messages is

1. OP $\to$ OR1
2. OR1 $\to$ OP,
3. OP $\to$ OR1, OR1 $\to$ OR2

4. OR2 → OR1, OR1 → OP
5. OP → OR1, OR1 → OR2, OR2 → OR3
6. OR3 → OR2, OR2 → OR1, OR1 → OP

whilst in Fig. 3 (data relay), the sequence is

1. OP → OR1
2. OR1→ OR2
3. OR2→ OR3
4. TCP/IP traffic to and from OR3
5. OR3 → OR2
6. OR2 → OR1
7. OR1 → OP

Even though the content of messages is not known, a global eavesdropper acquires important info about circuit members and sequence, that could help identify message origin in subsequent data relay phases. Circuit setup can then be viewed as a critical secondary channel.

2 Token Passing

We will now describe a new protocol for anonymous messaging, that is based on a ring topology and on a token passing approach. The basic idea is to have a fixed topology (a ring), so that communication has to flow around all nodes in the ring, and there is no need for a dangerous circuit setup phase. In this paper, we will limit the description to three nodes, ongoing research is being pursued to extend the method to an arbitrary number of nodes. We will first describe the protocol, and then address secondary channel and system setup issues.

Let us then suppose the group is composed of three members, namely A, B and C. Suppose also that the three members can communicate with each other as in a token ring LAN protocol. This is reminiscent of the IEEE token ring topology [10], where messages are exchanged as tokens traveling around the ring. In this case, we have a ring with 3 nodes (namely A, B and C), that are circularly connected, as in a ring topology.

We suppose each group member has a pair of asymmetric keys, and that the public keys are securely known to all group members. We will call the public keys PK(A), PK(B), PK(C), and the corresponding private keys SK(A), SK(B), SK(C).

Suppose now that A wants to anonymously send a message M_A to the group. A will then encrypt for B, sending $E_{PK(B)}(M_A)$ to B. We will say in this case, that A has "seized" the token, as in IEEE 802.5 (token ring). B does now know if the originator of the message is A, because A could also have forwarded a message received from C.

If, on the contrary, A does not wish to send a message to the group, A will send to B an encrypted dummy: $E_{PK(B)}$(dummy1). The dummy is recognizable as such , so B will know there is no message and will be able to insert his own message, if desired.

If a non-dummy message is received, B will forward the message to C, after re-encrypting for C. In this case B sends $E_{PK(C)}(M_A)$ to C. C does not know whether the originator of the message is B or A.

C will now forward the message to A, and send $E_{PK(A)}(M_A)$. A will receive and decrypt , and will recognize it as the message she had previously sent. So A will absorb the token, as in IEEE token ring, and will release a dummy. So A will send $E_{PK(B)}(dummy)$ to B. B will now have a chance to insert his own message, if desired, or pass a new empty token (with a newly generated dummy) to C. The dummy should be fresh, i.e. each new dummy should be different from previously used dummies. The above example is illustrated in the following three-party protocol:

1. $A \rightarrow B : E_{PK(B)}(M_A)$
2. $B \rightarrow C : E_{PK(C)}(M_A)$
3. $C \rightarrow A : E_{PK(A)}(M_A)$
4. $A \rightarrow B : E_{PK(B)}(dummy1)$

We will now discuss two issues that can be seen as related to a subtle type of secondary channel, where the adversary uses information about which node starts the process, and draws conclusions that may help identify the message source.

2.1   Starvation Avoidance

Consider the above three-party protocol. If, after absorbing the token, A will send a new message, instead of a dummy as in message (4), it will keep occupying the ring, denying others the chance to communicate. If the same happens again and again, only A will communicate and other group members will starve.

One could solve the problem as in token ring protocols, and force the node that ate the token to release a dummy afterwards, as in the above three-party protocol. This, however, will not work in this context, because it will destroy anonymity. To understand this, consider again the above three-party protocol. Member C will have received an informative message in (2) and will have forwarded an informative message in (3). Suppose now that, in the next round, C receives again an informative message, as described below:

1. $A \rightarrow B : E_{PK(B)}(M_A)$
2. $B \rightarrow C : E_{PK(C)}(M_A)$
3. $C \rightarrow A : E_{PK(A)}(M_A)$
4. $A \rightarrow B : E_{PK(B)}(dummy1)$
5. $B \rightarrow C : E_{PK(C)}(M_B)$

In this case C knows the message originates from B, if the rule of "mandatory dummy after eating token" was applied. In fact, in the previous round, C does not know if message (2) originates from B or from A. However, if it originated from B, seeing a non-dummy at step (5) would be impossible.

This is solved by having the member who absorbed the token flip a coin, and forward a dummy or a content message accordingly. So, in the latest example above, message (4) could be a dummy with probability $1/2$, or a new information message $E_{PK(B)}(M_A^1)$ with probability $1/2$. In this case the above situation does not occur, and the probability of starvation rapidly approaches zero as information flows around the ring: after n rounds, the probability of A never releasing a dummy, and B starving, is $1/2^n$.

2.2 Protocol Start-up

In the previous method, anonymity is destroyed if some group member can easvesdrop on all traffic, simply because the first group member sending any kind of communication is also the originator of the message. We then need to define a protocol start-up phase that will prevent sender detection via starter detection.

The issue is quite tricky, and easily overlooked. However, let's follow this line of reasoning:

-   Suppose there is no traffic on the network (power was just turned on and no previous messages were sent). Suppose also A sends a first encrypted info to B. This has to be a dummy, otherwise B knows for sure it originates from A (cannot have been forwarded from C).
-   Suppose now that after this first message from A to B, that everyone knows to be a dummy, an information-carrying message is sent from B to C. Then C knows it is from B, and not from A, since the previous message was a dummy.
-   The same reasoning goes on and on, and no one is able to start without being detected.

So it looks like the protocol is ok when it is up and running, but it cannot be started securely. How can this be solved? We propose the following solution: let any node start spinning a dummy token around the ring, and let A, B, and C wait an unpredictable amount of time, before they send their first message.

More formally, let each group member define a time interval [Low, High], that is not revealed to the other members (e.g. A could define [3 seconds, 10 seconds], while B could define [5 seconds, 8 seconds]). When the protocol starts, each member waits a random amount of time within his defined interval, then sends a message if desired. The time intervals are re-initialized periodically, so that they cannot be detected by observation.

In the above discussion, the very act of 'starting to speak' creates a secondary channel, even though the content of the message is not known (in fact the adversary is not even supposed to know if it is a message or a dummy).

2.3 Anonymity and Randomness

There seems to be some connection between anonymity and randomness. Well, there is a similar connection between secrecy and randomness. In a deterministic, randomness-free world, God can see all the sins (no secrecy), and similarly he will know all the sinners (no anonymity). We will address the issue more technically below.

For secrecy, randomness is needed for key generation. If our adversary can predict our pseudo-random numbers, she will bypass all our cryptographic tools, no matter how secure.

For anonymity, all protocols we know need some kind of true-randomness. Some, like the token passing method described in this paper, need it for a number of reasons, including the generation of cryptographic keys. Others, like DC-nets [6], that can work without cryptographic keys, need randomness for some other reason.

The fact that DC-nets need randomness is easily seen, even in the original 3-party description by Chaum [6]: each dining cryptographer needs to flip a coin to start the protocol. If our adversary can predict the coin flipping result, anonymity is lost. DC-nets also need to generate random numbers in order to avoid collisions, i.e. message generation by more than one party in the same round. Knowing who is allowed to send the message is the same as knowing the next message origin, if only one member is allowed to communicate at a time. Hence members will need to wait a random and unpredictable amount of time after a collision is detected, or some other form of system-wide initialization is needed. It looks like dining cryptographers also go along with some secondary channel that is related to the need for a start-up phase.

Shuffled-send methods [3, 5] require randomness to produce an unpredictable shuffle. This is also done in mix-nets, though in a less systematic way, by requiring onion routers to delay transmission until some suitable batch of messages is received, so that individual messages may be forwarded in some different, unpredictable order.

3   Conclusions

When dealing with anonymity, secondary channels are everywhere. Well, it's no surprise: one registers to some anonymity-preserving service, and part of the anonymity is instantly gone.

We have highlighted some cases that are relevant in well know anonymity approaches (Mix-nets and onion routing, and approaches based on DC-nets). We have also presented a new anonymous messaging protocol for three parties, and addressed possible solutions to secondary channels that arise in the start-up phase.

References

1. Chaum, D.: Untraceable electronic mail, return addresses, and digital pseudonyms. Communications of the ACM 4(2) (1981)
2. Dingledine, R., Mathewson, N., Syverson, P.: Tor: the second generation onion router. In: 13th USENIX Security Symposium, Berkeley, CA (2004)
3. Corrigan-Gibbs, H., Ford, B.: Dissent: accountable anonymous group messaging. In: CCS, pp. 340–350 (October 2010)

4. The Anonymizer, http://anonymizer.com
5. Brickell, J., Shmatikov, V.: Efficient anonymity-preserving data collection. In: ACM KDD, pp. 76–85 (2006)
6. Chaum, D.: The dining cryptographers problem: unconditional sender and recipient untraceability. Journal of Cryptology 1(1), 65–75 (1988)
7. Wolinski, D., Corrigan-Gibbs, H., Ford, B.: Scalable Anonymous Group Communication in the Anytrust Model. In: ACM European Workshop on System Security (April 2012)
8. ISO/IEC 8802-3:1990 [ANSI/IEEE Std 802.3-1990 Edition], Information processing systems Local area network Carrier sense multiple access with collision detection
9. ISO/IEC 8802-4:1990 [ANSI/IEEE Std 802.4-1990], Information processing systems Local area network Token-passing bus access method and physical layer specifications
10. IEEE Std 802.5-1989, IEEE Standard for Local Area Networks: Token Ring Access Method and Physical Layer Specifications
11. Jain, R.: FDDI Handbook: High-Speed Networking Using Fiber and Other Media. Addison-Wesley (1993)
12. Nemzow, M.: FDDI Networking: Planning, Installation and Management. McGraw-Hill (1994)
13. Goldschlag, D.M., Reed, M.G., Syverson, P.F.: Hiding routing information. In: Anderson, R. (ed.) IH 1996. LNCS, vol. 1174, pp. 137–150. Springer, Heidelberg (1996)
14. Syverson, P.F., Tsudik, G., Reed, M., Landwehr, C.: Towards an Analysis of Onion Routing Security. In: Federrath, H. (ed.) Anonymity 2000. LNCS, vol. 2009, pp. 96–114. Springer, Heidelberg (2001)
15. Goldschlag, D., Syverson, P., Reed, M.: Onion routing for anonymous private internet connections. Communications of the ACM 42(2), 39–41 (1999)
16. Sirer, E., Goel, S., Robson, M., Engin, D.: Eluding carnivores: File sharing with strong anonymity. In: 11th SIGOPS European Workshop (2004)
17. Di Raimondo, M., Gennaro, R., Krawczyk, H.: Secure off-the-record messaging. In: Proc. WPES (2005)
18. Clarke, I., Sandberg, O., Wiley, B., Hong, T.W.: Freenet: A distributed anonymous information storage and retrieval system. In: Federrath, H. (ed.) Anonymity 2000. LNCS, vol. 2009, pp. 46–66. Springer, Heidelberg (2001)
19. Bennett, K., Grothoff, C.: GAP - practical anonymous networking. In: Privacy Enhancing Technologies Workshop (2003)
20. Back, A., Möller, U., Stiglic, A.: Traffic analysis attacks and trade-offs in anonymity providing systems. In: Moskowitz, I.S. (ed.) IH 2001. LNCS, vol. 2137, pp. 245–257. Springer, Heidelberg (2001)
21. Freedman, M., Morris, R.: Tarzan: A peer-to-peer anonymizing network layer. In: 9th ACM CCS, Washington (2002)
22. Rennhard, M., Plattner, B.: Practical anonymity for the masses with morphMix. In: Juels, A. (ed.) FC 2004. LNCS, vol. 3110, pp. 233–250. Springer, Heidelberg (2004)
23. Levine, B., Shields, C.: Hordes: A multicast-based protocol for anonymity. Journal of Computer Security 10(3), 213–240 (2002)
24. Danezis, G., Dingledine, R., Mathewson, N.: Mixminion: Design of a type III anonymous remailer protocol. In: IEEE Symposium on Security and Privacy, pp. 2–15 (2003)
25. Gu, C., Tsudik, G.: Mixing E-mail with Babel. In: Network and Distributed Security Symposium, pp. 2–16 (1996)

Communication Setup in Anonymous Messaging
(Transcript of Discussion)

Francesco Bergadano

University of Turin

Hello everyone, I'll be talking about secondary channels in anonymous messaging. Actually I'm going to be considering two different approaches to anonymous messaging. One is the well-known Mix-net like approach, also called onion routing. This is well-known, so I will go only briefly over it. And the second approach is a new protocol based on token passing over a ring. They both have interesting types of secondary channels I want to discuss.

For onion routing I based my analysis on a relatively recent paper on the implementation of onion routing in the Tor system; I believe many of you have seen that. But in any case, what was known as Mix-nets in the previous literature, in these practical systems have become either onion proxies or onion routers. So all the IP packets travelling over the network first go to an onion proxy. Then the onion proxy does all the work for the user, encrypts the packet many times in an onion-like multiple encryption, and routes the packet, the encrypted packet, through the network, through a number of onion routers, and in the end the last onion router will finally get the plaintext IP packet, and forward it to the normal TCP/IP communication network. This is to protect anonymity, so in the end nobody knows who was the original sender of the packet. Every mix, every onion router, only knows the predecessor and the successor in the sequence of communication hops.

And it is well known, as the authors of the cited paper on Tor also admit, that onion routing is not strong against a global eavesdropper. If we have all these onion routers, we have senders and receivers, if somebody can see all this, if we are far enough away to see all the communication going on, we can simply analyse traffic to detect the sender. Looking at the slide, suppose for example that Sender 2 sends a packet to Receiver, and no other traffic is going on. Then we see that something is going from R1 to R2, then to R3 and finally to Receiver, and by simply looking at that we can see the path of the packets through the network, so we can tell at the Receiver's end that the Sender was Sender 2.

In reality things get more complicated because the network is busy, so there's packets running every way, and it becomes very difficult to analyse traffic. But still in principle one can do it. And as a consequence, even in the original Mix-net paper by Chaum, it is suggested that routers should buffer traffic, so as to accumulate a sufficient number of packets, and wait until the buffer is full enough. They should then send away the packets in a different order, so as to make it impossible to analyse traffic by changing the order with which the packets were sent. But that causes a delay, additional latency in the network. So you have a trade-off between latency and anonymity in onion routing.

B. Christianson et al. (Eds.): Security Protocols 2013, LNCS 8263, pp. 170–175, 2013.

In my paper, I have analysed another form of traffic analysis that is related to a start-up phase in onion routing approaches, such as Tor. In Tor everything is based on symmetric cryptography at some point, because you want to make it more efficient. In the original Mix-net paper everything was based on public key cryptography, but it was of course just a proof of principle idea. If you want to do it for real, as they did in Tor, you have to set up a symmetric key path between Sender and Receiver to make it fast. So when an onion proxy wants to communicate through a sequence of onion routers, before even starting to use a circuit, it has to set up the circuit. In order to set up the circuit the onion proxy first sends a circuit set up request to the first onion router and gets a response. There is a Diffie-Hellman key agreement, so after this phase the onion proxy and the onion router share a symmetric key. The same is done with steps 3 and 4 with onion router 2, and afterwards with onion router 3. After the set up phase the user, via the onion proxy, shares a key with each of the onion routers. So, from that point on, Mix-net operation can work with symmetric encryption.

When the circuit is set up then the communication will go through the routers, encrypted many times as in Mix-nets, and when it gets to the final onion router then it continues as normal TCP/IP traffic. By looking at these we can see that there is some possible traffic analysis again because the pattern used in circuit set up is different with respect to the data relay pattern. In fact, by looking at the figure, one notices that in circuit set up we have links 1 and 2 between OP and OR1, then links 3 and 4, etc, etc, whilst in data transmission traffic goes all the way to the final router, and then it comes back, so the two kinds of communication can be distinguished. So again, you can do some traffic analysis. So I will conclude here for onion routing, because the work is very well-known, but what I wanted to point out is that in onion routing in Mix-nets you can do traffic analysis of different kinds that endangers the very goal of anonymity we were looking for.

So now I'm going to move to the second part of the paper, and I'm going to be talking about token passing and a new protocol for anonymous group messaging. We use a ring topology and a token passing idea. We pass a token from one user to the next around the ring.

Frank Stajano: So besides Mix-nets there was another famous construction of Chaum paper.

Reply: DC-nets, yes.

Frank Stajano: Can you say how it is different?

Reply: Well, one of the goals of DC-nets was to allow for anonymity without encryption, in order to provide unconditional security for anonymity. This is not our goal. At the same time we can avoid some of the drawbacks of dining cryptographers such as the difficulty of media access, with the kind of contention that you get in dining cryptography. I'll get back to it in the end.

Anyway here the communication is anonymous because one cannot tell if a token is created by the predecessor, or just passed on.

Alec Yasinsac: Just to be sure I understand that, that's also true with the Tor network, when a message comes in an eavesdropper can't tell whether the message going out is a message that was forwarded, or a message that was created, right. So I mean, that's really a property of Tor as well.

Reply: In Tor, when there is a message one cannot tell who sent it in the first place because it was encrypted all the way. But actually in Tor I don't think the routers ever create a message, they only route the messages.

Alec Yasinsac: But the message could be created from a user who is a Tor node.

Reply: Yes.

Alec Yasinsac: You see my point is, if you have one message on a network it goes from router A to router B, and then the message goes from router B to router C, an eavesdropper has no way to know if that message that went from A to B terminated at B and a new message started to go to C, which is exactly the property that you're addressing.

Reply: There's maybe some similarity, but I think not exactly the same, because routers are routers, they're not users, they just forward messages.

Alec Yasinsac: On behalf of users.

Reply: On behalf of users, yes. Here the user can be the origin of a new message, or just a forwarding mechanism.

Michael Roe: In email remailers when the remailer buffers up a lot of messages and then sends them out in a different order then they came in, then because they're encrypted, and the eavesdropper can't tell which message coming in corresponds to which message coming out. But Tor has, I think, slightly weaker mathematics, because if you see the real time properties an eavesdropper who's got global surveillance of the network can, by looking at the correlation of the message coming in and going out, possibly match things up even though they're encrypted just by looking at the timing of when things come in and go out.

Reply: Yes. OK, so the whole idea is a kind of a whispering game, I don't know if British and American kids do that, but kids sit in a circle and you whisper some sentence to your neighbour, and your neighbour will whisper to the next. And at some point the sentence that is broadcast is not exactly the same that we started with. So you can say something anonymously, for example, I start out with some innocent looking sentence such as"moles love apples", then it's whispered to the next one and becomes "moles loves add-ons", and then "Bob loves add-ins", and "Bob loves Alice". And in the end the kid says "hey: Bob loves Alice!". Who said that? We don't know, it's anonymous. So this is the idea, we pass something around and we never know who injects the information in the process.

So here is the protocol, it's very simple. For the moment it's just a three-party protocol because it's ongoing work. I use public key cryptography here to make it simple, but I could have used secret keys just by setting up the keys first, or I could have used nothing at all, just relying on the physical security of point-to-point communication. In any case there is a message M_A sent from A, and, at step 1, A sends secretly to B message M_A. B reads the message, decrypts it, understands it, and forwards the message to C by re-encrypting it for C. So now C has the message, but C does not know who created the message, it could have been B, or it could have been somebody ahead in the ring, and B is just a forwarder of the message. This reminds us of IEEE token ring, because when we receive the message we don't just say, OK, I've got it, it's finished, but no, I forward the message anyways, so the message keeps going on, and it does a whole ring trip. When A gets the message again, A can realise she was the creator of the message, so A will absorb the message and free the network again. So A, after receiving her own message, sends out a dummy at step 4 so the network is free to use again, like in IEEE token ring. So this is very simple, and it should allow for anonymity.

I could not see any problem for a while, then by thinking about this for a while I realised there were some secondary channel issues. And basically there are two problems I want to discuss with you. One of them is anti-starvation, i.e. network availability issues. If the protocol is as I have described it, you realize that after A receives the message after one complete ring trip, A has to send a dummy, because if A sends a message again everyone else will starve. For networking, this is fine, but for security and anonymity it's not fine because then everybody knows things have to be that way, and this knowledge provides a secondary channel that completely destroys anonymity.

Imagine these are the messages that went around the network. When C receives message number 5, this is a content carrying message, it's not a dummy, it contains a real message. As a consequence C will know that the previous message number 2 was sent by A, because if it was sent by B, then message number 5 should be a dummy. If message 2 was sent by B, it would have returned here, and B would have released the dummy at this point. So, if we don't want starvation, and we adopt a classical anti-starvation policy, then there is no anonymity.

So what do we do? The solution is, after finishing a trip around the ring A at step 4 will not necessarily send out a dummy, but it will send out the dummy only with probability a half. So with probability 0.5, A will send a dummy, and with probability 0.5 it will use the network if it so wishes. In this case C cannot use this information as a secondary channel, but at the same time there is no starvation because with probability $1/2$ the network will be freed, so there is starvation only with probability $1/2^M$, after M trips around the ring. So this was one first problem that was easily overlooked, and we have solved it.

Here is another problem, even more subtle: the start-up phase. The protocol works fine when it's running. We imagine this token going round the ring, and it's been going round the ring for hours, then it's fine, it's no problem. But when you have to start, somebody has to start speaking, and starting to speak is another secondary channel. This is well known also in more recent works, such as Dissent, which was published just a couple of years ago, they have the same problem. If you want to do anonymity, but then you take action and you speak first, then everybody realises you want to say something, and anonymity is not there anymore. And here it's the same. If the network is idle, who will start to speak? A cannot start to speak, because otherwise B will receive an informative message and it will know it's from A, because that's the first message in history. So A cannot start. But then also B cannot start, nobody can start.

So what do we do? Again we have a probabilistic solution. It's like in this famous movie, this movie by Sergio Leone, I don't know if anybody has seen it, but in the final scene of the movie there is a showdown, and it's three gunmen at the showdown, not two as usual, but three, so it fits my protocol. And of course you should not draw your gun, because when you do that you're dead. So you have to wait, wait as in the movie, there is a long waiting time. It's about the unpredictability of gun drawing, nobody knows when the other ones will draw a gun. And it's the same here. The network has to start but nobody has to be able to predict when anyone will start speaking, because if we can predict when someone will start speaking, then there's no anonymity.

Frank Stajano: Start with the dummy.

Reply: Yes, that's what we do, exactly. We start spinning a dummy. The dummy goes around and everybody waits, how long does everybody wait, you don't know, everybody has to think of some time when they will start communicating, but this has to be secret. For example, every player chooses two randoms, low and high, two random times, system-wide, and then it will select a time within the interval, and start speaking only after that amount of time. If this is unpredictable to others then the anonymity is preserved.

Frank Stajano: But what does it mean if that is idle if you're already spinning a dummy in the network?

Reply: Idle in the sense that there is only a dummy going around, no information. It's a dummy talking, it goes around, the network is idle.

So we have seen some examples of secondary channels. In onion routing we have traffic patterns, traffic analysis can detect traffic patterns. I can detect when some packet is forwarded by a router, as a consequence I can know traffic sources. This was well known, but then we have seen a new kind of secondary channel analysis, which is linked to a start-up phase in Tor, known as circuit setup.

Then we have seen a different approach based on token passing, and we have seen that starvation-avoidance policies and network activation can cause problems that have to be addressed. We have also seen a very interesting link between anonymity and randomness. We have seen that in order to get anonymity you need random bits everywhere. For example, in Mix-nets you need buffering, and a random reordering of packets in order to avoid traffic analysis. In more recent work in Dissent, there is a so-called notion of 'shuffled send', for those who have seen it, and the message shuffles have to be random.

My approach here to anti-starvation and start-up in this token passing mechanism needs randomness, because, for example, I have to insert information only with some probability. I have to flip a coin to insert information only when we get heads, for example. In DC-nets there is a coin flipping primitive, which is at the basis of all communication, and also acquiring media access requires some kind of solution. For example, by a contention mechanism, and this also requires randomness, waiting for some random amount of time. So we get an intriguing question: it has been shown that one can obtain anonymity without cryptography, as in dining cryptographers, and also in cocaine auctions, and it has been shown that I don't need pubic key cryptography or secret key cryptography, to get anonymity. But the question is, can we also obtain anonymity without randomness, without unpredictable data that I have access to, but that others cannot predict, without secrets. I would tend to give a negative answer based on what we have seen here.

Future work: of course, this has to be extended to an N-party protocol, and it turns out it's not easy, because if we just extend what I have shown here to N parties a naïve extension doesn't work, so I'm working on a more involved protocol for N parties. Then I'd like to formalize a more precise adversary model, and provide further comparison with approaches based on DC-nets. OK, I'm done, any other questions?

Daniel Thomas: So with the alternative, probabilistically sending a dummy when you receive your own message back, if it's possible to say that two messages were sent by the same person, you don't know who the person was, because of the anonymous network, but you know that the same person sent them, because they have the same kind, can you do a correlation with whether the dummy was sent or not, and over the sequence of the messages eventually work out who it was who sent them?

Reply: So the question is, if I can tell two messages were sent by the same person, I don't know who it is, but they were sent by the same person.

Daniel Thomas: You know that sometimes the node sends and sometimes it won't. OK, if a dummy is never sent by a node, when it sees one of these messages, then it's not the sender of the message. But if sometimes it does send a dummy then it is the sender of the messages, can you over a period of time ...

Reply: So if you never see a dummy you know the same person is transmitting again and again.

Daniel Thomas: Yes, the same kind of message.

Reply: Interesting.

Daniel Thomas: Over time if you do that universally and to check probability, can you have, with some high probability, the one that's sending messages.

Reply: So we get some information we should not get.

Daniel Thomas: Yes.

Reply: I had not thought of it, thank you, yes. So that's still another channel. Yes.

Vanessa Teague: Could the same thing happen, if the sender is sending a dummy. Just go back to the slide, I understand that if B doesn't get message 4, then he doesn't know whether A was the originator of message A. But if B does get message 4, then can't B infer that A must have sent message A?

Reply: If B does get message 4 then, well the dummy could have been created here, too, right.

Vanessa Teague: Ah, so it's the dummy getting propagated in that case.

Reply: Yes, A does not have to transmit every time.

Towards a Stronger Location Integrity

Rubin Xu and Dongting Yu

Computer Laboratory, University of Cambridge, United Kingdom
{rubin.xu,dongting.yu}@cl.cam.ac.uk

Abstract. Currently in mobile location-based services the application relies solely on the coordinates provided by the phone's operating system to determine its location. The application residing on the phone then submits the resulting location data to the application server, leaving the protocol insecure as a dishonest user can inject fake data at the last step. In this paper we propose a new method that allows an application to independently verify the integrity of submitted data by checking its plausibility given surrounding Wifi access points. Instead of the traditional single channel of information, namely the submitted coordinates, the application can supplement a second channel to potentially filter out fraudulent location data.

1 Introduction

With an increasing number of mobile phones having GPS capabilities so too have the number of location-based services and applications increased. These services use a user's location in many ways: some to help provide a context to provide relevant information, some to provide local engagement, and some to verify physical presence. We see an increasing number of services relying on the accuracy of the location data, some even having financial incentives (imagine an airline offering discounts for travellers visiting the greatest number of airports), with little visible effort devoted to verifying the authenticity of these data. Academically, location privacy is an active research topic, but the integrity of location data has largely been little studied. Prior work on location integrity ([4], [2], [1], [3]) requires the deployment of trusted location beacons, and hence is only applicable in specialised use cases with a limited spatial coverage.

There are currently two popular methods to locate a mobile device: through computing GPS coordinates using satellite information, and querying a remote location provider with nearby Wifi access point (Wifi AP) and cellular tower identifiers [5]. After either of these methods, the mobile device then submits the latitude and longitude coordinates to the application server, which then uses this data directly. It is at this last step that the user can discard real calculated data and insert fraudulent coordinates, creating a fake physical presence.

Our threat model is as follows: an adversary who is trying to falsely appear at as many places as possible in the shortest amount of time or with minimal effort. This adversary is likely an everyday mobile device user who is dishonest when using the service, as lying to the application can bring some incentives for himself.

B. Christianson et al. (Eds.): Security Protocols 2013, LNCS 8263, pp. 176–179, 2013.
© Springer-Verlag Berlin Heidelberg 2013

He can easily modify the application itself or directly tap into the application's communication with its server. We do not assume larger cooperating attacks (adversaries sharing necessary information among them) or ones funded by a powerful adversary. After all, our method cannot provide absolute certainty but rather a boost in confidence. Also, as a lightweight method, we cannot prevent all types of location-spoofing attacks. For example, we do not prevent replay attacks so if a user physically shows up at a location once, he will be able to repeatedly lie for that location in the future. We consider these types of attacks to be out of scope.

We bring two contributions in this paper. First, we present a lightweight design that allows mobile applications to independently verify the integrity of received location data. No special hardware or modification to phone OSes is needed apart from software code in the mobile application and its server. An implementation can be easily made modular and used as a library to further reduce implementation hassle. Second, we present an example formula that can be used to calculate a score to indicate the plausibility of a submitted coordinate. Individual applications can set their own thresholds below (or above) which the location would then be accepted with integrity.

2   Design

We start with a description of the general design of our protocol. The mobile application first requests location information from the phone OS as usual. The phone OS proceeds with GPS, A-GPS, or Wifi (for an approximate location) and returns a coordinate to the mobile application. Now, instead of submitting this coordinate alone to the application server, we add that the application should collect the identifiers of nearby Wifi APs (they may have been collected just earlier, but that time was by the OS), and send this information as well. As before, this channel should be protected for confidentiality and integrity, for example with TLS.

After the application server receives the (claimed) coordinates and the set of Wifi APs, it checks the coordinates against its database of previous such submissions. If there are sufficiently close (i.e. Wifi signal range) submissions made prior by other users, then the submitted Wifi APs are compared against those previously-submitted lists. The rationale is that since these two submissions are fairly close, the current submission should at least report some APs previously seen in this area. Similarly, it is also possible to check the submitted APs against all of the APs database, with the rationale that an AP does not usually move, for a submitted AP that in fact exists elsewhere far away. For each 'correct' report of an AP, a score is added; optionally, a score is deducted for each report of an AP that has been reported elsewhere. In the end, a final score will result for this submission of location, and the application will then decide whether to accept it or not depending on an application-specific threshold.

We mentioned a formula to calculate the plausibility of a set of submitted Wifi APs and thus determine the integrity of the data. Optimising this formula itself is worthy of study, simulation, and field trials. We present a basic formula that illustrates the idea behind our design, as

$$score = f(m, p_1) \times f(m, p_2) \times \cdots \times f(m, p_n)$$

where a lower score indicates better plausibility, m is the coordinate of the mobile device (as given by the phone OS), p_n is coordinate set of each seen Wifi APs that are also previously reported (to be specific it is the coordinate set of most recently accepted submitted location that includes the matched AP), and

$$f(x, y) = \frac{|x - y|}{1 + |x - y|}$$

is the function to convert the distance between two points in space to a value in $[0, 1)$. Of course, either the score or $f(x, y)$ can be optimised. For example, $f(x, y)$ can be written as a piecewise-defined function to eliminate the long tail and better reflect the fact that Wifi APs will no longer be detectable after a certain distance due to signal attenuation.

In the above formula we choose to only consider the submitted APs that are previously reported, and not to penalise submitted APs that are close enough but not previously reported, or submitted APs that are previously reported as being elsewhere. Arguably getting APs right is already hard enough that no further penalties are necessary (it is very hard to correctly brute force an AP's MAC address). However, if such penalties were introduced, some care must be taken. We approximate the location of an AP to be the location of last accepted submission that reports this AP (or a weighted average location of last n submissions); this location is only an approximation and it is possible that the new submission is just out of the range of that AP. The submission in this case should not be falsely penalised.

3 Discussion

Our proposed scheme brings confidence to client-submitted location data without any changes to the existing mobile infrastructure, and can be realised as a generic service/library adoptable by different applications with ease. However some challenges still remain, as we outline below:

– **Bootstrapping**
 The continuous availability and accuracy of the Wifi AP database is critical to the correct operation of our scheme. If the database is to be built from scratch, the initial portion of submitted AP locations has to be trusted and assumed correct. More generally if some geographical location is seldom visited by previous queries, their initial explorers will play an important part in bootstrapping that part of the database. To avoid DoS attacks from malicious clients, it might be better to probabilistically update the AP database even if the submitted query is in conflict with known AP information.

- **Third-party Location Authority**
  To work around the bootstrapping problem, we could take advantage of existing maps of Wifi AP locations. Both Apple and Google are in possession of such databases, used for coarse-grained location services where GPS is unavailable. We can imagine them becoming a location stamping service where individual application provide current location coordinates together with a list of nearby Wifi APs, and the stamping service will digitally sign the location data if the submitted APs are consistent with their database.
- **Wifi AP Dynamics**
  In our model we have not explicitly considered the cases where an AP is moving in space (such as personal hotspots) or is temporarily unavailable as being powered off. The probabilistic nature of our scheme can associate lower weight to such transient APs, minimising their impact on the overall accuracy of the score.

  Another scenario is that multiple APs can occupy the same geographic coordinate but are yet distant to each other, because they live on different altitudes, for example different floors of a highrise building. A scheme that does not penalise absence of APs still works well in this scenario, as positive AP witnesses are sufficient to pass the location validation.

4   Conclusion

In this paper we present a lightweight design that allows mobile applications to verify the plausibility of user-submitted location data with no modification to phone OSes or third-party equipment. We have also provided an example score formula as an initial workable metric. Potential difficulties are outlined with possible solutions. We believe that our work is a practical proposal to verify location integrity.

References

1. Brands, S., Chaum, D.: Distance bounding protocols. In: Helleseth, T. (ed.) EURO-CRYPT 1993. LNCS, vol. 765, pp. 344–359. Springer, Heidelberg (1994), http://dx.doi.org/10.1007/3-540-48285-7_30
2. González-Tablas, A.I., Kursawe, K., Ramos, B., Ribagorda, A.: Survey on location authentication protocols and spatial-temporal attestation services. In: Enokido, T., Yan, L., Xiao, B., Kim, D.Y., Dai, Y.-S., Yang, L.T. (eds.) EUC-WS 2005. LNCS, vol. 3823, pp. 797–806. Springer, Heidelberg (2005)
3. Han, K., Kim, K.: Enhancing privacy and authentication for location based service using trusted authority. In: 2nd Joint Workshop on Information Security (2007)
4. Sastry, N., Shankar, U., Wagner, D.: Secure verification of location claims. In: Proceedings of the 2nd ACM Workshop on Wireless Security, pp. 1–10. ACM (2003)
5. Zandbergen, P.A.: Accuracy of iphone locations: A comparison of assisted gps, wifi and cellular positioning. Transactions in GIS 13, 5–25 (2009), http://dx.doi.org/10.1111/j.1467-9671.2009.01152.x

Towards a Stronger Location Integrity
(Transcript of Discussion)

Rubin Xu

University of Cambridge

Location data has been more and more accessible since the wide adoption of smartphones, and if you open up your smartphone you'll be surprised how many applications use your location data. A recent survey suggests that in Google Play, the official Android application store, more than 42% of applications ask for permissions to access your location data. Some of these applications use location data just to increase usability, for example, to provide contextual information about service around you. Others, namely location-based services, build their core functionality on top of your current location. For example, we have Foursquare, where a user can check in their current location and obtain information like promotions or reviews about service around him. Another one is Momo, a Chinese location-based service from which you can communicate with people around you. After you check in your current location, the app allows you to see people around you and start chatting with them, providing a way of socialising with new people.

So for applications where location is the key component of their functionality, we think that sometimes a user will have incentives to cheat. One example would be the Nando's 'around the world' challenge. Has anyone heard of it? Basically if you are able to prove that you have been eating at every single Nando's restaurant around the world, then they will allow you to dine at Nando's for free for the rest of your life. Well they haven't actually made clear how they're going to judge this, which I guess is kind of on purpose so you can't really claim the prize. But nevertheless you can imagine that hypothetically Nando's can use your Foursquare check in records as proof that you've actually been to these restaurants. So in this case the user will have an incentive to trick Foursquare into checking in at places where he isn't physically present.

Another incentive will be for spammers and phishers. They could fraudulently initiate you to push their spamming and phishing attempts. A third example would be that a normal user would actually try. Take Foursquare as an example, a normal user will actually trust when Foursquare tells you that this user has been checking into this particular place without realising that the actual location can be spoofed, hence facilitating actual privacy issues around location-based social networks. So, for example, the Momo, the Chinese location-based service, from which you can find out people around you, and the application actually tells you how far the people are away from you, then you can imagine an attack by a malicious user where the user fraudulently claims that he is in this place and then he collects the data about the people around him with precise distance between the current location and the user's location. And you repeat this process multiple

B. Christianson et al. (Eds.): Security Protocols 2013, LNCS 8263, pp. 180–188, 2013.

times, for three different locations at least, then you will be able to perform a triangulation attack on the service, finding out the exact location of every other user around you, which kind of is a violation of the privacy of other users.

Well we could argue that in this case it's kind of the flaw of the design of the protocol of this particular location-based service where they didn't provide enough randomisation, and they didn't actually take the privacy of other users into consideration. But the ability to spoof your current location data to actually inject false location into the system actually makes an attack much more dangerous because, I'm going to show you, a malicious user can actually automated a process and potentially find out people around the world, potentially every user on this particular location service around the world.

Right, so what are the ways of tricking applications into taking fraudulent location data. Well we have this hard way, you can reverse engineer the application, find out exactly how the application communicates with the server, and then you can initiate this protocol yourself but feeding in false location data. And note that in this case authentication or cryptography doesn't help at all because the adversary has complete visibility of applications, hence all encryptions, keys, and possible obfuscation, so an attacker will always be able to inject false coordinates if he has access to an application. Well, there's actually a much easier way. So Android's operating system allows to inject mock locations. The only thing you need to do is to enable this option in your mobile device's developer settings, and then you can simply invoke public APIs, which can be used to inject false location data. There are already plenty of apps that perform such tasks for you, and this is bad.

So I hope now you can see that we need some kind of location integrity in these scenarios. Most research we have seen so far focuses on location privacy where users don't trust applications: they assume that the application may leak their private location information. However, if we look from the other side then the applications do not necessarily trust the user because the user is able to inject fraudulent location information, interfering with the application and potentially other users.

So how can applications have confidence in user-submitted location data? Imagine that you are engineering a location-based service, and writing up the access control policy for it. What kind of properties do you want? The first thing is we want it to be practically deployable, so hopefully we don't need to invest in new infrastructure on which to base our trust. There exists previous research on topics related to location authentication, for example the Echo protocol from CMU where they perform location-based authentication which basically means that they are able to prove that a device is within a particular range of a trusted beacon by means of distance bounding using ultrasonic waves. This is not very scalable because they have to deploy these beacons to places where you want to have location integrity, and that's really not going to scale well. A similar requirement is that you want your location integrity verification to be globally available, well at least in populated areas of the planet where location-based services makes sense, so probably you don't need to worry about the Arctic, but you do want to have location integrity in big cities or populated areas.

A third desired property would be we want the implementation of location integrity verification to be lightweight. We definitely don't want to modify the existing smartphone's hardware to add more sensors, and hopefully we should be able to implement the verification scheme with minimal coding effort. In other words a stock mobile OS should already provide the information we need to perform the verification.

Perfect location integrity is a very difficult, if not impossible, problem and we are definitely not claiming that we've solved it. We just want to increase applications' confidence in user-supplied location data, and to raise the bar for attackers such that they need to spend some effort to spoof location. An adversary should not be able to spoof location coordinates of places he hasn't physically been to. It's possible for him to perform a replay attack whereby he makes submissions about places he actually did go to but is not currently in. We also consider the case where two colluding users can cheat by relaying their location data, but again the bottom line is we are not claiming we've solved the problem of perfect location integrity, it's just a way of boosting confidence.

Frank Stajano: You started with something about attacks on privacy from apps. Now you are talking about something you want to do, where you want to make sure that their location is the real one, so in some sense "whose side are you on?" Are you also trying to do something which is going to protect privacy for those who use the apps?

Reply: Well we don't explicitly talk about privacy. As in the previous example, the privacy violation is made dangerous because of the lack of location integrity verifications, such that an attacker can make automated attacks on a large scale. But we do not address location privacy.

Frank Stajano: Even if your thing works it doesn't mean that the attacker is going to use your thing, so it doesn't solve that problem, right?

Reply: Well the attacker is not going to use our scheme, the location service provider will be using it to prevent attackers from automating.

So our idea is quite simple: you just use your nearby Wifi access points as your location witness. This fits nicely with the three desired properties we just proposed. First of all you don't need to invest in new beacons, you just take advantage of existing, publicly available Wifi access points as your location beacon. They are globally available, well at least in populated areas of the world. And it's easily implementable in current mobile operating systems because the OS provides APIs to retrieve the list of available access points around you.

So in our scheme, an app will first request location from the operating system, the operating system delegates the request to location providers - peripheral devices in the mobile phones, who will then return the appropriate coordinates, and the OS passes this back to the app. In the meantime the app also requests the list of visible Wifi access points together with their MAC address and the signal strength from the OS. Then the application could submit its current location data together with the Wifi access points information to its server where validation will be performed. Basically we use these Wifi access points as the other channel to increase the confidence of submitted location.

Right, so how does the server verify the location information? It maintains a list of access points and their previously reported locations, and when a new request comes, the server will only consider the first N strongest Wifi access points information just to prevent a malicious user from submitting all possible access points with fake MAC addresses. Next, it will check if the reported access point is consistent with previously seen access points in the database. Here we have a bootstrapping problem. Initially the server will have no information about a new access point so it has to bootstrap itself by trusting the first few submissions in an unexplored area and that the submitted access point is genuine. After this initial phase it can proceed by checking if the user-submitted access point is consistent with the submitted coordinates, considering factors like the last seen date of the access point, the signal strength, and whether this Wifi is a fixed router or some mobile hotspot. By verifying the coordinates with the submitted APs, the server will be able to determine whether this is plausible or not, and if it is plausible then it will accept a query, and update its AP database accordingly.

Francesco Bergadano: So you don't actually have to connect to the Wifi?

Reply: You don't need to connect.

Francesco Bergadano: Only use the SSID?

Reply: Yes, you just need to passively scan the surroundings for available access points, and using their MAC address as keys to the database.

Feng Hao: So it can also easily spoof the Wifi access point.

Reply: Well everything can be spoofed, even if you can't physically spoof the Wifi access point you can do it in software, just reverse engineer the communication protocol and submit fraudulent access point data. So in this sense, yes you can spoof it. But, you have to submit the correct access point information to be able to pass the test.

Robert Watson: And I guess Google, and maybe also Apple, collect some information on access points, do you know how they go about verifying the integrity of things submitted. I guess they've crowdsourced it, and sometimes it's driving around in cars and so on.

Reply: I could only guess that most of Google's data is actually based down their street view cars so it's kind of trusted in some sense.

Robert Watson: Right, I was just curious if you had any information on whether they had some validation technique. I guess they must do something.

Reply: Well if we have the majority of the data correct then you can easily find out the outliers, using statistical techniques.

Alec Yasinsac: Please clear it up for me just to be sure I understand. What you're saying is the app will send to the location service and say, here's where I am, right?

Reply: And a list of access points as witnesses that I am actually here.

Alec Yasinsac: But they're not witnesses because they don't speak for you, you just say, I am here, and this is additional proof that I'm here because I know these access points are around me.

Reply: Yes.

Alec Yasinsac: But if I already know, so I could report, so I know now I'm here, I've got all the access points that I've connected to here, and if some of those are connected, I go back to the USA next week and I could report that I'm here.

Reply: Yes, so this is the replay attack I talked about before.

Alec Yasinsac: But it doesn't have to be a replay attack, because I don't necessarily have to be here.

Reply: But you have to have been here.

Daniel Thomas: So you're saying that it's easier for the person running the service to get hold of information than the attacker, so it's more work for them to find out this data.

Alec Yasinsac: That's my question, and additionally if the provider has to be able to protect that information too, because that database obviously would give them, the adversaries, a lot of data to be able to use to do this. But my question, I want to be sure I understood.

Feng Hao: And also one question I was wondering is why you send all this information entirely by the app because it makes spoofing quite easy. If you consider the alternative approach of sending information through the Wifi or the Internet to the server, if just some kind of handshaking between the server and the Wifi access point at least the server can know that the information source address is actually from this Wifi.

Reply: That's not entirely trivial to do because if you just communicate using IP stack then you don't know the source MAC address because there could be layers of routing around on top of that. I think the only thing you know is IP addresses, but you could also go through proxies so even IP addresses may not be reliable.

Feng Hao: I guess my question is, who will be the best witness in this case, and it can't be the app itself because app could be cheating, and a witness has to be something else.

Reply: Well the witness is the access point. It's just the way we ship the witness information via applications, hence, yes, this is open to spoofing attack.

Dongting Yu: To the app, the server in the backend is the trusted part of this protocol, and they're not an adversary.

Feng Hao: Yes, but it still relies on the wireless access point in the sense that wireless test points should be some trusted witness in some way if you built a protocol based on that assumption.

Dongting Yu: So the point is, if I were to spam a large area of the US, I don't know the Wifi access points in San Francisco, for example, so I cannot rapidly appear in many places within a short period to spam my neighbours.

Robert Watson: It's a world in which there's an open version database that lists the set of access points everywhere, which can be crowdsourced in the same way you can crowdsource street navigation and so on. Can you imagine some extensions to the model you have that use cryptography, or proof of liveness, or something that might help us with that. Could a Wifi access point then just for example agree that every access point then will provide a proof of liveness, and strengthen the protocol.

Reply: If you have guarantee on the freshness of your Wifi access point data then you can prevent replay attacks, but you will probably still face relay attacks.

Robert Watson: And I guess you need the distance bounding and so on.

Reply: Yes and distance bounding is going to be difficult, especially when we are talking about signal travelling at speed of light.

Frank Stajano: So why is the application upset if it gets the wrong location?

Reply: Because some of their core functionalities are based on the availability of user location, and surely they don't want fraudulent data.

Frank Stajano: If the user gets a benefit from the application, the user will provide the correct location. If the user want to the application then it's an adversarial game between the user and the application. Why does the application want to fight the user, what does the application gain by getting something that the user doesn't want to give?

Reply: Well there are always good users and bad users. A good user's incentives will be aligned with the application, but there are bad users like spammers and phishers who try to trick the application and others, whose incentives are not entirely aligned with the application itself.

Michael Roe: You might, for example, have an access control policy that says, this information about this location is only accessible to people who are really there, and you've got a bound on how many that's likely to be, which is no longer true if you can't authenticate that, and somebody will pretend to be in large numbers.

Frank Stajano: Well if you are granting benefits based on the application as opposed to just providing a service like Foursquare, then for granting benefits I would argue that you need a stronger form of authentication to just collecting Wifi access point here.

Bruce Christianson: But the question is, what could that possibly lead to.

Frank Stajano: Yes, so I just want to have a more concrete description of the scenarios in which this location service is used before I understand whether this is the appropriate strength to provide, because it looks to me that if the application is just giving me something which is made more useful by knowing where I am, like I'm going to tell you how to get to the station, and if you tell me where you are, I can tell you from where you are to the station, in fact if you lie, well tough, I'm just going to give you a wrong route and it's not going to be useful to you. Therefore either you give me the right location or I'm just going to give you incorrect information, that's fine. If instead it's something like Mike said, you know, if you're here I'm going to give you some extra benefit beyond the information from the application like, open the door?

Michael Roe: That's probably too strong, you know, sending information about the location or like who else is here, for example, then you might say, who is in this room is different from people who are elsewhere in the world, but people who are supposedly in the same room with us, it should be within line of sight are allowed to know that piece of information.

Robert Watson: Of course after the question if you're in the same room, you might have ID cards if you brought some identification, is the important property that we're in the same room, or is the important property that we're in the same location. And those are slightly different questions, because are we in the same room is a question that we might build the protocol among ourselves, and are we in the same location has to do with this sort of formal notion of you're at this point on the planet. And maybe if you're trying to solve one of those problems you don't need to solve the other problem.

Mohammed Almeshekah: There is a startup called Shopkick that tries to drive foot traffic to physical stores. They created a scheme to reward customers for physically being in the stores in an effort to provide incentives for customers to visit physical stores instead of only shopping online. Whenever you physically step into on of their participating stores the app will detect that by determining your location and then charge the physical stores a fixed amount per customer. So in this case, your location will cost some companies money and there is a huge incentive to determined the location with relatively high accuracy.

Frank Stajano: So in that case, for example, I would much rather suggest and scan a QR code of a screen in the shop that is constantly changing, which proves that you were in the shop at that time, as opposed to, you know, do it with a location Wifi.

Audience: Well they do ultrasonic sound beacon, the ones that you mentioned at the beginning of the talk.

Frank Stajano: Collecting something electronically that is there in that store as opposed to doing something based on location.

Mohammed Almeshekah: Yes, they do something similar with some beacons that are installed in the stores, however, they still dealing with some fraud cases.

Sandy Clark: That requires a user to be active to scan the QR codes but his is a passive.

Frank Stajano: It is active, which in my viewpoint is a feature because you only, from a privacy viewpoint, you only say that you're there, if you want to say that you're there. If you wanted to be passive and you thought that was a better idea, you could do it with Bluetooth for example, you could still get a Bluetooth token that was only available in that store.

Bruce Christianson: But again you've got to be careful about the threat model, because I could go to the store, scan the QR code, and relay that to 4000 people, who then ...

Frank Stajano: Well not if you change it every minute.

Bruce Christianson: Well how long does it take to change?

Robert Watson: This is like a guy with a one-time token, you have to forward stuff to giving your proximity, whether it's pressing a button or something to limit the use of numbers, then it's just information.

Frank Stajano: Well you know you're not going to have had the 4000 people in the shop at the same time if the shop is this size.

Bruce Christianson: Yes, the question is, what is the threat model.

Robert Watson: If it's advertising, well we know actually advertisers are kind of interested in it as long as people look at them.

Frank Stajano: Well what I am saying is, if you do the QR code version it doesn't really scale to the problem because you'd have to do that every minute to get a new one, right, and if you have one you can't keep on re-sending it, and if you try to send it to 4000 people then it's obvious that it's a fake, because you couldn't physically have 4000 people inside the shop.

Bruce Christianson: But what about 16 people.

Frank Stajano: Well 16 people, yes, but it just doesn't scale, so that's again, you can do the scan and you get 16.

Robert Watson: If you look at all the CCTV camera how long will it take before they recognise you are good? And it seems like, if there are two different questions you can ask yourself, and to ask one if you really require strongly that you know the person's physical location, you basically start with distance bounding. And the other if you can accept something you really have to limit what you use or make sure people don't try to rely on something you can't rely on. And suddenly you care about, well how much money is getting sold?

Frank Stajano: If it's something where you're basically getting a discount token for the store, so long as it doesn't scale to thousands of people I think that you can do it for 10 people and you have to redo it the next minute, then it's not too bad.

Robert Watson: There is an interaction with a business model though, for example, the store also has an online website and if you have time to go there in person, you get a discount on the website, and you get these sort of problems we've had with Groupon, and they went out of business because they didn't understand the scalability you associate with cheap communication.

Reply: Shall I carry on? So one way of computing a plausibility score is to compute the likelihood that the given submitted coordinates are close to the known sighted location of the access points. This formula is just an example, don't worry about the details too much. A possible improvement is that, we could do distance or rather travel bounding. If a user submits successful location data as time goes then you can find out their average travelling speed. And a possible upper bound for that is you can't really travel faster than a plane. An even more elaborate scheme is that the upper bound of travel speed is dependent on your local terrain, or local traffic, and if you are travelling a very short distance then you probably aren't travelling on a plane, and hence you can make the upper bounds a little bit more precise. And I said, replay and relay attacks are still possible, but we're not trying to achieve 100% integrity here, we just want to increase the confidence and raise the bar for attackers.

Right, because bootstrapping is difficult, we have to assume that the initial submission of access points from users are trusted. As Robert said, Google and Apple already have this database, so we could also imagine that in future Google may become a location authority, whose service is providing authenticated messages of location directly to the app server.

Final conclusions: we argue that location integrity is important, and in our scheme we propose to use Wifi access points as a location witness to increase the confidence of user-submitted location data. The details still need to be thought of carefully. Yes, bootstrapping is hard but Google and Apple already have this database and we probably could take advantage of that.

Back Channels Can Be Useful! –
Layering Authentication Channels
to Provide Covert Communication

Mohammed H. Almeshekah, Mikhail J. Atallah, and Eugene H. Spafford

Purdue University
305 N. University Street, West Lafayette, IN 47907, USA
{malmeshe,matallah,spaf}@purdue.edu
http://www.cerias.purdue.edu

Abstract. This paper argues the need for providing a covert back-channel communication mechanism in authentication protocols, discusses various practical uses for such a channel, and desirable features for its design and deployment. Such a mechanism would leverage the current authentication channel to carry out the covert communication rather than introducing a separate one. The communication would need to be oblivious to an adversary observing it, possibly as a man-in-the-middle. We discuss the properties that such channels would need to have for the various scenarios in which they would be used. Also, we show their potential for mitigating the effects of a number of security breaches currently occurring in these scenarios.

Keywords: Authentication, Server Impersonation, Back-channels, Phishing.

1 Introduction

Whereas many current research efforts in improving authentication seek to develop stronger credentials and better management of these credentials, we are not aware of a facility for giving users and their service providers a login flexibility beyond the usually implied "this username requests to access to the system." Service providers (such as banks, brokerages, etc) provide all-or-nothing access: a customer who merely wants to check her balances and positions (i.e., read-only access) cannot do so without implicitly obtaining the authority to carry out transactions (including money transfers), and the authority to administer the account (including changing the physical address of record, the email address of record, etc). Ideally, in this situation, there should be three levels of access: One that allows only viewing account balances, another that also allows carrying out transactions, and the highest one that also allows account administration. Compromising the credentials of the read-only level would not give the adversary full control over the user's account, and would limit the damage done during the time it takes for the victim and bank to realize that a phishing attack

B. Christianson et al. (Eds.): Security Protocols 2013, LNCS 8263, pp. 189–195, 2013.

has happened. Contrast this to the current deployed systems, where a victim of phishing would grant the adversary all of these privileges at once, even if the victim wanted "read-only" access (e.g., because the phishing email containing a link to a phishing site invited the victim to "view an important message").

A customer who knows she is "taking a risk" by logging in from a public place, with possibilities of shoulder-surfing and/or of hidden CCTV cameras, should really be given the option of a degraded form of login (the "read-only" kind). The question then arises, why is such a 3-level login facility not provided by financial institutions, even though the liability from a phishing attack often falls more on them than on the imprudent customer? The obvious answer is that no customer would want to memorize three passwords for each institution they do business with. Customers are having enough of a hard time managing their current passwords where the ratio is one-to-one. We argue that there is a way to have the benefits of the 3-level access, without the burden of increasing the number of passwords users have to manage.

2   Preliminary Solution

This section presents a simple first step towards achieving the goal of conveying extra information to the server, beyond the all-or-nothing access that is implicit in every login made in currently deployed systems. In what follows, for convenience we use financial institutions in our examples, but this entails no loss of generality as the discussion applies equally well to any service provider.

2.1   A Simple Proposal

We propose a login mechanism such that:

1. The interface is similar to those currently deployed, namely, with two fields, one for entering a username and the other for entering a password, and
2. What is entered in the password field does not tax the user's memory significantly more than in currently deployed systems, and
3. What a shoulder-surfer or eavesdropper observes when the user enters her credentials reveals no information as to what covert message is being sent, other than the usually implied "this username wants to login."

To achieve the second requirement, we propose that the user enters, in the password field, the regular password (the same thing users enter today) followed by a space, and then followed by a word that conveys the secret message to the bank. In the 3-level access example we discussed, this could be one of three words $\{w_1, w_2, w_3\}$ that are (i) trivially memorizable by the user, and (ii) have a natural total ordering in that particular user's mind. For example, the three words could be the names of the 3 first dogs of that customer, or of three soccer teams, or of three makes of cars. Accidental mis-typing (that results in a word that is outside the pre-agreed set) would result in a failed login, with the necessity to re-enter username, etc. The only constraint on these three words is that the edit distances among them should be greater than one typographic error. This is essential so that mis-typing one of them does not accidentally result in sending another one. A shoulder-surfer (or a ceiling CCTV camera) that captures what the user entered would of course be able to replay it, but would not get a higher access level.

The above simple scheme does not reveal to a shoulder-surfer the nature of the secret message being sent to the bank through the memorizable word. Even a shoulder-surfer who is a customer of the same bank (and we should assume such an adversary) may not know that the covert message pertains to a choice of access-level, because the bank customer may have chosen to use the covert-messaging facility for something completely different than access-level selection. We discuss below the possibilities of sending other covert messages to the bank.

2.2   Conveying Other Messages

Once financial institutions make such a login facility available, its possible uses include many other scenarios other than the 3-level access used above to intro-duce the rationale for such a mechanism. Some customers may not care at all about 3-level access: Such customers might decide to never click on an email link, therefore never fall prey to phishing. They might also never take any risk when logging in from public places. Such a customer may set her account up so that the trivially memorizable word(s) that comes after the password covertly con-vey to the bank different courses of action(s) that the bank is supposed to take following the login. The scheme can also be extended to provide k-level access, with $k > 3$, although the costs in storage and user memory increase accordingly.

Conveying Duress. One such possibility is conveying to the bank one of the following two messages: (i) "this is a normal login and I request full access"; or (ii) "I am under duress, pretend that access is granted but call the police immediately and inform them that I am under duress." As discussed in [1,2], if the user is under duress then the adversary will demand to know, under threat of violence, how the user conveys both messages (i) and (ii). As explained in [2], there is a way for the user to appear to comply while giving the adversary what will trigger message (ii) only (if the adversary attempts to use it). For example, the agreement with the bank could be that "bulldog" is the word for message (i), and any other dog breed is for message (ii). Typos result in denied access (no accidental police-calling because of a typo). An adversary who is given wrong information, such as poodle for message (i) and any non-poodle dog for message (ii), has no way to tell whether a signal will be sent to the bank or not.

Indirectly Exposing Phishing. There is no way for the victim of an ongoing phishing attack, made possible as a result of the user's unwisely clicking on a link in a phishing email from the "bank," to directly inform the bank of this fact. However, the user can unwittingly (and indirectly) alert the bank to this fact if one of the few covert messages in her repertoire is "I am doing this login because you solicited it in an email to me." If such a covert message is sent to the bank's server it indirectly alerts the bank of the high likelihood of an unfolding phishing attack. Because the bank knows whether it solicited a connection or not – many banks never send email-embedded links as a matter of policy – it can conclude whether the user has fallen for a phishing attack. As a result of that, an active man-in-the-middle attack resulting from the successful phish only compromises a degraded version of the login that (indirectly) alerts the bank. The bank can call the customer and ask for a change of password and provide advice so as to avoid a repeat occurrence of the episode. This is not a sure-fire defense and several things can still go wrong but it provides an improvement over the current situation where the bank is oblivious of such an attack, even though it may stand to suffer damages from it more than the customer; in some countries financial institutions are required to charge-back the customers' accounts when they fall prey to a phishing attack if the customers acted in good faith.

Phishing is characterized by the discrepancy between what the user thinks (that the bank sent an email urging access via a provided link) and the bank's state (that it sent no such link). Providing a way for users to express their state serves to indirectly alert the bank and prompt it to take some precautionary measures. Such measures can include contacting the user to verify a sensitive transaction and/or giving the user limited access thus minimizing the damage caused by an adversary. Furthermore, the bank can direct the adversary to a honeypot account and alert the user, using out-of-band communication channels, so that the adversary can be monitored and possibly identified for prosecution.

A more sophisticated system can be designed following the same structure in [2] where a third party monitoring user logins is only alerted if the user signals a solicited login as a result of a phishing attack. Such a third party would learn nothing about the identities and activities of the users during normal logins and will only be alerted in case of phishing. We can imagine such a security and business model of combatting phishing led by third-party companies.

2.3   Using Other Channels Than the Password Field

The password field is not the only channel for conveying a covert message to the server; we next give examples of other authentication channels that can be used for that purpose.

Biometrics. Some biometrics can be used as the communication channel depending on how much control the user has on the selection of the biometric and its mode of use. For example, when using an iris scan the user has limited choice, but when using fingerprints the user may send a covert message by the choice of finger to use. Furthermore, for a given finger the user may be able to convey a message through the tilt of the finger relative to the fingerprint reader.

Multi-factor Authentication. Two-factor authentication has been widely adopted, especially in financial institutions. It increases security but remains vulnerable to server impersonation and other sophisticated attacks such as those used by the Zeus malware [4]. Not only is our proposal still relevant in a world of multi-factor authentication, but the multiplicity of factors provides a new mechanism for covert communication. The choice by the user of which factors to use can be used as the covert communication mechanism. For example, if three factors are available and a minimum of two are required, then the user's choice of which factor to leave out sends a covert message to the server.

2.4 Channel Capacity

Psychological and user-acceptance considerations dictate that covert messages be encoded in unary: If three bits can be sent then three (and not the usual 2^3) distinct covert messages can be sent to the server. In fact we argue that, even if $k > 3$ bits can be sent (e.g., by the user's choosing of $k - 1$ out of k possible factors to authenticate), in practice it will not be practical for the typical user to send more than a very small number of bits (possibly as low as 3, but that number is best determined experimentally with user studies).

2.5 Credentials-Sharing

It is ill-advised to share access credentials (such as a password) with others, yet people do it all the time for the sake of convenience. For example, doctors or managers share their passwords with a nurse or secretary so they can avoid the inconvenience of using a (possibly unwieldy) patient-management or enterprise-resource-planning software system. For password-based systems, a service provider can gain a competitive advantage by offering those customers who choose to share their access credentials the ability to share lower forms of access credential (e.g., "read-only" with their tax-accountants).

3 Desiderata for a Better System

The scheme that implements the covert channel needs to have more sophisticated features than the simple ones discussed above. We discuss these features in the following paragraphs.

3.1 Obliviousness

An electronic eavesdropper should neither learn nor be able to re-use the recorded client responses (even for, e.g., repeating the low form of "read-only" login that the user executed). Achieving this means that the server, upon receiving a login request, must use a nonce that affects what the user's client software sends to the server. A replay would then be useless because at the next login the server will generate a different nonce and will expect a different response. The simple scheme's user interface would still be used, but it would need to be processed by client software (that would use it together with the nonce received from the server to generate the response sent to the server). Such obliviousness is best implemented within, for example, the browser itself, as using plugins would imply a lack of mobility, but this assumes the client is running trusted software.

3.2   Resistance to Server Compromise

An adversary who gets a copy of the information stored in the server's credentials file (e.g., /etc/passwd/) should not gain more information than in currently deployed systems. In the scheme discussed earlier, where a password is followed by an easy-to-memorize word, neither the password nor the easy-to-memorize words are vulnerable to a dictionary attack. This is of more importance with the latter as they are likely to be dictionary words (because they need to be trivially memorizable by the user).

3.3   Resistance to Persistent Adversaries

The scheme should assume that the adversary is persistent in seeking access to the user's account, and the adversary will continuously try until he succeeds unless specifically prevented by the underlying scheme. In the case of an attack involving coercion the adversary can demand all the possible login credentials and try them until he succeeds. In phishing attacks, the adversary might launch a number of different attacks through a different number of vectors, e.g., a phishing email, a Facebook message, and an IM message.

4   Further Remarks

A grand vision for authentication has been sought for a number of years, of users having a small number of identities to login to the many heterogeneous service providers, with full control on the user side [3]. Such a vision has been articulated in the National Strategy for Trustworthy Identities in Cyberspace (NSTIC), with cell phones serving as a central hub for client online identities [5]. Such a mechanism addresses many of the security and privacy problems associated with online identities, but it does not render unnecessary what we are proposing: A cell phone hub would become a more tempting target for evildoers, and would benefit from what we propose (especially in cases of physical coercion against the phone's owner).

The features and properties of a covert communication channel as we describe deserves further investigation along many dimensions, including:

1. *Cryptographic:* How to best achieve the desired obliviousness and resistance to server compromise, without degrading the ability and performance of the necessary credentials-checking at login time?
2. *Psychological:* Which parameters of such a system would be acceptable to users, and (if acceptable) would not cause too many errors and false alarms after deployment?

3. *Risk analysis and Economics:* Would such a system decrease the overall risk to the service provider, and by how much. What is its effect on the liability insurance rates of the service provider? Are here any hidden and costly unintended consequences?

Many questions will need answering, but we believe that the overall outcome of such investigations will be favorable to our general approach along all of the above-mentioned dimensions.

Acknowledgments. Portions of this work were supported by National Science Foundation Grants CNS-0915436, CNS-0913875, Science and Technology Center CCF-0939370; by an NPRP grant from the Qatar National Research Fund; and by sponsors of the Center for Education and Research in Information Assurance and Security. The statements made herein are solely the responsibility of the authors.

References

1. Clark, J., Hengartner, U.: Panic Passwords: Authenticating Under Duress. In: Proceedings: The 3rd Conference on Hot Topics in Security. USENIX Association (2008)
2. Stefanov, E., Atallah, M.: Duress Detection for Authentication Attacks Against Multiple Administrators. In: Proceedings: The 2010 ACM Workshop on Insider Threats, pp. 37–46. ACM (2010)
3. Anderson, R.: Can We Fix the Security Economics of Federated Authentication? In: Christianson, B., Crispo, B., Malcolm, J., Stajano, F. (eds.) Security Protocols 2011. LNCS, vol. 7114, pp. 33–48. Springer, Heidelberg (2011)
4. Trend Micro, How ZeuS/ZBOT Bypasses Two-Factor Authentication (October 2010), http://community.trendmicro.com/t5/Web-Threat-Spotlight/ZeuS-ZBOT-Variant-Bypasses-Two-Factor-Authentication/ba-p/16514
5. The White House, National Strategy for Trusted Identities in Cyberspace, NSTIC (2011)

Back Channels Can Be Useful! – Layering Authentication Channels to Provide Covert Communication (Transcript of Discussion)

Mohammed H. Almeshekah

Purdue University

Robert Watson: Can you just clarify the problem very slightly. Is the goal to make users use some passwords less frequently or you want them to have the ability to delegate?

Reply: Delegation is part of what we want to achieve. However, the main goal is to give users a ways to express their intentions and doubts through the password protocol itself. This will give them different levels of access. Why would users want to do that? Take as an example the case where users get an email to take some actions. The user might think that the real service provider might have solicited them, but when they convey this information to the server, in the case the server didn't solicit them, phishing attempt can be detected before any damage could happen. The main challenge of course is how users can convey this message in a way that is undetected by middle parties.

Frank Stajano: In duress situations there is still a distinguisher for the attacker who has the user in front of him. Either the credentials the user gave him work and allow access or does not work and access is denied. If the attacker asks the user for the credentials and release him this is fine, but if you are there at the cash point and he has a gun at your head, he can see that all the stuff that you supply still doesn't work.

Reply: So the service provider, the bank, should make the duress credentials work and present what is supposed to be presented while at the same time take some other actions to protect the user and his account.

Bruce Christianson: The duress password should present what is supposed to happen.

Reply: Exactly. The advantage here is that the bank would know what is happening right now is completely under duress and whatever activity on the account is not under the user's will. The main point here is the bank knows that duress is happening just before it happens, not just having to deal with the aftermath where it would be much harder to solve the problem.

Ariel Stulman: In the case of accessing a bank account, the attacker can simply ask the user to transfer some money and the check his account that the money has really being transferred.

Reply: This is a valid point. However, since the bank already know, at the authentication layer, that a duress is taking place some actions can be taken such as dividing the user's balances by 10. This will greatly reduce the damage.

B. Christianson et al. (Eds.): Security Protocols 2013, LNCS 8263, pp. 196–201, 2013.
© Springer-Verlag Berlin Heidelberg 2013

Also, the bank, can automatically have some procedures that can kick-in and issue a detailed audit trail logging all useful information (which would be a waste of resource if done for every account activity). Another possible action, is to temporarily disable overseas money transfer and show a message to the user account saying that they have to come physically to the branch due to some suspicious account activities, or something similar. Is it not a bullet-proof solution, and not sure if one can be provided to this problem, but it significantly reduces the damage to some more acceptable levels and changes the economics of the game.

Dylan Clarke: The whole point of a phishing attack is it only works if the user actually believes the email, so what would be to stop the attacker putting in the email, we believe your solicited password has been compromised so you must put in your unsolicited password?

Reply: Nothing prevents them from doing so. However, I think it give much more room for users to think "why are they soliciting and telling me my solicited password is compromised?". The other thing is that the scheme simplifies the user's login instructions and clearly distinguish between two type of credentials, solicited-credentials that are always used when logging in by following a link and unsolicited-credentials that is used whenever the user types the URL himself.

Sandy Clark: It won't work.

Reply: I don't see why not. Surely, we need further user studies examining how much does such a scheme reduce the compromise of the unsolicited-credentials.

Bruce Christianson: It would work if you could rely on users to just follow the protocol instead of acting irresponsibly. However, this scheme is solely used for the password scheme. When having a multi-factor authentication, the choice of factors could be used to convey a message.

Reply: The idea here is that the instructions are much simpler and clearer. Two different credentials for two different, clear and distinct usages.

Ariel Stulman: Not taxing the users memories is obviously a noble goal. However, trying to remember that this login for solicitation and this login for non-solicitation, etc is a challenging task?

Robert Watson: Not only that, but you're going to use these at different rates. There is the credential you use all the time, and there is the one you use once in a while. Chances are some password I will never use and probably cannot remember when I want to use it.

Ariel Stulman: Also, the question of which one is which during the time of use is challenging.

Frank Stajano: And which one of the two fingers? Probably, the one that is more worn out.

Ariel Stulman: Also, probably I will end up every time I want to login I will try the first one, then the second one until I found the right one.

Reply: I totally agree with you that there are some challenges. More field studies are needed and further investigation of other scheme that uses the same concept is an interesting area of future research. We try to argue here that there is a spectrum of interesting usage of covert communications and provide some preliminary schemes. Also, we present some recommendations and properties of such schemes for them to be useful and effective.

Bruce Christianson: It's a very nice protocol, the danger is obviously the things that people don't have to do very often. The rarer an actual fire is the more important it is to have fire-drills, so perhaps you can have some protocol where users regularly have to do the solicited or unsolicited.

Robert Watson: Especially duress, we ought to kind of apply duress for a short period of time.

Bruce Christianson: Yes, a mechanism by which the bank can apply duress for a short period to train the user.

Reply: But in the duress problem, it's not a major issue, all that the user needs in the example presented is to pick another word from the same dictionary other than what the user is regularly using. An example of the dictionary of fruits with the normal login word as "apple" all that the user need do is to give any other fruit other than apple.

Bruce Christianson: Do something different to what you usually do.

Reply: Yes, but in duress, going back to presented example, if the user picked poodle as their dog breed word, they don't need to remember the non-duress part, they could put any non poodle breed, so that's kind of easier for the user to remember. You will always use poodle to access and when you are under duress use any non-poodle breed.

Bruce Christianson: What about solicited versus non-solicited credentials.

Reply: It is a more challenging case. However, assuming the user gets enough solicitation email, which is currently the case, they tend to remember it. Also, another point is that users don't have to have different words in different domains. If we can design the system such that the service provider does not know the word itself (by obfuscating it using the password) the user can repeat the word across domains. We are currently investigating some ways of trying to achieve that.

Robert Watson: It's harder, the duress thing is probably easier to engineer. The question I have for you is, I think this protocol lacks some fundamental self-centredness effects still, which is the bank feels that they are the only person in the world that needs to authenticate you, and therefore thinks they should use special things to authenticate you, then they give you special procedures, or special devices, and so on.

Bruce Christianson: And why should they need to be authenticated?

Robert Watson: Right, absolutely, so then this very asymmetric and why the burden should be on me as the end user. Do you have any thoughts of how you might apply this in such a way that you could use it for a single sign-on, or of some method of authentication to other services, or integrate with existing token devices?

Reply: We actually haven't thought about that yet, but that's a really interesting question to look into.

Robert Watson: I mean, here in the UK you could not deploy this system with banks that now provide tokens to all customers. So you'd have to combine them to places such as these tokens.

Reply: But with tokens, an active man-in-the-middle, could just relay the messages back and forth, and just get access, as he's part of the session.

Robert Watson: So what the token gives you is something you have, that is subject to relays. If people were really looking for that protection, then they expect the bank authentication systems to use both systems, and that would be a simple composition of the two systems. But, is there is something stronger you could do by composing these two systems directly and actually integrate the protocols, then you get some new techniques. In other words, can you evolve the tokens somehow such that, in the duress attack, there's something you can do that's stronger than either of the two systems isolated.

Reply: We've been thinking a little bit of integrating this with the token itself exactly as you said. For example, can I put that message in the RSA ID and just add two simple buttons click representing the two cases of solicited and non-solicited, which subsequently can generate different codes.

Robert Watson: Yes, the straightforward thing to do is to have a "I'm under duress" button, but I think if I was putting someone under duress I would make sure they didn't press that. You would need still covert channels to communicate with the device. But I think this in interesting of how to integrate this with existing mechanisms for authentication.

Reply: I totally agree.

Steven Murdoch: One way of specifying a scheme for this is that most bank customers care about people stealing, and especially customers care about who will see how much money they have. And the way that they deal with this is a covert channel but it's only a single bit, and the meaning of this bit is sent by the bank. So the bank sends you a message to say, do you wish to login, or do you wish to do a transfer, or do you wish to do that, and then the user can either say yes and take the number, or they can say no.

Reply: But with a single so my question is the yes or no fixed, so 1 means, yes, and 0 means no, so anyone in the middle, if he gets 1 he could just change it to, or if he gets 0 he could just change it to 1.

Steven Murdoch: So the yes answer is you've taken a cryptographic hash of the cash, and in the no answer you didn't.

Dylan Clarke: Just to go back to your point about duress, and say people will have to do something different. But have you looked at any of the psychological studies on the fact that when they're distressed people tend to do whatever they're trained for, whether it's appropriate or not.

Reply: No we haven't yet. Unfortunately, we don't see a lot of work on duress, while this matter is becoming increasingly important as the convergence between our physical and digital lives is at rapid pace. So I think it would be a really interesting question to answer whether users will will tend to use what they are trained to use usually because they are under duress?

Dylan Clarke: There's one example that shows how serious that could be. There was a case in the US with a Police officer who trained extensively to do close quarter firearms disarms and he was an expert at it. One day he faced somebody who pulled a gun at close quarters, he grabbed him, took the gun off him, and then handed it back to him just like he did with his partner in training.

Reply: I hope he didn't kill him.

Dylan Clarke: No, his partner actually came round the corner and shot the other guy.

Bruce Christianson: So that second mechanism, that's the one you need.

Feng Hao: Just one small point on the phishing attacks. Yes, it's quite a nice protocol, but you also assume a lot of intelligence and good educational background for the kind of users you want to protect. So that tends to be one extreme side of the spectrum of the users, but it is usually not the kind of users that spammers and phishers want to target, because they want to catch the other extreme.

Reply: The major difference in this scheme is that users instruction are extremely simplified into two distinct black and white cases. If you do enter the URL yourself using your own personal computer, use the unsolicited part. In any other case use the solicited/suspicious part. It might not work for all users but certainly raises the bar and alleviates the burden on users on having to verify the origin of the email and the URL of the server they go to when they click the link, and that the certificate is valid, etc. In these cases most users have no clue what we are talking about, let alone being able to perform these tasks and verify that they are talking to what they think they are talking to.

Daniel Thomas: So currently banks tell users that they will never get any links, and people still do click on links.

Reply: That is one of the motivations of this work. There is a trade-off, users would like convenience and functionality. They would like to get an email from the bank with a direct link to their bank statements. The other point is that, it is not the case that all banks tell you that they will never send you an email with clickable links. In fact, one of the banks I bank with sends me a clickable link to my monthly statement. This leaves users confused, and the instructions of what to do with email links is not universal. The other point is that whenever there is a trade-off between convenience and security, convenience most of the time wins. Users would like technologies to help them and not make their lives harder.

Frank Stajano: The other point is that it's all very well telling the users, "don't do this", but if they follow the advice and then they can't get what they need to do, like checking their own bank account, they're just not going to follow the advice because they need to check their bank account, and that's more important. I mean, if the advice is, don't run JavaScript because it's dangerous, which is a very sensible piece of advice, and if I don't run JavaScript my bank's website doesn't work, what choice do I have? I'll have to run the JavaScripts, because I need to see my bank account. No matter how much I trust my system, it's not going to give me money instead of my bank.

Reply: So yes, there's a limit to giving users sensible instructions and then blame them if they don't follow them, because we have no remedy to offer them if they don't follow them for a good reason. This schemes proposes one of the ways to provide some remedies as we alleviate the damage by having a restricted access with the solicited part.

Robert Watson: The trick here is to at least align the interest in adopting your protocol with one of the two parties. Ideally this would be the bank because the bank would like to accomplish low levels of fraud. Then they have the system administrator problem, which is how do you get the users to conform to your policy, how do you get them to use the system correctly. So it would be nice if there is a structured argument specifically for why they actually need this protocol and what benefits does it produce.

Reply: That's part of the liability issuer we raised in the paper. Will the user be liable now if he doesn't communicate solicitation? Would that covert message change liabilities? Do we want to do so? That is an interesting question to ask.

Spraying Diffie-Hellman
for Secure Key Exchange in MANETs

Ariel Stulman, Jonathan Lahav, and Avraham Shmueli

Department of Computer Science
Jerusalem College of Technology
Jerusalem, Israel
stulman@jct.ac.il, {j.lahav,adshmueli}@gmail.com

Abstract. As the capabilities of mobile technology such as PDAs, smart-phones and tablets increases, *theoretical* ideas are materializing. One of these ideas under active development is a infrastructure free network, based solely on mobile devices (a.k.a. MANET - mobile ad hoc network). These networks would have the ability of running communications without the use of pre-existing infrastructure, allowing for a reduction of cost to carriers, setting up communication networks where no infrastructure is available (like disaster zones), etc. In this paper we propose an algorithm, based on the famous Diffie-Hellman key exchange (KE) algorithm, that will provide for confidentiality of KE during conversation initiation, from which a cryptographically secure channel can later be derived. The algorithm utilizes the constant fluctuation of MANET network topology to flush-out eavesdroppers (if they exist), assuming no prior knowledge and without active user intervention.

1 Introduction

Peer-to-peer applications are quickly gaining popularity, with many applications taking advantage of the multitude of channels (Bluetooth, WIFI, etc.) between devices for setting up closed networks. There are even SDKs that attempt to abstract the entire communication process (regardless of channel) and leave to the developers the task of application programming. [1] The next logical step, which is already emerging in some applications (see for example [2]), is complete mobile ad hoc networks, or MANETs, which allows for the connection of two parties through intermediate parties without pre-existing infrastructure. The network is based on mobile devices, such as smartphones, acting both as the end users for the communications and the routing agents for packets. Usage of such networks is advantageous in many perspectives, including, for example, the ability to bypass central routing hubs which are required for efficient '*big brother*' eavesdropping.

Of course, eavesdroppers are not limited to routing hubs, as they are able to anonymously join the MANET and monitor or taint all traffic passing through them. In order to achieve confidentiality, MANET developers turn to cryptography. Assuming that cryptographic keys were not setup in advance, key exchange

B. Christianson et al. (Eds.): Security Protocols 2013, LNCS 8263, pp. 202–212, 2013.

algorithms must be employed to allow for a secure channel between communicating parties. In this paper we wish to introduce a variant of the famous Diffie-Hellman (DH) key exchange algorithm [3], spraying Diffie-Hellman, which allows for a secure key exchange given an adversary that can manipulate packets in transit (section 2). Since man-in-the-middle (MITM) attack undermines DH's main claim of confidentiality, our algorithm will mitigate (within a predefined probability) this attack allowing for communication confidentiality as intended by DH protocol. This will be accomplished without prior agreement among communicating parties (section 4.1) and without user intervention in the confirmation protocol (section 4.1).

2 Spraying DH

2.1 Model

In our model, we place no limitations on the attacker. She can eavesdrop, control (stop or allow transmission) and inject data into the stream she controls. Thus, we must assume that on every route under her control, she can taint the data to initiate a MITM attack. We assume that attackers can collude, bringing under their control multiple routes. For the sake of simplicity, we will refer to all of the colluding parties as one entity.

We assume that there is no trusted third party coordinating or authenticating sender to receiver (or vice-versa), and that the only prior knowledge to work with is the address of both communicating parties. This address can be in a form of IP address in the network, the phone number allocated to the smart device, or the IMEI number embedded in the device by the manufacturer. In order to prevent network collisions, we do assume that this address is unique and cannot be spoofed. This assumption can be justified by the fact that although one can transmit a false address, this can only influence some of the network routing tables, but not all of them. This gives packets not traveling through malicious nodes the ability to be delivered to the correct recipient.

Definition 1. Let $R = \{r_1, r_2, \cdots, r_n\}$ be a non-cyclic route ($r_i \neq r_j \; \forall r_i, r_j \in R$) between the sender ($r_1$) and receiver ($r_n$) at the connection time.

Let $\mathbb{R}$ denote the set of all possible such routes, and $|\mathbb{R}| =$ the size of $\mathbb{R}$.

Let $A = \{a_1, a_2, \cdots, a_w\}$, such that $A \subseteq \mathbb{R}$ and all $a_i \in A$ are under the attacker's control. Let $|A| =$ the size of A.

Let $F = \{f_1, f_2, \cdots, f_m\} = \overline{A}$. That is $F \cup A = \mathbb{R}$ and $F \cap A = \emptyset$, denoting all the paths not under the attacker's control. Let $|F| =$ the size of F.

Based on the above definition, it is understood that $|A| < |\mathbb{R}| \implies |F| > 0$, meaning that at least one route between the sender and receiver is not under the attacker's control.

2.2 Algorithm

What allows an attacker, Eve, the ability of executing MITM attack against DH, is the ability of tainting the data passing through her. Without this ability, DH provides confidentiality as stated. By utilizing the inherent nature of MANETs of ever changing network topology, we are able to remove this ability from the attacker; thus, rendering her a passive attacker.

To accomplish this we notice that Eve cannot know in advance all of the paths between sender, Alice, and receiver, Bob. By utilizing more than one path for KE, we reduce Eve's capabilities to guesswork. She must, by chance, succeed in intercepting all channels between Alice and Bob to be able to taint the KE data.

KE Sending Protocol. Suppose we have a KE message, *msg*, that needs to be passed from Alice to Bob. Alice must go through the following protocol steps:

1. Alice appends a cryptographic hash (i.e. MD5, SHA1, etc.) to *msg*. The purpose of this hash is for Bob to be able to confirm that he received all parts of *msg* (see next step) untainted.
2. The derived *msg* (including the original *msg* coupled with its hash) is then divided into k smaller parts, such that $msg = msg_1 + msg_2 + ... + msg_k$.
3. Each msg_i is to be sent through a different network route, starting with Alice's immediate neighbors and making its way to Bob in separate paths.

KE Receiving Protocol. For Bob to be able to re-construct the message, he must:

1. receive and concatenate all micro-message parts of the information to re-compose *msg*.
2. Bob must now check the integrity of the data by recomputing the cryptographic hash attached to the message to see if it coincides with what was sent.

Under these conditions, in order for Eve to manipulate the key in such a way so a MITM attack can be conducted later, she must intercept all of the micro-messages (msg_i), re-build *msg*, change the data, compute the hash, break the new *msg* and resend it to Bob. One micro-message that escapes interception, alerts Bob to the possibility of MITM, for which appropriate measures can be taken. This is functionally equivalent to reducing Eve's capabilities to eavesdropping, without the ability of tainting the data.

Some More Details. Step 3 of the sending protocol, describes the dispersement of msg_i through different routes starting from Alice's adjacent neighbors. This dispersement (or, spraying) of msg_i among available routes, $\mathbb{R}$, can be done by having Alice randomly select an adjacent node, $r_2 \in R$, for each msg_i and allow the routing to commence from there. This will give a probability of

$$P = 1 - \left(\frac{|A|}{|\mathbb{R}|}\right)^k \tag{1}$$

that the channel will not be compromised (a positive result); whether a secure channel is actually setup, or an attack attempt is detected and thwarted. This is based on the probability that at least one msg_i will get through some $f_j \in F$ to alert Bob as to the existence of MITM.

Alternatively, she can evenly spread all msg_i among her neighbors, picking as many routes as possible. By having Alice spray micro-messages in an even fashion on all available routes, we get a positive result probability of

$$
P = 1 - \begin{cases} 0 & k > |A| \\ \dfrac{\dbinom{|A|}{k}\dbinom{|F|}{0}}{\dbinom{|\mathbb{R}|}{k}} & k \leq |A| \end{cases} \tag{2}
$$

Intuitively, random spread should have a higher secure channel setup success rate (see figure 1). This can be explained by the fact that if there are insecure routes originating at Alice's neighbors, they get a higher probability of being selected if one was forced to spread micro-messages.

Consider, for example, the scenario where Alice has four neighbors, of which one $\in A$ and three $\in F$. In addition, suppose that k=3; that is, msg is divided into three micro-messages. If we assume random-spread, there is a

$$
\left(\frac{3}{4}\right)^3 = \frac{27}{64} = 42.19\% \tag{3}
$$

chance of setting up a successful secure channel. Using even-spread under the same conditions, the chances of setting up a secure channel drop to

$$
\frac{\binom{1}{0}\binom{3}{3}}{\binom{4}{3}} = \frac{1*1}{4} = \frac{1}{4} = 25\% \tag{4}
$$

The chances of being fully compromised, however, are also higher when random spread is used. For the above scenario random spread would have a

$$
\left(\frac{1}{4}\right)^3 = \frac{1}{64} = 1.56\% \tag{5}
$$

chance of being compromised. Even-spread, based on Equation 2, would guarantee that the channel isn't compromised.

If, however, we consider an alternative scenario where Alice has four neighbors, of which three $\in A$ and one $\in F$, and again we suppose that k=3, the situation is reversed. Using even-spread there is a high probability that Alice will be fully compromised. In addition, there is some probability that the attack will be detected. Success, however, is impossible. Using random-spread, however, increases the possibility of being attacked, but leaves the possibility of success open.

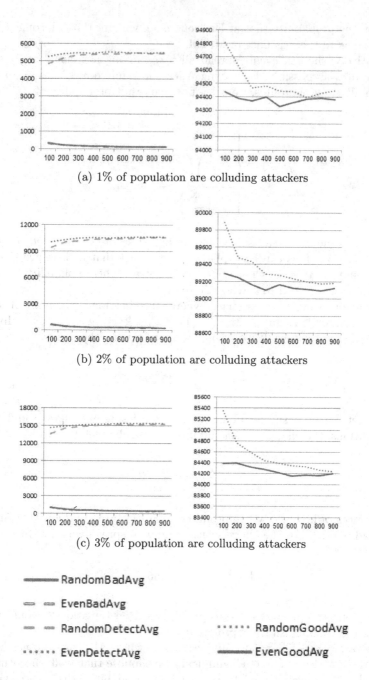

(a) 1% of population are colluding attackers

(b) 2% of population are colluding attackers

(c) 3% of population are colluding attackers

RandomBadAvg

EvenBadAvg

RandomDetectAvg   RandomGoodAvg

EvenDetectAvg   EvenGoodAvg

Fig. 1. Comparison of random vs. even spread for 100000 channel setups for different network population sizes. Graphs on left show that even spread is better or equal to random spread when attack is present (fewer successful attacks (Bad) and more detected attack attempts (Detect)). Random spread, however, is more successful in setting up a secure channel (right).

In some link-state based routing protocol, like OLSR [4], nodes have enough information about the structure of the network so they can find several different routes to the destination. This allows for the pre-planning of up to nine forward hops using the SSRR (Strict Source and Record Route) IP option [5]. Assuming a capable attacker will try to place herself at the location x_i such that $max(x_i \in F_1 \wedge x_i \in F_2 \wedge \cdots \wedge x_i \in F_h)$ increasing $|A|$, she will try to control the route convergence points; the location near the sender (i=1) or near the receiver $(i = n_j)$. Therefore, by pre-planning routes and distancing automatic route selection from a convergence point, we presume security will be increased dramatically.

3   Previous Work

Strong cryptographic algorithms in place today for securing data transmission heavily depend upon the secrecy of the cryptographic keys. Both in symmetric and a-symmetric schemes, one of the weak links lies in the key coordination between sender and receiver. As many MITM attacks are centered around this weakness, key exchange algorithms that allow for secure key coordination are of utter importance. Today, key coordination in public networks is based on a trusted third party using public key infrastructures (PKI) [6], such as in SSL [7] and TLS [8], on out-of-band coordination techniques in private networks, such as in SSH [9], or on a combination of both such as in IPsec [10].

The most famous in-band, no-third-trusted-party key exchange algorithm is the Diffie-Hellman (DH) algorithm [11,12], standardized in [3]. The DH scenario environment, allows for the coordination of a symmetric key between two parties with an eavesdropping adversary not being able to deduce the key. In [13] it was shown, however, that an adversary who has the ability to manipulate communication packets, can execute a MITM attack compromising the confidentiality of future data transmission. This is accomplished by orchestrating two separate exchanges, one between the sender and attacker, and the other between the attacker and receiver. Thus, all communication from the sender can be decrypted by the attacker and re-encrypted for the receiver. In this scenario, neither the sender nor the receiver is aware of the MITM and there is a loss of confidentiality.

In order to mitigate this threat, authenticated DH variants, that authenticate communicating parties to each other, were developed. In STS, a-symmetric public key certificates are used to authenticate communicating parties [14]. Zimmerman et. al. [15] developed ZRTP which provides confidentiality, protection against MITM attacks, and, in cases where the signaling protocol provides end-to-end integrity protection, authentication. It uses ephemeral DH with hash commitment, and allows the detection of MITM attacks by displaying a short authentication string (SAS) at initial startup for the users to read and verbally compare over the phone.

Both methods have their downsides with regards to pre-required knowledge to overcome MITM attack. In STS [16], pre-shared certificates must be known in advance in order to validate communicating parties. In ZRTP prior knowledge of the communicating parties voices must be known. The security is built upon the fact that each party recognizes the other side's voice and thus verifies their authenticity. In [17] it was shown that use of voice synthesizers can overcome ZRTP security mechanisms and conduct a MITM attack.

4   Discussion

4.1   Overcoming Problems

The algorithm described above has been able to overcome some problems existent in related algorithms used within the MANET architectures.

Prior Knowledge. The prior knowledge that communicating parties must have before commencement of the session is a key issue in protocol selection for a specific architecture. On the one extreme, pre-shared key (PSK) protocols, like SSH [18], require that the key be correlated "by hand" out-of-band. This scheme is perfectly suitable on VPNs where parties "meet" and "setup" a network. In our model, however, where communicating parties might have never met (i.e., A tells B about C, and provides his address. B and C have never met, and could not have pre-shared a key for communication exchange), this scheme is excluded. Other algorithms, like ZRTP, use SAS for the authentication mechanism. This requires that both sides recognize each other prior to session setup, which precludes a party from referring one friend to another. In addition, as [19] stated and has been shown in [17], voices can be spoofed with a synthesizer, overcoming authentication.

By utilizing the inherent architecture of the network, we can detect with high probability the existence of a MITM attack without prior cooperation between communicating parties; thus, terminating the connection and protecting its parties.

User Intervention. It is quite accepted among protocol (and application) developers that minimal user intervention is essential for the success of the proposed product. The more a user must interact with the protocol, the less likely he will do so; reducing the overall security of the product.

In ZRTP it is required, in every conversation, that both users run SAS and recognize voice for the shared secret to be computed and authenticated. Many people will be inclined not to do so. On the contrary, sooner or later they will view it as a burden and try to do away with this feature. This, obviously, totally voids the ability of ZRTP to detect MITM.

In our algorithm, user intervention is not required. It is the protocol that detects MITM based on concatenation of msg parts, and can be pre-configured to terminate connection setup if MITM is detected. Of course, the option can be presented to the user as to allow communication regardless of the threat, but this is just an augmentation to the protocol and not an essential part.

Forward Security. Perfect forward secrecy [16], PFS, is defined as the ability to protect the secrecy of exchanged keys from earlier runs even in the event of disclosure of long-term secret keying material. This amounts to a conversation remaining secret even if some long term keying material is compromised. Ephemeral DH is known to have perfect forward security. This is based on the fact that for each conversation a different key is agreed upon based on a onetime random number chosen by each party. Compromising the data from one conversation does not compromise any other conversation as no long term keying material exists. Under these definitions SDH adheres to PFS as it reduces to the ephemeral DH algorithm.

In addition, in contrast to ZRTP where compromise of current key opens all future conversations to MITM attack, as future key is derived from current key stored by the communicating party, in SDH this isn't true. For every conversation a new ephemeral key is negotiated and isn't based on previously stored information.

4.2 Cost and Shortcomings of SDH

Overhead. Features, no matter how effective, all come at some cost. For every feature introduced into the protocol in order to achieve some goal, be it security, authenticity, reliability etc., a cost must be endured. SDH is no different. For this scheme to work we must increase the overhead of conversation handshake. As msg is divided into more parcels or packets, the optimum packet size isn't used. Since the same amount of data is sent, the overhead increases in a linear fashion as a direct function of the number of micro-messages msg is divided into.

For example, suppose we had a ratio of

$$\rho = \frac{headers}{data} \tag{6}$$

then by splitting msg into i micro-messages we get an linear increase by a factor of i

$$\rho' = \frac{i * headers}{data} \tag{7}$$

since the overall data sent is constant but each parcel has its own header.

The difference between (7) and (6), $\rho' - \rho$, is the additional overhead incurred at the sender's side, but there is other overhead as well. Since multiple paths are used for each msg_i, only one would actually take the optimal path between communicating parties. All others are forced into sub-optimal paths, and this is also an overhead incurred by the protocol. Of course, there is a direct correlation between the level of security achieved and the overhead incurred. The more we divide msg into micro-messages and the bigger their dispersement among different paths, the greater the probability that MITM will be thwarted. We leave exact calculations and estimations to future research.

Bottle Necks. SDH assumes that convergence points around the sender and receiver are the vulnerable portions of the path between communicating parties; thus, the spraying embedded in the algorithm. This, however, might not necessarily be the case. It is possible that there are bottle necks on the path between parties. These bottle necks would require that all traffic between parties converge and pass through these nodes, allowing for an attacker to compromise the connection. Suppose, for example, that there are only x *intercity* connection points. All traffic between the two cities must pass through one of these x nodes, regardless of the multiple paths SDH started with.

Single Side Mitigation. SDH exhibits an interesting phenomenon; specifically, single side mitigation. Spraying is done on the sender's side, without any control on the path micro-messages will take once released. It is quite possible that although spread out at the beginning of the journey, paths will converge long before reaching their destination. This would stipulate that albeit an attacker close to the sender is turned passive, an attacker near the receiver, however, will still have the ability to intercept communications with much less effort. Thus, it would seem that the algorithm's capabilities are influenced by the attacker's position.

This, however, might not be a problem. All KE algorithms (including DH) require the receiver to respond with some un-forseen data. At this point, the receiver would employ the same spraying technique, causing a nearby attacker to loose the ability of influencing the communication. Now, for an attack to succeed, we must have colluding attackers strategically placed near moving targets, a feat difficult to execute "on the fly".

We leave the investigation of this phenomena ("single side mitigation") to future research.

Shortcomings. There is one major deficiency with SDH that must be further looked into. SDH, just like DH, does not take care of authentication; rather, it creates confidentiality (which is the basis for authentication). This implies that one does not know to whom one really is talking. We assumed that the network addresses cannot be spoofed, and network routing cannot be influenced. This is true for most part, since routing information is widespread and constantly being updated by all around. Thus, the probability of being able to taint everyone's information all of the time is small. But theoretically speaking, if an attacker were able to do that, the SDH does not provide authenticity. It would be possible for the key exchange to be conducted with a different partner than was intended. To achieve authentication of parties as well, we must incorporate mechanisms that will operate above the actual connection. We leave that to further research.

5   Conclusion and Future Research

In this paper we proposed an algorithm, SDH, that allows for secure key exchange with zero prior knowledge between sender and receiver. In today's emerging mobile wireless networks, this type of capability is of utter importance. As CAs are being hacked and certificates forged, with governments and criminals listening in on communication lines, the chain of trust is compromised and must be augmented. We believe that SDH can be a step in the right direction towards privacy.

In addition, we provided two possible spraying methods (random spread and even spread) and showed that on average even spread is better. Albeit, the difference between the two diminishes as the population size increases.

There are still many questions left open for future research, including estimation of protocol cost, the ability to force bottlenecks, augmenting the protocol with authenticity to overcome identity mis-match, examining the feasibility of running packets through completely different network paths, etc.

References

1. Alljoyn, Qualcomm (2012), https://developer.qualcomm.com/ mobile-development/mobile-technologies/peer-peer-alljoyn
2. The serval project (2010), http://www.servalproject.org/ (access date: September 6, 2012)
3. Rescorla, E.: Diffie-Hellman Key Agreement Method. RFC 2631 (Proposed Standard), Internet Engineering Task Force (June 1999), http://www.ietf.org/rfc/rfc2631.txt (access date: September 6, 2012)
4. Clausen, T., Jacquet, P.: Optimized Link State Routing Protocol (OLSR). RFC 3626 (Experimental), Internet Engineering Task Force (October 2003), http://www.ietf.org/rfc/rfc3626.txt (access Date: September 6, 2012)
5. Postel, J.: Internet Protocol. RFC 791 (Standard), Internet Engineering Task Force, updated by RFC 1349 (September 1981), http://www.ietf.org/rfc/rfc791.txt (access Date: September 6, 2012)
6. Cooper, D., Santesson, S., Farrell, S., Boeyen, S., Housley, R., Polk, W.: Internet X.509 Public Key Infrastructure Certificate and Certificate Revocation List (CRL) Profile. RFC 5280 (Proposed Standard), Internet Engineering Task Force (May 2008), http://www.ietf.org/rfc/rfc5280.txt (access date: September 6, 2012)
7. Freier, A., Karlton, P.: The Secure Sockets Layer (SSL) Protocol Version 3.0. RFC 6101 (Proposed Standard), Internet Engineering Task Force (August 2011), http://www.ietf.org/rfc/rfc6101.txt (access date: September 6, 2012)
8. Dierks, T., Rescorla, E.: The Transport Layer Security (TLS) Protocol Version 1.2. RFC 5246 (Proposed Standard), Internet Engineering Task Force, updated by RFCs 5746, 5878. (August 2008), http://www.ietf.org/rfc/rfc5246.txt (access date: September 6, 2012)
9. Ylonen, T., Lonvick, C.: The Secure Shell (SSH) Protocol Architecture. RFC 4251 (Proposed Standard), Internet Engineering Task Force (January 2006), http://www.ietf.org/rfc/rfc4251.txt (access date: September 6, 2012)
10. Kent, S., Seo, K.: Security Architecture for the Internet Protocol. RFC 4301 (Proposed Standard), Internet Engineering Task Force (December 2005), http://www.ietf.org/rfc/rfc4301.txt (access date: September 6, 2012)
11. Diffie, W., Hellman, M.E.: New directions in cryptography. IEEE Transactions on Information Theory 22(6), 644–654 (1976)
12. Hellman, M., Diffie, W., Merkle, R.: Cryptographic apparatus and method. USA Patent 4 200 770 (April 29, 1980)
13. Rivest, R.L., Shamir, A.: How to expose an eavesdropper. Commun. ACM 27(4), 393–394 (1984), http://doi.acm.org/10.1145/358027.358053 (access date: September 6, 2012)
14. O'Higgins, B., Diffie, W., Strawczynski, L., de Hoog, R.: Encryption and isdn - a natural fit. In: Proc. ISS 1987, Pheonix, March 15-20, pp. 863–869 (1987)

15. Zimmermann, P., Johnston, A., Callas, J.: ZRTP: Media Path Key Agreement for Unicast Secure RTP. RFC 6189 (Proposed Standard), Internet Engineering Task Force (April 2011), http://www.ietf.org/rfc/rfc6189.txt (access date: September 6, 2012)

16. Diffie, W., Van Oorschot, P.C., Wiener, M.J.: Authentication and authenticated key exchanges. Des. Codes Cryptography 2(2), 107–125 (1992), http://dx.doi.org/10.1007/BF00124891 (access date: September 6, 2012)

17. ser. Cryptologic Quarterly, vol. 26(4), United States' National Security Agency, NSA (2007)

18. Cusack, F., Forssen, M.: Generic Message Exchange Authentication for the Secure Shell Protocol (SSH). RFC 4256 (Proposed Standard), Internet Engineering Task Force (January 2006), http://www.ietf.org/rfc/rfc4256.txt (access date: September 6, 2012)

19. ERK. On the security of short authentication strings (March 2007), http://www.imc.org/ietf-rtpsec/mail-archive/msg00608.html (access date: September 6, 2012)

Spraying Diffie-Hellman for Secure Key Exchange in MANETs (Transcript of Discussion)

Ariel Stulman

Jerusalem College of Technology

I want to talk about key exchange algorithms in MANETs and mobile ad hoc networks, and do some background, which I'm sure everybody knows. Everything started with a joint research project with Flinders University in South Australia. They built a practical MANET for Android call Serval, and in the communication between us it was agreed that we took on ourselves the security aspect of the system. So this arrangement induces a requirement on the algorithm, it has to be practical.

The Diffie-Hellman key exchange algorithm, everybody knows, it's one of the most famous algorithms out there. This is a famous picture taken out of Wikipedia. We have A and B, Alice and Bob, trying to communicate. Each one has to pick a secret key, they have some common knowledge, that's public knowledge, that's the yellow paint. Each one of them goes and picks a secret key, which is the paint that each one knows. Each one combines separately his own paint, it's obviously mathematical equations not paint, and they get a different paint. Now they send it out one to the other, and then they can generate a common secret without actually transferring the key from one side to another. As long as the adversary is sitting in the middle doesn't know the secret key, it's got to be computationally infeasible for him to compute this shared key, and this is something that Diffie-Hellman gives us without any problem.

The problem is, as everybody knows, man-in-the-middle. B could be a man-in-the-middle, and then he'll just set up a secret key with A, with Alice, and set up a secret key with C, and then just be the man-in-the-middle transferring everything around, and save it in cleartext, such that everything passing through him, is cleartext. We have two separate common keys, and then Diffie-Hellman is broken. This is famous. So we sat and we thought what could be done. Firstly, Diffie-Hellman's strong point is if an attacker is passive and is only listening to the channels. The only problem is if we have an active attacker that can orchestrate a man-in-the-middle attack, or any other kind of attack, like relay attacks, or impersonation attacks, if it can orchestrate an attack then it's broken. So a lot of algorithms out there trying to take Diffie-Hellman and play around with it to get around this problem, and most of them go in the route of, let's add authentication, you should know who you're talking to, am I talking to B, am I talking to C. If we add authentication into the actual key exchange algorithm then we solve the problem.

B. Christianson et al. (Eds.): Security Protocols 2013, LNCS 8263, pp. 213–222, 2013.
© Springer-Verlag Berlin Heidelberg 2013

There are two famous solutions. One of them is by Diffie himself, STS. The other is ZRTP, Zimmermann real time protocol. And the idea was that either we add certificates, which is what station to station protocol did. They add a certificate to actual communication and that identifies you to other side. What Zimmermann did in ZRTP is that he used a short authentication string protocol. The first time you set up communication, out of the supposed secret key we generate some kind of short sentence, three words, four words, whatever, and you're supposed to use your voice and say, I see on my screen apple, orange, and I don't know what. And the other side will also see the same words, and that will authenticate the fact that it's secure from side to side. If you have a man-in-the-middle, so in that sense he would have a different key with Alice and a different key with Bob, so then the two, Alice and C, would not see the same words, and they'll say, there's something wrong here, and they will stop the communication. But NSA used voice synthesisers to prove that this is easily broken. Just by him saying the generated words, and then I just go and synthesise his voice. In a sense ZRTP, which is what is used today - actually incorporated Serval right now - that's the standard they use today in MANET security, is obviously broken if we can synthesise the voice.

The problem with everything as usual is prior knowledge. If there are certificates or user intervention, all these things are obviously not good ideas. The more we demand out of users, the less they are inclined to do it, like we spoke right now. If I asked, if I demanded of a person to add password plus, plus, plus, he just wouldn't do it. So if I go and I tell them, every time you give a call say: apples and oranges, and pears, and next time say: Oxford and Cambridge. He just won't do it. He'll just say, I don't care, and just go on. So this obviously is not good. So we were thinking how can we go and do this automatically. Now on the Internet today everybody knows TLS, or SSL, or whatever protocol you use, it's automatic, you don't deal with it, you go the bank, you write HTTPS, or you link using a hyperlink, or whatever it is, and then it just happens. But in order to do that we have to have trusted third parties, some certificate authority, and your browser has to be pre-installed with the certificate, and the signatures, and everything else. But in MANETs that's not practical, because if we were going to set up right now a MANET right here, a mobile ad hoc network, so there is no trusted third party. I can sit in the corner and just hack everybody around, and nobody would know. There's no trusted third party in something that is set up ad hoc. So what can we do to try to setup all a secure connection?

The architecture we're talking about is some kind of network, and let's suppose that this little guy right here is trying to communicate with that guy, and we have two adversaries in the middle, and they're trying to break the system. So the question is how can we go and set up the key exchange between this one and that one without these two actually seeing what's happening. Now we are assuming that obviously the cryptography works, which means that if I set up a key exchange then I'm home free. The question is how do we get the keys to the other side. So we thought of the following. What we first do is append some kind of hash to the message, the purpose of the hash at the other end is if the attackers do get the message, or at least part of the message, and that hash will change, I will be able to detect it on the other side at the receiving end. So we append some kind of hash, and then we split the message. Instead of one key exchange message, I'll take it and split it into N parts, with N obviously varying, I don't know what it is exactly, 2, 3, 4, 5, 10, 15 parts, exactly the same message, instead of sending as one piece we'll send it over the system in N pieces, and we're going to try to send every piece through a different route in the system, which is not something difficult to do since I know that I'm attached to X number of people I can upfront, even TCP, or any other protocol you know, send this piece through him, and that piece through him, that piece through her, and then let it go on by itself. The truth is that in TCP itself I could even specify nine steps ahead, I could say, go from here to there, from there to there, and then go, or any other way. In a sense I am taking a sub optimal path, because the standard routing algorithm will look for the optimal path, but by taking a sub optimal path what I am doing is I am spreading risk around, and by spreading around I am trying to circumvent those two attackers.

Now the actual spreading algorithm, we have two possible spreading algorithms that we have thought of, and there can be many variations of these two, but we have the random and the even spread. The random spread will just say, each message part randomly go and pick one of your neighbours and say, you take it. And then for the next message part he can randomly go and pick any one of those neighbours and take it again. So it could be that the same neighbour will actually get all the pieces, or parts of the pieces, just randomly spread. I have to define success before I say the probability of success, but success means if I detect that I'm being attacked, because I can just go and shut down the communication, or if I'm able to set up a key exchange. Failure is that if I am attacked. So if we think about it for a second, if I go and send N parts in N different routes, or randomly selected routes, for an attacker to be able to orchestrate an attack he must be able to intercept every one of those pieces. If even one piece gets through, then when the receiving side would get all the pieces, reconstruct the message and see that the hash doesn't match, something is wrong, somebody is tampering. And by doing that I just shut down the communication and say let's start again. So in order for the attacker to succeed every piece must go through an attacker. If we have A attackers, and we have from a total of R possible routes, and you have K parts, that's a very low probability of being attacked. This depends on, if you have one neighbor and you're sending packets through them, it's a very high probability of being attacked. But if you're sitting in a stadium, or you're sitting in an airport or any other place, then you have hundreds of people around you where you can connect to, it becomes a very high probability of success.

Other possible spreading methods, and in a second I will talk about the advantages and disadvantages of any one of these methods, is evenly spreading the message, the packet. I'm going to pick a message part, look for some neighbor whom didn't I use yet, so send it through him. The next message part I'm not going to send through him, I'm going to send through someone else. Purposely, upfront, try to spread the messages as much as I can amongst my neighbours, and then let it go on by itself. Here the probability obviously changes because my binomial probability is A choose K, so for an attack to succeed I want all K parts to go through A, and zero parts to go through the good paths, so the probability obviously changes.

Now we ran simulations on this kind of architecture, and we tried it with a whole bunch of percentage of attackers, which means that we increased the population, but we left an amount of colluding attackers percentage-wise constant, which means, for example, up here what we did for these two. We sent 100,000 communication set ups, and we said, let 1% attackers out of a population of 100, 200, 300, 400, and the amount of attackers we increased so it should be the same percentage of attackers, which obviously doesn't have to be that way, if you have three attackers and you increase the population then the percentage decreases, but if, suppose we just keep it the same percentage of attackers and we just increase the population and see what happens. So we did it for 1% of attackers, 2%, 3%, 4%, we did a whole bunch of these things, and we got very interesting results. What you see on the right side is approximately 95% were able to succeed which means that all packets went through non-attackers, every one of them. That means we actually were able to set up a key exchange. What we see on the left side is either attacked or detected, I made attack red and I made detected green, because detected is also OK, it's an OK result. But you can see that it went down below 1%, even less, of actually attacked. Now the attackers are colluding attackers, which isn't something that's easily done. If you have 900 people and 1% attackers, so we need a lot of attackers that collude at real time to be able to do this. So we see the results are pretty good.

The only thing is, let's talk about the differences we see between even spreading random spread. So when we randomly spread the messages so the chances of being attacked are actually higher, because it randomly could happen that I will send all message parts to the same person, and he happens to be an adversary. And when I evenly spread the messages, and not pick a neighbour that I've picked before, so my chances of being attacked decrease. And that's how we look at the attack vector, we looked at random and even spread, we see that random spread actually has a worse blue line, a bit worse than the even spread, you have a higher chance of being attacked. We looked at the amount of detected attacks, it's worse because what happens is that if I go and I send everything through one attacker, my chances of detecting that I'm being attacked decreases. And if I go and I spread actual messages then my chances of detecting an attack increase because at least one packet was able to get through, and able to detect the attack. So there's a trade-off here, what's more important, I'm not sure yet. But what's more important, we want to detect an attack, or get actually be able to thwart an attack. These were pretty much the results we got. Question?

Daniel Thomas: What's the structure of the graph which you ran simulation on?

Reply: Random. It means a MANET, when you walk into the airport, that's random. I mean, we could sit right here and it's, change the seats around and it's random again. So the simulation that we did, and we're still running tests and simulations, and stuff like that, we just generated random graphs with different population sizes, and randomly selected attackers, and we just kept a ratio, we wanted it to be 1% attackers, 2% attackers, 5% attackers, whatever it is, and then see what happens by setting up the graph, and now flowing through the system and see what happens.

So now we do the other side, the receiving end, this is just the other way around to make sure that we detect everything. So first we have to reconstruct all the message parts. Next thing we do is that we check the hash. A hash mismatch it indicates a message tampering. Colluding attackers would have to change every message part, recompute the hash, and resend that in order for them to succeed in an attack. Because if they just changed one message part then I will detect it on the other side, so a hash mismatch is what stops tampering. I could have a denial-of-service, that's true, because if he just gets one and just changes it every time I won't be able to set up a communication. But as far as I'm concerned denial-of-service is better than being attacked, that's a better system. And once we have the key, we can deduce a shared secret.

Rubin Xu: So you can actually build a threshold encryption system on top of that, such that you don't need to retransmit each time you get a hash mismatch?

Reply: You could, we were thinking of actually incorporating into the actual application, talking about future research, all kinds of levels of thresholds of being attacked, you can talk anyway if you don't care. If you care then we can have the application flash red, or flash green, and above that do whatever you want to build a whole layer of authentication, authorization, whatever you want, above this system. Obviously it's still preliminary, it's not complete, but you can do above, build a whole level of things above this. What's interesting here is that we're using the actual fluctuating architecture of the network to be able to get security, and not some prior knowledge or prior I don't know what, because if I am trying to call some common friend that we have, suppose that you told me that his phone number is 12345679, I don't have any prior common knowledge of that person, so how can I set up a communication. But by utilising the fluctuating topology of the network, I can try to set up such a communication.

If all message parts arrive and the hash matches then we have no attacker influence of data, and we have security achieved. When I say security I mean our common shared secret. If the hash does not match, at least some data was influenced by the attacker, then the attacker is detected, which is also a good result, it's not a bad result. The only bad possibility is that all message parts were influenced by the attacker, and hash matches, it means that they intercepted all the parts, they did what they want, and then they recomputed the hash and sent that, that's a bad result, and then I'm attacked. The thing about it is that's it improbable due to ever-changing topology in the network it is very hard or improbable for some attackers to position themselves in such a way that every message part in some randomly chosen path would go through them in real time.

Chaminda Alocious: You talked about that you divide the message into parts, so what if you encrypt the whole message first and then you divide these message into parts, and then you communicate and send it to the receiver, what's different between that one and your approach?

Reply: Well you say encrypt the message first, so how do you decrypt a message without a common shared secret.

Chaminda Alocious: With a shared key. You can use the elliptic curve cryptography to decrypt each and every part on the receiver end because you have a shared key.

Reply: That's prior knowledge, we're talking without prior knowledge. If you have a shared key, so we solved the problem before we started. I can't encrypt something that the other side can't decrypt, and he can't decrypt it if we don't share a secret. So what we're trying to do is actually gain a shared secret without prior knowledge.

As I said, it's very improbable for them due to the ever-changing topology in a network, and everybody should think of an airport, not a stadium, people sit there for an hour, or two or three, so that's not changing. But think of an airport, people just moving around all the time, so the topology is actually changing all the time, so in order for them to attack you think of a government trying to attack someone, it will have to have, I don't know, 20 agents walking around with you all the time, all around you in some kind of ring, so if you look around you will probably see them. And they've got to make sure that there's nobody else within communicating distance, and if we do this over Wifi, which is what we did, we set up the system over Wifi which has a distance of more than two feet, it's not 100 meters, but it's something like 50 metres, 40 metres Wifi, so then it's very hard for an adversary in a very busy place to actually execute an attack, even if they collude. So that was the actual basic idea.

So some conclusions. Well what we were able to do is allow for a key exchange over insecure channels without user intervention; I'm not dealing with security, I'm just calling the other guy, let the system deal with it. We do it without prior knowledge; I don't know anything, I don't have any shared secret, I didn't share any secret with them before. And because Diffie-Hellman allows a perfect forward secrecy and we're just using Diffie-Hellman, so we were able to gain perfect forward secrecy. The idea here is in a sense was we were able to take an active attacker and turn them into a passive attacker. And once we're passive, then we're home free again. The problem with the protocol is that it relies heavily on the correct routing algorithms of the network, which means that if the attacker was able to influence the network to route everything to them, then in a sense they are becoming a breakpoint, a bottleneck, and then if all the packets, all the message parts were being routed to an attacker, and then he will send out a new key, he used the network to attack.

Looking at open problems for the research, the first one to consider is the overhead, how much does this cost. And it turns out it's not such a big problem. So it's true that I'm using a lot of message parts instead of one, and it's true that I'm using sub optimal paths instead of the optimal path, because actually by spreading it out, only one is the optimal path, everything else is sub optimal, but this is a one time thing per conversation, which means it's just a key exchange. So it's not a factor of the length of the conversation, it's a one-time thing so it's not such a big problem. And bottlenecks, what happens if there's bottlenecks, that's really an open problem, because suppose you try to call somebody in a different city and there's only three or four, or five connections, so if an adversary sits on those five connections, we have a bottleneck and everything has to flow through him. And the question is, two questions. One, can an attacker force a bottleneck, which means suppose there isn't a bottleneck, when you look at the graph it's actually a nice good connected graph, but can he do something to the network to force everything to actually flow through him. And this is something that could be a big problem because if you talk about MANETs, so MANETs in a sense have the characteristics that everybody goes and he announces I'm here, and there is no big brother that you have to log into. So suppose that somebody announces, I am Bob, and I announce that I am Bob, so slowly what happens is there will be a ripple effect, and at some point the ripples will meet and we're going to have a contradiction. An attacker could only influence a small part of the network for a certain amount of time before it's overrun by the real answers, and that's really the open question, can an attacker force such a bottleneck. And if he can force it can I detect it? which means if I add to the protocol some kind of detection, that if I hear from the right side that someone is saying he's Bob, and on the left side someone saying he's Bob, so I'm standing right at the connection of the ripple, can I then announce someone is trying to attack Bob, in a sense go and knock down Bob and say, listen don't communicate secret with Bob right, something is wrong. So that's another question we have open right now, can we give a network a bottleneck factor. So as far as graph theory is concerned it's not so difficult to look at a network and say, OK, there's three bottlenecks, that's not such a big deal. The question is can you do in real time without an overhead using smartphones that don't have high processors and do it all the time. This is something that we're dealing with right now.

Another question is, what happens if we have a single side mitigation for Diffie-Hellman. Suppose that we have Alice and here we have Bob, suppose all the colluding attackers are all standing right here. In a sense, that we have actually, we know there are two conversion points in the graph that we must go through. One conversion point is right there, that's one conversion point, and the other conversion point is right here. The sender and the receiver are conversion points by definition, so if an attacker can go and place themselves in such a conversion point, can he influence the system. Now what I mean by single side mitigation, it means that if it's true that Alice tries to send to Bob, and these attackers are all sitting at this conversion point, right here, that's a conversion point, so they will be able to influence the information that Bob receives. But Bob, part of a key exchange algorithm has to send back information, and he's going to spread it out. So if he goes and he has even one more out here, or even if he goes and he tells it to go through a couple of steps, or I don't know what. So it could be that by spreading it out one way and not two ways, does that break our scheme, or doesn't it break the scheme, I'm not sure yet. I think it doesn't because as long as Bob can get out even one message part, not through his converging attackers, then he is home safe. That's an open problem.

And the last problem is obviously authentication, replay attacks, impersonation attacks. So replay attacks, it's not so difficult to get around if you add a nonce or something, you know, one time nonce, into the key exchange, you get past replay attacks. But impersonation attacks are a bigger problem because if Eve goes and says, I am Bob, let's talk, then how can I know it's not Bob. But spreading Diffie-Hellman we talked about does not provide authentication, it provides confidentiality, which is a level below authentication. Above that we can try to build an authentication scheme, you know, you can add using a password, you can add, authentication is actually not a problem, it doesn't have to be done necessarily with two of the same exact and do them both together. So we have to know that our scheme does not give authentication, it gives just confidentiality, and if you can do something with it, build above it so that could be something good to do.

Anyway that's it, that's the scheme, Questions?

Petr Svenda: In wireless sensor networks there is something called secrecy authentication protocol, which is similar to selecting different routes to the target node. We are not using the Diffie-Hellman because the nodes can't compute Diffie Hellman efficiently at the moment, so it is based on plaintext key exchange or symmetric cryptography, but in the part of selecting routes over which you propagate key shares, you will take many different paths. Ross Anderson was co-author of the paper that proposed secrecy amplification protocols. The different secrecy amplification protocols that were published are differing in the way how they are selecting the paths for key shares propagation. In wireless sensor networks you really like to save node's energy and don't like to try all possible paths because it's too (energy) expensive. But you might maybe try and go only with the close (w.r.t. communication range) or fast (in your scenario) neighbours.

Reply: Trying all pairs is very expensive, but we might not need to if we decide that we would do studies right now, what is the N, the K, how many parts do you need to split that's good enough, it would give me the results I'm looking for. I'm not sure of the numbers yet. But there is some interesting results which I don't know how to explain yet. For some reason, I mean, the hypothesis that we had is that as I increase the population, even if I keep the percentage of attackers steady, I would see a downward slope because at some point there becomes so many possibilities that the chance of an attacker succeeding decreases, even though I'm increasing the number of attackers, but not the percentage. For some reason it's smoothing out, and I don't know how to explain this yet, it reaches a kind of plateau, some kind of asymptotic edge as population increases, I don't have an explanation yet, I'm trying to figure out why is it doing that, why is it not doing what we're assuming it's supposed to do. And is it true for success too, I mean, notice it's decreasing as the population increases, and then it plateaus out, and I don't know why yet. But that's also an open problem because I wasn't going to assume I was going to see that, I don't know why.

Audience: It might be the case because what you have already shown that there are attackers that surround some part of the node, and there is no other way to communicate with these nodes.

Reply: I agree that that could be it, but, and when I increase the population, so, even if I increase the number of attackers I should be seeing a downward sloping anyway, because if I go and I have now instead of 900 people I got 2000 people, so sooner or later there will be more possible paths. It was all random, which means that I increased the number of nodes and then told the simulator just place them randomly within some pre-defined area, which means I defined some kind of box. This is the area, place them out, and then just take a look what the graph that I can build and go on, if I can't really explain this plateau yet, I hope to have a better answer next time, but right now, that's it.

Shishir Nagaraja: So what is the edge actually on this, what does the edge between two nodes mean?

Bruce Christianson: When are two nodes connected?

Reply: It's communicating distance. If we talk about over Wifi then it's 40 meters, and there's actually a connection between me and you.

Shishir Nagaraja: It's the signal strength? So if I have a high power broadcasting antenna here I would be closest to everybody then any two people sitting next to each other.

Reply: Even if you are connected to everybody, it doesn't mean that the other person is also not connected. Why should I send through you, I could send it through him, him, and him. And if you go and you try to spoof the packets and send out your own, there will be a contradiction. And once there's a contradiction then the system is rebooted, it's reset.

Bruce Christianson: The argument is if you're connected to everybody sooner or later somebody is going to pick him as the next node. The longer the path is the more chance that that will happen.

Reply: But that's OK, as long as one message path doesn't go through him I'm in business, and that's what I want. I need everything to go through you for an attack to succeed, and the chances of that are very small, even if you're connected to everyone.

Shishir Nagaraja: If the nodes are trying to conserve power then I could become the centralised point of the network.

Reply: So then that's the question I suggested before, can one force a bottleneck? You want to be a bottleneck, and the question is can you force it. And I'm not sure by a high powered receiver and transmitter you will become the central bottleneck because I am purposely choosing not to send it through the optimal best path. I'm purposely choosing sub optimal paths in order not to go through some flashy system.

Audience: But then it's a matter of cost.

Reply: Right, I mean, everything is a matter of cost, what we're paying here is sub optimal paths. But we're paying it only for a small fraction of the conversation because once we set up the key, then from now on it's on the optimal path, I'm never going to use sub-optimal again.

Bruce Christianson: Shishir's argument is even if you have a 90% chance of avoiding him at each step, if there are enough steps your chance of avoiding him for any part of the message is low.

Daniel Thomas: And if there's more than one attacker doing the same thing, then it goes down much faster.

Bruce Christianson: That's right.

Reply: Right, if you have a lot of colluding attackers that are actually strategically placed on the topology of the network, then you can actually break the system. But the question is, why should this happen. The protocol doesn't say anywhere that I have to pick the highest power guy next to me.

Bruce Christianson: No, it's the fact that he's a neighbour to everyone that gives him the advantage.

Shishir Nagaraja: Yes, because he's got a higher degree there.

Bruce Christianson: Everybody thinks that he's the nearest neighbour, that's the trick.

Reply: That's a good point.

Audience: So everybody is doing a broadcast, is that right?

Reply: Well that's what happens in MANETs anyway, what happens in MANETs, when I want to talk to someone in a MANET I broadcast it to my neighbour who broadcasts it to his neighbour, and it's propagated until it reaches the destination, that happens, it's nothing to do with authenticity, or with the confidentiality, it happens by the actual system, that's the way the system works. And we set up a MANET right here, a mobile ad hoc network, so then I pass it to Sandy, who passes it to Frank, who passes it to, so even if you have a high power receiver and you can see everything, that doesn't help you, as long as I don't pass everything through you.

Steven Murdoch: So this scheme, you're splitting keys over space. You could also do the same thing over time, so you could run this protocol over five days?

Reply: Yes, but that's not practical, if I'm trying to call my mother, five days from now is not a good idea.

Bruce Christianson: Well you could plan ahead.

Audience: With a no prior knowledge here don't you require special software at every two communicating points, such that they divide the message and recombine the message?

Reply: Yes and no, because I need special software to actually set up the MANET, so I can just incorporate it into that software, when you dial to the other side it should do it with this protocol. I mean, there is no, when you want to set up an ad hoc network you need some software that does it, so part of the dialling will actually be to spread it out. Thank you very much.

On the Origin of Yet another Channel

Petr Švenda and Václav Matyáš

Masaryk University, Brno, Czech Republic
{svenda,matyas}@fi.muni.cz

Abstract. Cryptanalysis of a cryptographic function like stream, block or hash function usually requires human cryptanalytical skills and labour. However, some automation is possible – e.g., by randomness testing suites like NIST/Diehard that can be applied to test statistical properties of cryptographic function outputs. Yet such testing suites are limited to pre-defined statistical functions. We propose a more open approach based on a combination of software circuits and evolutionary algorithms to search for unwanted statistical properties like next bit predictability or random data distinguishability. Design of a software circuit acting as a testing function is automatically evolved by a stochastic optimization algorithm and uses the potentially unknown "other channel" leaking information during cryptographic function evaluation.

We tested this approach on candidate algorithms for SHA-3 and eStream competitions with comparable (but slightly worse) results as STS NIST and Diehard tests w.r.t. the number of rounds of the inspected algorithm, where tests are still able to detect unwanted statistical properties in output. Additionally, the proposed approach is not limited only to assess randomness-like properties in function output, but can be also used for other tests like whether a function is invertible or how its avalanche effect degrades.

1 Unguided Hunt for Weaknesses in Cryptographic Functions

The main motivation for this work is to provide a tool with the crucial ability to automatically probe for unwanted properties of cryptographic functions that signalize flaws in the function design. Such properties might be (note that we intentionally target a broad range of cryptographic functions):

- predictability of next output bit (stream ciphers),
- corrupted avalanche effect (hash functions, stream ciphers),
- distinguishability of function outputs from truly random data (block ciphers), etc.

Typical cryptanalytical approach against new cryptographic function is usually based on application of various statistical testing tools (STS NIST, Diehard) as the first step and then application of established cryptanalytical procedures (algorithmic attacks, differential cryptanalysis) combined with an in-depth

B. Christianson et al. (Eds.): Security Protocols 2013, LNCS 8263, pp. 223–237, 2013.

knowledge of the inspected function. The first step can be at least partly automated and (relatively) easy to apply, but will detect only the most visible defects in function construction or apply only to a limited number of algorithm rounds. The second approach usually yields much stronger insight and detects more defects, but usually requires extensive human cryptanalytical labour. Additionally, general statistical testing tools are limited to a predefined set of statistical tests. That on one hand makes the follow-up analytical work easier if the function does not pass a certain test, yet on the other hand severely limits the potential to detect other defects.

We designed and tested an automated process that can be used in a similar manner as general statistical testing suites, but additionally provides the possibility to construct (again automatically) new tests. We represent "tests" as a hardware-like circuit with a software emulator to execute the circuit over given inputs and to compute outputs and evolutionary algorithms (EAs) to design the circuit layout ("wires" and "gates"). Although such an automated tool will not (at least for the moment) outperform a skilled cryptographer on particular cryptographic function, it still has two main advantages:

- It can be applied automatically against multiple different cryptographic functions with no additional human labour, a working implementation of the inspected function is sufficient.
- It may discover and use unanticipated information leakage "channels" from the function than those usually assumed by cryptographers.

We implemented the tool (more details given in Section 3) and tested our idea on SHA-3/e-Stream candidate functions (details are given in Section 4). Results are very similar to those obtained from NIST and Diehard test suites w.r.t. the number of rounds of the inspected function where tests were able to find some defects. Based on experience with behaviour and significance of results, we add detailed discussion about potential extensions, expressive power of a circuit and interesting behaviour detected (Section 5). Conclusions are given in Section 6.

2   Previous Work

Numerous works tackled the problem of distinguisher construction between data produced by cryptographic functions and truly random data, both with reduced and full number of rounds. Usually, statistical testing with a battery of tests (e.g., STS NIST [Ruk10] or Dieharder [Bro04]) or additional custom tailored statistical tests are performed. The STS NIST battery was used to evaluate fifteen AES (round 2) candidates, demonstrating some deviation from randomness in six candidates [Sot99]. In [TDcc06], detailed examination of eStream Phase 2 candidates (full and reduced round tests) with STS NIST battery and structural randomness tests was performed, finding six ciphers deviating from expected values. More recently, the same battery, but only a subset of the tests, was applied to the SHA-3 candidates (in the second round of competition, 14 in total) for a reduced number of rounds as well as only to compression function of algorithm

[DEKS10]. Additionally, custom-built statistical tests based on strict avalanche criterion and others were used, resulting in estimation of relative security margins of candidates w.r.t. the number of rounds. [SDEK10] proposed a method to test statistical properties of short sequences typically obtained by block ciphers or hash algorithms for which some from STS NIST can not be applied due to insufficient length. Probabilities expressed by p-values are calculated for each short subinterval and an improved method based on recalculation of expected probabilities is provided. Example results applied to selected block and hash functions are presented. 256-bit versions of SHA-3 finalists were subjected to statistical tests using a GPU-accelerated evaluation [Kam12]. Both algorithms and selected tests from STS NIST battery were implemented for the nVidia CUDA platform. Because of massive parallelization, superpoly tests introduced by [DS09] were possible to be performed, detecting some deviations in all but the Grøstl algorithm.

Stochastic algorithms were also applied in cryptography to some extent, focusing initially mostly on simple transposition and substitution ciphers or problems like efficient knapsack algorithm. A nice review of usage of genetic algorithms in cryptography up to year 2004 can be found in [Del04], a more recent review of evolutionary methods used in cryptography is provided by [PG11]. TEA algorithm [WN95] with a reduced number of rounds is a frequent target for cryptoanalysis with genetic algorithms [CVn05, Hu10, GHD07]. In [GHD07] a comparison of genetic techniques is presented, with several suggestions which genetic techniques and parameters should be used to obtain better results. We adopted the genetic programming [BNKF97] technique with steady-state replacement [LLL08]. An important difference of our approach from previous work is the production of a program (in the form of a software circuit) that provides different results depending on given inputs. Previous work produced a fixed result, e.g., bit mask in [CVn05, Hu10] that is directly applied to all inputs.

Structure of a software circuit resembles artificial neural networks (NN) to some extent. Notable differences are in the learning mechanism and in a high number of layers used in our software circuit (NN usually use only three). Recently, deep belief neural networks (DBNN) were proposed [HOT06] with the learning algorithm based on restricted Boltzmann machines that also use five or even more layers. Still, a software circuit uses mutation and crossover to converge towards an optimum instead of back propagation in case of classical NN or lay-by-layer learning algorithm for DBNN. Also, different functions may be computed inside every node in case of software circuit instead of weighted sum of DBNN.

3   Software Circuit Designed by Evolution

A software circuit is a software representation of a hardware-like circuit with nodes ("gates") responsible for computation of simple functions like AND or OR taking inputs and providing outputs. Nodes are positioned in layers where outputs from the previous layer are provided as inputs to the nodes in the following layer by connectors ("wires"). Input to the whole circuit is simulated as an output of the first layer of nodes and output of last layer is taken as the output of whole circuit. Connectors might connect node to all nodes from a previous layer or only to some of them.

Examples of such a circuit might be a Boolean circuit where functions computed in nodes are limited to logical functions or artificial neural networks where nodes compute the weighted sum of the inputs. Besides studying complexity problems, these circuits were used in various applications like construction of a fully homomorphic scheme [Gen10] or in design of efficient image filters [SSV12].

3.1 How to Design Circuit Layout

Circuit evaluation can be performed by a software emulator that propagates input values, computes functions in nodes and collects outputs; or possibly directly in hardware when FPGAs are used [SSV12]. Circuit design can be laid out by an experienced human designer, automatically synthesized from the source code or even automatically designed and then improved by an optimization algorithm. We use the last approach and combine a software circuit evaluated on a CPU (or also on GPUs) with evolutionary algorithms (EAs). The main goal is (somehow) to find a circuit that will reveal an unwanted defect in the inspected cryptographic functions. For example, if a circuit is able to correctly predict the nth bit from a key stream generated by a stream cipher just by observing previous $(n-1)$ bits, then this circuit serves as a next-bit predictor [Yao82], breaking the security of the given stream cipher. Note that a circuit need not to provide correct answers for all inputs – it is sufficient if a correct answer is provided with a statistically significant probability better than random guessing.

When combined with evolutionary algorithms (broader term than genetic algorithms, covers also stochastic algorithms inspired by nature evolution), the whole process of circuit design consists of the following steps:

1. Several software circuits are randomly initialized (randomly selected functions in nodes, randomly assigned existence of connectors between nodes) forming population of candidate individuals. Every individual is represented by one circuit. Note that such a random circuit will most probably not provide any meaningful output for given inputs and can even have disconnected layers (no output at all).
2. If necessary, generate new test vectors used later by a so-called fitness function for evaluation.
3. Every individual (circuit) in the population is emulated and the outputs obtained are evaluated by the fitness function that will assign a rating based on how well this individual performs in solving a given task (e.g., what fraction of inputs were correctly recognized as being output of stream cipher rather than completely random sequence).
4. Based on the evaluation provided by the fitness function, a potentially improved population is generated by mutation and crossover operators (genetic algorithms) from individuals taken from the previous generation. Design of

every individual (circuit) may be changed by changing operations computed in nodes or add/removing connectors between nodes in subsequent layers.

5. Repeat from step 2. Usually hundreds of thousands or more repeats are performed, therefore the evaluation of a single circuit in step 3 must be fast enough (currently, we are in the milliseconds range).

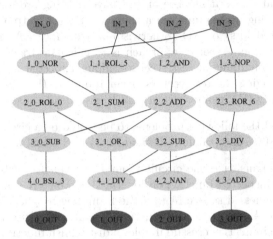

Fig. 1. Software circuit with input nodes (IN_x), inner nodes, output nodes (x_OUT) and connectors. Note that not all input or output nodes need to be used, and that not all inner nodes need to output any value.

3.2   How to Evaluate Circuit Performance?

Evaluation of a circuit performance is a crucial yet tricky part of the proposed process. Evaluation of a circuit is so called "supervised teaching" – we have pairs of inputs and expected outputs (given by a "teacher"). Outputs from a circuit for given inputs are compared with expected outputs and circuit performance is then graded accordingly. When done incorrectly, the process will not provide a circuit solving the expected problem. The progress may fail at least on two fronts:

1. Improperly defined problem to be solved by circuit. For example, if we define a problem to be solved so that there is more than one correct answer (e.g., to find a preimage for a given hash function output) and yet we insist only on one particular preimage being correct (although other values also provide same hash), the circuit will not be able to converge towards a working solution, even though the hash function is invertible. Alternatively, a problem may be too hard to be solved, yet a working solution for a limited number of rounds still would be of interest from the cryptanalysis perspective. Finally, a circuit may seem to be solving the problem, yet we do not learn anything about the function itself – so called "overlearning". E.g., if we ask the circuit to distinguish between a function output and a completely random value, but we do not change the test vectors, then we just learn which particular

test inputs belongs to which category and achieve a very good performance on the testing set, but not on new verification data.

2. Unsuitable settings for EAs to progress towards a better solution (usually caused by an improper fitness function or insufficient amount of computational time). EAs work well where a gradual improvement with small steps towards a better solution is possible. Problems for which you either have a solution that solves it at once or you have nothing are not suitable. For example, defining fitness function as binary YES (all output bits of circuit match expected bits) or NO (otherwise) will hamper EA chances to find a working solution. A better approach is to calculate fraction of bits that match over many different tests vectors (input, expected output). Last but not least, changing the test vectors either too often (EA fails to adapt) or too infrequently (EA will overlearn) can lead to dead ends.

So far, we adapted the following problems to be tested by a circuit, with results presented for the first one (random distinguisher) in Section 4:

1. Random distinguisher – the circuit input is a sequence of bytes produced either by the inspected function or generated completely randomly and the output is the guessed source (e.g., if the Hamming weight of circuit output is higher than $\frac{1}{2}$ than it is the function output, otherwise it is a random sequence). A circuit is successful if able to distinguish function outputs from random sequences significantly better than by random guessing. Truly random sequences were taken from the Quantum random bit generator service [STS+08].

2. Next bit predictor – the circuit input is a vector of n bits taken from an output of the function (e.g., stream cipher) and the expected circuit output is the value of the $(n+1)th$ bit. The problem can be relaxed to the prediction of multiple bits, Hamming weight or other property of following byte(s). A circuit is successful if able to predict correct value(s) significantly better than by random guessing. A typical target would be some keyed function with an unknown key, yet unkeyed functions can be targeted as well – caution must be taken to prevent a circuit simply learning the unkeyed function itself and using it to compute the expected output.

3. Strict Avalanche Criterion detector – the avalanche effect property of function F (e.g., hash) expects half the bits to flip in the output on average, even for a single bit change in the input. The input for the circuit is a sequence of bytes X. Expected output from the circuit is such a sequence Y that will produce significantly more (or less) bit flips than expected when processed by a function (Hamming_distance$(F(X), F(Y)) >> |X|/2$). A special care must be taken not to let the circuit just learn the function itself.

Note that an interpretation of a circuit output might not be just an exact match to the expected value. Even when only Yes or No is expected, one can let the circuit to encode its answer into a bit value/Hamming weight/majority value of the circuit output, as such a less strict matching allows for multiple ways how the circuit can signalize Yes answer and gives more flexibility to the EA.

3.3 Practical Implementation

We implemented our evaluation software circuit both on CPU and GPU combined with the GAlib optimization library [GL207]. Significantly larger test vectors are possible (10^5 instead of 10^3) with a GPU implementation (nVidia CUDA), where many different evaluations can be executed in parallel with negligible performance impact. On average, a 70x speedup w.r.t. CPU implementation was achieved. Additionally, we use BOINC infrastructure to perform distributed computation with more than a thousand CPU cores and 16 nVidia GF 465 cards. One well described problem of neural networks is difficulty to understand the resulting solution. To ease understanding of our software circuits, we implemented an automatic removal of nodes and connectors that do not contribute to the resulting fitness value, transformation into the Graphviz dot format for visualization and also transformation into a C program source code that executes the functionality of a particular circuit without the need to run a circuit emulator. For a start, we used following elementary operations for nodes: no operation (NOP), logical functions (AND, OR, XOR, NOR, NAND), bit manipulating functions (ROTR, ROTL, BITSELECTOR), arithmetic functions (ADD, SUBS, MULT, DIV, SUM), read specified input even from internal layer (READ) and produce constant value (CONST). Typical initial settings for software circuit parameters were: 5-8 layers, 16-32 input nodes, 16-32 nodes in internal layer, 1-16 output nodes. Typical settings for EA parameters were like: 20 individual in population, 1000 test vectors (CPU version), 0.05 probability of mutation, and 0.5 probability of crossover.

4   Results for eStream/SHA3 Candidates

The approach described above was tested on candidate function for eStream [ECR04] and SHA-3 [SHA07] competitions. The big advantage came with availability of implementations with the same programming interface (API) for all candidates – one can automatically test (e.g., random distinguisher) on large number of functions without need to change (significantly) corresponding code.

Presented results serve as a baseline over multiple functions rather than the best result we can achieve against a particular function. Because of the significant number of inspected functions parametrized additionally with different numbers of rounds and multiple parallel runs for every such a combination, we were not able to optimize for best results for every separate function. Indeed, we were able to obtain improvements (better distinguishing rate) for selected functions where we selectively applied more optimizations. For example, when circuit with memory (see Section 5) was used against Decim limited to three rounds, distinguishing success rate raised from 0.53 to 0.62.

4.1 eStream Candidates

From 34 candidates in the eStream competition, 23 were potentially usable for testing (renamed or updated versions, problems with compilation). For a start, we limited ourselves to only 7 of these (Decim, Grain, FUBUKI, Hermes, LEX, Salsa20, TSC) having structure allowing reduction of complexity by decreased number of rounds in a straightforward way.

In this work, we aim to obtain a software circuit capable of correctly distinguishing between a stream of bytes generated by an eStream candidate function with an unknown key, and a stream of truly random bytes. We worked with three scenarios with respect to the frequency of key change:

1. Key is fixed for all generated test sets and vectors. Even when test sets change, new test vectors are generated using the same key.
2. Every test set was generated using a different key. All test vectors in a particular test set are generated with the same key.
3. Every test vector (16 bytes) was generated using a different key.

Table 1. Results for eStream candidates

Function name (total rounds)	Rounds detectable by NIST (run/set/vector)	Rounds detectable by circuit (run/set/vector)
Decim (8)	5/5/2	3/3/1
FUBUKI (4)	0/0/0	0/0/0
Grain (13)	2/2/0	2/2/0
Hermes (10)	0/0/0	0/0/0
LEX (10)	3/3/3	3/3/3
Salsa20 (20)	2/2/0	2/2/0
TSC (32)	10/10/10	10/10/10

4.2   SHA-3 Candidates

Similarly, we tested also SHA-3 competition candidates. From 51 candidates for the first round, only 42 were potentially usable for testing due to compilation problems, source code size, speed etc. We limited ourselves to 18 candidates that can be easily limited in complexity by decreasing the number of internal rounds, and while the full (unlimited) version produced a random-looking output, their most limited version did not. Following candidates were considered: ARIRANG, Aurora, Blake, Cheetah, CubeHash, DCH, Dynamic SHA, Dynamic SHA2, ECHO, Grøstl, Hamsi, JH, Lesamnta, Luffa, MD6, SIMD, Tangle and Twister.

4.3   Discussion

Detailed results including the circuits found, analysis of some of them and details for the STS NIST settings can be found in this paper's supplementary data[1] and [Ukr13]. The following main points were observed:

---

[1] Detailed results can be found at http://www.fi.muni.cz/~xsvenda/papers/spw2013/ .

Table 2. Results for SHA-3 candidates

Function name (total rounds)	ARIRANG (4)	Aurora (17)	Blake (14)	Cheetah (16)	CubeHash (8)	DCH (4)	Dynamic SHA (16)	Dynamic SHA2 (17)	ECHO (8)	Grøstl (10)	Hamsi (3)	JH (42)	Lesamnta (32)	Luffa (8)	MD6 (104)	SIMD (4)	Tangle (80)	Twister (9)
Rounds detectable by STS NIST	3	3	1	5	1	1	7	12	2	3	1	6	3	7	9	1	22	7
Rounds detectable by software circuit	3	2	0	4	0	1	7	10	1	2	0	6	2	7	8	0	22	6

1. The circuit providing good distinguishing results for the particular combination of function, number of rounds and used key usually significantly decreased in success rate when function or even key is changed. Therefore, the whole process of the evolution to particular combination is to be perceived as a test in some cases.
2. Not all operations and connectors are relevant for the circuit performance. Irrelevant components can be automatically pruned out, easing understanding of the circuit.
3. STS NIST is better in detection of statistical deviances than proposed approach for multiple SHA-3 candidates, but usually only one more round.

5   Increasing the Expressiveness of the Circuit

Previous section provided us with the baseline results for a wide range of functions. We laid out the following metrics to measure the success of the proposed approach:

1. Proposed approach should have the power to express statistical tests used in STS NIST battery (i.e., test from NIST can be encoded in the form of software circuit, but not necessarily automatically by genetic programming).
2. Proposed approach should provide at least same results (w.r.t. number of rounds of limited function) as the STS NIST battery. Preferably, there should be at least one (cryptographic) function with the number of rounds limited to N, where STS NIST fails to detect significant defects in sequence, but proposed approach succeeds.
3. Proposed approach may fail to achieve same results as the STS NIST, but then should provide other significant advantage like smaller computation or memory requirements or requiring significantly less input data (thus allowing for use as function's online tester).

4. Proposed approach should provide better distinguishing success rate when combined with STS NIST then STS NIST provides alone (approach is providing additional test coverage not provided by STS NIST, even when approach alone cannot distinguish with better probability than STS NIST).

Generally, we achieved points 1 (when extension with memory is considered, see Section 5) and 3, in some cases achieved point 2 and failed yet to achieve point 4. Basic version of the proposed approach uses inputs only 16-32 bytes long. Note that constructing a distinguisher between function output and truly random data based on as short a sequence as 16 bytes is significantly more difficult than the same task for a long sequence. First, longer sequences decrease the impact of small fluctuation of both random data and function's output (e.g., if there is inbalance of number of zeroes and ones by only one bit in 16 bytes, it is 1/128 of whole input, making it relatively significant difference, even when one can completely expect such a situation in truly random data. Contrary, if 1 000x1 000 000 bits are used (STS NIST), such a difference is insignificant). Second, function's output can produce periodic behaviour easily detectable in longer data stream, but completely invisible in 16 bytes only. Indeed, when data for STS NIST battery is generated in such a way that changes key every 16 bytes, proposed approach provides exactly same results on the tested functions.

To further improve performance of the evolutionary circuit, we propose additional extensions of the basic version presented before. Note that as modification of a circuit is based on evolutionary algorithms, performance may be increased by application of generic techniques for faster convergence towards the optimal solution, like modification of EA parameters. We will not cover these techniques here. Note that increasing the circuit expressiveness may actually decrease the convergence speed for easier problems as search space is usually increased by such a technique.

We can divide such techniques into several groups:

- Techniques to increase amount of data processed by the circuit: READX, memory (block-based, bit-based), circuit providing formula with expected occurrence counter
- Techniques to increase expressivity of circuit: loops, circuit of circuits
- Techniques to increase complexity of functions used by the circuit: linear genetic programming inside node, code fragments inside node, complex instruction from known tests

5.1 Techniques to Increase an Amount of Data Processed by the Circuit

Previous results were provided for the situation where the circuit performing distinguisher was based on 16 input bytes only – significant disadvantage w.r.t statistical batteries processing from tens up to hundreds of megabytes of data. With such a setting, it is a significantly harder situation for the evolutionary circuit to find a working distinguisher. Therefore, we propose several techniques for how circuit expressivity and amount of data used can be expanded.

Possibly the easiest way to provide more data to circuit is to introduce additional instruction (called READX) which provides one of the input byte from the circuit's inputs directly to the function node with READX instruction. One may perceive such an instruction as a direct wire between node and requested input. Such an input can be already encoded by the circuit, but for the price of several NOP instructions. With a special instruction, input is directly accessible and more importantly, length of circuit's input can be more than the size of input layer as READX can obtain any value from it. Human interpretation of circuit with READX instruction is straightforward. However, if the input data should be enlarged by e.g., one hundred input bytes, then one hundred READX instructions must be present in the circuit to process all inputs by the circuit (but not all inputs bytes are relevant for a distinguisher).

More promising, but also more complicated (also from the perspective of the interpretation of well performing circuit) is introduction of a *memory*. Instead of circuit processing whole input in a single run, input is divided into B blocks with same length N and processed one by one. Circuit is extended by additional M inputs and M outputs (same number). Outputs from a processing block B_i are provided as inputs for the block B_{i+1}, together with N inputs from test vector. Such an extension provides possibility to extract some statistics from input block B_i, store it into the memory M and later combine with statistics from following blocks. Most importantly, test vector length can be significantly increased and all input bytes are directly processed by the circuit. Final output (distinguisher) is then based on memory and last input block. We already obtained preliminary results for such a modification which shows better results (better distinguishing ratio) than single-run circuit. Note that longer input test vector also increases circuit's execution time accordingly.

Finally, one can incorporate circuit into bigger framework which will perform part of the computation and evaluation separately. If evolutionary circuit is providing working distinguisher, this distinguisher must be based on some redundancy in input stream of a tested function which is not present in truly random data. Such a redundancy is expressed (if found) by some formula encoded inside the circuit. Circuit's output is then interpreted not directly as distinguishing verdict (truly random data or function data), but only as classificator of input data into one of several categories $C_1, ..., C_n$ (e.g., if circuit provide one output byte, then classifies into 256 categories). If multiple inputs are given to a circuit and classified, particular distribution over categories C_i is obtained. The goal is to find such a circuit, which will provide significantly different distribution D_f of categories C_i for inputs coming from the tested function f then a distribution D_r produced by the inputs taken from truly random data. If such a circuit can be found, input stream of data (multiple inputs) is signalized as a function's output if significant deviation from pre-computed distribution D_r is detected in D_f and signalized as truly random data otherwise (with given confidence level). Fitness function is again defined as a ratio of correctly classified test vectors from presented test set. Note that test vectors now need to be extended from single input block to multiple input blocks taken from same source (function or random data) – single input block would provide only very crude distribution D. Also, much longer input data are naturally provided to circuit to facilitate decision.

5.2 Techniques to Increase Inner Functions Complexity

Set of operations available to software circuit design can be extended from elementary operations like Boolean functions or simple arithmetic operations to code fragments automatically extracted by parser from implementation of inspected function with hope of achieving better results than NIST/Diehard batteries. Previously described circuit constructions used very simple operations like AND, MULT or SUM in the circuit processing nodes. When a circuit needs some more complex operation, it needs to be constructed from these simple blocks, occupying multiple layers and connectors. Potentially, a better performance in weakness hunting can be obtained if the set of allowed operations is extended by the more complex ones. As a particular cryptographic function is inspected, sub-operations of this function might be viable candidates for such complex operations. However, selection of such an operation requires some knowledge of the function itself, hampering advantages of fully automated approach.

We propose to keep with the fully automated approach and let sub-operations be extracted from an existing implementation of the inspected function automatically. Once extracted, evolution algorithm is allowed to select these fragments as the function for processing nodes and emulate these fragments on inputs if selected. Note that by partial execution, we do not aim to replicate exact behaviour of target code (same output for same input), but rather to provide similar code that can be applied over any input data provided by rest of circuit.

For practical verification of this idea, we choose implementation of target function (e.g., stream cipher) in the Java language with advantage of human-readable bytecode generated directly by Java compiler and disassembler (javac g, javap - c). Resulting file with text representation of bytecode is automatically parsed and any subpart of code described by triple *[method_name, start_instructi-on_offset and end_instruction_offset]* can be emulated by simple stack-based execution machine.

Several challenges need to be tackled with such a partial execution:

- Handling of method inputs – in regular program execution, method arguments are pushed to stack before method call. If method is to be executed from the middle, stack with arguments has to be filled by other means. In our implementation, part of values provided by previous layer via connectors is stored into stack before partial execution is performed.
- Bottom of the stack is reached before end of execution – because not all instructions in method are executed (e.g., push), bottom of the stack might be reached prematurely as the current instruction to be executed expects value(s) on stack whereas there is (are) none. In our implementation, we simply ignore the instruction in case that not enough arguments are present on stack.

- Handling of global arrays – in case when global arrays are used to load and store values during execution, such memory structures must be prepared and set before first access. In our implementation, part of values provided by previous layer via connectors is used. Also, instruction is ignored when data necessary for emulation are not present.
- Form of the output from a partial execution emulated by given node. More specifically, which byte (or multiple bytes) should be provided as node's output? In our implementation, we simply take value at the top of the stack as output.

Note that challenges described above are solved in ad-hoc manner and may fail to execute many instructions from original code. Still, if target function itself uses e.g., finite field multiplication (FFMul in AES) partial execution described above will enable software circuit to directly execute such an operation.

Once execution stack described above is available, fragments can not only be taken from existing code, but can also be generated randomly. Every fragment in the node will then consist of several bytecode instruction emulated over node's input – technique known as linear genetic programming.

Another option is are to use parsers like the ANTLR parser generator [PQ94] or ASTParser [KT06], alternatively BytecodeParser [God12] working directly on the bytecode level, thus easing emulation later. Optionally, one may use language supporting reflection and allowing for runtime code modification. However, this will decrease the evaluation speed of a single circuit (w.r.t. C/C++ performance) and prevent a GPU-based acceleration. Note that a large number of candidate circuits needs to be evaluated; otherwise EAs are unlikely to find a viable solution.

6 Conclusions

We proposed a general design of a cryptoanalytical tool based on genetic programming and applied it to the problem of finding a random distinguisher for several stream ciphers (with a reduced number of rounds) taken from the SHA-3 (18 functions) and eStream (7 functions) competition. Baseline with results was established for these functions. In general, the proposed approach proved to be capable of matching the performance of the NIST statistical testing suite in scenario where the tested function key is changed for every test vector, and close matching results when key is changed less often. When a key is changed less often, alonger sequence with the same key is produced and available for inspection by statistical testing suite where a basic version of the proposed approach is not able to deal with inputs longer than tens of bytes. Therefore, we proposed several extensions, like circuit with memory or more complex function in the node capable to process very large inputs.

Future work will be devoted to evaluation of extension proposals and their comparison with basic version of proposed approach.

Acknowledgements. This work was supported by the GAP202/11/0422 project of the Czech Science Foundation. The access to computing and storage facilities owned by parties and projects contributing to the National Grid Infrastructure MetaCentrum, provided under the programme "Projects of Large Infrastructure for Research, Development, and Innovations" (LM2010005) is highly appreciated. Martin Ukrop provided data from the experiments with SHA-3 candidate function evaluations.

References

[BNKF97] Banzhaf, W., Nordin, P., Keller, R.E., Francone, F.D.: Genetic programming: An introduction: On the automatic evolution of computer programs and its applications. Morgan Kaufmann Publishers (1997)

[Bro04]   Brown, R.G.: Dieharder: A random number test suite, version 3.31.1 (2004)

[CVn05]   Castro, J.C.H., Viñuela, P.I.: New results on the genetic cryptanalysis of TEA and reduced-round versions of XTEA. New Gen. Comput. 23(3), 233–243 (2005)

[DEKS10] Doganaksoy, A., Ege, B., Koçak, O., Sulak, F.: Statistical analysis of reduced round compression functions of SHA-3 second round candidates. Technical report, Institute of Applied Mathematics, Middle East Technical University, Turkey (2010)

[Del04]   Delman, B.: Genetic algorithms in cryptography. PhD thesis, Rochester Institute of Technology (2004)

[DS09]   Dinur, I., Shamir, A.: Cube attacks on tweakable black box polynomials. In: Joux, A. (ed.) EUROCRYPT 2009. LNCS, vol. 5479, pp. 278–299. Springer, Heidelberg (2009)

[ECR04]   ECRYPT. Ecrypt estream competition, announced November 2004 (2004)

[Gen10]   Gentry, C.: Computing arbitrary functions of encrypted data. Commun. ACM 53(3), 97–105 (2010)

[GHD07]   Garrett, A., Hamilton, J., Dozier, G.: A comparison of genetic algorithm techniques for the cryptanalysis of TEA. International Journal of Intelligent Control and Systems 12(4), 325–330 (2007)

[GL207]   Galib 2.4.7, a c++ library of genetic algorithm components (2007)

[God12]   Godbillon, S.: Bytecodeparser - java bytecode parser and emulator (2012)

[HOT06]   Hinton, G.E., Osindero, S., Teh, Y.-W.: A fast learning algorithm for deep belief nets. Neural computation 18(7), 1527–1554 (2006)

[Hu10]   Hu, W.: Cryptanalysis of TEA using quantum-inspired genetic algorithms. Journal of Software Engineering and Applications 3(1), 50–57 (2010)

[Kam12]   Kaminsky, A.: GPU parallel statistical and cube test analysis of the SHA-3 finalist candidate hash functions. In: 15th SIAM Conference on Parallel Processing for Scientific Computing, PP 2012 (2012)

[KT06]   Kuhn, K., Thomann, O.: Eclipse ASTParser (2006)

[LLL08]   Liu, L., Li, M., Lin, D.: Replacement strategies in steady-state multi-objective evolutionary algorithm: A comparative case study. In: Proceedings of the 2008 Fourth International Conference on Natural Computation, ICNC 2008, pp. 645–649. IEEE Computer Society, Washington, DC (2008)

[PG11]   Picek, S., Golub, M.: On evolutionary computation methods in cryptography. In: MIPRO, 2011 Proceedings of the 34th International Convention, pp. 1496–1501 (2011)

[PQ94]   Parr, T.J., Quong, R.W.: ANTLR: A predicated-ll(k) parser generator.
           Software Practice and Experience 25, 789–810 (1994)
[Ruk10]   Rukhin, A.: A statistical test suite for the validation of random number
           generators and pseudo random number generators for cryptographic appli-
           cations, version STS-2.1. NIST Special Publication 800-22rev1a (2010)
[SDEK10]   Sulak, F., Doğanaksoy, A., Ege, B., Koçak, O.: Evaluation of randomness
           test results for short sequences. In: Carlet, C., Pott, A. (eds.) SETA 2010.
           LNCS, vol. 6338, pp. 309–319. Springer, Heidelberg (2010)
[SHA07]   NIST SHA-3. SHA-3 competition (announced November 2, 2007)
[Sot99]   Soto, J.: Randomness testing of the AES candidate algorithms. In: NIST
           (1999)
[SSV12]   Sekanina, L., Salajka, V., Vašíček, Z.: Two-step evolution of polymorphic
           circuits for image multi-filtering. In: IEEE Congress on Evolutionary Com-
           putation, pp. 1–8 (2012)
[STS+08]   Stevanović, R., Topić, G., Skala, K., Stipčević, M., Rogina, B.M.: Quantum
           random bit generator service for Monte Carlo and other stochastic simula-
           tions. In: Lirkov, I., Margenov, S., Waśniewski, J. (eds.) LSSC 2007. LNCS,
           vol. 4818, pp. 508–515. Springer, Heidelberg (2008)
[TDcc06]   Turan, M.S., Doğanaksoy, A., Çalik, Ç.: Detailed statistical analysis of syn-
           chronous stream ciphers. In: ECRYPT Workshop on the State of the Art
           of Stream Ciphers, SASC 2006 (2006)
[Ukr13]   Ukrop, M.: Usage of evolvable circuit for statistical testing of randomness.
           Bachelor thesis, Masaryk University, Czech Republic (2013)
[WN95]   Wheeler, D., Needham, R.: TEA, a tiny encryption algorithm. In: Preneel,
           B. (ed.) Fast Software Encryption. LNCS, vol. 1008, pp. 363–366. Springer,
           Heidelberg (1995)
[Yao82]   Yao, A.C.: Theory and application of trapdoor functions. In: Proceedings
           of the 23rd Annual Symposium on Foundations of Computer Science, SFCS
           1982, pp. 80–91. IEEE Computer Society, Washington, DC (1982)

On the Origin of Yet another Channel
(Transcript of Discussion)

Petr Švenda

Masaryk University

Good afternoon, I will talk on the origin of yet another channel. The reason why we choose such a title is that we will use something borrowed from the nature—the genetic programming technique—and we will search for another side channel in a cryptographic function. I will be focusing on the randomness testing of the function outputs. I will give you a brief overview of how existing statistical batteries like STS NIST or Diehard are doing such testing. Then I will present our idea based on a software circuit combined with the genetic programming. I will show you some results for candidates from the eStream competition for stream ciphers and also some from SHA-3 competition. Some discussion about interesting results we were getting will go afterwards. And finally some possible extensions to obtain yet better results.

The first question to ask is why we should bother to test some properties of randomness in any function output. The answer is that if the function is planned to be used as a pseudorandom generator then we like to ensure that the properties of the bits and bytes coming from this generator are similar to what you would expect from a truly random number generator. It can be also a requirement by third parties as was the case for the AES or SHA-3 competitions where this reason is partially same as the first one: sometimes you like to use AES as a pseudorandom generator. And the third reason is that if the function behaves in such a way that there are significant deviations from the statistics of the truly random sequence, it may signal some inner defects of the functions. Of course, passing the statistical tests is not any proof that the function is without defects. You can use at least two main different approaches to study cryptographic functions: human cryptanalysis or the fully automatic approach, statistical testing.

How is to work with existing statistical batteries like STS NIST or Dieharder? At first you will take the function you are interested in, for example AES, you will seed this function with a key, and then you will generate a long stream of output data. For these batteries you generate at least tens of megabytes. Dieharder requires several hundreds of megabytes of data. Testing suites contains several tests, dozens of them in every battery. An example of a simple test is the assertion that the number of binary ones in the stream should be similar to number of binary zeroes. Another test is based on taking the data you have and playing the Scratch game with it and then count how many times the first player will win, and how many times the second player will win. If the results you are not too different from what one would expect for truly random data then you say that given data passed the test.

B. Christianson et al. (Eds.): Security Protocols 2013, LNCS 8263, pp. 238–244, 2013.

What we would like to achieve is having a mechanism that generates new tests automatically, because designing the tests by hand is time consuming. The first step is to realize that tests can be expressed as an algorithm. If it is an algorithm then we can express it as a hardware-like circuit. We will not use a real hardware circuit, but software emulation, which is more or less the same. There are several issues that need to be solved. The first thing is who will design such a circuit? We will use genetic programming as a designer. The second thing is what will be the question or the task that the circuit should solve? We formulate this question to be a random distinguisher as circuit should be able to distinguish data coming from two different sources: the tested function and truly random generator. Because we will use genetic programming, we need to be able to compare the qualities of candidate solutions (circuits). We will use a set of multiple test vectors for comparison.

Basic goal we would like to achieve is to have a circuit-encoding distinguisher at least as good as the existing statistical batteries, but generated automatically. Later on I will tell you how and whether we succeeded.

At first I will briefly discuss the software circuit. You have the input nodes where you put some input data. Then you have nodes inside, each computing one operation taken from the set of different predefined operations. You have also connectors (wires) which transport output data from one node in the previous layer to another node in the next layer. Node output may come to multiple nodes, the same as in ordinary hardware circuits. In a hardware circuit, you usually have physical limitations forcing you to have no crossings of the connectors (wires), but that's no limitation for the software circuit as connectors are only simulated. You put your input data to first layer; let it be manipulated by functions in the following layers and then read the output in the last layer. We developed the open software tool EACirc to generate and simulate such circuits; you may like to take a look at that.

The basic assumption is that if there is some defect in the functions output we should be able to find a circuit that is able to distinguish between the data produced by the defective function and the data produced by the truly random generator.

We took truly random data from two different quantum random generators (QRNG service - HU, Germany and QRBG service - Ruer Boškovic Institute, Croatia) and we used it to generate 500 test vectors. Test vectors were 16 bytes long, so we need 500x16 bytes from the truly random source for every test set. Then we took target function like Salsa20, AES or any other function, and generated a data stream, forming another 500 test vectors. Then we take these test vectors one by one, put them as inputs for the circuit, let it run and read the output. The output is some sequence of the bits that needs to be interpreted. For example if the Hamming weight of the output byte is bigger than 4 then the circuit is "signalising that the input data comes from the truly random generator, otherwise it comes from the tested function. We let it run for all test vectors (1000 total in our example, half coming from random source, second half from tested function); counting how many times it correctly thinks the input data are coming from the random source, how many times it correctly thinks the source was the tested function. A successful circuit should do better than random guessing.

Still, someone has to design this circuit. We use genetic programming for that, a supervised stochastic optimisation technique inspired by natural evolution. In short, you are maintaining the population of candidate solutions – distinguishing circuits in our case. At the beginning, you usually generate them randomly and initial population is usually no better than random guessing. But due to simulated natural selection, solutions improve over time. We started with something like 20 candidate solutions, taking one candidate circuit, loading into circuit emulator and letting it run with 1000 input test vectors. Because we know what the correct answers should be, we can compute how well the circuit was performing and assign a fitness value. After testing all our circuits we know which circuits are bad performers, which are better, and which are the best. For the next generation we will drop some of the circuits that are bad, and instead of them we will insert new circuits generated by mating (crossover and mutation) of other well-performing circuits.

I need to stress that the speed of circuit evaluation is critical because we need to evaluate candidate circuits many times. It has to be done for every generation, for every individual and for every test vector. Usually you have at least thousands of generations (we were using 30,000 of generations), tens of individuals in the population (20 in our case) and we were using 1000 test vectors. Therefore, in our settings for a single experiment, we need around 600 million of evaluations. We developed both CPU and GPU implementations and used resources mainly from our Metacentrum grid to carry these computations.

What is the comparison methodology we were using? We targeted some selected algorithms from the eStream competition at the beginning. We selected algorithms in which the number of rounds can be easily reduced. The reason is that usually the statistical testing batteries are not able to find any defects in a function with a full number of rounds, but they can find some defects if you will the number of rounds. And that is still a reasonable result because if the number of rounds where the statistical battery can find some defect is very close to the total number of rounds then something is potentially wrong with the function. We generate and run these ordinary testing batteries (STS NIST, Dieharder) and put these results aside for future comparison with the proposed approach. We then prepare input data for our software circuit as I have already described to you. The genetic programming was left running for several hours or sometimes days, trying to find a circuit that performs reasonably well as a distinguisher between truly random data and function output.

An important setting influencing the results is how often you change the key used for generating the test vectors. We tested three scenarios. The first one fixes the key for the whole experiment. In the second case we change the key for every test set. In our case the key remains fixed for 500 test vectors. And in the third scenario the key changes for every test vector. For every 16 bytes generated you have to supply a fresh new key. Key change frequency influences the length of data generated by a single key. So if you will go with the third extreme scenario then the output stream generated by the function seeded with same key is only 16 bytes long.

Lets take a look on some example results. Grain is one of the eStream candidates. What you can see are the results for the three described scenarios w.r.t. key exchange frequency. First two columns are the results from the testing batteries with 0 means that no test passed. You can clearly see that the Grain function limited to only two rounds has very defective output. The third column is our software circuit, which is showing whether we are able to find a distinguisher better than random guessing.

Here are the aggregate results for the seven eStream functions we were testing. The green box for the given number of algorithm rounds mean that the statistical testing batteries say with a high certainty that output is significantly different from the truly random data. The first column is Dieharder battery, the second column is the STS NIST battery and the third column is our approach. For some functions our approach detects deviances in the same number of rounds of tested functions, for some functions we are a bit worse, for Decim for example. I will get to that later on. The left group of columns is for the scenario when key is fixed for the whole output stream, so the Dieharder battery will get from 200 to 250 megabytes of data produced from a single key, quite a large dataset. If we change the key more frequently, results remains more or less the same. But the results change dramatically once you are changing the key for every test vector. What you can see is that testing batteries are performing much worse than were performing before, lowering the number of rounds where you can see defects detected.

I will now show you how genetic programming usually works on the proposed problem. Take an example of Salsa20 limited to 2 rounds only. On the x-axis of the figure you have the number of generation and when evolution starts. Circuits are just randomly guessing as they are just randomly generated circuits and you don't expect that they are able to distinguish reliably between the function's output and truly random data.

But after some time, genetic programming will learn something about the function output and start to perform better. There are still some fluctuations because we are exchanging the test sets from time to time and some test sets fit better or worse with the given circuit. Still, the average distinguishing success rate is increasing. After several hours of genetic programming, the resulting circuit is able to distinguish between truly random data and Salsa20 output limited to two rounds with a good success rate, forming a reasonably good distinguisher.

I will not talk about the details why this particular circuit works; honestly I don't understand fully why and how it's working. We put significant effort to ensure that it's not just a bug in the code and that results are real by making independent verification using statically generated C programs performing the circuit functionality. We also generated a visual representation of a circuit rendered later by Graphviz. For every particular setting and every tested function, we ran evolution 30 times in parallel to get robust results, also on-average behaviour of the otherwise stochastic evolution. What was interesting was that we were getting different results (different distinguishing circuits) each time. Sometimes, the success rate was the same, but the circuits that were coming out from the genetic programming had different inner structure. For example, first circuit has different unused input bytes than the second circuit. Such diversity is well known property of solutions found by genetic programming. You often get different solutions solving the same problem.

Lets take a look on more interesting results from the experiments done so far. We tested what will happen if we do not construct the test set as half of vectors taken from the function output and the second half from random data, but both taken from the random source, being literally indistinguishable. As a result, every time the test set is changed, population of candidate solutions starts by random guessing. But what is getting better when distinguishing between two truly random groups over the time? The reason is overlearning on the vectors in particular test set, a common problem in artificial intelligence. Once the test set is changed, the success ratio goes down. For fun, we took one half of random data from the Germany-based generator forming the first group, and the second half from the Croatia-based generator. Fortunately, we were not able to distinguish between these two sources, hinting that both are possibly random. But the situation was quite different for the real functions like Salsa20. The graph provides results for the period where the test set was changed 300 times and in some parts the success rate doesnt drop to random guess over a period of more than 30 test vector changes, yet suddenly drops afterwards. As such event repeat with some periodicity, it is probably related to some periodic defect in the output stream.

Having described the whole process, what is then the new test that can be added to existing testing batteries? Is it a particular circuit that was found after several days written down as program in some imperative language? The answer is most probably no, because this circuit was found for a particular function we were inspecting, and sometimes even for a particular key. What you should add as another test is the whole described process including the evolution with genetic programming. If such a battery test is run and after several hours can find a distinguisher better than random guessing, then there is some problem with the function output.

So what is the comparison to statistical batteries? There are advantages, but also disadvantages. The first advantage is that it's a new approach and we don't need to have a fixed test for all tested functions, but we have dynamic construction for particular function with possibly better results. The proposed approach is also able to work on very short sequences like 16 bytes whereas Diehard takes more than 200 megabytes (but Dieharder can possibly detect deviations on smaller amount of data as well). But working on very short sequences is also disadvantage as deviations like repetitions with longer periodicity cannot be detected. In a minute, I will present how we can fix that. For the disadvantages, there is no proof of test quality or coverage, similar to the situation with the testing batteries. Second, it may be hard to analyse the result because it might be unclear what the circuit is actually doing (though we are working on automatic analysis). Finally, the proposed approach can have a longer running time, depending on the learning period use. Our initial goal was to be at least as good as statistical batteries, hopefully better. The results so far show that statistical testing batteries are still sometimes better than we are for a particular algorithm, but this advantage is decreasing with the frequency of key exchange. If we force Dieharder to work on the stream with 200 megabytes consisting effectively of independent short blocks generated by a different key each, then it can detect deviations in a lower number of rounds with the same results as our approach.

What you can do at the moment is to let the evolution run even longer, therefore providing more data to evolution overall and waiting for a possibly better result. We can also add more layers; adjust the setting in a simulator and so on, but I would not expect significantly better results than we currently have, because Dieharder and STS NIST are basing their results on megabytes of data while we are working only with 16 bytes. But working on only 16 byte blocks is usually a limitation and the obvious next step is how to supply more data than we are currently working with. Here is an idea of what we are currently implementing, named as circuit with a memory. Instead of working with one short input supplied to circuit only once, you designate some of the input nodes as nodes accepting memory inputs and rest of the input nodes as accepting input bytes as usual. Same number of output nodes are designated as the memory outputs, rest as circuit ordinary outputs. Instead of executing given circuit only once, you are executing the circuit multiple times with memory outputs provided as memory inputs for the next iteration. Ordinary inputs are taken fresh from longer data stream. With such settings, circuits can process some statistics from every new fresh input block and combine it with information already stored in memory for previous blocks. As a result, one can process a longer stream limited only by the number of iterations we will perform.

A different way to increase the descriptive power of a circuit is to insert more complex operations inside circuit nodes. We implemented an emulator of a stack-based machine similar to Java bytecode execution and the code extraction from real Java implementation of the tested function. The idea is that if you like to find some weakness in a tested function, say AES, then it may be helpful to incorporate parts of the AES code directly inside the circuit, e.g., multiplication over Galois field. And we can still do this fully automatically. So we take the AES implementation in Java, compile it into the bytecode, parse the bytecode, extract some fragment of bytecode instructions and finally emulate this fragment as one operation inside some node in a circuit.

Finally, there are other goals possible for circuits to perform than random distinguishing. For example, one can use circuit to check violation of strict avalanche criterion by manipulating tested function inputs. If successful, some internal problem is detected.

In conclusion, we come up with a new idea for how to generate tests for automated statistical testing. We have so far comparable results to STS NIST. We are lagging for longer sequences, but we have ideas how to hopefully fix this. What we definitely need is a more detailed analysis of the results we are getting, because it took longer than we expected to implement all necessary software stuff and we had little time to inspect why the circuits are actually working (what bits in inputs are relevant for final decision). Also I would expect that once we switch to significantly longer sequences with techniques like circuit with memory, we will get better results for the scenarios where key is not changed frequently. That's all from my side.

Michael Roe: It might be that the periodicity in success rate of distinguisher circuit that you see for Salsa20 is actually periodicity in the random number generator you're using for the generation of the second random stream or for performing the mutations/crossover of the genetic algorithm.

Reply: We took special care not to be trapped in such a situation. When we were in need for the random data for the genetic algorithms, we were using the truly random data taken from the quantum generator services (QRNG service - HU, Germany and QRBG service - Ruer Boškovic Institute, Croatia). Such a service was also used as the random number generator for the genetic algorithm itself and also for the keys that were fed into the tested functions. But your remark is correct; you need to be very careful about using a randomness source as it is not used only for the keys, but also for other purposes influencing the quality of distinguisher found.

Verifiable Classroom Voting:
Where Cryptography Meets Pedagogy

Feng Hao, Dylan Clarke, and Carlton Shepherd*

School of Computing Science
Newcastle University
{feng.hao,dylan.clarke,c.g.shepherd}@ncl.ac.uk

Abstract. In this paper, we propose – and have implemented – the first *verifiable* classroom voting system. The subject of secure classroom voting has so far received almost no attention from the security community. Though several commercial classroom voting systems have been available, none of them is verifiable. State-of-the-art verifiable voting protocols all rely on finding a set of trustworthy tallying authorities (who are essentially cryptographers and computer experts) in the first place, and hence are completely unsuitable for classroom voting. Our system design is based on "self-enforcing e-voting" – a new paradigm that was first presented at SPW'12 (Hao, Randell and Clarke). A self-enforcing e-voting scheme provides the same End-to-End (E2E) verifiability as other e-voting schemes but without involving any tallying authorities. The removal of tallying authorities brings several compelling advantages in real-world voting scenarios – here, classroom voting is just one example. We have piloted the use of the developed verifiable classroom voting system in real classroom teaching. Based on our preliminary trial experience, we believe the system is not only scientifically valuable, but also pedagogically useful.

1 Introduction

Classroom voting is a powerful new pedagogy, which was first developed for the physics classroom by Harvard University's Eric Mazur in his influential book: *"Peer Instruction: A User's Manual"* [1], and subsequently extended by other academics to teaching mathematics and other subjects [2].

In this teaching technique, the teacher first poses a set of multiple-choice questions to a class of students, gives them a few minutes to discuss in small groups and asks them to vote for the best answers. Typically, a student submits the vote using a special hand-held device (known as the "clicker" [2,3]) that sends radio frequency signals to a special receiver installed in the classroom. The receiver tallies votes in real time and displays the results over a projector, providing instant feedback to the students and the teacher alike. Several studies have reported success of using this

---

* The work was supported by Newcastle University Innovation Funds and partly by the ERC Starting Grant (SEEV), No. 306994.

B. Christianson et al. (Eds.): Security Protocols 2013, LNCS 8263, pp. 245–254, 2013.

technique to retain the students' attention, to increase the classroom interactions and to improve the student learning outcome [2, 3].

There have been several commercial classroom voting systems available, e.g., iclicker[1], TurningPoint[2] and eInstruction[3]. In particular, the TurningPoint voting system has been adopted and trialed by a number of universities in the UK, including Newcastle University. (The first author had an opportunity to participate in a demo of the TurningPoint system at Newcastle University. This research work was motivated by that experience.)

However, a notable limitation with TurningPoint – and in fact all existing classroom voting systems – is that the voting results are not verifiable. There is no means for students to check if their votes have been recorded and tallied correctly. The integrity of the results may be affected by many factors: e.g., hardware malfunction of the voting device, lost signal in the radio frequency transmission, software bugs, malicious attacks where an adversary tampers with the back-end software to arbitrarily modify the results.

One might question why we should care about the verifiability at all – if the tallying results turn out to be wrong, it is probably not too big a deal. After all, the classroom voting result is not as sensitive as that in political elections. However, we believe verifiability is still important. First of all, it provides confidence on the accuracy of the tallying results. If any hardware failure or a software bug causes the tallying procedure to go astray, the error in the result will be caught publicly if the system is verifiable. Second, though classroom voting questions are usually not sensitive, there are exceptions: for example, when the system is used as a module assessment tool to rate a lecturer's teaching performance. By taking security into consideration in all conditions, we can make classroom voting more widely useful. Finally, by making the system verifiable, students will have an opportunity to learn and practise the fundamental "trust-but-verify" principle in routine classroom voting. This can prove relevant when they later participate in more serious national elections.

Besides a lack of *verifiability*, there are other limitations with the existing classroom voting systems. They generally use proprietary devices as voting clients. This however not only imposes vendor lock-in but also creates serious logistical issues – simply transporting the physical devices into and out of the classroom can be a laborious task. In addition, they require installing a proprietary receiver in the classroom. This seriously limits the portability of the system, as voting is confined to only designated classrooms.

2   System Design

In this section, we will propose a *verifiable* classroom voting system and show a concrete implementation. Our system addresses all the problems we explained above.

---

[1] http://www.iclicker.com
[2] http://www.turningtechnologies.co.uk
[3] http://www.einstruction.com/

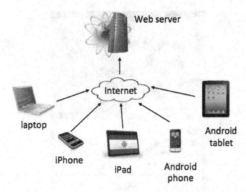

Fig. 1. Verifiable classroom voting system using mobile devices as voting clients

2.1 Overall Architecture

Figure 1 shows the overall architecture of our system. At the client side, students use their own computing devices to vote. We have developed two voting clients – an Android app [5] and an iOS app [4] – to support voting from iPhone, iPad, Android phone and Android tablet. In addition we provide a generic web voting interface, so people with any other types of smart phones (e.g., windows 8, blackberry etc) or a laptop can still vote, as long as the device has a web browser and is connected to the Internet.

2.2 System Configuration

There are three roles involved in the use of the system: administrator, coordinator and voter. The administrator is responsible to maintain the availability of the web server. A coordinator – usually a teacher – is someone who coordinates voting in a classroom. The system can accommodate many coordinators at the same time. Finally, voters are usually students in a class.

Classroom voting is arranged according to *voting sessions*. A voting session consists of a list of voting questions. We support four types of questions in the system:

1. Single-answer question: students can only choose one answer. (e.g., *which is the largest country in the world? A: Russia; B: China; C: America; D: India*)
2. Multiple-answer question: students can choose multiple answers. (e.g., *which of the following countries are members of Commonwealth? A: Singapore; B: India; C: Austria; D: Canada*)
3. Free numeric input question: there are no given answers and students are free to enter any numeric value (e.g, "*Enter the value of π to the two decimals*")
4. Free text input question: similar as above, except that the entered answer can be any text (e.g., "*Enter the name of the largest ocean on earth.*")

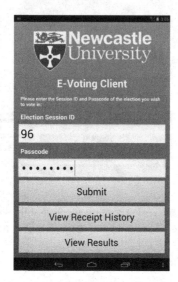

Fig. 2. Login screen for the voting client

The system is only verifiable when the voting questions are of the first two types (our verifiable voting protocol requires knowing the names of the candidates before the election). However, we still support the latter two types of questions, as we consider them useful features, even though the voting results cannot be verifiable in the cryptographic sense.

When a coordinator creates a voting session, there are a few options he needs to configure.

– Whether using a group passcode or individual passcodes.
– The maximum number of students in the class, denoted as N.
– The auditing factor F, which allows each student to audit a vote up to F times (by default $F = 5$)
– The security level L bits (by default $L = 128$)
– The length of the receipt R characters (by default $R = 5$)

A group passcode is a single passcode available to all students in the class. In this setting, the teacher informs students of a session ID and the group passcode, which are needed to log into the particular voting session (see Figure 2). However, one drawback with this authentication mechanism is that one student can vote multiple times by re-using the same passcode. In many circumstances, this is not an issue as there is no incentive for students to double-vote. However, in some cases when voting involves sensitive questions such as rating a lecturer's performance, a group passcode would be inadequate. Individual passcodes should be used instead.

In the individual passcodes scheme, each student is assigned a unique passcode. The web server first generates N random passcodes (recall that N is the maximum number of students in the class). The coordinator then prints out all

N passcodes, each on a paper slip. The paper slips are physically mixed up in front of the students before being distributed to the class. One student can only take one passcode. After voting is finished, the public bulletin board will show how many passcodes have been used. This number should be matched to the actual number of students in the class (e.g., based on a signed class attendance sheet). Any significant discrepancy would suggest something wrong (e.g., ballot stuffing), which demands further investigation.

2.3   Voting Protocol

To implement the system, we adopt the Direct Recording Electronic with Integrity (DRE-i) protocol [7], which is under the category of "self-enforcing e-voting" protocols [6]. The DRE-i protocol provides the same end-to-end verifiability as other verifiable voting protocols but without requiring any tallying authorities.

The protocol has three phases: setup, voting and tallying. The setup phase involves pre-computing cryptograms for all electronic ballots, as specified in [7]. Depending on the size of the class and the number of questions, this phase usually takes several minutes to complete.

The second phase is voting. Figure 3a shows the initial voting interface of the Android app for a single-answer question. To cast a vote, a student follows two stages: 1) selecting an answer; 2) confirming or canceling the previous selection.

In the first stage, the student makes a selection: let us assume he selects "Yes". In the next interface, the app shows that "Yes" had been selected and asks the student to "Confirm" or "Cancel" (Figure 3b). There is also a third button "Receipt", which leads to the display of a stage-1 receipt (Figure 3c). The student can verify the receipt by checking that the same content on the receipt has been published on the public bulletin board (a publicly accessible website).

The second stage handles the student's choice of "confirm" or "cancel". Suppose the student chooses to "cancel (essentially, this is to perform voter-initiated auditing [7]). The voting interface will show that the previous selection has been canceled (Figure 4a); the student can proceed to the next question (if any) or re-try the same question. There is also a button "Receipt", which leads to the display of the stage-2 receipt for the cancellation case (Figure 4b). A student can repeat the same cancellation operation up to F times (recall that the value F is configurable). On the other hand, if the student chooses to "confirm", the interface will show the vote has been casted (Figure 4c), together with a stage-2 receipt for the confirmation case (Figure 4d). Same as before, to verify the stage-2 receipt, the student simply needs to check that the content on the receipt matches that published on the public bulletin board. This requires no knowledge of cryptography. As long as all receipts are available on the public bulletin board, anyone with cryptographic knowledge and computing skills will be able to verify all receipts in a batch.

The third - and last - phase is the tallying process. When all students have casted their votes, the coordinator would end that particular voting session through a web interface. The voting results are immediately available. Figure

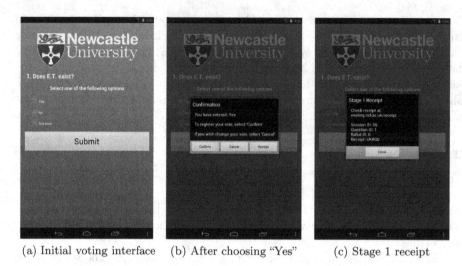

(a) Initial voting interface   (b) After choosing "Yes"   (c) Stage 1 receipt

Fig. 3. Stage 1 voting interface and receipt

5 shows an example of the tallying results in a bar chart. The same results are also available on the voting website, together with all receipts (i.e., audit data). We provide an open-source Java program on the voting website to facilitate any interested party to cryptographically verify the integrity of the results based on the audit data.

3   Trials

3.1   Usability Trial

We conducted a voting trial workshop at the School of Computing Science, Newcastle University, on 3 September, 2012. The participants were mainly MSc students who had just submitted their dissertations. We provided pizza catering for all participants. With this workshop, we aimed at "three birds with one stone": to trial our newly developed verifiable classroom voting system; to serve as a farewell party for MSc students as many of them would leave shortly; and finally to give some MSc students a chance to present interesting results in their dissertation projects and let all participants vote for their favorite presentation using the classroom voting system.

There were in total around 40 participants who were mainly MSc students. Five students presented their dissertation projects, and afterwards we asked all participants to vote for the most "entertaining" presentation. In this case, the integrity of the voting result must be ensured, so we used the individual passcodes scheme as described in Section 2.

(a) Case A: user chose cancellation

(b) Case A: receipt for cancellation

(c) Case B: user chose confirmation

(d) Case B: receipt for confirmation

Fig. 4. Stage 2 voting interface and receipt

During the trial, participants had two ways to vote: 1) using an Android app [5] (version 1.0.0); 2) using a web interface at http://evoting.ncl.ac.uk. (At the time of the trial, the iPhone app was still under development, so iPhone users had to use a web interface to vote.) At the end of the workshop, we received 26 completed questionnaires, among which 17 participants voted through the Android app, and 9 through the web interface.

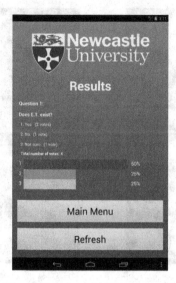

Fig. 5. Display of tallying results

The feedback questionnaire consisted of 10 statements and respondents were asked to indicate their agreement or disagreement on a Likert scale from 1 to 5 (i.e., "strongly agree", "agree", "neutral", "disagree" and "strongly disagree"). The statements were as follows:

1. Joining a new session was easy.
2. I understood how to join a new session.
3. I understood how to answer questions.
4. Answering questions was easy.
5. I understood how to check the receipt.
6. I understood why I might want to check the receipt.
7. I felt confident that my answers had been recorded correctly.
8. I understood how to view the results.
9. Viewing the results was easy.
10. I felt my answer was sent anonymously.

We summarize the received 26 questionnaire answers in Table 1. There was no obvious difference in the answers between those voting through the Android app and those through the web interface, so we combine all answers in one table.

In general, the feedback was encouragingly positive. Participants generally found our verifiable voting system easy to use (see Table 1). However, some people expressed "neutral" opinions about the security of the system. Despite that we designed the system to be *verifiable* and we physically shuffled the passcodes to ensure *anonymity,* roughly half of the participants indicated they were not sure whether the vote had indeed been correctly recorded and whether the voting was anonymous. These are useful lessons, which teach us that e-voting is not only a security problem, but also a subject of of psychology and voters' perception of security. We do not believe anyone should immediately accept a new voting system just because it is verifiable or has security proofs. But we do believe that, given a verifiable voting system with all important security elements accounted at the outset of the design, the public confidence in the new system – and their acceptance – will gradually grow.

Table 1. Summary of the 26 received questionnaire answers

Question	Strongly Agree (1)	Agree (2)	Neutral (3)	Disagree (4)	Strongly Disagree (5)	Average score (nearest option)
1	17	7	2	0	0	1.42 (*Strongly agree*)
2	15	9	2	0	0	1.5 (*Strongly agree*)
3	18	8	1	0	0	1.42 (*Strongly agree*)
4	21	4	1	0	0	1.23 (*Strongly agree*)
5	7	11	5	3	0	2.15 (*Agree*)
6	4	14	5	3	0	2.27 (*Agree*)
7	4	10	8	2	2	2.75 (*Neutral*)
8	10	10	5	1	0	1.88 (*Agree*)
9	11	10	3	1	1	1.96 (*Agree*)
10	3	10	10	3	0	2.5 (*Neutral*)

3.2 Pedagogical Trial

Following the success of the usability trial in September 2012, we made several improvements to the Android app to make it more user-friendly. Also, we provided an iOS app [4] for those using iPhones and iPads to vote. In October and November, 2012, we first trialed the system in real classroom teaching on the "Cryptography" (BSc final year) and "System Security" (MSc first year) modules, in which the first author is the module leader. On 10 January 2013, at the last (revision) lecture of "Cryptography", the first author prepared ten revision questions for the class, gave students 15 minutes to discuss among themselves and asked them to vote for the best answers. At the end of the lecture, a student survey was conducted using the same voting system to collect the feedback. The survey questions and the tallied answers (within brackets) are summarized below:

Question-1 Does the voting make the lecture more fun?
    Answers: Yes (26), No (2)
Question-2 Does the voting help you learn?
    Answers: Yes (26), No (2)
Question-3 Do you find it useful to have a small group discussion before voting?
    Answers: Yes (25), No (3)
Question-4 How do you think that the amount of voting used in this lecture should change?
    Answers: More (10), Less (1), Remain the same (16)

Question-5 Do you recommend classroom voting for teaching the same module next year?

Answers: Yes (26), No (1)

The survey results clearly indicate the pedagogical value of the developed classroom voting system. The vast majority of the students in the class found the classroom voting system quite "fun" to use. We believe "fun" is a critical factor in learning – by making learning a fun process, we are able to better retain the students' attention in the class and improve their learning outcome. It is also worth noting that we used about a quarter of the time in a lecture (1 hour) for classroom voting. We were initially concerned if that was too much. But based on the feedback, 16 out of 27 expressed that was an adequae percentage; another 10 (nearly one third) students actually wanted more voting in the class. This is further evidence to show that students generally liked the system.

4   Conclusion

In the paper, we have presented a pioneering classroom voting system that is verifiable. This system serves as a good example to demonstrate the power of the underlying "self-enforcing e-voting" paradigm. Through putting the system into the real classroom teaching and collecting the student feedback, we show that the system has also demonstrated great pedagogical potential to enhance the students' learning experience in a traditonal classroom environment.

References

1. Mazur, E.: Peer Instruction: A User's Manual. Prentice Hall Series in Educational Innovation, NJ (1997)
2. Cline, K., Zullo, H.: Teaching Mathematics with Classroom Voting - With and Without Clickers. Mathematical Association of America (2011)
3. Bruff, D.: Teaching with Classroom Response Systems - Creating Active Learning Environments. Jossey-Bass (2009)
4. Link to the iOS app for the verifiable classroom voting application, https://itunes.apple.com/us/app/id565080670
5. Link to the Android app for the verifiable classroom voting application, https://play.google.com/store/apps/details?id=uk.ac.ncl.evoting
6. Hao, F., Randell, B., Clarke, D.: Self-Enforcing Electronic Voting. In: Proceedings of the 20th Security Protocols Workshop (SPW 2012), Cambridge, UK (2012)
7. Hao, F., Kreeger, M.N.: Every Vote Counts: Ensuring Integrity in DRE-based Voting System. School of Computing Science, Newcastle University. Technical report No. 1268 (2012)

Verifiable Classroom Voting:
Where Cryptography Meets Pedagogy
(Transcript of Discussion)

Feng Hao

School of Computing Science
Newcastle University, UK

Hi, good afternoon everyone. We have come to the last talk. I know many of you are probably desperate for a pint in the pub, so I will make your life easy and keep the talk short. This talk is about "verifiable classroom voting". If you look for the literature on this subject, you will probably find none. The reason should become clear later in the talk. This work is in collaboration with Dylan Clarke, and Carlton Shepherd. Dylan is an RA working with me and Carlton is a third year undergraduate student in the School of Computing Science, Newcastle University.

Here is the outline for the talk. First, I will give you some background on classroom voting. I will explain what classroom voting systems are currently available. However, none of those available systems is "verifiable". Next I will describe our solution. And in addition to describing the theoretical design, we will present a prototype implementation of the design. Furthermore we will present our trial experience of applying the prototype in a real classroom environment to enhance the students' learning process. That has received good student feedback. Finally I will conclude with suggestions for future research.

First of all, what is classroom voting? Here is one example.

Question: (3+4)+2=2+(3+4) illustrates which of the following properties?

    a Commutative
    b Associative
    c Reflexive
    d Transitive
    e Distributive

Can someone tell me your answer to this question?
Audience: A.
Audience: Also B.
Reply: Any more answers? Imagine that you ask this question to a class of young students. Many may feel shy to give an answer, because they are afraid to get it wrong and hence be embarrassed. (The correct answer is A.) Interestingly, in one study, school teachers were asked the same question, and it turned out that 48% of them got it wrong.

B. Christianson et al. (Eds.): Security Protocols 2013, LNCS 8263, pp. 255–264, 2013.
© Springer-Verlag Berlin Heidelberg 2013

What can you do to encourage students to actively participate in the discussion? The solution is to remove that barrier of possible embarrassment. You don't ask any individual student to answer a question; you ask them to do it as a group. For example, we can do a-show-of-hands, but counting hands is too slow. You can do better with electronic technology.

This is how a typical electronic classroom voting system works. You have a voting device, which may use infrared light communication. So there must be a receiver, which is usually installed high above in the ceiling to obtain a clear sight of light. Alternatively, you may use voting devices that use radio frequency communication. The system normally displays the voting results over a projector using PowerPoint. When you finish sending your votes, all these votes will be tallied by the receiver. There is a Powerpoint plug-in that queries the results from the receiver and displays them over a projector.

Currently, there are several commercial systems available. Many people may have heard of *TurningPoint*, which is very popular in the UK. Many universities have been trialling the use of TurningPoint in a classroom. In the US, *iclicker* is commonly used in universities. Another system is called *eInstruction*. Here, I only list three, but actually there are quite a few. Technically, all these systems work basically the same.

There are several problems with all these systems. The first is a lack of verifiability. And in fact that was what initially motivated our work. I attended a demonstration of *TurningPoint* in Newcastle University. The instructor demonstrated the working of the system. Impressive. But then I asked: "how do I know the results you show on the screen are actually correct?" He thought a bit and said: "you have to trust us". Well, as a security researcher, I was not convinced. This is just one problem. Another problem is related to the system maintenance.

If you think about the handset, the maintenance of the handsets is not an easy problem. Someone has to maintain those handsets – if one is malfunctioning, you have to replace it. In addition, transporting handsets from one classroom to a different room is not easy. Finally, you must have a fixed receiver installed at the classroom. That means you are limited to conducting voting only in that classroom. If you want change to a different classroom, you need to buy another receiver. The cost can scale up linearly.

The maintenance and cost issues are obvious. Almost everyone agrees. As for the lack of verifiability, some people may disagree that is a problem. They may say, "What's the point? They are students. They should accept whatever the teacher tells them. What's the point of having security and verifiability?"

Well, we think security and verifiability are important. A few weeks ago, I met Steve Schneider at the University of Surrey. He told me quite an interesting example, so I borrowed the same example here. During a university admission day, Steve gave a lecture to the 6th form students, who were interested in entering the university. And he distributed all these TurningPoint handsets to the students and asked them to vote: "Do you think the school uniform should be made compulsory?" Students were excited because they have strong views on this subject. The participation was active and high. They sent all votes by pressing the "clickers". Steve said, "OK. Let's see the voting result." So he showed this result to the students. (79% voted "Yes" while 21% voted "No".)

There was an immediate gasp from the audience. Steve went on to explain what happened: he actually swapped the answers, but no one else knew it. That is the point - if one is able to manipulate the tallying results arbitrarily without being noticed, how can you trust the tallying results are actually correct? I think that is a quite good example to explain why we need verifiability. So far we only talk about problems. Next, I am going to talk about solutions.

Sandy Clark: Did you know that there is a device that will allow you to use one clicker to beat all clickers in a room by jamming all other clickers' response? It's about 30 dollars. It's on hack-a-day, if you're interested.

Reply: That is interesting. I would like to add that to the slides.

Frank Stajano: My feeling to this initial problem setting is that this is an important problem, and that this is an attempt to fit a technological solution to what is really an anthropological and sociological problem that should be solved at that level first. The problem is that the students are embarrassed to say what is the correct answer according to them because it might be wrong, and they might look stupid. Then I think that as educators what we need is to make them feel that making mistakes is OK in the process of learning, and they should be willing to engage and make mistakes, and not be ashamed of making mistakes. And just giving them a technological solution that allows them to hide just so they can express the answer without being embarrassed about mistakes doesn't solve the problem that they could be embarrassed. And we should teach them not to be embarrassed.

Sandy Clark: I agree with you in principle, but there is a problem in that. Some studies done with primary school teachers involve asking them, you know, how do you respond when you ask a girl a question, and how do you respond when you ask a boy a question. They will tell you that they respond in both the same way. But when you videotape them and show them, they responded differently. And it's not only in the training, is the social pressure of the teachers, but then it's also peer pressure, so you have a lot of girls who are afraid to speak up.

Frank Stajano: Then what we want is to liberate those girls.

Sandy Clark: Yes, we do, but it's, that is a long-term solution that we want to get to, but this is an immediate solution.

Frank Stajano: This is just a band-aid.

Sandy Clark: But hey, anything that can help.

Bruce Christianson: This is something that gets them through the first term.

Sandy Clark: Right, this sort of thing develops the confidence to just speak up later.

Frank Stajano: So if I'm asking a question in my algorithms class, say, is this going to be linear, $n \log n$ or n^2, and some people will say something. Then I want to say, well you guys, you think it's $n \log n$, why, or how would you deal with that. I have to ask the question to someone. If they're all anonymous how can I follow this up, and go through the reason?

Reply: Actually I will come to that. If you know the response from the audience, you can actually structure your next question accordingly. For example, if you have a question and you realise that almost everyone in this classroom got it wrong except one student, what I did in my class is that I asked who voted for this answer. There was one student raising his hand. He looked quite shy and a bit embarrassed. But then I said that you were the only one who got it right; can you explain it to the rest of the class why you chose this answer? You could immediately see the change on his face. He suddenly became quite energetic. When I asked him to explain it to the rest of the class, he was very happy to do that.

Frank Stajano: But then when you reveal that that was the wrong answer he would feel very bad.

Reply: In that case probably.

OK, let me move on. We had a student response survey on the use of the system and I will explain that later. This is the overall architecture of the solution that we propose. Basically for the voting we don't want to have any custom-built hardware. The voting device could be smart phones, tablets or laptops – in fact, any computing device, as long as it can connect to the Internet. Of course if you have smart phones we provide apps that give you good usability. All communication is through the Internet and the votes are tallied at the web server. You are not limited to one classroom. It can work anywhere as long as your device can connect to Internet. You can even vote at home. So that is the architectural view of the system.

The underlying voting protocol is called self-enforcing e-voting, which is something I talked about last year. After the workshop last year I was quite fortunate to receive an ERC starting grant to investigate this idea further. Recall that self-enforcing e-voting is a system that provides end-to-end verifiability, but without any tallying authority.

If you look at the literature for the past 20 years, you will find that verifiable e-voting schemes all assume trusted tallying authorities. That is exactly the assumption that we challenge. I designed a self-enforcing e-voting protocol three years ago in 2010, and I put the paper on the IACR eprint. Then I submitted the paper to conferences like Oakland, CCS. But it was all rejected. The reviewers basically said, for 20 years everyone assumes tallying authorities are needed to tally votes, and you argue that's a bad idea, so you must be wrong. But anyway I think it is starting to change because people realize that the tallying authorities are actually not as indispensable as many have thought. And we demonstrated that by removing the tallying authorities from the whole system, you get a system that is much simpler and more efficient. You look at security aspects; they are the same as those depending on the tallying authorities. Then you ask: what's the point of having the tallying authority if you can be better off without them?

The way to achieve that is by using a combination of pre-computation strategy, and some novel encryption techniques so that you can cancel out random factors when you multiply the ciphertexts. But I'm not going to go into the details of that. And for the technical details, you can read our technical report.

I thought the best way to show how the system actually works is to give you a demo. Can I ask one question? How many of you have Android phones? Can you raise your hands? How many of you have iPhones? Alright. Just have a try. If you have an Android phone you can download our app and try it out. The name of the app is Newcastle University evoting. At some time in future, probably next year, I want to remove the Newcastle name so it's going to be generic and available to everyone. If you use iPhone, there is also an iPhone app you can try out. Just search for Newcastle University evoting. Who doesn't have a smart phone? You can still vote if you have your laptop. You can go to this address, http://evoting.ncl.ac.uk. It's essentially the same thing but the usability is not as good as the apps. Once you get the app all you need to do is to have a session ID and a passcode. I'll just give you five minutes, and at the end of five minutes I will reveal the results of the election.

Steven Murdoch: Is this actually a talk about mobile phone malware? (laughter)

Reply: At least you know where it's coming from.

Sandy Clark: So Frank, I thought that one way that you could actually use this when you're asking some questions without singling out someone who acted one way or another would be to have thought through what would cause someone to choose the wrong answers. Then you can simply say, those of you who chose A, well A is not the right answer, but this is probably what you were thinking, and this is what led you this way. Try, what happens if you think about it like this.

(chatter)

Just cast your vote and I will finish the election and show the results. Then I can show you how to verify.

(chatter)

Virgil Gligor: This says in progress ...

Reply: Yes, that's a good point, I will come to that.

Virgil Gligor: We have started in progress.

Reply: No, that is only the first stage. There are two stages.

(chatter)

Reply: Finished? So if you used mobile phone app, the app would have kept a history of the receipts, and then you can verify.

Virgil Gligor: Shall we go to the next question?

Reply: Yes. With the web interface I have to admit the interface could be improved, but so far we have been focusing on the app interface.

Alec Yasinsac: You're sure my answers won't become public?

Reply: OK, we'll see. (laughter)

Audience: Can we cheat?

Reply: Sure, you can actually double vote. Feel free to do that. All done, everyone, OK. So now all I need to do is to finish the session. Now you can refresh your app and you will see the results. I will also display the results here. Right, so this is the tallying results for the first question: is cryptography is a science, an art, or both? It is a sensitive question and some people may have strong opinions. But it seems that we have quite a balanced view here: cryptography is both a science, and an art. If you ask individual views, sometimes people may strongly disagree. Here, we take the view of the majority and hence avoid the potential conflict. That is the first question. Basically the system supports four types of questions, and I have four questions here which correspond to the four types.

The first one is type-I, which is called a single-choice question. You're only allowed to choose one answer. And for the type-II, that is called a multiple-choice question. You can choose more than one question. And here we got a few tallies. I'm actually surprised that six people choose Zimbabwe, but actually its commonwealth membership had been terminated some time ago if you watch the news. For the type-I and type-II questions, they are verifiable. There are receipts on the bulletin board, which you can all verify. But for the last two questions, they are not verifiable. Still we support them because they are useful. So the third question is called free numeric input - you enter whatever numeric input and the system will just tally it. It is not possible to make it verifiable because we don't have pre-defined candidate names. In this case, yes, most people chose 27 for the number of countries in the EU, which is the right answer.

Frank Stajano: What does it mean, it is not possible to be verifiable?

Reply: Because to make the system verifiable you need to know what the candidates are, so that you do this pre-computation. But with the free numeric choice you don't know what are the candidates.

Frank Stajano: Well it's not possible in your system or it's not possible in general?

Reply: If you remove the requirement on privacy, yes, it is possible (for example, everyone speaks aloud). But if you want to have verifiability and privacy at the same time, you've got a problem. So that is the third question. And the last question is called free text input. For the free text input, it's entirely up to the student to enter whatever they want, and this can be a little bit tricky because a student can write anything they want (laughter), sometimes something you would not expect.

Ariel Stulman: Can't you just ask Google the answers?

Frank Stajano: Exactly.

Ariel Stulman: Why bother with anything, when you have these clickable things and you can search Internet. If you ask how many countries are in the European Union, what I would do is first ask Google, how many countries. Then I enter the answer.

Ariel Stulman: Or try Wikipedia.

Reply: Remember that this is just one example. There could be other cases that you use this type-4 question. for example, you may ask a student to write free comment about this lecture, or feedback on what need to improve. And in fact I am going to show you one session to see what students said.

Ariel Stulman: What I would do would be to just chat with my neighbour, and ask him what he has to say.

Alec Yasinsac: I think your point here is, if what you're doing is inspiring them to go onto Google and find the answer, that's just as good as if they knew it off the top of their head.

Reply: Exactly.

Virgil Gligor: Not really, because they may go to the Wikipedia and get the wrong answer. (laughter)

Alec Yasinsac: But then you show the history ...

Reply: OK, I need to watch the clock so let me carry on. That is a simple demo of how the voting works, and how it actually worked in my classroom. I conducted some usability studies among the MSc students, about 40 of them. About 30 students gave their responses. For example, I asked them to answer the four questions. Here each question corresponds to one of the four colour bars. In the first question, students generally find it quite easy to vote. Just get the app, enter the session ID, passcode, and then start voting. It is quite easy to do that. And for the next set of questions I wanted to see how students felt, if it was easy or difficult to check the receipts. In general they felt easy, but not as easy as compared to the previous slide. But in general I think the responses are still quite positive. In the third question, I wanted to ask the students to express their opinions about anonymity, and that is something quite interesting. If you think about it the voting should be anonymous as you just enter a random password. But the students were quite cautious and felt that the voting was not really anonymous. Probably they were thinking about the IP address got logged by the campus wi-fi network. Given that those MSc students took the security as the specialist, so it actually makes sense. Unfortunately I don't know how to address this problem. One possible solution, as I talked with the University staff, is to have a special Wi-Fi network just for voting, so anyone can go to Wi-Fi without needing any campus login.

Ariel Stulman: And use Tor?

Reply: Yes, that's another way. But the signal is often not good. That is a usability trial. So far so good. And I also did some trials with final year undergraduate students. In one last lecture on revision, I actually set an election of 10 questions. I asked students to vote for the best answers, and at the end of the lecture I asked them to provide feedback about the voting experience. The first question is, "does the voting making the lecture more fun?" You can see that about 95% of students said yes, and about 5% said not really. "Does voting help you learn?" Again, the vast majority, 95%, said yes. And "do you find it useful to have small group discussion before voting?" This is something I found quite useful. Instead of just asking everyone to vote straightway, I said, don't rush to vote; talk to people sitting next to you, and try to reach some agreement on the best answer for that question before you vote. I want students to actually take some time, even a few minutes, to discuss among themselves, and take some consideration before sending the vote. And it turns out that students like that kind of group discussion, because usually in the classroom everyone is passive and quiet, and now I give them the freedom to talk to each other. They found it a quite different experience, and they like it. Finally I asked them: "do you recommend classroom voting for next year?" Most people said yes, which is really good. And also, that was a one hour lecture, but I used 15 minutes for voting. My worry was that I may have used too much time, but it turns out that was not a problem. Nearly 60% students said that the time was about right. 35% students said they wanted more because they found it quite fun, which is quite interesting.

Sandy Clark: Students probably liked it as playing a game.

Reply: Yes, I mean, it's a system in which they can interact with their peers and express opinions, and like playing a game. They like it, and wanted to have more in their future classes.

However there are some usability issues. Actually if you have your smart phone you can go to session 109. So far you have seen quite good results but I also want to show you some negative aspects. In the last question, I asked them, "write your free comment about how to improve classroom voting". They are quite straightforward. Some said the interface sucks, because there are too many confirmations; a lot of steps to go through; and there are too many popups. In a sense, all these complaints are actually just one complaint, which is: verifiability degrades usability. We say we want to make the system verifiable but that comes at a cost. By making the system verifiable you push the receipt to the voter, to the student. But sometimes the student just doesn't want to take the receipt. They may say, "yes, we trust you". So that is the kind of a mental model among the students, and we are still trying to figure out how to address that.

Here is the conclusion. We have designed and implemented a verifiable class-room voting system. We believe it is the first, and is the only "verifiable" class-room voting system available. If you look at all the previous voting systems like Helios, they are completely unsuitable for a classroom setting, because for all those systems you need to find a set of cryptographers as tallying authorities to start with. But in the classroom setting, how can you do that? It is impossible. So the only way to have a practical and realistic classroom voting system is that you need to make the elections self-enforcing. You make the system verifiable, but without involving any tallying authority. Our work is only a start, and is still in the preliminary stage. In fact we implemented the system just a few months ago. At the moment, I have one student extending the system to the whole campus of Newcastle University, so anyone with a Newcastle University campus login will be able to create elections.

So far that is what we have been doing, but in the longer term we want to make the system freely available to all the universities in the UK, then in Europe, and finally the rest of the world, because we see the value of this kind of system. Not only the value as scientific research, but also the value in using it for education and the pedagogy. It might sound quite cool, but to make the system available worldwide, you have to think about computation. If you do a simple calculation you may realise that the potential computational load is massive because it involves a lot of cryptographic operations. That is a challenge that we are going to face in the future. We've got a grant to support further research in this direction. Initially I thought classroom voting is just a small hobby project but once the system was developed and trialled in the actual classroom I realised it is actually more useful that what I initially thought. We will continue to improve the system and will try to make it available to other universities as well. That is the end of my talk. Thank you.

Jeff Yan: Well actually it looks like the one question is missing in your student survey. Did any of them bother to check whether the vote has been recorded, and how many students have checked that?

Reply: My guess is that very few, but the point is that the information is on the public bulletin board. If you want to check all the information is there, but I agree, there should be some mechanism to actually encourage people to check receipt. That is a hard problem, I mean, it applies to all e-voting schemes in general. You provide a mechanism for people to check, but then you also need a mechanism to encourage them to check, or put incentive. I don't know how to solve that problem, but that is quite a general problem.

Alec Yasinsac: Well if they're not using it, it suggests that it's not needed. That is the challenge here.

Reply: That's a very good point because the point of having verifiability in the system is that people can check. If people don't bother to check, and then the verifiability doesn't really make much sense.

Bruce Christianson: Ask the question about the 6th form uniform and then see. (laughter)

Reply: On the other hand if you think about elections, here we only talk about classroom voting. But you also think about larger scale elections. The point of an election is to convince the losers. So at least the losers would have an incentive to check. Still they are a small population so there should be a separate mechanism to encourage more people to do the checking. It's not a technological issue, it's about the incentive.

Bruce Christianson: Well it's a good application there for the location protocol because you want to restrict voting to just people who are in the classroom. But is there an easy way to stop people from voting multiple times or not?

Reply: Yes, so in this case I don't stop voting multiple times. If you vote twice it will be guaranteed that it is counted twice, because that's what verifiability is for. Authentication is a different matter. Actually we have two mechanisms for authentication. So far we just used one, which is a group password. That is one password for everyone. We have another mechanism implemented in the system which is called individual passwords. For individual passwords, what we did in our election trial is that we physically print those passwords on pieces of paper, and mix them together in a sweet box. Everyone takes one random piece of paper to vote. And at the end of the voting you can count how many people have actually voted, and how many confirmed votes shown on the bulletin board. The two numbers should match.

Bruce Christianson: And it's clear from the physical characteristics that it's anonymous, but how to do that online?

Reply: That's a big question, and I hope I will come back with an answer in future research.

Fig. 1. Offsite backup options (seen on Cambridge Security Group whiteboard)

B. Christianson et al. (Eds.): Security Protocols 2013, LNCS 8263, p. 265, 2013.

Author Index